- Benefit from the experience of others and save money doing so.

- This book provides 'step-by-step' instructions on how to shop gluten free, where to shop gluten free, what to shop for, where to receive help and why eating gluten free is essential.

- Receive updated information and discover the abundance and availability of gluten free foods.

- This book answers the most common and technical questions and provides information to help you develop the necessary skills to maintain a gluten free diet and feel confident and comfortable doing so.

- Once diagnosed with celiac disease, it is essential to follow a strict gluten free diet.

- Celiac disease is an adverse reaction to a complex group of certain gluten-proteins (prolamins) involving the immune system. Individuals suffering from celiac disease have a genetic predisposition to the reaction from these prolamins (gliaden in wheat, horedin in barley and secalin in rye).

- At present time, the treatment for celiac disease is to eliminate all grains that contain these toxic gluten proteins, all byproducts of these grains and any food that contains these grains and/or grain byproducts.

- It sounds easy in theory but when put into practical use, can be quite frustrating and overwhelming.

- Learning your ingredients and understanding how to read labels is imperative. This book was put together to help you do just that.

- I was amazed at how much my health improved simply by changing my diet to gluten free.

Guide Books Publishing Company
2113 Washington Lane,
Bensalem, PA. 19020   USA

www.GlutenFreeCentral.com

Please pass the word about this book's availability to your doctor, pharmacist, medical practitioner, nutritionist, dietitian, health care professionals, local market, health food grocery store, food distributors, food manufacturers, and fellow celiacs and dietary organizations.

Copies of your personal corresponding gluten free letters from manufacturers, distributors, health care professionals, chemists, organizations and other specialists would be useful and appreciated.

Published by Guide Books Publishing Company

ISBN: 0-9722596-5-1

Library of Congress Control Number: 2002093952

Gluten Free

Reference
Guide
The Complete Book of
Terms & Definitions

By Jan Marie Silcox

TABLE OF CONTENTS

DEDICATION

I dedicate this book to everyone who has inspired me, especially my father, for which his pride is wonderfully inspiring, beyond, belief.

ACKNOWLEDGEMENTS

I thank my son Jason for his love, encouragement and patience. Thanks to my friends and family (especially my sister Linda), Tish, Carol, Lynnette, Ron, all the other gluten free dieters I have met along this journey and to the people at the Natural Food Store in Penndel PA.

Special thanks to Barbara Busco, The Good Family, Dr. Salowe, Kerry Schwoyer and Donna Anderson for their encouragement and emotional support and to that Higher Power for which this book has become possible.

My personal thanks to everyone who has responded with interest and encouragement to the thousands of phone calls, letters and e-mails in order to make this book possible.

I would also like to thank anyone who has purchased this guide. My wish is that you receive the benefits, which were intended. Your support is appreciated!

DISCLOSURE

This book contains my personal opinions and ideas, me being, of course, the author Jan Marie Silcox. **I compiled this book with years of accumulated knowledge and experience with the intentions of helping others**.

The information in this book should be, used as a general guideline. Consult your doctor about any decisions regarding your health and diet and for updated information about celiac disease and the gluten free diet.

I wrote this book with the understanding that I am not promoting or recommending any treatments. The reader is in no way obligated to make any additional purchases and **in this book, I do not make dietary suggestions or give medical advice.** I do however provide information I have created or gathered, along with helpful resource contacts.

INTRODUCTION

I understand how inconvenient, frustrating and overwhelming the gluten free (GF) diet can be. The gluten free (GF) diet's complexities are one of the reasons I have put this guidebook together. Although I must declare the longer, you are on the gluten free diet the easier it gets.

My diagnoses of celiac disease (CD) and dermatitis herpetiformis (DH) seemed somewhat typical. **Celiac disease (CD) was, overlooked and misdiagnosed**. I went years with subtle discomforts. However, when I got food poisoning, my symptoms dramatically worsened and celiac disease (CD) developed into the degenerative stage. My stomach pains became unbearable.

With much persistence and a family history of intestinal cancer for motivation, **I pleaded with a gastroenterologist to perform an endoscope.** During the exam, Dr. Salowe noticed how inflamed my stomach was and how flat my villi were, a small bowel intestinal biopsy was performed along with blood work, and I was finally diagnosed. What a relief! [With my family's history of cancer, I considered myself lucky.]

Respectfully speaking there were two significant statements my doctor made "I hope you like fruits and vegetables because you'll need to change your diet to gluten free." He also confessed not knowing much about celiac disease and said; "you must learn about celiac disease and the gluten free diet enough to teach me." I put together literature he now gives his patients.

The day I was diagnosed with CD my world changed. Living life as a celiac for me was quite a struggle in the beginning. Now I consider it a gift. Besides eating healthier, I enjoy the work associated with the GF diet.

Within three days on the GF diet, my stomach felt better. It took 16 days for my intestines to start to relax. I went from being malnourished to gaining weight normally within two months. My body started readjusting itself within six months, several more changes took place for about another year and then within two years my system balanced out completely.

I now live a healthy life with an incredibly strong immune system. Every celiacs' progress differs and relapses can occur without a strict adherence to the gluten free diet. For most celiacs, **health improvements begin within days of starting a strict GF diet** and the small intestine usually heals completely within three to 12 months. Of course the quicker the body will heal, depends, on the severity of damage, the health of a patient when diagnosed and how strict the GF diet is maintained.

I had to learn the gluten free GF diet well. Processed foods of any nature caused my intestines distress. I began the GF diet by eating only whole foods, that I was certain were GF. For me this meant preparing foods from scratch and then eventually purchasing prepared GF foods. I can now handle a great variety of GF processed and prepared foods.

I have always had an interest in whole foods and their nutritional impact on the human body. My awareness became an obsession with my diagnosis of celiac disease, I was compelled to care for my body the best way I could. **I read everything I could get my hands on about CD** and the GF diet. I came across information that was, factual, contradictory and some that was good ole' common sense.

I am, considered a 'sensitive celiac'. The least little bit of gluten contamination affects me. [I rarely cheat!] **As my body healed and my energy level increased,** I became motivated to help others in their times of need. Needing food! Needing food! Needing food! Every time I would meet a newly diagnosed celiac, I was reintroduced to the difficulties of the

GF diet. After all learning, eating and staying on the diet is the cure.

Because of the overwhelming demand to make this guide available, I compiled this book with my personal experiences, notes, opinions and charts. I kept this book as simple as possible yet also informative and **I tried to answer the most frequently asked simple and complex questions.**

I hope by sharing this information with you, you find eating gluten free (GF) easier. I was amazed at how much my health improved by simply changing my diet to GF. My hopes are that you will feel as vibrant and healthy as I do.

Good health!

SPECIALTY GLUTEN FREE ITEMS

Although all food items need to be verified gluten free (GF), there are certain **GF food items made by specialty food companies** that are available only through special resources. [Special resources include **health food** grocery stores, **ethnic** grocery food stores and gluten free **mail order** companies.]

A list of specialty gluten free food items may include **pasta** (e.g. corn pasta, rice pasta, bean pasta and potato pasta), **baked goods** (e.g. breads, bagels, muffins, brownies, cakes, pies and pancakes/waffles), **flours** (e.g. rice flour, arrowroot flour, potato starch-flour, corn flour, cornmeal, bean flour and tapioca starch/flour), **snacks** (e.g. pretzels, taro or potato sticks, crackers, puffs, rice cakes and cookies) **baking mixes** (e.g. bread, bagel, muffin, brownie, cake, pie crust and pancake/waffle mixes), **nutritional bars and/or drinks**, **cereals** (e.g. whole grains or prepared cereals) and certain **condiments** (e.g. spreads, dips, flavorings, baking powder and bullion).

DETAILS & SPECIFICATIONS

Celiac disease (CD), also known as coeliacs, gluten sensitive, nontropical sprue, enteropathyand celiac sprue is a genetically predisposed disease caused by a toxic reaction to the proteins (prolamins) found in certain gluten cereal grains (wheat, barley and rye).

Celiac disease (CD) is a permanent autoimmune disorder and disease of mal-absorption. This digestive disease damages the small intestines and interferes with the absorption of nutrients from food, when people with CD eat intolerable foods (e.g. foods with a certain type of gluten protein).

Symptoms of CD (before diagnosis and/or with contamination) are variable in combination and severity and vary from person to person. Symptoms of CD may include any of the following: bone pain, moodiness, poor appetite, weight loss, lactose intolerance, offensive flatulence, sensitivities, brain fog, fatigue, vomiting, anemia, nausea, diarrhea, hyperactivity, depression, nutrient deficiencies and stomach bloating, pain, gurgling and cramping.

If there is a strong clinical suspicion of CD, diagnosis can be, done quickly through blood tests to screen for specific antibodies to gluten or most accurately by an endoscope used to examine the small bowel and obtain a biopsy. [The test will be negative if the patient is already on the GF diet.] **Suggestions are all family members and offspring of celiacs be tested.** [DH may be diagnosed along with CD. Treatment for both is the GF diet.]

Treatment for CD & DH is non-medical (e.g., the lifelong strict avoidance of foods containing forbidden gluten grains and byproducts of these grains). [Gluten should, never be reintroduced to the diet.] For some, treatment may involve being, monitored by a physician to evaluate progress and to detect changes, which may need additional treatment. Antibody tests can be, used as a guide in monitoring a patient's adherence to the GF diet. Visiting a nutritionist familiar with celiac disease may be helpful.

Some patients find it necessary to restore health with **supplements** (e.g., acidophilus to help restore intestinal flora, a good multivitamin and mineral complex, zinc to help boost the immune system, digestive enzymes to help break down food, calcium for the bones, folic acid, vitamin B complex, additional vitamin B 12, vitamins A, K, C and D, and possibly iron).

Newly diagnosed celiac patients may be **temporarily intolerant of lactose**. Patients who have had active CD for years before diagnosis may also have associated immune related conditions. Food intolerances and chemical food additive sensitivities may be responsible for a wide spectrum of **neurological issues** (ADD and ADHD) in many children. A diet both, casein free and gluten free has been known to help.

There always seems to be controversy about which grains are safe for celiacs on the gluten free (GF) diet. According to my research, the **forbidden grains** include **wheat** (the most toxic), **rye, barley,** and possibly **oats.** [Advanced testing indicates 'pure' oats are not harmful to those who have CD and/or DH disease. Oats used in test studies are 'pure' and uncontaminated.] Other forbidden grains include **bulgur, diploid, durum, einkorn, emmer, far, hexaploid, kamut, mir, seitan, semolina, spelt, tetraploid, tsampa, triticale** and **triticum.**

Acceptable grains safe for celiacs include **corn, rice, wild rice, quinoa, millet, sorghum, amaranth** and **buckwheat.** [Buckwheat is not a wheat relative.] **Job's tear, tef** and **ragi** are closely related to corn and therefore are also consider safe.

When choosing questionable grains individual tolerance should dictate use. [Sensitivity to specific GF grains may indicate additional food allergies.]

For free information about grains write to **The** *U.S. Department of Agricultural Research Service,* Western Regional Research Center, Albany CA 94710. Ask for literature about grains and their relationship to celiac disease and the gluten free diet.

For **updated information** about the acceptable and forbidden grains for individuals with celiac disease, dermatitis herpetiformis **write, call or visit** the web sites of **the '***Celiac Associations/Groups* 'on page 214.

SUGGESTIONS & TIPS

Purchasing a gluten free food list will help resolve most GF issues. [See page 215 for details about obtaining the ***Gluten Free Food Product List*** '*the manufactures list of commercially prepared gluten free foods'*.] Ingredient mixtures and formulas can change at any time. **An 'updated' annual gluten free food list is imperative.**

There are usually phone numbers and addresses printed somewhere on the label of food products. Use them to call or write with questions or concerns about any product. [I personally call regularly with a variety of ingredient and manufacturing questions.] **Keep in mind not all manufacturers are knowledgeable or informed in the area of GF foods**, nor are most receptionists, especially about compound ingredients.

If the gluten free purity of a product is questionable, you must avoid it.

Create a list of essential addresses and phone numbers along with the names of any person who has been helpful and friendly to you. Record your favorite travel agencies, places to stay (e.g. receptionist, driver and tour guide), restaurants (e.g. food staff, chef, host and owner), local market, and health food grocery store (e.g. owner, manager and ordering-personal).

Purchase a few good gluten free recipe books. There are many GF recipes books in public libraries you can borrow free (e.g., look in the food allergy section). After learning the diet well, convert your old recipe favorites to GF.

Until you develop label-reading skills, purchase only foods labeled gluten free.

CAUTIONS

Some products may appear gluten free according to their label, but are not. This is confusing and difficult especially to the newly diagnosed and gluten sensitive.

Hidden sources of gluten can be found in commercially prepared products made with ingredients that are processed from gluten grains (e.g., flour, pasta, cereal, bread and other baked goods) and undefined ingredients (e.g. colorings, flavorings, fillers, additives, gums, stabilizers, preservatives, enzymes, starch, sweeteners, emulsifiers, thickeners and food agents).

Although not life threatening, contamination a concern for commercially prepared foods: 1.) Inadequately cleaned equipment and surfaces. 2.) Gluten contamination in the environment. 3.) Wheat flour used as filler or to keep foods separated or to dust conveyor belts and airborne.

Learn your ingredients well, read every label, every time, avoid foods that are questionable and bring the resourceful side of your personality with you shopping.

Gluten free living does get easier!

MENU PLANNING

- ❖ Keep a diary. Record foods that agree and/or disagree with your system.
- ❖ Stock your kitchen well with GF foods and stock your medicine cabinet well with GF prescription and nonprescription medications.
- ❖ Make extra GF meals and refrigerate or freeze some for another meal.
- ❖ Use leftover GF dinner for lunch the following day.
- ❖ Prepare GF baked goods ahead of time, freeze some and use as needed.
- ❖ Premix dry GF ingredient mixes for muffins or bread then freeze in individual containers and use as needed. (Add wet ingredients before baking.)
- ❖ Stock up on essentials (e.g. pasta, flour, cereal, baking mixes, baking ingredients, baked goods and some condiments). (See "specialty food items')
- ❖ Stock up on GF sale items. Most health food stores offer discounts on cases or volume buying.
- ❖ Store GF bread in the freezer, and use as needed.
- ❖ Put waxed paper between each slice of GF bread, GF pizza crust, or GF tortilla shell before freezing for easy separation.
- ❖ GF bread slices taste better toasted.
- ❖ Have a separate toaster for GF breads, to avoid contamination.
- ❖ Clean preparation areas well before preparing GF foods (e.g. counters, grills, cutting boards, kitchen utensils and appliances and attachments).
- ❖ Always keep a small travel bag packed with your favorite GF snacks.
- ❖ A strict adherence to the GF diet is simply easier with whole foods and processed GF foods made with basic ingredients.
- ❖ After grocery shopping, mark your GF food items with a permanent marker or with tiny unique stickers, for easy GF identification.
- ❖ Store GF food items separate, from foods containing gluten.
- ❖ Avoid contaminating GF condiments with utensils (e.g., leaving crumbs or other gluten containing foods behind). [Avoid this by not double dipping, using a separate utensil every time and/or if possible getting separate condiments.]
- ❖ Consider purchasing GF condiments (e.g. catsup, honey and mustard) in squeeze bottles and/or pourable containers to prevent contamination.
- ❖ Keep a few good GF recipe books on hand. Copy and save your favorite GF recipes separately. Creating GF recipes will get easier!
- ❖ Measure GF ingredients accurately when, following recipes.
- ❖ Add natural GF flavorings to GF recipes to add flavor and nourishment (e.g. applesauce, crushed pineapple, fresh and dried fruit, spices, herbs, shredded raw vegetables, nuts, seeds, yogurt, unrefined sugar, fruit spreads, molasses, maple syrup and honey).
- ❖ Store GF flours and starches in the freezer, tightly sealed.
- ❖ Store baked goods in sealed containers while still warm to retain moisture. [Allow the baked goods to cool before freezing.]
- ❖ On the internet, type in the words 'gluten free' or 'celiac disease' and see what comes up. Go from there!

The following are basic gluten free meal suggestions.

The meal suggestions are menu-planning ideas only and not considered daily-recommended requirements. Although all food items need to be gluten free, there are certain GF food items (e.g. pasta, flours, baked goods, baking mixes and cereals) only available through specialty resources. (See "specialty food items".)

SNACK MEAL SUGGESTIONS

Jerky (e.g. turkey or beef).	Crackers (e.g. rice, bean, corn or potato).	Pudding (e.g. rice or tapioca).	Gelatin with fresh fruit.
Dip (e.g. bean, or vegetable).	Toast with fruit spread.	Chocolate or carob chips.	Tortilla chips.
Pure water with added sweetener & lemon or lime citrus juice.	Fruit juice (e.g. apple, cranberry, berry or pineapple).	Vegetable juice (e.g. carrot, tomato or vegetable blend).	Apple sauce or crushed pineapple.
Cereal.	Cookies.	Corn nuts.	Candy.
Potato chips.	Mixed fruit cup.	Herbal tea.	Marshmallows.
Puffs (e.g. rice or potato).	Frozen pudding pop.	Frozen fruit bar.	Fruit smoothie.
Potato sticks.	Corn chips.	Rice cakes.	Popcorn cakes.
Coffee or tea.	Milkshake.	Popcorn.	Yogurt.

Fresh vegetables (e.g. avocados, broccoli, carrots, cauliflower, celery, cucumbers, green beans, peppers or tomatoes).

Fresh fruit (e.g. apple, apricot, banana, cantaloupe, cherimoya, cherries, grapes, cranberries, grapefruit, guava, honeydew, kiwi, kumquat, mango, nectarine, orange, papaya, peach, pear, persimmons, pineapple, plantain, plum, pomegranate, raspberries, strawberries, tangerine or watermelon).

Seeds (e.g. pine nuts, pumpkin, sesame, squash or sunflower seeds).

Nuts (e.g. almond, Brazil, cashew, hazel, macadamia, pecan, pistachio or walnut).

Nut butter (e.g. almond, cashew, hazelnut or peanut butter).

Fruit dried (e.g. apricot, banana, coconut, date, fig, pineapple, prune, or raisins).

Fruit spread (e.g. apple butter, pumpkin butter, berry preserves or marmalade).

Pickled vegetables (e.g. beets, chow chow, pickles, or sauerkraut).

Sweeteners (e.g. honey, maple syrup, molasses or rice bran syrup).

Trail mix (e.g. mix-together nuts, seeds, dried fruit, crispy cereal & sweetener).

Cheese (e.g. dairy cheese or non-dairy cheese).

Meal Replacement (bars or drinks).

LUNCH/DINNER MEAL SUGGESTIONS

Cooked **fish, meat,** or **poultry** with cooked **beans& grains** or steamed **vegetables.**	Fresh **salad** greens, cooked **beans / grains** & broiled **fish, meat** or **poultry** & **dressing.**	**Asian dishes** (e.g. fried rice, stir-fry's, risotto, vermicelli, chow mien or teriyaki).	**Sandwich** (e.g. tuna, egg salad, sliced meat, chicken salad or nut butter with fruit spread).
Frankfurter, or **burger,** seasoned **beans&** French-fries.	Broiled **poultry, fish,** or **meat** with **seasonings,** sauce or **gravy.**	Cooked **pasta, rice** or **potatoes,** with **sauce** or **dressing.**	Steamed **vegetables** with **sauce, gravy** or **dressing.**
Baked **potato** stuffed with **vegetables, sauce** & grated **cheese.**	Fresh **salad greens** with broiled **seafood, fish, poultry** or **meat& cheese.**	Fresh **salad greens** with grated fresh **vegetables** & **dressing** & seeds.	**Crackers** with sliced **cheese** & **fish, meat, seafood** or **poultry.**
Fresh **vegetables** with **Hummus, bean dip** or **spread.**	**Crackers** or chips with **bean dip hummus** or **spread.**	Salads (e.g. **egg, coleslaw, tuna** or **chicken** salad).	Homemade soup, Bisques, or **chowder** with **chips** or crackers
Baked potato, sweet potato, or **yam** with grilled **meat, poultry, fish** or **seafood&** a steamed **vegetable.**	**Vegetarian & Indonesian dishes** made with fruits, vegetables, **beans& grains.**	**Mexican dishes** (e.g. nachos, chili, tamales, ensalada, burritos, tastadita, enchiladas, tacos or quesadillas).	Roasted **fish, meat** or **poultry** with cooked **rice, pasta** or **potatoes** & a steamed **vegetable** with **dressing.**
Fresh **salad greens** with sliced hard-boiled **eggs& dressing.**	**Irish Dishes** (e.g. casseroles, stews, pot roast or potato dishes).	Cooked **potato** with steamed **vegetables&** grated **cheese.**	**Bisques, soup** or **chowder** with a **sandwich.**
Cooked **pasta, rice** or **potatoes** with **pesto.**	**Cottage cheese** with dried **fruit** or fresh fruit.	Cooked **pasta** or **rice** with beans, cheese & oil.	**Italian Dishes** (e.g. spaghetti, lasagna or pasta).
Packaged or **prepared meals.**	**Pizza** crust with toppings.	**Baked dish** with a piece of **bread** or **muffin.**	**BBQ chicken, pork** or **tofu.**
Polenta with pizza **toppings.**	**Macaroni & cheese.**	**Leftovers.**	Open faced sandwiches.
Franks & beans.	**Seasoned beans.**	**Seasoned rice.**	**Chicken nuggets.**

BREAKFAST MEAL SUGGESTIONS

Eggs, with fried **potatoes, toast & bacon** or **sausage**	A piece of **cake** with **frosting** or fruit spread.	Corn **muffins** topped with **butter** or **syrup**.
Toast, corn **muffins**, or **bread** with butter, cream cheese or fruit **spread**.	**Pancakes, French toast,** or **waffles** with fruit, **sauce** or **syrup**.	**Rice cakes topped** with nut butter& dried fruit, chopped nuts or seeds.
Frittata or **omelet** with **hash brown** or home fries & **toast** with butter or spread.	Hard or soft boiled **eggs**, with hash brown or **home fries & toast** with butter or spread.	**Eggs** with steamed **vegetables** (e.g. asparagus or spinach).
Cold **cereal** with **milk** (dairy or nondairy).	**Yogurt** with dried or fresh **fruit.**	**Muffins** with cream cheese **frosting**.
Hot **cereal** (buckwheat, rice, cornmeal, millet, or quinoa) with **milk** (dairy or nondairy) & **fruit**.	Bean or corn **tortilla wrap stuffed** with cheese, beans, eggs or sautéed vegetables.	**Pudding** (e.g. tapioca or rice) with **dried fruit** (e.g. figs, currants, dates apricot, coconut or prune).
Nutritional bar or drink.	A piece of **pie**.	**Instant breakfast** drink.

Make a list of personal family GF recipe favorites!

TERMS & DEFINITIONS
INTRODUCTION

This section is an alphabetically arranged list of various food ingredients and terminology relating to celiac disease (CD), dermatitis herpetiformis disease (DH) and the gluten free (GF) diet, with which you may or may not be familiar.

There is no need to get a degree in gluten free dialogue. The definitions in this book will help you understand any gluten free reading material associated with celiac disease, along with understanding all the gluten free ingredients used in recipes.

Following each word(s) is its brief definition and a supposition if the food product is gluten free (GF).

The words and/or terms being defined are printed in '**bold**'. These **bold**-words (which are not underlined) are considered unsafe, forbidden, questionable, or they may possibly be gluten free (GF).

Words underlined and printed in '**bold**' are considered gluten free (GF), safe, acceptable or questionable.

[In a 'definition statement' if a 'single' word is underlined, then that particular ingredient 'only' is gluten free (GF).]

All individually '*italicized*' words listed in a definition-statement are themselves also defined separately. [Research further, by also reading these definitions.]

There is a broad spectrum of gluten free (GF) cautions applicable to any food. Not 'every' gluten free 'caution' can possibly be listed in this book.

The food 'terms & definitions' are based on 'ordinary' foods, with which most people are familiar.

In this list, selected amounts of foods are prepared with special gluten free ingredients, obtainable 'only' through 'special gluten free resources'. (See *Gluten Free Resource Guide*.)

In each definition, where applicable, there is a statement pertaining to gluten free (GF).

To make referencing comprehensive yet quick & simple, these statements are brief & general.

Relevant **gluten and/or gluten free statements** listed in each definition include, but are not limited to the following:

* **GF**. In its purest form it is gluten free.
* **Check for GF purity**. Although it is gluten free you need to make sure it is 100% pure GF.
* **Verify GF**. It needs to be identified and verified as GF.
* **Obtainable GF**. It is usually not gluten free, but is obtainable gluten free through special resources.
* **Questionable**. There may be concerns. You need to look into it. Avoid unless verified GF.
* **Avoid unless source is known**. Avoid it & avoid any food it is in unless its source and/or all of its components are verified GF.
* **Question the source**.
* **Caution**. Examine it carefully. Possible health concerns.
* **Avoid if possible**. It should be avoided for health issues or because of possible gluten free concerns.

* **Risky**. It is most likely not gluten free. It is uncommon to find it gluten free.
* **Avoid**. Avoid it. Avoid byproducts of it. Avoid it in all foods. Avoid all food with it.

The safety of every food item is not possible to check with label reading alone. **Law does not require the listing of all food-components or of classes of ingredients and/or foods on labels** and then there is the possibility of cross contamination. [There are no specific definitions for some ingredient terms listed on labels.]

If you would like the labeling laws for processors to change, write the **Food & Drug Administration 5600 Fishers Lane, Rockville MD 20857**.

Let the FDA know you have a restricted diet, label reading is essential to your health and you would like everything going 'into' or 'on' all products listed on the label in the ingredient section.

Let the FDA know about any other food concerns you might have (e.g., irradiated food, genetically modified food, pesticides used on foods and chemicals used in foods).

For updated information about the dermatitis herpetiformis, celiac disease, acceptable and forbidden grains and the gluten free diet write, call or visit the web sites of the 'Celiac Associations/Groups' on page 206.

The terms & definitions section of this book is concentrated for your convenience. Below are a couple of suggestions to enhance your search.

1) When researching a specific food such as 'rice germ' you can find additional information about 'rice germ' if you look up 'rice' and also look up 'germ'.
2) If you can't find a particular food item in this book such as 'white sauce', try being more general by breaking the phrase down and looking up part of the word (e.g., the word 'sauce').

Throughout the definitions section you will see 'refer to A & F charts'. These are the 'allowable' and 'forbidden' food charts found in the back portion of this book.

Most commercially prepared food products contain the manufactures name, phone number and/or address. This is consumer contact information you can use to find specific product information. Purchasing the **Gluten Free Food Product List** 'the manufactures list of commercially prepared gluten free foods' would prove invaluable. This annual book is simple to use and contains thousands of gluten free grocery food store items and countless manufactures names and phone numbers. To purchase this book see page 207.

Selecting products with the least amount of basic ingredients is the least complicated and most likely, the safest, for anyone on a restricted diet.

Certain undefined ingredients are defined in hypoallergenic foods (e.g. spices, seasoning, flavoring and coloring). Some ingredients are specifically defined in many natural and organic foods.

Read labels carefully and look for **red-flag** items (e.g. gluten grains and their byproducts and forbidden flavorings, colorings, vinegars, fillers, gums, emulsifiers, stabilizers, cereal proteins, sweeteners, binders, preservatives, starch, food starch, additives, certain fats/oils and other food additives and agents).

You can purchase gluten free (GF) specialty items at regular, health food and ethnic food stores, or through gluten free mail order companies. In each definition, where applicable, are instructions on where to purchase these 'specialty' gluten free items.

The *Gluten Free Resource Guide 'a consumers guide for living gluten free',* contains a list of the names of gluten free (GF) mail order companies, along with other must have information (e.g. illustrations, charts, book recommendations, various resources, menu planning, sample letters, the do's & don'ts of the gluten free diet and practical information on how to shop, dine, travel and stock a pantry gluten free). To purchase this book see page 207.

Learn your ingredients well, read every label, every time, avoid foods questionable and bring the resourceful side of your personality with you shopping.

The terms & definitions section contains an abundance of information. Learn useful facts and particulars by reading this section in book-format. Especially review the following words: absorption, acute, anemia, artificial, base, baked goods, basic, biopsy, books, buckwheat, blood test, bread, catering, cereal, celiac disease, common name, codex alimentarius commission, cosmetic, celiac shock, commercially prepared, dermatitis herpetiformis, drug store, diagnosis, diarrhea, disease, filler, envelope, FDA, flavor, flour, food list, fruit, GMO, genus, grain, gluten, gluten free, gluten testing, glutinous, generic, grocery food store, health food, ingredients, hidden ingredient, hypoallergenic food, immune system, imitation, intestine, kitchen supplies, leavening agent, lactose intolerant, label reading, mail order, mill, meal replacement, manufacture, metabolize, mixes, malnutrition, malabsorption, medication, newly diagnosed, plain, nonspecific ingredient, nutritionist, oil, organic, pure, packaging material, peptides, prepared food, PDR, pasta, protein, pharmaceuticals, pastry, plant, recipe, processed food, quinoa, residue, restaurant, seasoning, snack, self diagnose, sensitive celiac, stock, strain, stuffing, sweeteners, special occasion, special ingredients, specialty companies, specialty resources, travel, supplement, substitute, symptoms, synthetic, traditionally prepared, topical medication, thickener, unusual name, unidentified ingredient, villi, vinegar, USDA, USP, vending machine, weight gain, wrappers, xanthan gum and yeast.

Note: The statements and/or the reliability of the sources of information, in the terms & definitions section are believed-to-be true at the time of printing this book. American, Canadian and European regulations have some differences in how they define certain ingredients.

TERMS & DEFINITIONS

100%: 100% is a term used for products containing a specific *food* or *ingredient*. The term 100% does not mean *'pure'*, only the word 'pure' on a *label* means *pure*. Products *labeled* 100% generally contain other *ingredients* (e.g. *filler*). Choose 100% pure GF *foods*. Verify 100% pure foods are GF. (See *ingredients*)

A & F Charts: (See *allowable* and *forbidden charts*)

Abalone: A type of *fish*. *Pure fresh* and *plain* are GF. (See *fish*)

Absinthe: A type of *spice*. *Pure spices* are GF. (See *spice*)

Absorption: Absorption is the process in *digestion* where *nutrients* are absorbed into the body. When consumed, *food metabolizes* through the *digestive system* and then transforms into energy. Individuals with *active celiac disease* may have trouble absorbing *nutrients*, because *villi* damage. *Celiac* patients on the *gluten free diet,* in general, absorb *nutrients* properly. (See *villi, nutrients, supplements* and *CD.*)

Acacia Gum: (See *arabic gum*) GF.

Acceptable Grains: (See *gluten free grains.*)

Acetic Acid: Acetic acid is a type of *natural* or *synthetic pH adjusting agent*. It occurs naturally in *apples, cheese, grapes, milk, peaches, pineapples, strawberries* and *apple cider vinegar*. Caution. GF.

Achar: Achar is a term for *chutney*. (See *chutney.*)

Acid: Acids are a type of *compound substance* releasing hydrogen ions when in *solution*. Acids are one of the main *ingredients* in *baking powder*. Verify GF. (See *alkali.*)

Acid Calcium Phosphate: A type of *leavening agent*. GF.

Acidophilus: Acidophilus is a type of good *bacteria* that helps treat intestinal disorders. You can take acidophilus to help maintain the *nutritional* balance of the *digestive system*. Acidophilus is available in a *supplemental* form and in some *yogurt* and other fermented milk products. Verify GF. (See *villa, flora* and *supplement.*)

Acid Reacting Materials: These materials may contain *chemical compounds* and *acid*. Verify GF.

Acidulant: A type of *preservative* used to make *food* more *acidic*. Verify GF. (See *preservative.*)

Acorn: *A type of nut. Raw* and *plain* acorns are GF. (See *nut.*)

Active Celiac Disease: Active celiac disease is *celiac disease* is celiac disease in an *acute stage.* Active celiac disease causes distress and possibly physical symptoms. The patient typically becomes ill and symptoms may worsen. Celiacs in either an active or inactive stage must stay on the GF diet for life. (See *acute* and *disease.*)

Active Dry Yeast: Active dry yeast is a certain type of dry *yeast* activated when dissolved in warm water. Types of active dry yeast include regular or protected active dry *yeast- PADY* and quick or instant active dry yeast- *IADY*. Some *yeast* are labeled 'gluten free'. (See *yeast.*)

Acute: *Celiacs* and/or *sensitive celiacs* just before *diagnosis* may react acutely after ingesting *gluten*. After ingesting even the smallest amount of gluten, these individuals may react briefly, severely and quickly with diarrhea and/or other minor *symptoms*. [Celiacs who follow a strict adherence to the GF diet commonly build up a degree of tolerance over time, but people with CD must maintain a GF diet for life.] (See *symptoms, sensitive, gluten sensitive* and *acute stage*.)

Acute Stage: Acute is the first stage of a *disease*. The acute stage is the beginning point in a *disease* where the body begins to weaken. Patients with CD in the acute stage might not show any immediate signs from the consumption of *gluten*. Patients in the acute stage of celiac disease will recover with a strict adherence to the GF diet. (See *four stages of disease, celiac disease* and *disease*.)

Additive: Additives are any non-nutritive *natural* or *synthetic substance* added to food during *manufacturing*. Types of additives may include *colors, chemical compounds*, spices, gums, *vitamins, minerals, seasonings, wax, fillers* and *flavors*. [Look up each individually.] Although generously added, additives as *'ingredients'* in processed foods are not always listed. The source of all additives is questionable. [Selecting products with the least amount of additives is the least complicated and most likely the safest.] (See *pure, ingredient, agent, substance* and *organic*.)

Adipic Acid: A type of *acid* derived from *beets*. GF. (See *acid*.)

Adrak: (See *ginger root*.) GF.

Aduki Bean: (See *adzuki bean*.) GF.

Adulterated: Adulterated is a term for *food* made less *pure* by the addition of *substances*. [Adulterated *substances* are frequently inferior.] {Some of these adulterated substances may include *artificial*

ingredients, chemical compounds, additives, fillers, food agents and *waxes*.} [Look up each individually.]

Adzuki Bean: Adzuki beans are a type of *bean* sweet, small and red in color with a white striped ridge. GF. (See *bean* and *adzuki bean flour*.)

Adzuki Bean Flour: An excellent *bean-flour milled* from the *whole* adzuki *bean*. Check for GF purity. (See *bean flour* and *adzuki bean*.)

Aerate: To allow air to circulate through a *food*. This can be done *mechanically* or *chemically* (e.g., with air or gas). *Dry ingredients* in *baked-good mixtures* are best aerated *mechanically* using a *sifter* or wire *whisk*. (See *sift, whisk, oxygenate* and *aerating agent*.)

Aerating Agent: (See *propellant*.)

Agar: Agar is a type of colorless and flavorless *powder* or granular *marine algae*. Agar is a *natural emulsifying, stabilizing, gelling* and *thickening* agent. Agar can replace *gelatin* in some *recipes*. Agar will not gel when mixed with *acetic acid*. Caution: agar contains *laxative* properties. Caution: agar may cause flatulence. GF. (See *condiment*.)

Agar Gum: (See *agar*.) GF.

Agave: Agave is a type of *sweetener/syrup* derived from a certain type of *aloe*. GF.

Aged Cheese: Aged cheeses are any ripened *'mature' cheese*, as opposed to an *un-ripened immature 'fresh' cheese*. Aged cheese matures from a variety of processes including subjection to *bacteria*. Choose <u>pure</u> <u>unflavored</u> types of aged cheese including some brands of <u>cheddar</u>, <u>Muenster</u>, <u>Parmesan</u>, <u>Romano</u>, <u>provolone</u> and <u>Swiss</u> cheese. Verify

GF. Avoid all aged *veined cheeses.* (See *cheese* and *dairy*.)

Agent: *Food* agents are any *chemical* or *natural substance,* causing an effect in and/or on *food.* Question all. (See *additive*)

Albacore: Albacore is a type of *tuna fish. Fresh pure* and *plain* albacore is GF. (See *tuna* and *fish*.)

Albumin: Albumin is a type of water-*soluble protein coagulated* by heat. Albumins are in *animal* and *plant tissue.* Albumins can be *egg* or *milk* based. GF.

Alcohol: Alcohol is an *intoxicant beverage* produced by the *fermentation* of *sugar* or *starch.* Gluten free alcohol includes certain brands of potato *vodka, rum, gin, brandy, tequila,* corn *whiskey* and some *wines. Certified* and *medical distilled alcohols* are GF. Properly distilled alcoholic beverages are gluten free (e.g., any distilled alcohol 80 proof or more is gluten free). *Pure distilled* alcohols include *whiskey, rum, gin, vodka, scotch, brandy, bourbon, vermouth* and pure *liqueurs. Distilled* alcohols with *additives* are not gluten free. Avoid *ale, beer, lager* and *malt wines.* [Look up each kind individually.] Question all flavored alcohols. {Alcohol may contain added *preservatives, dyes, colorings, flavorings* and other *additives.*} (See 'alcohol' in A & F charts.)

Alcohol Free: Alcohol free is a term used to state the *food* or *beverage* does not contain *alcohol.* The term alcohol free does not guarantee *alcohol* was not used as an *extracting agent.* (See *alcohol* and *extracts*.)

Alcohol Vinegar: Alcohol vinegar is a type of *diluted distilled alcohol.* Caution. Verify GF. (See *vinegar* and *alcohol*.)

Ale: Ale is a type of forbidden *alcohol* brewed from malt and hops. (See *alcohol* and *beer*.)

Alfalfa: Alfalfa is considered a *vegetable. Pure fresh* and *plain* alfalfa is GF. Individuals with *weakened immune systems* are advised to avoid alfalfa sprouts. Avoid if possible. (See *sprout* and *weakened immune system*.)

Algae: Algae is a type of aquatic *organism* obtained from fresh or salt water. Check for GF purity.

Alginate: *Salt* or *ester* derived from *alginic acid (seaweed).* Alginate is a *thickener* and *emulsifier.* GF.

Alginates Gum: A type of *gum* derived from *seaweed.* GF.

Algin Gum: Algin gum is a certain type of *gum.* GF. (See *gum*.)

Alginic Acid: Alginic acid is a type of *seaweed.* GF. (See *alginate*.)

Alkali: Alkalis are *acid neutralizing substances* used to make *food* less *acidic* or more *alkaline.* Alkali *substances* are one of the main *components* in *baking powder.* Verify GF. (See *acid*.)

Allergen: Allergens are *substances* having the potential to cause an allergic reaction in certain people. The FDA has not formally defined 'allergens', but the FDA does list foods that cause serious allergenic responses. [The FDA allows processors to voluntarily *label* their products with 'incidental' potential allergenic foods other than the most commonly known.] At present time, the FDA has no allergenic labeling regulations for the term 'gluten free'.

The FDA expects processors to abide to the policy on hypoallergenic foods. [If you would like these laws to change, write the FDA and let the FDA know you have a restricted diet, *label* reading is essential to your *health* and you would like gluten listed as an allergen.] (See *FDA* and *hypoallergenic foods*.)

Allergenic Foods: (See *allergen*.)

Allowable & Forbidden Charts: Throughout the definitions section you will see 'refer to A & F charts'. These are the 'allowable' and 'forbidden' food charts found in on pages 197-207. The A & F charts were, designed for quick and easy referencing. All foods and food ingredients in the A & F charts are defined individually and extensively in this terms and definitions section. All food items in the A & F charts need to be verified gluten free.

All-Purpose Flour: The use of the term 'all-purpose flour' refers to flour made from *forbidden wheat grains*. The term '*all-purpose flour*' listed as an *ingredient* is usually *wheat flour* unless *specifically identified*. All-purpose flour is a type of *grain flour* usually *milled* from soft or hard *wheat grains*. Avoid. [A certain type of GF all-purpose flour is available only through specialty companies or can be *homemade* with *specialty ingredients*.] (See *flour* and *specialty companies*.)

All-Purpose Potato: A type of *tuber* used in a wide range of recipes. To cook all-purpose potatoes: bake, fry, boil or steam. GF. (See *potato*.)

Allspice: A type of *spice*. *Pure* allspice is GF. (See *spice*.)

Almond: Almonds are a type of *nut*. *Raw* and *plain* almonds are GF. (See *nut* and *blanch*.)

Almond Butter: A type of *nut butter ground* from *raw* or *roasted almonds*. Check for GF purity. (See *almond* and *nut butter*.)

Almond Meal: Almond meal is a type of *meal/flour* milled from almonds. Use almond meal as a *flavoring* or *binder* in *baked goods*. *Raw* almonds can be home *milled* in a *coffee mill*. Check for GF purity. (See *almond* and *meal*.)

Almond Milk: Almond milk is a type of *nondairy milk*. Almond milk is prepared from *raw almonds*. Almond milk is easy to *home-make*. {Almond milk may contain added *filler, flavors, gums, alcohol, grain byproducts* or *enzymes*.} Verify GF. (See *non-dairy milk* and *almond*.)

Almond Oil: A type of *oil* obtained from *almonds*. The best is *distilled* almond oil. Check for GF purity.

Aloe: Aloe is a type of *vegetable*. *Pure fresh* and *plain* aloe and aloe juice and gels are GF. Question the source of *gum* added to some aloe juice and aloe gels.

Aloo: (See *potato*.) *Plain* are GF.

Alta: *Whole-wheat flour*. Avoid.

Alum: GF.

Aluminum: Caution. GF.

Aluminum Cookware: Aluminum cookware is reactive to *acid* and *alkaline food*. Do not use *ascorbic acid* with *aluminum cookware*. (See *ascorbic acid, aluminum foil, cookware* and *stainless steel*.)

Aluminum Foil: *Cook* GF *food* separate on a piece of *aluminum foil* to avoid *contamination* (e.g. toast). (See *aluminum cookware*)

Amaranth: Amaranth is a type of GF *seed*. Amaranth is not a *grain* or member of the *grass plant family*. Amaranth is considered a *'grain'* because of its 'grain-like' similarities. Amaranth is extraordinarily nutritious and high in protein and calcium. Whole amaranth seeds are available at health food grocery stores and by mail order. (See *grains* and *amaranth flour*.)

Amaranth Flour: Amaranth flour is a type of *flour milled* from *amaranth* seeds. Amaranth flour blends well with other *flour*. Check for GF purity. (See *amaranth*.)

Amasake: Amasake is type of *beverage* made from *rice*. <u>Some are GF</u>. Question added *sweeteners*. Verify GF. (See *beverage*.)

Amazake: (See *amasake*.)

Amberjack: A type of *fish*. *Fresh pure* and *plain* amberjack are GF.

American Cheese: American cheese is a specific type of *cheese* made from cow's *milk*. American cheese is one of the most popular cheeses. American cheese is available in individually wrapped *slices* or fresh *sliced* at the *deli* department of the grocery store. Question the possibility of *contamination* at the deli department with the *equipment* (e.g. food slicing machines) and preparation area. They must both be free of *gluten* contaminants. Verify GF. (See *cheese*.)

American Dietitian Association: To locate a registered dietitian in your area call or write the American Dietitian Association. The phone number is 312-899-0040. The mailing address is 216 W Jackson Blvd. Chicago, IL. 60606-6995. (See *dietitian*.)

Amino Acid: *Organic acids* are the building blocks for *protein*. GF.

Aminos: (See *liquid aminos*.)

Amioca: (See *waxy cornstarch*.)

Ammonium Bicarbonate: Ammonium bicarbonate is an *alkali dough strengthener, leavening* and *texturizing agent*. Ammonium bicarbonate is an ingredient in some *baking powder* mixes. GF.

Ammonium Carbonate: Ammonium carbonate is an *alkali dough strengthener, leavening* and *texturizing agent*. Ammonium carbonate is in some *baking powder* mixes. GF.

Ammonium Hydroxide: A type of *chemically* made *alkaline*. Caution. GF. (See *alkali*.)

Amylase: Amylase is a type of *enzyme* found in *plants* and *animals* converting *starch* and *glycogen* into *simple sugar*. GF. (See *enzyme*.)

Anasazi Bean: Anasazi beans are tiny mottled maroon and white *pinto bean* relative. GF. (See *bean*.)

Anchovy: A type of *fish*. *Pure fresh* and *plain* anchovies are GF. Anchovies may be *salt cured* or packed in *oil*. <u>Choose *plain* unseasoned</u> anchovies. Verify GF.

Anchovy Paste: A type of *condiment paste* made with *anchovies* and *filler*. Question added *filler*. Avoid unless source is known. (See *anchovy* and *paste*.)

Anecdotal Reports: Anecdotal reports are subjective testing and/or reports. These reports are based on hearsay, as apposed to scientific facts and investigations. Anecdotal reports are sometimes gathered or obtained from other *celiacs*.

Anemia: Anemia is a type of blood deficiency in which there are too few red blood cells or too little hemoglobin in the red blood *cells* because of poor health. Anemia may develop from a poor *diet*, *malnutrition* problems and/or *absorption* difficulties. *Celiacs* may be *anemic* when first diagnosed.

Angelica: A type of *herb*. *Pure* angelica is GF. (See *herb*.)

Angostura: A type of *spice/herb*. *Pure* is GF. (See *herbs* and *spices*.)

Animal: Animals are any living non-*plant organism* with independent movement. Animals rely on *plants* for *nutrition*. Although an animal may consume *gluten* in its *diet* there has been no research indicating this as being harmful to *celiacs* on a GF *diet*. Therefore, all *pure fresh* animal foods (e.g., *eggs*, *meat*, *poultry*, *fish* and *seafood*) are GF no matter what the animal consumed. Concerns for gluten are in the *preparation* or *processing* of animal foods (e.g. *omelets*, *hot dogs*, *chicken patties*, *fish sticks* and *fish cakes*). [Look up each source individually.] Choose *pure fresh* and *plain* animal *foods*. Check for GF purity. (See 'meat, fowl, fish and seafood' in A & F charts.)

Anise: Anise is a type of *spice*. *Pure* anise is GF. (See *spice*.)

Annatto: Annatto is a type of *natural dye* obtained from a certain *seed pulp*. Caution. Verify GF.

Antibodies: Antibodies are a certain type of *protein* produced by B *cells* in the body, in response to the presence of *antigens*. *Antibodies* are the primary form of immune response in resistance to *disease*. Antibodies act by attaching themselves to a foreign *antigen* and weakening or destroying it. If there

is a strong clinical suspicion of *celiac disease*, diagnosis is through blood *tests* to screen for specific antibodies to *gluten*. The *blood test* for *celiac disease* looks for *antibodies* to an *enzyme* called *transglutaminase*. [The blood test will be negative if the patient is already on the GF diet.] (See *biopsy*, *blood test* and *antigen*.)

Anti-Browning Agent: A food *substance* used to prevent *foods* (commonly *fruits* and *vegetables*) from browning. Caution. (See *agent*)

Anti-Caking Agent: A food *substance* used to prevent *foods* from lumping or clumping together. Anti-caking agents keep powdered food substances free-flowing. (See *agent*)

Anti-Foaming Agent: A food *substance* used to prevent or reduce foaming. Caution. (See *agent*)

Antigen: Antigens are a certain type of *protein* on the surface of a *cell* or bacterium stimulating the production of an antibody. *Antibodies* are the primary form of immune response in resistance to *disease* and act by attaching to a foreign antigen and weakening or destroying it. If there is a strong clinical suspicion of *celiac disease*, diagnosis is through blood *tests* to screen for antibodies to *gluten*. The *blood test* for *celiac disease* looks for *antibodies* to an *enzyme* called *transglutaminase*. (See *biopsy*, *blood test* and *antibodies*.)

Antimicrobial Agent: A food *substance* used to prevent the growth of *bacteria*, *mold* or *yeast* in *foods*. Caution. Verify GF. (See *agent*)

Antioxidant: Any *natural* or *chemical additive inhibiting oxidation* and thus prevents *food* from spoiling. Antioxidants are also *substances* used internally to rid the body of *toxins*. Caution. Verify GF.

Appenzeller Cheese: A type of solid *Swiss cheese* made from cow's *milk*. Verify GF. (See *cheese*.)

Appetizer: Appetizers are types of *food* served before a main course. Appetizers are a type of side dish, *hors D'oeuvre* and sometimes finger *food*. Most appetizers are not GF. Avoid unless source is known. (See *special occasion*.)

Apple: A type of *fruit*. *Raw fresh* and *plain* are GF. Apples make one of the best *travel foods*. (See *apple cider vinegar* and *fruit*.)

Apple Cider: Apple cider is a type of *beverage* pressed from *raw apples*. [Caution: pasteurization for the elderly, very young and people with a *weakened immune system*.] Caution. Check for GF purity.

Apple Cider Vinegar: Apple cider vinegar is a type of *vinegar* made from *fermented* freshly pressed *apple juice*. The best apple cider vinegar is *raw, unfiltered, organic, pure* and *natural* with the '*mother*' and without *preservatives*, added *clarifiers, enzymes* or *preservatives*. Apple cider vinegar is great for travel. Store apple cider vinegar in a cool dark place up to three years. Avoid *apple-flavored vinegar*. Choose 'pure' apple cider vinegar. Verify GF. (See *vinegar*.)

Apple Dried: Dried apples are a type of *dried fruit* made from sliced *raw apples*. Check for GF purity. (See *dried fruit*.)

Apple Flavored Vinegar: Apple flavored vinegar is a type of *distilled* white *vinegar* with added *flavorings*. Avoid. [Apple flavored vinegar is not the same as *apple cider vinegar*.] (See *apple cider vinegar*)

Apple Juice: Apple juice is a type of fruit *juice* pressed from *raw apples*. Question added *spices* and sweeteners. Choose 100% *pure* naturally sweetened or unsweetened. Verify GF. (See *juice*.)

Applesauce: Applesauce is a type of *natural dessert* made from *cooked pureed raw apples*. Most *applesauce is safe*. Question added *spices* and sweeteners. Choose 100% *pure* naturally sweetened or *unsweetened* applesauce. Applesauce makes a great *travel snack food*. Verify GF.

Appliance: Appliances are any hand held or stationary *kitchen tool* using electricity. Clean all appliances and appliance attachments well in between uses. (See *toaster*.)

Apricot: Apricots are a type of *fruit*. *Raw fresh* and *plain* apricots are GF. (See *fruit*.)

Apricot Dried: Dried apricots are a type of *dried fruit* obtained from *apricots*. Check for GF purity. (See *dried fruit*.)

Apricot Kernel: *Apricot seeds.* Verify GF. (See *apricot kernel oil*.)

Apricot Kernel Oil: *Oil* obtained from *apricot kernels*. Verify GF.

Arabic Gum: Arabic gum is a *gum* derived from *acacia* trees. GF.

Arabinogalactan Gum: *Gum* derived from larch trees. GF.

Aragum Gum: Aragum gum is derived from *acacia* and *corn*. GF.

Arame: *A type of seaweed. Pure* and plain arame is GF. (See *seaweed*.)

Arepas: *Posole* made from *starchy corn* slaked in lye. Verify GF.

Aromatic: Containing a pleasing aroma. (See *aromatic rice*.)

Aromatic Rice: A type of *long grain rice* with a pleasant *aroma* and *flavor*. GF. (See *rice* for specifics.)

Aromatic Wines: Questionable. (See *wine* and *vermouth*.)

Arrowroot: Arrowroot is the starchy *root* of a tropical plant. GF. (See *arrowroot powder*.)

Arrowroot Flour: (See *arrowroot powder*.) GF.

Arrowroot Powder: Arrowroot powder is a type of GF *powder* made from finely *milled* dried *arrowroots*. Arrowroot powder is a tasteless *thickening* and *coating agent*. Arrowroot powder is excellent for *sauces* not requiring high heat. Choose *100% pure* arrowroot powder. Arrowroot powder is obtainable at *health food* and *ethnic grocery food stores* and by *mail order*. (See *thickeners*)

Arrowroot Starch: (See *arrowroot powder*.) GF.

Artichokes: A type of *vegetable*. *Pure fresh* and *plain* artichokes are GF. (See *vegetable*.)

Artificial: Artificial is a blanket term for a variety of *ingredients* made with *natural* or *synthetic chemicals*. Artificial *substances* are from sources other than the *plant* part it names. Artificial ingredients can also be *natural substances*, but derived from sources other than the *food* it is *imitating*. Artificial substances are generally *unnatural*. Anything artificial is questionable. Caution. Avoid artificial foods if possible. (See *sensitivities*.)

Artificial Color: Artificial color is a blanket term for a variety of *artificial substances* used to add *color* to *foods*. Caution. Question the source. (See *artificial*.)

Artificial Flavor: Artificial flavor is a blanket term for a variety of *substances* used to *flavor* to foods. {Artificial flavors may contain added *sweeteners, colorings, preservatives, alcohols, oils* and *emulsifiers*.} Caution. Question the source. (See *artificial* and *extract*.)

Artificial Ingredient: (See *artificial*.)

Artificial Sweetener: Artificial sweetener is a blanket term for a variety of *substances* used to *sweeten* foods. Caution. Question the source. [Look up each individually.] The majority of artificial sweeteners are GF. (See *artificial* and *sweetener*.)

Arugala: A type of *vegetable*. *Pure fresh* and *plain* arugala is GF.

Asadero Cheese: An un-*aged* cow's *milk* cheese similar to *Monterey jack*. Verify GF. (See *cheese*.)

Asafetida: Asafetida is a type of *seasoning* commonly packaged with *wheat* or *rice flour filler*. Question the source of the *filler*. [The filler in asafetida is commonly *rice flour* in health food stores and *wheat flour* in ethnic stores.]

Ascetic Acid: A type of *acid* obtained from *wood*. Caution. GF.

Ascorbic Acid: *Vitamin C powder*. Ascorbic acid is a *component* and *leavening agent* usually derived from *corn* or *synthetic* prepared. Do not use *aluminum cookware* with ascorbic acids. Verify GF. (See *acid aluminum* and *stainless steel*.)

Asiago Cheese: A type of semi-firm *cheese* made from cow's *milk*. Verify GF. (See *cheese*.)

Asian Noodles: Asian noodles are *noodles* made from *beans, potato,* *cornstarch, rice* and/or *wheat.* Question the source. (See *pasta.*)

Asparagus: A type of *vegetable. Pure fresh* and *plain* asparagus are GF. (See *vegetable.*)

Asparagus Bean: A type of *bean* used *fresh* or *dried.* GF.

Aspartame: Aspartame is a type of *synthetic sweetener.* It is *'specifically identified'* as an *'ingredient'.* Caution. Verify GF. (See *artificial sweeteners* and *sensitivities.*)

Assorted Flavorings: (See *artificial flavorings.*)

Atole: Atole is *milled corn.* Verify GF. Atole is also a *meal* made with *masa, fruit* and *milk.* Verify all ingredients are GF.

Au Natural: Au natural is a term for *food* in its *natural* state. All au natural foods need to be verified GF. (See *natural.*)

Avenin: A type of *plant protein* (*prolamin.*) found in *oat.* (See *oat* for acceptability and *prolamins.*)

Avidin: Avidin is derived from *eggs.* GF.

Avocado: A type of *vegetable. Pure fresh* and *plain* avocadoes are GF.

Avocado Oil: A type of *oil* obtained from *avocadoes.* Verify GF.

Azuki Bean: (See *adzuki bean.*) GF.

Baati: *Wheat flour* balls. Avoid.

Baby Food: Call the baby *food companies* you favor and request their *allergen/gluten free* food list.

Baby Formula: (See *baby food.*)

Baby Lima Bean: Baby lima beans are a type of small *lima bean.* GF.

Backpacking Food: Backpacking foods are typically *instant* lightweight *foods* designed to take up little room while cross-country *traveling.* These types of foods make great *travel foods.* Only a few backpacking foods are GF. (See *instant* and *travel.*)

Bacon: Bacon is *cured* and *smoked pork.* Choose *100% pure* bacon. Choose bacon free of *nitrates* if possible. Avoid *canned bacon, bacon bits* and *imitation bacon.* {Bacon may contain added *flavors* and *sweeteners.*} Avoid *bacon flavored* with *forbidden barley malt.* Verify GF. (See *bacon bits.*)

Bacon Bits: Avoid. [You can *home make* bacon bits by crumbling *cooked* GF bacon slices.] (See *bacon* and *imitation.*)

Bacteria: Bacteria are types of parasitic *microorganism* without distinct *nuclei* or organized *cell* structure. Bacteria are what cause *animal* and *plant tissue* to age, decay, *mold, ferment* and disease in a *natural* process. A type of good *bacteria* (*acidophilus*) helps treat intestinal disorders. (See *good bacteria, acidophilus* and *sensitive.*)

Bacteria Ripened Cheese: Any *aged cheese matured* by the process of subjection to *bacteria.* Some bacteria ripened cheeses are GF. Verify GF. (See *cheese.*)

Badam: (See *almonds.*) GF.

Baffle: *Wheat* flour balls. Avoid.

Bagels: Bagels are chewy dense round *doughnut*-like *baked-goods* made with *yeast* and *wheat dough.* Avoid. You can *home make* GF bagels with *specialty* GF *ingredients. Commercially prepared* bagels are available only through specialty companies. (See *special resources* and *specialty ingredients.*)

Baingan: (See *eggplant.*) GF.

Bake: Baked foods are baked in an *oven* on the baking rack. Do not bake GF *foods* in the same dish with other

foods containing *gluten*. (See *baked-goods, oven, toaster oven* and *cook*.)
Baked Beans: (See *seasoned beans*.)
Baked-Goods: Baked goods are *foods baked* in an *oven*. Baked-goods are typically *prepared* with a moist *batter* or *dough mixture*. Types of baked goods include *breads, brownies, cakes, doughnuts, muffins* and *pies*. {Baked goods may contain added *starches, emulsifiers, flavorings, colorings, preservatives, sweeteners, stabilizers, acidifiers, antioxidants, yeast food, buffers, alkalis, dough conditioner, enzymes, humectants* and *leavening, maturing, antistalin, bleaching, antistaling, antifoaming* and *antimycotic* agents.} Baked-goods are normally prepared with *forbidden wheat flour*. Most *commercially prepared* baked-goods are not GF. If a baked-good is truly GF it will be *labeled*. There are excellent *recipe books* available to *home bake* GF baked-goods with specialty GF *ingredients*. Some of these recipe books provide easy to make GF *baked-good* recipes with a variety of *substitutions* and alternative *baking* suggestions. (See *recipe books*.) Avoid all baked goods unless verified GF. [Read the labels of all baked goods. Certain brands of rice and potato breads contain *wheat*.] *Commercially prepared* GF baked-goods are available through *specialty companies* and/or specialty bakeries. (See *gluten free resource guide, bakery, specialty resources, special ingredients* and *books,* and also see 'breads, brownies, bakes, pies and muffins' in A & F charts.)
Baker's Chocolate: Baker's chocolate is a type of *unsweetened*

chocolate used in *baking*. Some are GF. {Bakers chocolate may contain added *sweeteners (malt), oils/fat* and *lecithin*.} Verify GF.
Baker's Yeast: Baker's yeast is a general term for *yeast* used for *baking*. Verify GF. (See *yeast*.)
Bakery: Bakery's are businesses that custom bake *baked-goods* right on the premises. The majority of bakery items contain *gluten* and/or are *contaminated* with *gluten*. [GF bakery baked-goods must always be question for gluten *contamination* from in the environment (e.g., *wheat flour* airborne or residue on counters and equipment).] Avoid bakery items unless you can find a bakery that bakes only *gluten free* baked-goods on a designated day, free of possible *gluten* contaminants. Gluten free bakery items are available only through *special bakeries*. There are some bakeries that bake only gluten free baked-goods (some of which are also dairy free). These bakeries usually create GF special requests such as wedding cakes. Some GF bakeries sell GF baked goods both wholesale and retail and may even express delivers. (See *gluten free resource guide* and *baked goods*.)
Baking Potato: (See *russet potato*.)
Baking Powder: Baking powder is a type of *powdered mixture* consisting of an *acid* and *alkaline*. Considered a *yeast substitute*, baking powder is a *leavening agent mixture* that reacts with *liquid* to make *baked-goods* rise. *Double acting baking powder* has a two stage *leavening* process. {Baking powders may contain a *filler* base, aluminum and an *anti-caking agent*.} Store baking powders airtight away from moisture.

Question the source of any added *filler*. You can *home-make* baking powder or choose commercially prepared GF baking powder. There are several GF baking powders available and some are labeled GF. Choose aluminum-free baking powder if possible. Question the source. (See *yeast substitute* and *condiment*.)

Baking Soda: Baking soda is an *alkaline powdery* white *substance* produced by a *compound* (*sodium bicarbonate*) made from *sodium carbonate* (a natural *mineral salt*) with *carbon dioxide*. Baking soda is a *leavening agent, yeast substitute, pH-balancing agent, absorption agent* and *preservative*. When baking soda is combined with an *acid ingredient*, it produces *carbon dioxide* gas bubbles immediately when moistened. [If using baking soda in pre-mixed dry GF baking mixtures, store them away from moisture because liquid will activate its properties.] Store baking soda in a cool, dry dark place. Choose *100% pure* baking soda *U. S. P.* Baking soda is available at all grocery food stores. [Caution: baking soda will remove *vitamin C* from *foods* and may destroy some B *vitamins*. Do not use in boiling water to soften foods (e.g. beans).] Verify GF. (See *leavening agent* and *baking powder*.)

Balsamic Vinegar: Balsamic vinegar is a type of *vinegar* made from *grape juice* aged in different types of wood barrels. The best balsamic vinegar is made in Modena, in northern Italy from white Trebbiano grape juice. Choose authentic balsamic vinegar with an API # and the letters MO imprinted in the bottle to assume no added *sulfites, flavors* and/or *colors*. *Refrigerate* balsamic vinegar after opening. Check for GF purity.

Bamboo Shoots: A type of *vegetable. Pure fresh* and *plain* are GF. (See *vegetable*.)

Banana: Bananas are a type of *fruit. Pure fresh* and *plain* bananas are GF. (See *fruit*.)

Banana Chips: Banana chips are a type of *dried fruit* made from dried *banana* slices. Avoid banana chips *coated* with forbidden *sweetener*. Verify GF. (See *dried fruit*.)

Banon Cheese: A type of semi-soft *chevre cheese* made from goat's *milk*. Verify GF. (See *cheese*.)

Bar: (See *meal replacement bars*, cand*y bars* and *alcohol*.)

Barley: Barley is a type of *forbidden cereal grain* from the *grass plant family*. Barley has a *gluten prolamin* that is toxic to celiacs. *Horedin* is the *gluten prolamin* in barley. Other *forbidden* types of barley include; whole barley, hulled barley, black barley, pearled barley, barley flakes, barley flour, barley malt, malted barley and barley grits. Avoid barley grains and barley grain relatives. Avoid *byproducts* of barley grains. Avoid food made with barley grains and barley grain *byproducts*. (See *grains, byproducts* and *horedin*.)

Base: Base is a term used for the main *ingredient* to which others are added. The base of all *ingredients* and/or *foods* need to be questioned and verified GF. (See *ingredients, chemical compound* and *components*.)

Basic: Basic is a term for foods minimally prepared without extras. Basic is a term generally used to describe foods with only the most important *ingredients*. [I find reading labels on healthier foods containing 'basic' *ingredients* easier. Foods in *health food grocery stores* seem to have fewer *ingredients* and most of these *ingredients* are common and recognizable.] Basic foods need to be verified GF. Question basic *foods* and *ingredients* for the possibility of *contamination* and *hidden ingredients*. (See *pure, natural plain* and *whole foods*.))

Basil: A type of *herb. Fresh* and *pure dried* basil are GF. (See *herb*.)

Basmati Rice: A type of *long grain aromatic rice*. Basmati rice is either *long grain brown* or *long grain white*. GF. (See *rice* for specifics.)

Bass: A type of *fish. Pure fresh* and *plain* bass are GF. (See *fish*)

Batter: Batter is a term for a thick *liquid mixture* used to make *baked-goods*. Batter *mixes* are normally used to replace *yeast* mixes. Instead, a non-*yeast leavening agent* is used. Batter mixes are also used to *coat* certain *foods* before *frying*. {Batters may contain a *cornmeal, bean flour, rice flour* or *wheat flour base*.} Most batter *mixes* contain a *wheat flour* base and are therefore not GF. There are excellent *recipe books* available to *home make* batter mixes with GF *ingredients*. If a batter-mix is truly GF it will usually be *labeled*. The gluten free purity of batter mixes and foods coated with batter are always questionable. Avoid unless source is known. *Commercially prepared* GF batter mixes are available through *special resources*. (See *specialty resources, special ingredients* and *books*.)

Batter Bread Mix: Batter bread mixes are a type of thick liquid *batter mixtures* poured into a baking pan, as opposed to kneading a more solid *dough mixture*. Avoid unless source is known. GF batter bread mixes are available through *specialty companies*. (See *batter*.)

Bayberry: A type of *fruit. Pure fresh* and *plain* bayberries are GF.

Bay Leaf: A type of *herb. Fresh* and *pure dried* bay leaves are GF.

BBQ: BBQ is a term used to describe food cooked over heat on a *grill*. To prevent possible contamination, do not place GF *foods* directly on a BBQ grill unless cleaned, instead *grill,* on top of *aluminum foil*. (See *aluminum foil*.)

BBQ Sauce: BBQ sauce is a type of *sauce* coated on *foods* prepared to be *grilled BBQ*-style. {BBQ sauces may contain *mustard, thickeners, vinegar, sweetener, flavorings* and *colorings*.} Question ingredients in BBQ sauces. Several BBQ sauces are GF. Question the source. (See *sauce* and *BBQ*.)

Bean: Beans are *edible seeds* from a variety of *plants*. [Beans are not referred to as seeds in this book.] Beans are also termed *legumes*. All *pure fresh* and *dried* beans are *naturally* GF. There are countless varieties of beans. [Look up each type of individually.] Beans are extremely versatile and *nutritious*. You can eat a selection of beans *fresh, dried, cooked* or *milled* into *flour*. Beans are excellent in *soups, dips* and *salads*. Beans are easier to *digest* when *cooked* in *soups* with *vegetables*. Most beans are interchangeable according to taste and the *recipe*. (See 'beans' in A & F charts.)

Bean Canned: *Canned beans*. Beans are *cooked* and sold in cans. It is easy to home cook *whole-dried* beans. Choose <u>plain</u> <u>canned</u> <u>beans</u> *preserved* in *salt* or *kombu*. Most *plain* canned beans are GF. Verify GF. (See *seasoned beans*.)

Bean Cracked: *Whole dried beans* partially *milled*. Cracked beans are crushed more than split beans. Check for GF purity. (See *bean dried* and *bean split*.)

Bean Curd: (See *tofu*.) Verify GF.

Bean Dried: *Dried* beans are *beans* grown into a dried bean and/or are *dried* from *fresh beans*. Dried beans are *whole*, *split* in half, *cracked*, *flaked* or *milled* into *bean flour*. [Look up each type individually.] Most *whole dried beans* need to be *soaked* overnight before *cooking*. {Dried beans may be *polished*, *dyed*, *flavored*, *roasted* or *parboiled*.} <u>Choose</u> <u>pure</u> <u>whole</u> <u>unadulterated</u> <u>beans</u>. Verify GF. (See *bean* and *pressure cooker* and also see 'beans' in A & F charts.)

Bean Flakes: *Whole dried beans* rolled flat. Check for GF purity. (See *bean dried* and *bean cracked*.)

Bean Flour: Bean flour is a type of *flour milled* from *whole dried-beans*. All beans are GF and therefore <u>pure</u> <u>bean</u> <u>flours</u> <u>are</u> <u>GF</u>. Bean flours are excellent as a portion of a GF *flour mixture* used in *baked-goods*. Bean flours add moisture and improve texture to *baked-goods*. You can home mill bean flours with *whole-dried beans*. Caution: the term 'bean flour' is unreliable, because of the possibility of the addition of *forbidden wheat flour*. Avoid bean

flours mixed with added *forbidden flours*. <u>Choose</u> <u>100%</u> <u>pure</u> <u>bean</u> <u>flours</u>. Check for GF purity. (See *bean, bean dried, garbanzo bean flour* and *soy flour*.)

Bean Fresh: *Fresh* beans are an *edible bean/seed* in its *pod* eaten as a *vegetable*. All fresh beans are GF, but avoid fresh beans prepared in *forbidden sauces* and *gravies*. (See *bean* and *vegetable*.)

Bean Pasta: Bean pasta is a type of *pasta* made from *processed beans*. Caution: the term 'bean pasta' is unreliable, because of the possibility of the addition of *forbidden wheat flour*. <u>Choose</u> <u>100%</u> <u>pure</u> <u>bean</u> <u>pasta</u>. Verify GF. (See *bean* and *pasta*.)

Bean Split: Split beans are *whole dried beans* split in half. The beans are usually broken to shorten cooking time. Check for GF purity. (See *bean dried* and *bean split*.)

Bean Sprout: Bean sprouts are any of various types of *sprouts* grown from *beans*. [Look up each individually.] All beans are GF and therefore all bean sprouts are GF. You can sprout beans easily with *whole-dried* beans. Irradiated beans will not sprout. (See *sprout* and *beans dried*.)

Bean Thread: Bean thread is a term used for a type of thin *pasta* made from <u>beans</u> and possibly *forbidden flour*. Avoid unless verified GF. (See *bean* and *pasta*.)

Beech: A type of *spice*. *Pure* beech is GF. (See *spice*.)

Beechnut: *A type of nut. Raw* and *plain* nuts are GF. (See *nut*.)

Beef: Beef is a type of *meat* from cattle (e.g. cows, heifer, bull and steer). *Pure fresh plain meats* are naturally GF. Question anything used in or on the beef. (See *meat* and also see 'meat' in A & F charts.)

Beer: Beer is a type of *beverage brewed* from *forbidden grains*. Avoid. (See *alcohol*.)

Beeswax: A type of *additive*. GF.

Beet: A type of *vegetable*. *Pure fresh* and *plain* are GF. (See *vegetable*.)

Beet Fiber: A type of *fiber* derived from *beets*. Verify GF.

Beet Greens: Beet greens are a *vegetable* from the tops of beets. *Pure fresh* and *plain* beet greens are GF. (See *vegetable*.)

Bellelay Cheese: A type of semi-soft *cheese*. Verify GF. (See *cheese*.)

Bel Paese Cheese: A type of semi-soft *cheese* similar to *mozzarella*. Verify GF. (See *cheese* and *mozzarella*.)

Bengali Bean: A type of small *lima bean*. GF. (See *bean*.)

Benzoic Acid: A certain type of *preservative*. Caution. GF.

Benzoin Gum: A certain type of *gum* obtained from specific trees. Caution. GF. (See *gum*.)

Benzyl Alcohol: An *additive* used as a *carrier* or *extraction solvent*. Caution. Verify GF. (See *alcohol*.)

Bergamot: A type of *spice/herb*. *Pure* are GF. (See *herbs* and *spices*.)

Berries: Berries are a type of *fruit*. All *pure fresh* and *plain* berries are GF. Different types of berries include *blackberries, strawberries, blueberries* and *raspberries*. Question any added *sweeteners* or *sauces especially* in *frozen* and *preserved* berries. GF. (See *gum*.)

Besan: (See *garbanzo bean*.) GF.

Beta-Carotene: The *naturally* occurring yellow coloring found in some *plants* and *animals*. Verify GF.

Beverage: Beverage is an umbrella term for anything drinkable. [Beverage usually refers to any drink other than *water*.] Choose 100% pure GF vegetable and fruit juice, coffee, soda, fruit drinks, dairy milk, non-dairy milk (e.g. *almond, coconut, rice, soybean* and *sunflower seed milk*), herbal tea and regular tea. [Look up each type individually.] Avoid tea with *barley, flavored coffee* or *tea, malted milk* and some *instant drinks*. {Beverages may contain added *flavorings, sweeteners* & *colorings*.} Question the source of *additives*. Although an abundant of beverages are GF, the source of all beverages need to be verified GF. (See 'beverages' in A & F charts.)

BHA: (See *butylatedhydroxyanisole*.) Caution. GF.

Bhatura: *Wheat flour bread*. Avoid.

Bhindi: Okra. (See *soy okra*.)

BHT: (See *butylated hydroxytoluene*.) Caution. GF.

Bicarbonate of Soda: (See *baking soda*.) GF.

Bierkase Cheese: A type of soft *ripened cheese*. Verify GF.

Bigeye: A type of *fish*. *Pure fresh* and *plain* are GF. (See *fish*.)

Bilberry: A type of *fruit*. *Pure fresh* and *plain* are GF. (See *fruit*.)

Binder: Binders are any *natural* or *artificial substance* binding *ingredients* together, especially *baked-goods*. Natural types of binders include *pectin, applesauce, eggs* and a variety of *gums*. [Look up each individually.] Verify GF.

Biopsy: A biopsy is a medical procedure where sample-*tissue* removed from a patient is tested. If there is a strong clinical suspicion of *celiac disease*, diagnosis can be quick through blood *tests* to screen for specific antibodies to *gluten* and most accurately by an *endoscope* used to examine the *small bowel* and obtain a biopsy. *Dermatitis herpetiformis* disease is diagnosed with a skin biopsy of a lesion. (See *intestine, gastroenterologist, celiac disease* and *dermatitis herpetiformis disease*.)

Biotin: Biotin is a *natural substance* found in every living *cell*. (See *cell*.)

Birch: A type of *spice/herb*. Pure are GF. (See *spices* and *herbs*.)

Birch Beer: Birch beer is similar to *root beer*. Risky. Avoid unless source is known. (See *root beer*.)

Biscotti: Biscotti's are a hard type *biscuit cookie baked-good* made with *wheat flour*. Avoid. *Commercially prepared* GF biscotti are available through *specialty companies*.

Biscuit: Biscuits are individual size *batter bread baked-goods* made with *wheat flour*. Avoid. *Commercially prepared* GF biscuits are available through *specialty companies*.

Bisque: Bisque is a type of thickened *soup*. Avoid unless the source of all ingredients is known. (See *soup*.)

Bitter Melon: A type of *fruit* considered a *melon*. *Pure fresh and plain* are GF. (See *fruit*.)

Bitters: Bitters is made with *alcohol*. Risky. Verify GF.

Black Bean: A type of small *bean*, black in color with a sweet robust flavor. Black beans are excellent in *salads* and *dips*. GF. (See *bean*.)

Blackberry: A type of *fruit*. Pure *fresh* and *plain* blackberries are GF.

Blackened: Blackened is a method of *cooking* (e.g., *fish, poultry* or *meat* are blackened in a hot skillet). *Plain* blackened *fish, poultry* or *meat* are GF. Question added *seasonings*.

Black-Eyed Pea: A type of small beige *bean* having a small black spot midpoint. GF. (See *bean*.)

Blackfish: A type of *fish*. Pure *fresh* and *plain* blackfish is GF. (See *fish*.)

Black Gram: (See *urad bean*.) GF.

Black Pepper: (See *pepper*.)

Black Rice: Black rice is a type of *rice* with a black outer layer (*bran*) and possibly black *endosperm*. GF. (See rice for specifics.)

Black Soybean: A type of soybean, black in color and more *nutritious* than the abundant tan colored soybean. (See *soybean* for specifics.)

Black Strap Molasses: Black strap molasses is a type of *molasses* made from *sugar cane*. Black strap molasses is *thicker* and more concentrated than other light or dark molasses made from *sugar cane*. Try to avoid molasses with *sulfites* if possible. Verify GF.

Black Turtle Bean: A type of *black bean*. GF. (See *black bean*.)

Black Walnut: A type of *tree nut*. A black *walnut* is from a certain walnut *tree*. GF. (See *nut* and *walnut*.)

Blade Mill: Blade mills are a certain type of *mill* used to *grind whole-dried* foods (e.g. *beans, seeds, nuts* and *grains*) by the force of a blade. Blade mills create heat during the *milling* process. Heat shortens the *milled* products shelf life and decreases its *nutritional* value. [Avoid nutritional loss by milling *fresh* and/or storing extras for short amounts of time.] Not all blade mills will mill large beans (e.g. *garbanzo beans*) because the shoot may be too small. The best blade mill is heavy-duty blade, with an open or large shoot opening for various size foods. (See *mill* for additional details.)

Blanch: Blanch is a culinary term used for soaking foods briefly (as a rule between 15 seconds to one minute.) in *boiled* water, to loosen the skin or kill *bacteria* and *enzymes*.

Blancmange: A type of *pudding*. Avoid. (See *pudding*.)

Bleach: To *whiten* with *chemicals*, or by age. Bleached food lacks *nutrition*. (See *bleaching agents*.)

Bleached Flour: A type of *wheat flour bleached*. Avoid. (See *flour*)

Bleaching Agent: Bleaching agents are *substances* (possibly *chemicals*) used to *bleach* or *whiten* foods (typically *flour*). Caution. (See *whitening agent* and *agent*.)

Blend: To mix wet *ingredients* with a fork, *whisk* or *blender*. Clean tools well in between uses. (See *blender*.)

Blended Vinegar: Blended vinegar is a combination of one or more *vinegars*. Question every type of *vinegar* used in this *mixture*. (See *vinegar*)

Blender: A blender is a type of hand held or stationary *kitchen appliance* used to *blend* wet *ingredients*. Clean the blender and all attachments well in between uses.

Bleu Cheese: Blue cheese is a type of *veined cheese*. Avoid all *veined cheese*. [*Wheat bread* inoculates the *cheese* with blue *molds*.] (See *cheese*.)

Blintz: A type of *pancake*. Avoid. (See *pancake*.)

Blood Test: A blood test is a medical procedure where sample blood is removed from a patient and tested. If there is a strong clinical suspicion of *celiac disease* diagnosis can be done quickly through blood tests to screen for specific antibodies to *gluten*. [The blood test will be negative if the patient is already on the GF diet.] Celiac patients have high levels of specific antibodies in their blood when they consume the type of gluten toxic to celiacs. The blood test for *celiac disease* looks for *antibodies* to an *enzyme* called *transglutaminase*. [*Antibody* test for IgA and IgG antigliadin *antibodies* in serum, including *antibodies* to the varying fractions of *gliadin* are measured.] Healthy celiacs should have negative values for the *antigliadin antibody*. If the value of *antigliadin antibody* is high, there is cause for concern. [A more accurate test for CD can be performed by an endoscope used to examine the *small bowel* and obtain a *biopsy*.] (See *biopsy, antigliadin, antibody* and *gastroenterologist*.)

Blueberry: A type of *fruit*. Pure *fresh* and *plain* blueberries are GF.

Blue Cheese: (See *bleu cheese*.)

Blue Cheese Dressing: A type of *dressing* made with *blue cheese*. Avoid. (See *blue cheese* and *dressing*.)

Blue Corn: Blue corn is a type of *corn* blue in color. GF. (See *corn*.)

Bluefish: A type of *fish*. *Fresh pure* and *plain* bluefish are GF. (See *fish*.)

Bluegill: A type of *fish*. Pure *fresh* and *plain* bluegill are GF. (See *fish*.)

Bluegreen Algae: *A type of seaweed*. Pure is GF. (See *algae*.)

Bocconcini Cheese: A type of *fresh mozzarella cheese* in small balls packaged in *whey* or water. Verify GF. (See *mozzarella* and *whey*.)

Boil: To cook in boiling water or *liquid*. [Do not reuse boiling water previously used to cook *gluten-*

containing food, instead cook GF foods first or separate.] (See *steam*.)

Bolted: Bolted is a term used for *ground grains sifted* (e.g., the coarse and fine particles have been separated). The *bran* is soft and therefore more often than not removed. Question the type of grain bolted (e.g. *wheat*). (See *unbolted* and *sifted*.)

Bolted Flour: Avoid. (See *bolted*.)

Bonbel Cheese: A type of semi-soft *cheese* usually *coated* with *paraffin*. Caution. Verify GF. (See *paraffin*.)

Boniato: (See *sweet potato*.) GF.

Bonita: (See *tuna*.)

Books: Books will inform and connect you to the *gluten free* world. Books are one of the most useful tools on your journey into foodstuff and good health. There are many GF *recipe* books available to *home-make* GF *recipes*. There are also excellent books about *celiac disease*. There are brilliant illustrated *children's* books about coping with food *allergies*. For a superior list of books containing gluten free facts, resource information and/or recipes, order the *Gluten Free Resource Guide 'a consumers guide for living gluten free,'* through *Guide Books Publication Company*. After each book recommendation is a brief description about the book. These reviews will help you in choosing books appropriate for you. [These books (most of which are best sellers) are recommend because of their information content, creativity, usability and accuracy.] *Guide Books Publication Company* also publishes an annual gluten free food list of *commercially prepared* GF *food products* in a book format The title of this book is *Gluten Free Food Product List 'the manufactures list of commercially prepared gluten free foods'*. This too is an essential book for *celiacs* and everyone following the *gluten free diet*. With the food product-list book, all you need to do is look up any food item and obtain the brand name that manufactures it GF. To purchase any of these books write for details, visit the web site or see the ordering form on pages 206 and 207. [Look up *gluten free food product list* and *gluten free resource guide*.]

Botanical: Botanical is the scientific study of *plants*. Botanical is a term used for products made from and/or anything relating to *plants*. (See *plant* and *plant parts*.)

Bouillon: Bouillon is a type of concentrated-*broth* in *liquid*, *powder* or cubed form. You cannot pour broth through a strainer to remove foods containing liquid. This process does not remove *gluten*. The *peptides* in *gluten* are too small to strain. {Bouillons may contain added *yeast* and *seasonings*.} You can *home-make* b*ouillon* and freeze it in ice cube trays, then place the cubes in freezer containers and use them as needed. Question all ingredients in bouillon. Some are bouillons are GF. Some GF bouillons are labeled. *Commercially prepared* GF bouillon is available through *specialty companies*. (See *specialty companies*, *yeast, broth* and *gravy*.)

Bouillon Cubes: (See *bouillon*.)

Boursault Cheese: A type of *triple cream cheese*. Verify GF. (See *triple cream cheese*.)

Boursin Cheese: A type of *flavored triple cream cheese*. Question added *flavorings*. Avoid unless verified GF. (See *cream cheese*.)

Bows: A type of *pasta* shaped into tiny bows generally made with *forbidden flour*. Avoid. (See *pasta*.)

Boysenberry: A type of *fruit*. *Pure fresh* and *plain* boysenberries are GF. (See *fruit*.)

Braise: To cook *food* at a high temperature to brown the outside, then the temperature is lowered and the *food* is *cooked* slowly.

Bran: Bran is the name for the outer *coating* of any *cereal grain*. [Even though *bran* is considered the *shell* of a *grain*, in this book bran is not referred to as *shell*.] The bran part of a *grain* adds *fiber* and *nutrients* to *foods* especially *cereals* and *baked-goods*. [Removing the bran from a *forbidden gluten grain* does not render the *grain* GF.] Types of bran include <u>*corn*</u>, *wheat*, *rye*, *oat* and <u>*rice*</u>. [Look up each individually.] GF rice bran is available through *special companies*. (See *cereal grains* and *rice*.)

Brand: Brand is the name (generally *trademark*) of a *manufacturer* or product or the product itself. Although some companies *manufacture* their own products, most companies owning the brand name do not produce the product. [The same *manufacturer* may *manufacturer* the same food carrying several different company labels (e.g., brand *labels* form several different *trademark* brands).] (See *manufacturer* and *label*.)

Brazil <u>**Nut**</u>: A type of tree *nut*. *Raw* and *plain* are GF. (See *nut*.)

Bread: Bread is a type of *baked-good* considered a food staple. Most *commercially prepared* breads are prepared with *forbidden grains* and *forbidden grain byproducts*. <u>*Bread* truly GF will be labeled</u>. You must read the labels of all breads. [Breads labeled potato or rice bread may contain wheat flour.] You can *home make bread* with allowable GF *specialty ingredients*. There are many superior *recipe books* available to *home bake* GF *bread*. *Commercially prepared* GF breads are available through *specialty companies*. (See *baked-goods*.)

Breadcrumbs: Breadcrumbs are coarse *crumbs* made from soft or hardened (stale) *wheat bread*. Avoid. *Commercially prepared* GF breadcrumbs are available only from *specialty companies*. You can *home-make* GF breadcrumbs with <u>GF bread, *cornmeal*, *rice flour*, *corn flour*</u> or crumbled <u>*corn flakes*</u> or <u>*potato chips*</u>. (See *bread* and *bread*ing.)

Bread Flour: Bread flour is a type of *flour* made from *hard wheat grains*. Avoid. (See *flour*.)

Bread Improver: A food *substance* used to improve the quality of *bread*. Caution. (See *additives*.)

Breading: Breading is made from crumbed or cubed *bread* obtained from soft or hardened *wheat bread*. Avoid. [Breading is not the same as breadcrumbs.] Commercially prepared GF breading is available only by *specialty companies*. You can *home-make* GF breading from GF bread or obtain *commercially prepared* GF breading through specialty resources. (See *bread* and *bread*crumbs.)

Bread Machine: A bread machine is a type of *kitchen appliance* used to *bake bread* from *scratch*. You can purchase GF bread machine bread mixes or *home make* GF bread mixes from scratch. [Caution: bread machines are costly and may over bake GF breads. Bread machines take some getting used to and mistake breads will be made! There are an abundance of cost effective *homemade* GF *bread recipes* that take minutes to prepare without a bread machine.] For a superior collection of recipe books, see the *resource guide*. (See *bread, batter breads* and *recipe books*.)

Breakdown Product: Breakdown products are any *substance* remaining after *metabolization*.

Breakfast Cereal: Breakfast cereals are a type of *cereal* as a rule made with *cereal grains* and served at breakfast time. Most *commercially prepared* breakfast *cereal* is *forbidden*. (See *cereal*)

Bream: A type of *fish*. *Fresh pure* and *plain* are GF. (See *fish*.)

Brew: To brew something is to use the process of *boiling, steeping* and/or *fermenting foods* into a *beverage*. Types of *foods* used in the brewing process include *grains* (e.g. *barley, wheat* and *rice*), *plants* (e.g. *tea*) and *beans* (e.g. *coffee*). Avoid food and beverages brewed from *forbidden grains*. Avoid *beer*. (See *beverage* and *alcohol* and also see 'beverages' in A & F charts.)

Brewer's Yeast: Brewer's yeast is a type of *non-leavening yeast* used in *brewing beer*. Avoid unless source is known. (See *yeast*.)

Brick Cheese: A type of semi-solid Wisconsin *cheese* made from cows *milk*. Verify GF. (See *cheese*.)

Brie Cheese: A type of semi-soft *ripened* cow's *milk cheese*. Verify GF. (See *cheese*.)

Brine: Brine is a type of *liquid solution* of *salt* and water used to *preserve* foods. {Brine solutions may contain added *sweeteners* and *seasonings*.} (See *preservative*.)

Bringal: A type of *spice/herb*. *Pure plain* are GF. (See *herbs* and *spices*.)

Broad Bean: (See *fava bean*.) GF.

Broil: To cook *food* directly under a high heat source. You need to broil *food* on a clean *grill* or put *aluminum foil* under the *food* to avoid *contamination*. (See *cook*.)

Bromated Flour: A type of *wheat flour* with added *bromic acid*. Avoid.

Bromelain: Bromelain is a type of *protein digestive enzyme* derived from *pineapples*. GF. (See *pineapple* and *supplement*.)

Bromic Acid: A *chemically* made *oxidizing agent*. Caution. GF.

Brominated Vegetable Oil: A certain type of *vegetable oil* to which *bromine* is added. Caution. Verify GF. (See *vegetable oil*.)

Bromine: A volatile *chemical* element. Caution. GF.

Broth: Broth is the *liquid strained* from *cooked meats, fish, poultry* and *vegetables*. You can *home-make* broth and freeze it in ice cube trays then place the individual cubes in freezer containers and use them as needed. {Broth may contain a little added *thickener, flavorings* and *seasonings*.} Question all broths. There are some *commercially prepared* GF broths available at *regular* and *health food grocery stores*. You cannot pour broth through a strainer to remove foods containing liquid. This process does not remove *gluten*. The *peptides* in *gluten* are too small to strain. (See *bouillon* and *gravy*.)

Brown: To cook *food* quickly over or under high heat resulting in a brown exterior. You need to brown *food* on a clean *grill* or put *aluminum foil* under the *food* to avoid *contamination*. (See *cook*.)

Brown Flour: Brown flour is a type of *wheat flour*. Avoid. (See *flour*)

Brownies: Brownies are a type of dense chewy *cake*-like *baked-good* made with *wheat flour*. Avoid. You can *home make* brownies with GF *ingredients*. *Commercially prepared* GF brownies and brownie mixes are available only through *specialty companies*. (See *baked-goods* and *special resources*.)

Brown Lentils: Brown lentils are a type of *lentil beans* brown and/or green in color. GF. (See *lentil*.)

Brown Rice: Brown rice is a type of GF grain. Brown rice is any *whole-grain rice* with the outer *coating* (*bran*) still intact. The *bran* is what contains most of the *nutrients*. Brown rice is more *nutritious* than *white rice* because white rice is rice with the bran removed. You can *mill whole* brown *rice grains* into a rice *grain-flour*. [Brown rice is less likely to be *polished, enriched, enhanced* or *converted*.] (See *rice* for details and specifics and see *brown rice flour*.)

Brown Rice Flour: Brown rice flour is a type of *rice* grain *flour milled* from *brown rice* grains. *Short brown rice grains mill* into the best *rice flour*, as opposed to *long grain brown rice grains* or any *white rice grains*. Check for GF purity. (See *flour* and *brown rice* for specifics.)

Brown Rice Noodles: Brown rice noodles are *noodles* made from *brown rice* grains. Check for GF purity. (See *pasta*.)

Brown Rice Pasta: Brown rice pasta is *pasta* made from *brown rice*. Check for GF purity. (See *pasta*.)

Brown Rice Syrup: (See *rice syrup*.)

Brown Split Pea: A type of *dried pea* brown in color that is *split* in half. GF.(See *bean* and *split pea*.)

Brown Sugar: Brown sugar is a type of white *cane sugar* and *molasses mixture*. Brown sugar is available either light or dark brown. {Brown sugar may contain added *invert sugar* or *invert syrup*.} You can replace brown sugar with a mixture of *white sugar cane sugar* and *molasses* or *unrefined sugar cane sugar*. You can purchase certain GF brands of brown sugar at *regular grocery food stores*. Caution. Verify GF. (See *sugar* and *molasses*.)

Bruise: Bruise is a term meaning to crush lightly. Bruising release some of the foods *flavors*. [Recipes often call for bruised *garlic* bulbs.]

Brussels Sprouts: Brussels sprouts are a type of *vegetable*. *Pure fresh* and *plain* are GF. (See *vegetable*.)

Bryndza Cheese: A type of semi-soft *cheese* made from sheep's *milk*. {Bryndza cheese may contain *brine* used in *curing*.} Verify GF. (See *cheese* and *brine*.)

Bucheron Cheese: A semi-soft *chevere cheese* from goat's *milk*. Verify GF. (See *chevere cheese*.)

Buckwheat: Buckwheat is a type of GF *seed* considered a *grain* because of its *grain* like similarities. Buckwheat is not *wheat* or *cereal* *grain* or a member of the *grass plant* family. Buckwheat is the common name for a *plant* family and its *genera*. [*Wheat* is not a relative to any members of the *genus buckwheat*. *Wheat* is the *common name* for *cereal* grasses of the *grass family*.] Buckwheat makes an excellent hot *cereal* or side dish. Buckwheat contains high levels of *oxalic acid*. Caution: question for possible contamination (e.g. if buckwheat was grown in the same field as *wheat* and *contamination* during processing). Check for GF purity. (See *gluten free grains* and all the other *buckwheat* products.)

Buckwheat Flakes: Buckwheat flakes are whole *buckwheat seed/grains* partially *cooked*, then rolled flat. Check for GF purity. (See *buckwheat*.)

Buckwheat Flour: *Flour milled* from *buckwheat groats*. Buckwheat *flour* is excellent as part of a *flour mixture* for *baked-goods*. Check for GF purity. (See *buckwheat*.)

Buckwheat Grits: Coarsely *ground buckwheat groats*. Check for GF purity. (See *buckwheat* for cautions.)

Buckwheat Groats: Un-*roasted buckwheat seeds/grains* not *ground*. GF. (See *buckwheat*.)

Buckwheat Hulls: Buckwheat hulls are the inedible outer *coating* (*hull*) of *buckwheat*. (See *buckwheat*)

Buckwheat Pasta: Buckwheat *pasta* is prepared from *buckwheat flour* and possibly a *mixture* of *buckwheat flour* and *wheat flour*. Avoid unless source is known. Risky. (See *buckwheat*.)

Buckwheat Whole: Whole buckwheat is the un-hulled *buckwheat seed/grain*. Whole buckwheat seeds will *sprout*. Check for GF purity. (See *buckwheat*.)

Buffalo: Buffalo is a type of *meat*. *Pure fresh* and *plain* buffalo is GF. (See *meats*.)

Buffer: Buffers are any *substance* used to reduce the impact of another. (See *substances*)

Bulb: Bulbs are the round organ part of a *plant* that grows underground. Types of bulbs include *onions, garlic* and *scallions*. [Look up each individually. *Raw* and *plain* are GF. (See *vegetable* and also see 'bulbs' in A & F charts.)

Bulghur: (See *bulgar*.) Avoid.

Bulgur: Bulgur is a type of *dried, precooked, parboiled* and *cracked wheat*. Avoid.

Bulk Food: Bulk food is a type of volume buying. Some regular and *health food grocery stores* and *mail order* companies offer discounts on cases or bulk buying. Bulk food is also a term for large quantities of food. Some *health food grocery stores* have containers with open bulk *food*. These open bulk foods are risky because of the possibility of *cross contamination*. When purchasing *food items* from open-bulk question if the foods are mixed or miss labeled or contaminated with scoops used previously for *gluten foods* (e.g. scoops *contaminated* with *forbidden flours*). There is little consumer product information on bulk foods. Ask!

Bulking Agent: Bulking agents are *substances* adding bulk to *food*. Bulking agents include *flour* and *filler*. Question the source.

Bun: Bun is a type of soft *sandwich bread*-like *baked-good*. Most *commercially prepared* buns are prepared with *forbidden grain*s and *forbidden grain byproducts*. Buns truly GF will be labeled. You must read the labels of all breads. You can *home make buns* with allowable GF *specialty ingredients*. *Commercially prepared* GF buns are available through *specialty companies*. (See *baked-goods, bread* and see *recipes*.)

Bundi: Bundi are *beans* used for making bean *flours* (e.g. *garbanzo* and *soy flours*). Verify GF.

Burdock: A type of *vegetable*. *Pure fresh* and *plain* burdock are GF.

Burfi: (See *cheese* cubes.)

Burger: Burger refers to a prepared food product that is usually cooked and used sandwich style. {Burgers may contain added ground *meats, vegetables, meat substitutes, seasonings* and possibly *fillers*.} You can *home make* burgers with *pure ground meat, poultry, vegetables* and GF *seasonings*. All ingredients in any prepared food needs to be verified GF. Question *vegetarian* burgers for added *wheat byproducts* and other meat replacement foods. Only a few companies produce *vegetarian* burgers that are GF. (See *patties* and *hamburger*.)

Burrito: Burritos are a type of bean filled *tortilla meal*. Question if the *tortilla* is made with *forbidden wheat flour*. Question the *meat seasoning* and all other *ingredients*. Varieties of frozen *commercially prepared* GF burritos are available through *specialty companies*. (See *specialty companies* and *special resources*.)

Butter: Butter is a type of *dairy* product churned from pure *cream*. You can freeze butter especially unsalted butter, which has a shorter

shelf life than *preserved salted* butter. Most *pure plain* stick butter is GF. Check for GF purity. Try to avoid *light* or *reduced calorie butters*, instead use less, or *substitute* with *natural oils*. (See *dairy*.)

Butter Bean: Butter beans are a type of small *dried lima bean*. GF.

Butter Flavoring: Butter flavoring is a type of *flavoring agent* made with *natural* and/or *artificial flavorings*. {Butter flavoring may contain added *sweeteners, seasoning* and *starch*.} Some butter flavorings are GF. Caution. Question the source. (See *butter*)

Buttermilk: Buttermilk is type of *dairy* product produced from the *liquid* left after the churning of *butter* from *cream*. Check for GF purity. (See *butter* and *dairy*.)

Buttermilk Powder: Buttermilk powder is *buttermilk* from which almost all the moisture has been removed. *Commercially prepared* GF buttermilk powder is available at *health food grocery stores* and *by mail order*. Verify GF. (See *buttermilk*.)

Butternut: A type of *nut*. *Raw* and *plain* butternuts are GF. (See *nut*.)

Butterscotch: Butterscotch is a type of *candy*. Risky. Avoid unless source is known. (See *candy*.)

Butter Substitute: Butter substitutes are *natural* and *artificial ingredients* used in place of *butter*. {Butter substitutes may contain added *sweeteners, flavorings* and *starch*.} Butter substitutes cannot replace butter in *baking*. There are some butter substitutes available GF. Caution. Verify GF. (See *nonstick spray* and *artificial ingredients*.)

Butylated Hydroxyanisole (BHA): A type of waxy *solid substance* that acts as a *preservative, stabilizer* and *antioxidant*. Caution. GF.

Butylated Hydroxytoluene (BHT): A type of waxy *solid substance* that acts as a *preservative, stabilizer* and *antioxidant*. Caution. GF.

Byproduct: Byproduct is a term used for any *substance* reproduced as a secondary result of the *manufacturing* of something else (e.g. *wheat-alcohol, barley-malt, rice flour* and *rye-whiskey*). Avoid all byproducts derived from any of the *forbidden grains*. Byproducts derived from GF grains are acceptable. (See *grain byproducts*.)

Cabbage: A type of *vegetable*. Pure *fresh* and *plain* cabbage is GF.

Caciocavallo Cheese: A type of *stretched-curd cheese* made from cow's *milk*. Verify GF. (See *cheese*.)

Cackle: A type of *fish*. *Fresh* and *plain* are GF. (See *fish*.)

Cactus: A type of *vegetable*. *Fresh* and *plain* are GF. (See *vegetable*.)

Caerphilly: A type of semi-firm *cheese* made from cow's *milk*. Verify GF. (See *cheese*.)

Caffeine: Caffeine is a type of natural stimulant found in *food* (e.g., found in *coffee, tea, chocolate* and *cola*). [Look up each individually.] Caffeine itself is GF. (See *beverage* and *decaffeinated*.)

Caffeine Free: (See *decaffeinated*.)

Cake: Cakes are types of *confection-baked-goods* considered *desserts*. Most *commercially prepared* cakes are prepared with *forbidden grains* and *forbidden grain byproducts*. Cakes truly GF will be labeled. You must read the labels of all cakes. You can *home make cake* with allowable GF *specialty ingredients*. There are many superior *recipe books* available to *home bake* GF cake. *Commercially prepared* GF cakes and cake mixes are available through *specialty companies*. [To find a bakery that will create & express deliver GF cakes- see bakery.] (See *bakery, baked-goods* and *recipes*.)

Cake Flour: A type of soft-*wheat flour bleached*. Avoid. (See *flour*)

Cakes (Rice or Popcorn): Rice and popcorn cakes are types of *commercially prepared* crunchy *snack food* made from puffed *rice* grains or *popped corn* grains. [Look up each type.] These *snack* cakes are an excellent bread *substitute* for some *sandwich*-like creations. {Popcorn and rice cakes may contain added *flavorings, sweeteners, coatings, nuts* and *seeds*.} Question added *forbidden grain byproducts*. Many popcorn and rice cakes are GF. *Plain unflavored* popcorn cakes are some of the safest. Verify GF. (See *snack foods* and *sandwich*.)

Calcium Ascorbate: (See *ascorbic acid*.)

Calcium Biphosphate: A type of *leavening agent*. Caution. GF.

Calcium Chloride: Chloride *salt* of calcium. Caution. GF.

Calcium Disodium: A type of *additive*. Caution. GF.

Calcium Hydroxide: Slaked lime. Lime water. A type of lye. Caution. GF.

Calcium Pantothenate: Pantothenic acid. A type of B vitamin. Caution. GF.

Calcium Phosphate: A type of *leavening agent*. Caution. GF.

Calorie: Calories are units of energy produced in the body from the *digestion* of *food*. [People increase their caloric intake to gain weight. People decrease their caloric intake, along with exercise to lose weight.] *Celiacs* will generally gain weight normally, once the diarrhea stops and the *villi* start to grow back (typically within one to three months after maintaining a strict GF diet). (See *villi, digestive system* and *diet*.)

Calzone: Calzone is a type of *filled pizza*. Avoid. (See *pizza*.)

Camembert Cheese: Semi-soft *cheese* made from cow's *milk*. Verify GF. (See *cheese*.)

Camphor: A type of *spice/herb*. *Pure* are GF. (See *herbs* and *spices*.)

Camping Food: Camping food is a type of *instant* lightweight *food* designed to take up little room while hiking and for easy *preparation* while living outdoors. These types of foods make great *travel foods*. Only a few camping foods are GF. (See *instant, backpacking* and *travel*.)

Canadian Bacon: (See *ham* and *bacon* for details and specifics.)

Canadian Wild Rice: Canadian wild rice is a specific type of wild rice. GF. (See *wild rice*.)

Candy: Candy is a variety of *confection*. Candy are various types of sweet *snacks* made with *sweeteners* and typically other sweet and/or snack food *ingredients*. {Candy may contain added *filler, gum, emulsifiers, stabilizers, flavorings, coatings, preservatives, colorings* and other *food agents*}. Always question the source of *sweetener*. Risky candy may include *caramel candy, chewing gum, filled chocolate, licorice, jellybeans* and candy made with *butterscotch toffee, flavored syrups, malt, fillings* and *crunchy rice cereal*. [Look up each type of candy individually.] Caution: *flour* is frequently used during processing to *dust* candy to prevent sticking and to aid in molding. A variety of candy are GF especially hard candy. Question all candy. (See 'candy' in A & F charts.)

Candy Bars: Candy bars are a type of individually *wrapped snack* foods made with *sweeteners* and typically other sweet and/or snack food *ingredients* (e.g. *nuts, seeds* and *grain byproducts*). A limited amount of candy bars are GF. Question all ingredients in candy bars. (See *candy* and also see *meal replacement bars*.)

Cane Sugar: Cane sugar is *sugar* derived from the *sugar cane* plant. Check for GF purity. (See *sugar* for types and cautions.)

Cane Syrup: Cane syrups are *syrups* derived from *cane sugar*. Caution. {Cane syrups may contain added *sweeteners*.} Verify GF. (See *cane sugar* and *syrup*.)

Cane Vinegar: Cane vinegar is a certain type of *vinegar* made from *cane sugar* that is sweet tasting. Caution. Verify GF. (See *cane sugar* and *vinegar*.)

Canned Bacon: Avoid. (See *bacon*.)

Canned Beans: (See *beans canned*.)

Canned Food: Canned foods are cooked foods stored and preserved in cans. [Some foods are cooked right in the can.] There are many canned GF foods. [Look up each type of canned food individually.] Most 'plain' canned *fruits* and *vegetables* are GF. {Canned foods may contain *thickeners* and *grain byproducts*} Question all ingredients in canned foods. Canned foods are convenient for *travel*. (See *canning*.)

Canned Fruit: (See *fruits canned*.)

Canned Vegetables: (See *vegetable canned*.)

Cannellini Bean: Cannellini beans are an extremely versatile type of white *kidney bean*. GF. (See *bean*.)

Canning: A method of *preserving*. (See *preserve* and *canned food*.)

Canola Oil: A type of *oil* obtained from *rapeseeds* (*canola seeds*). Caution: most canola seeds are *GMO*. Check for GF purity. (See *GMO*, *oil* and *sensitive*.)

Cantal: Cantal is a type of semi-firm *cheese*. Verify GF. (See *cheese*.)

Cantaloupe: A type of *fruit* considered a *melon*. *Fresh pure* and *plain* cantaloupes are GF. (See *fruit*)

Capers: Small *seeds/buds pickled*. Question the type of *brine* or *vinegar* used for *pickling*. Question the source. (See *pickled*.)

Caprino Romano Cheese: An *aged* firm *Romano cheese* made from goat's *milk*. Verify GF.

Capsule: Capsules are one of the many forms in which medication and/or supplements are concentrated for ingestion. [Medication is often encapsulated.] *Gluten* is a minor problem in *pharmaceutical* products, most commonly in capsules. You should avoid gluten in all amounts. (See *medication* for details.)

Caramel: Caramel is a type of *coloring*, *flavoring* and *sweetening agent* made from certain *sweeteners* (e.g. burnt *sugar*, *corn dextrose*, *malted corn*, *lactose*, some *molasses*, *invert sugar*, *wheat dextrose* or *barley malt*). The source of *caramel* as an *'ingredient'* in *food* and

beverages is always questionable. Avoid unless source is known.

Caramel Candy: A type of *candy* made from *caramel*. Question the type of *sweetener* used. Caution. Avoid unless source is known. (See *caramel* and *candy*.)

Caramel Color: Caramel coloring is a *coloring agent* derived from the caramelization of corn *syrup* or *barley malt syrup*. Caution. Always question the source. Avoid unless source is known. (See *caramel*.)

Caramel Flavor: Caramel flavoring is a *flavoring agent* derived from the caramelization of corn *syrup* or *barley malt syrup*. Caution. Always question the source. Avoid unless source is known. (See *caramel*.)

Caraway Seed: A type of *seed*. *Raw* and *plain seeds* are GF. (See *seed*.)

Carbohydrate: Carbohydrates are *organic compounds* derived from *carbon*, hydrogen and oxygen. Sources of carbohydrates include *sugar*, *starch* and *cellulose*. All are questionable. [Look up each individually.]

Carbohydrate Gum: A type of gum derived from *tree* bark. GF.

Carbonate: Carbonates are a type of *mineral* (e.g., a *salt* or *ester* of *carbonic acid*). *Liquids* become gaseous when *carbon dioxide* is added. GF. (See *carbonated drinks*.)

Carbonated Drinks: Carbonated drinks are certain type of *beverage* with added carbonation (*carbon dioxide*). Carbonated drink is an umbrella term for a variety of *flavored soft drinks*. {Carbonated drinks may contain added *flavorings, sweeteners & colorings*.} Question the source of all ingredients. Several carbonated drinks are GF. Verify

GF. (See *beverage* and also see '*beverage*' in A & F charts.)

Carbonation: (See *carbonate* and *carbon dioxide*.)

Carbon Dioxide: A type of gas. Formula CO2. GF. (See *carbonate*.)

Carbonic Acid: Carbonic acid is a type of weak-*acid* formed when *carbon dioxide* is dissolved in water. GF. (See *carbonate*.)

Carboxymethycellulose (CMC): A type of *gum* derived from *cellulose*. GF. (See *cellulose* and sodium *carboxymethylcellulose*.)

Cardamom: Cardamom is a type of *seed* used *dried whole* or *ground* into a *spice*. The *pure ground spice* and *raw* seed is GF. (See *spice* and *seed*.)

Cargo Rice: A term used for *rice* with its *bran* removed. Check for GF purity. (See *white rice* for specifics.)

Caribou: A type of *meat*. *Pure fresh* and *plain* are GF. (See *meat*.)

Carnauba Wax: Carnauba wax is a type of *wax* obtained from a *palm* tree. Caution. GF.

Carob: Carob is type of GF *pod* of the locust *tree*. Carob is also a term for a type of *ground powder* obtained from the *dried roasted pods*. Carob is *naturally caffeine free* and sometimes termed carob *flour*. *Pure* carob *powder* can *substitute chocolate powder* in most *recipes*. Carob *powder* is used to make *carob chips* or a *carob powdered drink mix*. All the ingredients in a carob food mixture need to be verified GF. (See *chocolate, flour* and *powder*.)

Carob Bean Gum: A type of *gum* derived from locust beans. GF. (See *carob* and *gum*.)

Carob Chips: Carob chips are a type of *candy chips* made with *carob powder*. {Carob chips may contain added *sweeteners, oils/fats* and *lecithin*.} Most carob chips are not GF. Avoid unless source is known.

Carob Flour: (See *carob*.) GF.

Carob Pod: A type of *fruit*. Fresh *pure* and *plain* are GF. (See *carob*.)

Carob Powder: (See *carob*.)

Carolina Rice: A type of American *rice* grain. GF. (See *rice* for additional details and specifics.)

Carotene: (See *beta-carotene*.) GF.

Carp: A type of *fish*. *Pure fresh* and *plain* are GF. (See *fish*.)

Carrageen Gum: A type of *gum* derived from *Irish moss*. Verify GF. (See *Irish moss* and *seaweed*.)

Carrier: Carriers are types of *liquid solvent* that *isolates* or *extracts* components from certain *plant parts*. Types of carriers include <u>*water*</u>, *alcohol, glycerin, oil/fat* and <u>*chemical*</u> <u>*compounds*</u>. Question the source of all carriers. Carrier is also a term used for any *substance* used to transport another (e.g. *salt, sugar, powder, flour* or starch). Question the source of carrier bases used as a carrying agent to transport flavors. Caution: carriers are often used to carry *flavorings* in foods (e.g. *sauces*). [Look up each source individually.] (See *extracts*.)

Carrot: A type of *vegetable*. Fresh and *plain* are GF. (See *vegetable*.)

Carrot Tops: Carrot tops are a *vegetable* from the tops of carrots. *Pure fresh* and *plain* are GF. (See *vegetable*.) A type of *vegetable*.

Carubin: (See *locust bean gum*.)

Casabo: Casabo is a type of *fruit*. *Fresh* and *plain* are GF. (See *fruit*.)

Cascara Sagrada: A type of *spice*. *Pure spices* are GF. (See *spice*.)

Casein: A type of *protein* in *milk*. GF. (See *milk* and *casein free*.)

Casein Free (CF): Casein free is a term meaning free of *casein* and *milk protein*. [*Casein* is not *gluten*. Casein free does not mean *gluten free*.] (See *milk*, *protein* and *gluten free*.)

Cashew Nut: *A type of nut. Raw and plain nuts are GF.* (See *nut*.)

Cashew Nut Butter: *Nut butter ground* from *cashews*. Verify GF. (See *cashew* and *nut butters*.)

Cashew Nut Milk: Cashew nut milk is a type of *nondairy milk*. *Cashew* nut *milk* is prepared from *cashew nuts*. You can *home-make* cashew nut milk easily. {Cashew milk may contain added *fillers, alcohol, flavorings, enzymes gums* or *grain byproducts*.} Verify GF. (See *non-dairy milk* and *cashew*.)

Casing: Casing is an outer *covering* customarily obtained form *animal byproducts* (*intestines*). Casings are used to make *sausage*. Verify GF.

Cassava: Cassava is the *root plant* from which *tapioca* is prepared. GF. (See *tapioca flour* and *root*.)

Cassava Flour: (See *tapioca flour*.)

Cassava Meal: (See *tapioca flour*.)

Cassava Starch: (See *tapioca flour*.)

Casserole: Casseroles are a type of *meal baked* in one dish. Casseroles are generally not GF. You can *home make* casseroles with GF *ingredients*. (See *meal*)

Castor Oil: Castor oil is a type of *oil* obtained from the *seeds* of the castor *plant*. Caution. GF.

Castor Sugar: A finely granulated British *sugar cane sugar*. GF.

Catalyst: Catalysts are *substances* initiating or increasing the rate of a *chemical* reaction without itself undergoing any change.

Catering Companies: Catering companies do not deal with scores of *gluten free* requests, although catering companies do get specific plate requests from people with different restricted dietary needs. Prior to any special occasion, you need to call the catering company ahead of time and talk with the preparation chef/cook and/or food staff. Be clear and specific with your *food* request (e.g., instructing the chef to *broil* your *chicken* on a separate plate thus avoiding cross contamination or to prepare your *salad* dry without *croutons* or *dressing*). Safe catered *foods* may include *fresh fruit*, plain *vegetable salads*, steamed *vegetables*, baked, roasted, grilled or *broiled fish*, *poultry* or *meat*, cooked *rice*, soft-boiled *eggs*, *pure fruit juice*, *lemon water* and *baked potato*. [All of these foods need to be *basic* and *plain*, without added *dressings, sauces, flavorings, croutons* and *gravies*.] You can bring a stylish personal travel bag filled with GF *dressings, seasonings, spices* and other *condiment* essentials. Caution: the wait staff are more often than not 'hurried' while serving dinner. You will receive better service if you arrive on time or a bit early and talk with the preparation and serving staff about your pre-requested GF meal. Caution: examine the food well. [Always examine your food. Sometimes you will be served the same food as everyone else, the only difference may be the food staff rinsed the *forbidden sauce, gravy* or *dressing* off the food items and consider this *'plain'*.] (See *restaurant* and *travel*.)

Catfish: A type of *fish. Pure fresh* and *plain* catfish is GF. (See *fish*.)

Catnip: A type of *herb*. *Fresh* and *dried pure* are GF. (See *herb*.)

Catsup: (See *ketchup*.)

Cauliflower: A type of *vegetable*. *Fresh pure* and *plain* cauliflower is GF. (See *vegetable*.)

Cayenne: A type of *spice*. *Pure spices* are GF. (See *spice*.)

CD: (See *celiac disease*.)

Ceci Bean: (See *garbanzo bean*.)

Celery: A type of *vegetable*. *Fresh pure* and *plain* celery are GF.

Celery Salt: A type of *seasoning salt* made with *ground celery seeds*. (See *seasoning salt*.)

Celery Seed: *A type of seed* ground into a *spice*. The *raw* seeds and *pure ground spice* are GF. (See *seed*, *spice* and *celery salt*.)

Celiac: A term used for individuals with *celiac disease*.

Celiac Disease (CD): Celiac disease is also known as celiac sprue, enteropathy, ideopathic steatorrhea, gluten sensitive, coeliacs and nontropical sprue *disease*. Celiac disease is an adverse reaction to a *complex* group of specific *gluten proteins* (*prolamins*) involving the *immune system*. Celiac disease is a permanent *autoimmune disorder* and *disease* of *malabsorption*, caused by a *toxic* reaction to certain *gluten proteins* (*prolamins*) found in certain *gluten cereal grains*. Individuals with celiac disease have a genetic predisposition to the reaction from these prolamins (e.g. *gliadin* found in *wheat*, *horedin* found in *barley* and *secalin* found in *rye*). [There are also *gluten prolamins* found in <u>oat</u>, <u>corn</u>, <u>oats</u> and <u>rice</u> but these do not have the same *toxic* effect to individuals with celiac disease.] Celiac disease is a *digestive* disease that damages the small *intestines* and interferes with the *absorption* of *nutrients* when certain individuals consume intolerable food such as the *protein 'gluten'* in the offending grains (e.g. *wheat, barley, rye* and possibly *oats*). [Advanced testing indicates 'pure' oats are not harmful to those who have CD and/or DH disease. Although the oats used in test studies are *'pure'* and uncontaminated.] Celiac disease is reversible and symptoms as a rule disappear with a strict gluten free gluten free (GF) diet. You should start to notice some relief of symptoms within the first few days of a strict GF diet. On the GF diet, your *immune system* will feel stronger, but that does not mean you can stop eating GF. Celiac disease is a *disease* people do not outgrow. [Do not reintroduce gluten to the diet.] At present time the *treatment* for *celiac disease* is to eliminate all *grains* containing the *gluten proteins toxic* to celiacs, all *byproducts* of these *grains* and any *food* containing these *forbidden grains* and/or their *grain byproducts*. The cure for CD is to avoid *gluten* for life. With *active celiac disease* in the *degenerative stage* a strict GF diet 'must' be followed or other diseases and even death are possible. (See *gluten*, grains, *forbidden grains, gluten free, symptoms, biopsy, villi, newly diagnosed celiac, sensitive celiac, disease, gastroenterologist* and *special resources*.)

Celiac Shock: Celiac shock is a term used for someone with *celiac disease* having an *acute* reaction to even the smallest amount of *gluten*. (See *sensitivities, sensitive celiac, acute* and *celiac disease.*)

Cell: Cells are considered the smallest independently functioning *component* in the composition of an *organism*. Cells consist of one or more *nuclei*. (See *organism*.)

Cellophane Noodles: A type of transparent *pasta* made from *brown rice*. Verify GF. (See *pasta*.)

Cellulose: Cellulose are types of *bulking agents* and *gums* obtained from *plant fibers* (e.g. *algae, cotton byproducts, wood* and other *plants*). [Look up each individually.] Question the source of *cellulose*. Caution. (See *gum*.)

Celtose: Celtose is a type of *spice*. *Pure spices* are GF. (See *spice*.)

Cereal: Cereal is a term used for a type of breakfast *meal* usually prepared from *cereal grains*, served at breakfast time. Most *commercially prepared cereals* are not GF. Cereals are more often than not made with *forbidden gluten grains,* relatives of *forbidden grains* and *byproducts* of *forbidden grains*. {Cereals may contain added *colorings, flavorings* and *sweeteners*.} Question all *cereal*. [Even question rice crisps for a *forbidden barley malt* coating.] *Commercially prepared cereals* that are GF are generally labeled. Very few GF breakfast cereals are available at *regular grocery food stores*, most are available at *health food grocery stores* or by *mail order*. Several *commercially prepared* GF cereals are available at *health food grocer stores* and by *mail order*. (See *grains, cereal grains, cream of rice, breakfast cereal, gluten free, whole grains* and also see 'cereal' in A & F charts.)

Cereal Binding: Avoid.

Cereal Grain: Cereal grains are any *edible grain (seed/kernel)* from a *plant* of the *grass plant family*. Cereal grains are used to make *breakfast cereal, pasta* and *flour*. *Forbidden gluten* cereal grains include *barley, rye, wheat* and possibly *oats*. [See oat for acceptability.] *Gluten free* cereal grains include *corn, rice, sorghum* and *wild rice*. *Amaranth, millet, quinoa* and *buckwheat* are 'not truly' cereal grains, but considered gluten free cereal grains because of their grain-like similarities. [Look up each grain and/or seed individually.] Avoid all *forbidden gluten* cereal grains and relatives of these *forbidden grains*. Choose only GF cereal grains. (See *cereal, byproducts* and *grains*.)

Cereal Protein: Cereal protein refers to the *protein* from any *cereal grain* (e.g. *wheat, oats, barley, rye, corn* and *rice*). [Look up each individually.] Question the source. (See *cereal grain* and *protein*.)

CF: (See *casein free*.)

Chalupa: A chalupa is a type of *meal* similar to a *burrito*. Question if the *tortilla* contains *forbidden wheat flour*. Question the source of *seasoning* and all other ingredients.

Chamomile: A type of *herb*. *Fresh* and *pure dried herbs* are GF.

Champagne: Champagne is sparkling *wine* made from *grape* juice. Question added *flavorings*. Avoid *sulfites* in champagne if possible. Verify GF. (See *wines*.)

Champagne Vinegar: Champagne vinegar is a type of *vinegar* made from *champagne*. Verify GF. (See *vinegar* and *champagne*.)

Channa: (See *fresh cheese*.)

Chapatis: Chapatis is a type of *wheat flour bread*. Avoid.

Chappati: (See *flatbread*.)

Char: A type of *fish*. *Pure fresh* and *plain* are GF. (See *fish*.)

Chard: A type of *vegetable*. *Fresh* and *plain* are GF. (See *vegetable*.)

Charlock: Charlock is a type of *vegetable*. *Fresh* and *plain* are GF.

Chaval: (See *rice*.)

Cheddar Cheese: Cheddar cheese is a type of semi-firm *aged cheese*. Cheddar cheese comes in white and yellow *colors* and *naturally flavored* from mild to extra sharp. Choose *pure* cheddar cheese white in color instead of yellow (the only difference is the added *coloring* which is frequently *annatto*). [Look up each kind individually.] You can *freeze* cheddar cheese but it crumbles when defrosted. {Cheddar cheeses may contain added *flavors*, *colors* and *preservatives*.} You can *shred* cheese by hand ahead of time, *refrigerate* it in containers and use as needed. Verify GF. (See *cheese*.)

Cheese: Cheese is a type of concentrated form of *milk produced* from the milk of *animals* (e.g. cows, sheep, goats, buffalos, reindeer, camel, mares or yaks). Cheese is either *fresh* (*un-ripened/immature.*), or *aged* (*ripened/mature*). Types of GF *cheeses* may include certain brands of *cheddar*, *Swiss*, *Romano*, *Parmesan*, *Gorgonzola*, *Edam*, *Gouda*, *Jarlsberg*, *Monterey jack*, *Muenster* and some *bacteria ripened* cheese. [Look up each individually.] You can replace cheese with all or a portion of *tofu* in some *recipes*. {Cheese may contain added *filler*, *flavorings*, *acidifiers*, *antimycotic* *agents*, *bleaching agents*, *buffers*, *coatings*, *colorings*, *seasonings*, *spices*, *preservatives*, *alcohol*, *emulsifiers*, *gums* and *enzymes*.} Choose *pure plain unflavored* and *unseasoned* GF *cheese*. Question all *processed cheese, processed cheese foods* and *cheese spreads*. Avoid all *veined cheese*. Avoid cheese with forbidden *grain byproducts*. You can *shred* cheese by hand ahead of time, *refrigerate* it in containers and use as needed. (See *dairy* and also see 'dairy' in A & F charts.)

Cheese Cake: Cheese cake is a type of *dessert*. Cheese cake is a dense rich *cake* made with *cream cheese* in a *wheat cracker crust*. You can *home make* GF cheesecake with special GF ingredients. (See *baked-goods*, *recipes* and *specialty foods*.)

Cheese Cubes: Cheese cubes are various types of *cheeses* cut into individual chunk size pieces. Question the source of precut cheese cubes. (See *cheese*, *deli* and *contamination*.)

Cheese Sauce Mix: Cheese sauce mix is a type of *dry* cheese *seasoning* mix. Cheese sauce mix is highly questionable. Risky. Avoid unless source is known. (See *seasoning mix* and *cheese spread*.)

Cheese Shredded: You can *shred cheese* by hand, ahead of time, *refrigerate* it in containers and use as needed. Question the source of shredded cheese. (See *cheese*.)

Cheese Slices: Cheese slices are individually *wrapped cheese slices*, or *fresh* sliced *cheese* sliced at the *deli* counter. Pre sliced cheese from the deli is always questionable because of the possibility of *contaminated* deli *equipment* (e.g.

food slicing machine and deli preparation area. [Both must be free of *gluten contaminants*.] Question the source of sliced cheese. (See *cheese* and American cheese.)

Cheese Spread: Cheese spread is a type of spreadable *cheese* made with *real* or *imitation* cheese. {Cheese spreads may contain added *oils/fats*, *emulsifiers*, *thickeners*, *stabilizers*, *colorings*, *preservatives* and various *food agents*.} All cheese spreads are questionable. Caution. Risky. Avoid unless source is known. (See *dip*.)

Chelator: Chelators are *substances* that *bind* or trap *trace minerals*.

Chemical: Chemicals are *substances* produced by the process of chemistry, where changes in structure, composition and properties take place. Caution. Verify GF. (See *substances, chemically, synthetic chemicals, chemical compound* and *organic chemicals*.)

Chemical Compound: Chemical compounds are formed by the composition of two or more *chemicals* produced by chemistry. Caution. Verify GF. (See *compound* and *chemical*.)

Chemically: Chemically is a term used to describe *food* altered with chemicals, as opposed to a *physical method*. Question the chemicals used. Caution. (See *denatured, mechanically* and *chemical*.)

Chemically Modified: Any *substance* specially processed using *chemicals* (e.g., *cornstarch modified* is chemically modified). Caution. Verify the source of food is GF.

Chenna Cheese: A type of *fresh un-ripened cheese* made from buffalo or cow's *milk*. Verify GF. (See *cheese*.)

Cherimoya: A type of *fruit*. *Fresh* and *plain* are GF. (See *fruit*.)

Cherry: A type of *fruit*. *Fresh* and *plain* cherries are GF. (See *fruit*.)

Cheshire Cheese: Verify GF. (See *cheese*.)

Chestnut: A type of *nuts*. *Raw* and *plain* nuts are GF. (See *nuts*.)

Chevre Cheese: A type of semi-firm *cheese* made from cow or goat *milk*. [*Pur chevre* on the *label* ensures it is made from the *milk* of goats only.] Verify GF. (See *cheese*.)

Chewing Gum: Chewing gum is a type of *candy*. {Chewing gum may contain added *sweeteners* and other food substances.} Chewing gum is *dusted* with a type of *powder* to prevent the chewing gum from sticking to the *wrapper*. Chewing gum is questionable. (See candy and also see 'candy' in A & F charts.)

Chicken: Chicken is a type of domesticated *fowl*. All *fresh* and *plain fowl* are naturally GF. To cook chicken: *bake, bake, boil, grill, steam, fry, microwave, roast* or *broil* plain and then *season* with GF seasonings. Avoid chicken *dusted* with *forbidden flours*, pre-*seasoned* and/or self basted. Verify GF. (See 'poultry' in A & F charts.)

Chicken Nuggets: Chicken nuggets are a type of *breaded chicken* side dish. The *breading* is usually made with *forbidden grain byproducts* and therefore should be avoided. You can *home make* chicken nuggets with specialty GF breading. There are some *commercially prepared* GF chicken nuggets produced by specialty GF companies that are available through *specialty resources*. (See *special resources, breadcrumbs* and *chicken*.)

Chickpea: (See *garbanzo bean*.)

Chicory: A type of *spice*. *Pure spices* are GF. (See *spices*.)

Chicos: (See *dried sweet corn*.) GF.

Chilaquila: Chilaquila's are a type of *meal* similar to a *burrito*. Question if the *tortilla* contains *wheat flour*. Question the source of *seasonings* and all other *ingredients*. *Commercially prepared* GF chilaquila's are available through *specialty companies*.

Children and Gluten Free: The gluten free diet is especially difficult for children. I suggest reading a few books written by parents who have been in similar situations. There are many good easy reading books that provide practical advice and emotional support from parents and families coping with children with severe allergies, celiac disease, Autism, food allergies, attention deficit disorders and sensitivities to *gluten, dairy, eggs, corn, peanuts* and *soy*. (See *gluten free resource guide*.) [You can purchase enjoyable children's books through 'The Food Allergy and Anaphylaxis Network' at #1-800-929-4040. You can call this non-profit organization and ask for their booklet about managing food allergies. In it, you will find offers for brilliantly illustrated children's books.] It is a good idea to keep a small *travel bag* on hand always packed with a few of your child's favorite GF *snacks*. If you have a child with *food intolerances*, you need to inform anyone providing care for them, including your immediate family, their school and any caretakers and friends of your child. On outings, send a GF care pack for your child, clearly marked with their name and most importantly packed with their favorite GF *foods* (e.g., gluten free foods you know they will eat). Send extra GF snacks so your child can share. Leave extra GF *nutritional bars, meal replacement drinks, snacks* and some kinds of *prepared meals* with your child's caregiver for emergencies. (See *gluten free resource guide*.)

Chili: Chili is a type of *seasoned meal* customarily *prepared* with *beans*. {Chili may contain added *seasonings, seasoning mixes, rice* and *thickeners*.) The source of all ingredients need to be verified GF. Risky. Few *commercially prepared chili* at *food places* are GF. (See *soup, restaurant* and also see 'chili' in A & F charts.)

Chilies: (See jalapeno *peppers*.)

Chili Powder: A type of *seasoning blend* used in *chili*. Question the possibility *filler* in the chili *seasoning*. Question the source. (See *seasonings* and *chili*.)

Chilla: (See *pancake*.) Avoid.

Chilton: Chilton is a *forbidden grain*. Avoid. (See *grains*.)

Chimaeras: A type of *fish*. *Pure* and *plain* are GF. (See *fish*.)

Chimichanga: Chimichanga's are a type of *burrito meal*. Question if the *tortilla* is contains *wheat flour*. Question the source *seasonings* and all other *ingredients*. *Commercially prepared* GF chimichangas are available through *specialty companies*. (See *special resources*.)

China Bean: (See *black-eyed pea*.)

Chinese Food: Chinese food is a specific type of *ethnic food*. All *prepared foods* need to be questioned. Always question

Chinese food for the possibility of contamination (e.g., the same *oil* used to *deep-fry* all *fried* Chinese foods and the woks are customarily only rinsed in between uses, causing *residue* build up). {Chinese foods may contain added *thickeners*, *seasonings* and *sauces*.} Chinese *foods* generally use *cornstarch* as a *thickener*. Avoid all Chinese crisp *noodles*, fortune *cookies*, *pastry* wrappers, *forbidden pasta* and *breaded* foods. Avoid *MSG* if possible. Verify the source of all ingredients in Chinese foods are GF. Verify the preparation area and equipment are contaminant free. (See *restaurant*.)

Chinese Rice Vinegar: A type of *rice vinegar* made from *wheat*, <u>*sorghum*</u> and <u>*millet*</u> instead of <u>*rice*</u>. Avoid. (See *vinegar*)

Chips: Chip is a term used for *French fries*. (See French fries). Chips are also, a type of *snack* food made from sliced <u>*potatoes*</u> and <u>*taros*</u>, and processed <u>*corn*</u> or other *grains*. {Chips may contain added *colorings*, *seasonings*, *preservative*, *flavorings* and other *food agents*.} Chips can be *baked* in an oven but are customarily deep *fried* in *oil*. Avoid chips *deep-fried* in *oil* used previously to fry *forbidden gluten foods*. Avoid chips made with *forbidden grains* and *forbidden grain byproducts*. Avoid chips dried on conveyer belts *dusted* with *forbidden flour*. Several brands of *commercially prepared* chips are GF. <u>Choose</u> <u>100%</u> <u>*pure*</u> GF <u>*potato*</u>, <u>*corn*</u> or <u>*taro*</u> chips. Verify the chips and added seasonings are GF.

Chive: A type of *herb*. Fresh and *dried pure* are GF. (See *herb*.)

Chlorella: *A type of seaweed. Pure* and *plain* are GF. (See *seaweed*.)

Chlorophyll: Chlorophyll is *plant* pigment (color) found in *algae*, some *bacteria* and in certain *plants*. Chlorophyll is what is responsible for capturing the light energy needed for photosynthesis. (See *algae*, *bacteria* and *plants*.)

Chocolate: Chocolate is a type of natural flavoring obtained from *roasted cocoa seeds*. *Pure* cocoa/chocolate is naturally GF. Chocolate contains *caffeine*. [*Caffeine free* <u>*carob*</u> can *substitute* chocolate.] Chocolate is available in *solid* or *powdered* forms. Chocolate is also a term for a type of *candy* made from chocolate. {*Prepared* chocolate may contain added *sweeteners*, *alkalis*, *buffers*, *emulsifiers*, *fats/oils*, *lecithin*, *stimulants*, *cocoa butter*, *milk powder* and various other *ingredients*.} Always question chocolate candy with added *caramel*, *toffee*, *butterscotch*, *flavored syrups* and *fillings*. Always question the source of added *sweeteners*. (See *candy*, *carob* and all the other *chocolate* products.)

Chocolate Chips: Chocolate chips are a type of *candy* food in small *chips* pieces. Always question the ingredients. (See *candy* and *chocolate* for details and specifics.)

Chocolate Milk: Chocolate milk is a type of milk with added chocolate flavored powder or syrup. Always question the source of added *flavoring*. *Commercially* prepared chocolate *milk* is risky. (See *milk*, *chocolate*, *chocolate powder* and *chocolate syrup*.)

Chocolate Powder: Chocolate powder is a *powdered* form of *chocolate* (*cocoa*). Chocolate powder is also a type of *instant powdered drink mix*. Both can be added to *milk* to make *flavored chocolate milk*. Some *commercially prepared* chocolate powders are GF. Verify GF. (See *chocolate* and *powder*.)

Chocolate Syrup: Chocolate syrup is a *liquid* form of *chocolate* (*cocoa*). Chocolate syrup is also a type of *instant liquid drink mix*. Both can be added to *milk* to make *flavored chocolate milk*. {Chocolate syrup may contain added *sweeteners* and *flavorings*.} Some *commercially prepared* chocolate syrups are GF. Verify GF. (See *chocolate* and *syrup*.)

Chola: (See *garbanzo beans*.) GF.

Chowder: Chowder is a type of chunky *seafood soup* frequently prepared with *potatoes*. {Chowders may contain added *thickeners*, *flavorings* and *seasonings*.} Question all chowders. There are very few *commercially prepared* GF chowders. They are available at *regular* and *health food grocery stores*. Avoid unless the source of all ingredients is known. (See *soup* and see 'chowder' in A & F charts.)

Chronic Stage: Chronic stage is the third stage of a *disease*. This is the point in a *disease* where the body is significantly deteriorating. [Patients with CD in the chronic stage might show signs from the consumption of *gluten* over the period of years from not yet being *diagnosis*.] The body sometimes suffers transformations from long-term changes in the body. Patients in the chronic stage of *celiac*

disease as a general rule will recover with a strict adherence to the GF diet. (See *four stages of disease, celiac disease, symptoms* and *disease*.)

Chub: A type of *fish*. Fresh and plain chub is GF. (See *fish*.)

Chutney: Chutney is a type of *fruit relish*. {Chutney's may contain added *seasonings, preservatives, sweeteners, thickeners, vinegar* and *firming agents*.} Question the source of all ingredients in chutneys. Several chutneys are GF. Question the source. (See *dip* and see *relish*.)

Cider: (See *apple cider* and *apple cider vinegar*.) Verify GF.

Cider Vinegar: (See *apple cider vinegar*.) Verify GF.

Cigarettes: Cigarettes are made from *tobacco leaves*. GF.

Cilantro: A type of *herb*. Fresh and pure dried are GF. (See *herb*.)

Cinnamon: A type of *spice*. Pure is GF. Question *powdered* cinnamon for *filler*. (See *spice* and *seasonings*.)

Citrange: A type of *fruit*. Fresh and plain *fruits* are GF. (See *fruit*.)

Citrates: A type of *salt* or *ester* of *sulfuric acid*. GF.(See *sulfuric acid*.)

Citric Acid: Citric acid is a type of *acid* derived from *citrus fruit* or *synthetically* prepared. GF. (See *acid* and *citrus fruit*)

Citron: A type of *fruit*. Fresh and plain are GF. (See *fruit*.)

Citrus: Citrus a term used for a certain group of *fruit* containing *citric acid*. Types of citrus *fruits* include *oranges, lemons, limes* and *grapefruits*. [Look up each type of fruit individually.] All pure fruits are GF. (See *fruit* and *rind*.)

Citrus Rind: The *rind* of *citrus fruit*. GF. (See *citrus fruit* and see *rind*.)

Citrus Zester: A type of *kitchen utensil* used to cut extremely thin slices from *citrus rinds*. (See *rind*.)

Clam: A type of *seafood. Fresh* and *plain* clams are GF. (See *seafood*.)

Clarified Butter: Clarified butter is *butter* that has been heated and then most of the *milk solids* are removed. Verify GF. (See *butter* and *dairy*.)

Clarifying Agent: Clarifying agents are *substances* used to make *food* clearer. Types of clarifying agents include *gums, gelatins* and *chemicals*. [Look up each individually.] (See *agents*)

Classes: Classes is a term for related *organisms* classified into groups, according to their identifiable characteristics. [*Potatoes* are produced by *plants* of the *genus* Solanum of the family Solanaceae. The common white potato classifies as Solanum tuberosum.] Avoid all classes of *grains* containing the *forbidden gluten toxic* to *celiacs*. Avoid all relatives of *wheat, barley* and *rye*. (See *gluten, grains, common name* and *genus*.)

Clear Flour: A type of *straight flour* milled from hard *wheat*. Avoid.

Clove: A type of *spice. Pure spices* are GF. (See *spices* and *seasonings*.)

CMC: (See *carboxymethycellulose*.)

Coagulating Agents: Coagulating agents are *substances* used to *thicken liquids*. Question the source. (See *thickeners*.)

Coarse Sugar: Coarse sugar is a type of roughly *granulated sugar.* Coarse *pure granulated sugar cane sugar* is GF. Verify GF. (See *sugar*.)

Coating: Coatings are any *substance* used to *coat food.* Types of coatings include *batter, breadcrumbs, glycerin* and *gluten.* [Look up each individually.] Caution: *gluten* is sometimes used to coat *rice grains* for sheen. Caution: *chemicals* are often used to coat whole foods to prevent *mold* (e.g., *fresh fruits* and *vegetables*). Some coatings are not visible. Question the source of all coatings. Question foods for possible coatings, especially *whole foods.* (See *whole foods, plain* and *pure*.)

Cocktail Sauce: Cocktail sauce is a type of *raw shredded horseradish* and red *sauce condiment* usually used on *seafood.* {Cocktail sauce may contain added *seasonings, ketchup* and *vinegar*.} Question all the ingredients. Some are cocktail sauces are GF. (See *sauce*.)

Cocoa: Cocoa is a type of flavoring obtained from *roasted cocoa seeds.* Cocoa is referred to as chocolate. GF. (See *chocolate*.)

Coconut: Coconut is really a type of *fruit* referred to as *nut. Fresh pure* and *plain* coconut is GF. (See *coconut shredded*.)

Coconut Dried: (See *coconut shredded*.)

Coconut Milk: *Coconut* milk is a type of *nondairy milk* made from shredded coconut. *Coconut* milk is easy to *home-make.* {Coconut milk may contain added *filler, alcohol, flavorings, enzymes, gums* and *grain byproducts*} Verify GF. (See *nondairy milk* and *coconut*.)

Coconut Oil: A type of *oil* obtained from *coconuts.* Pure coconut oil is GF. Coconut *oil* is solid at room temperature. Coconut oil needs no *refrigeration.* (See *coconut*.)

Coconut Shredded: Shredded coconut is *fresh coconut* shredded. *Commercially prepared* shredded coconut has most of the moisture removed. {Shredded coconut may contain added *sweeteners*.} Choose *plain unsweetened* coconut if possible. Avoid shredded coconut with *sulfites* if possible. Verify GF.

Cod: A type of *fish*. *Fresh* and *plain* cod are GF. (See *fish*.)

Codex Alimentarius Commission: This is an organization of the *Food* and *Agriculture Organization*/World Health Organization. The CAC is dedicated to *nutrition* and *foods* for special dietary needs (e.g. *gluten free foods* for *celiacs*). The commission uses the standard of allowable *gluten* content in products of less than .03% total *protein*. They consider .03% as not being dangerous. [These are standards only and these standards do not advise the consumption of *gluten*.] It is much safer to consume *foods* without any *gluten*. Avoid all gluten in all amounts if possible.

Coeliacs Disease: (See celiac disease.)

Coffee: Coffee is a type of *beverage* prepared from *ground coffee beans*. Choose coffee made with *100% pure* GF coffee beans and/or *naturally decaffeinated coffee*. Coffee can be fresh ground or instant. Question added *flavorings* in coffee or flavorings added to *coffee beans*. {Coffee may contain added *stimulants*.} Question all *instant* coffee and coffee *substitutes*. [For your convenience, there are coffee cup funnels and single coffee filters available to make pure GF coffee, one cup at a time.] Coffees from *vending machines* are risky. Verify GF. (See *coffee beans*.)

Coffee Bean: Pure plain coffee beans are naturally GF. Coffee beans are the beans from which coffee is ground. Question *flavored* and *coated* coffee beans. Choose *100% pure* coffee beans. *Decaffeinated* coffee beans should be naturally *decaffeinated*. For your convenience, you can *mill whole* coffee beans *fresh* with a *coffee mill*. (See *coffee* and *coffee mill*.)

Coffee Grinder: (See *coffee mill*.)

Coffee Mill: Coffee mils are a type of small *kitchen appliance* used to *grind whole coffee beans*. You can also use a coffee mill to *mill* soft *dry ingredients* (e.g. *quinoa, millet* and soft *seeds*). Choose a coffee mill with a removable lid to make cleaning easy. Clean out leftover *residue* with a *dry pastry brush*. To avoid *contamination mill* GF *foods* only, in the same mill. It is practical to have two coffee mills. [One *mill* for *spicy ingredients* (e.g. *dried jalapeno peppers* and *cori*an*der seeds*) and a second *mill* for non-spicy *ingredients* (e.g. *millet, quinoa, coffee beans* and *rice*).]

Coho: A type of *fish*. *Fresh* and *plain* are GF. (See *fish*.)

Colby: A type of semi-soft mild *cheddar cheese* made from cow's *milk*. Verify GF. (See *cheese*.)

Cold Cuts: (See *lunchmeat*.)

Coleslaw: Coleslaw is a type of cold *salad* made with shredded *cabbage*. {Coleslaw may contain added *seasonings, vinegar* and *mayonnaise*.} Question all ingredients. (See *salad*.)

Collard Greens: A type of *vegetable*. *Fresh* and *plain* are GF.

Colloidal: A suspension of particles in a solution.

Coloring: Coloring is a blanket term for a variety of *substances* used to *color* foods. Colorings are *natural* or *artificial substances* that add color to *foods* or *beverages*. Some types of *natural* coloring *agents* include *annatto*, *carotene*, *red beet*, *paprika*, *spices*, *vegetables*, *turmeric*, *caramel* and *amaranth*. [Look up each individually.] Some colorings are from *chemical* or *synthetic* substances. The term coloring listed as an ingredient is not always defined. Question the source of all colorings. Caution.

Colour: (See *artificial coloring*.)

Colts Foot: A type of *spice*. *Pure* are GF. (See *spice*.)

Colzo Shoot: A type of *vegetable*. *Fresh* and *plain* are GF.

Comfrey: A type of *spice*. *Pure* are GF. (See *spice*.)

Commercially Prepared: Commercially prepared food is a term used for foods that are not *homemade* but manufactured. Commercially prepared foods are *manufactured* in large quantities with a profit-making point-of-view. *Manufacturing foods* is a business with profit and supply and demand being top priorities. Commercially prepared food is normally produced for the general public majority not for individuals with special needs. All commercially *prepared food* is questionable for the possibility of *gluten*. Only a small number of companies *manufacture* commercially prepared *specialty* GF *food* items. There is an abundance of commercially prepared GF foods available at *regular grocery food stores*. Some commercially prepared GF *specialty* items are available at *regular grocery food stores* but most *commercially prepared specialty* GF *foods* are available at *health food*

grocery stores or by *mail order*. (See *special resources*.)

Common Name: Common name is a term used for the common name that describes a widely found species of *animal* or *plant*. [A 'common name' may be an *ingredient* and/or *substance* shared by two or more other *ingredients* or *substances* having an equal relationship.] The common name is a non-*specialized* name used by most ordinary people with no special knowledge (e.g., *wheat* is the common name for cereal grasses of the *grass family* and *buckwheat* is the common name for a plant family and its *genera*). (See *genus* and *unusual name*.)

Common Starch: Common starch refers to *cornstarch*. GF. (See *cornstarch*.)

Communion Wafer: Communion wafers are a type of *forbidden* thin white *wheat wafer* served at a religious ceremonies. There are *commercially prepared* GF communion wafers available through *specialty companies*.

Companies: (See *manufacturers* and *distributors*.)

Complete Protein: Complete proteins are types of *proteins* having all the necessary *protein components*. Question the source.

Complex: Complex is a term for multifaceted or *compounded* things having a composition of many parts or elements. Complex ingredients are not simple. (See *simple*.)

Component: Components are parts of food (e.g., an individual unit of *food* combined from one or more other units of *food* to form an *ingredient*). Food components may be *natural* or *artificial*. [Law does not require the listing of all *food components* on *labels*.] Question the source of all *food/ingredient* components. (See *ingredient*.)

Compote: Compote is a type of *fruit spread*. This spreadable *fruit* is prepared with *cooked* pieces of *fresh* or *dried fruit*. {Compotes may contain added *sweeteners* and other *food agents*.} Question the source. (See *fruit* and *dried fruit*.)

Compound: (See *chemical compound* and *compounded*.)

Compounded: *Prepared* specifically from *raw ingredients* in a specific format. (See *compound* and *chemical compound*.)

Compounded Ingredients: (See *compounded* and *raw ingredients*.)

Compounded Medication: Compounded medication is a type of *medication* custom *prepared* (*compounded*) from basic *ingredients*. Compounded medication is specifically *prepared* for individual needs (e.g., prepared *gluten free* for *celiacs*). *Compounded medication* can be *compounded* through special resources. To get a referred *compounding pharmacy* in your area, call *The International Academy of Compounding Pharmacists* at 1-800-927-4227. [Areas include all of the USA and Canada.] (See *medication*.)

Compressed Yeast: Compressed yeast is a type of *fresh yeast* condensed into a *solid* form. Caution. Verify GF.

Concentrates: Concentrates are *liquid* to semi-liquid *food* with most of the *liquid* removed. Most of the *water* or *liquid* has been removed and/or evaporated. Question the source of all concentrates.

Condensed Foods: Condensed foods are *foods* that have been *concentrated*. (See *concentrates*.)

Condiment: Condiments are single or *prepared seasonings* or *flavored mixtures* used to adjust or improve the taste of *foods/meals*. [Condiments are *components* to *food*.] {Condiments may contain added *fillers, vinegars, grain alcohols, stabilizers, emulsifiers, preservatives, colorings, stabilizers, sweeteners, flavorings, additives, dyes* and *food agents*.} A good number of condiments are not GF. Question the source of all condiments. Always question condiments for *hidden ingredients,* especially in *spices, sauces, gravies, dips* and *spreads*. Avoid condiments with *forbidden grains* and *forbidden grain byproducts*. Question added *filler*. [*Fillers* are not always listed as an *ingredient* on labels.] Question all *dried herbs, dried spices, ketchup, dressing, sauce, marinade, dip, dry seasoning mixes, mustard, BBQ sauce, tamari sauce, ground spices, mayonnaise, bouillon, gravy, gravy extracts, miso, spice blends* and *soy sauce*. [Look up each individually.] *Contamination* occurs easily in condiments from *utensils* (e.g., leaving *forbidden crumbs* behind). [Avoid this by not double dipping and if possible purchasing separate condiments.] I suggest choosing your favorite condiments from a GF food product list and verifying their GF purity and always having them on hand. (See 'condiments' in A & F section.)

Confection: (See *sweeteners*.)

Confectioners Sugar: A type of *cane sugar sweetener* finely

granulated into a *powder.*
{Confectioner sugar may contain added *cornstarch.*} Verify GF. (See *sugar* and *sweetener.*)

Constipation: A type of *gastrointestinal* upset causing infrequent and difficult bowel movements (e.g., hard, solid and sometimes painful stools). *Diarrhea* is more common for patients with CD to experience than constipation. (See *symptoms* and *diarrhea.*)

Contamination: *Toxic gluten* contamination for celiacs, as a rule, is not life threatening. *Symptoms* of contamination vary in severity and symptoms, from person to person. Contaminated foods are considered un-*pure*. In this book, the term contamination refers to *gluten free foods* made impure with *forbidden gluten grains* or *forbidden grain byproducts*. Obvious contamination can occur by using the same *oil* previously used to *deep fry gluten* containing *food* and from *gluten residue* remaining on kitchen *equipment* and *appliances* (e.g., inadequately cleaned kitchen *utensils surfaces, sifters, grills, toasters* and *woks*). Question the possibility of contamination with *hidden ingredients* (e.g., *foods* produced in an environment not free of *gluten* contaminants). A major concern of contamination is *wheat flour* used as a *filler* or to keep *foods* separated or to *dust* conveyor belts and even airborne. [Law does not require the listing of all *food components* on labels.] Question *cross contamination* when purchasing *ingredients* from open-*bulk* (e.g. scoops used previously for *gluten*

containing *flours*). (See *cross contamination* and *hidden sources.*)

Convenience Stores: Convenience stores are just that 'convenient.' They carry a limited amounts of GF food items (e.g. *fresh fruits* and *vegetables*, hard-boiled *eggs, yogurt, milk,* some *beverages,* c*andy* and a few *prepared snacks, canned* goods and possible a select few *deli* items). You will have more of a selection of GF foods if you go into a *grocery food store* instead of a convenience store. (See *grocery food store, specialty food items* and *travel.*)

Converted Rice: Converted rice is *rice parboiled* before the *bran* is removed. {Converted rice may contain *additives.*} Verify GF. (See *rice.*)

Conveyer Belt: Conveyer belts transport *processed foods* during *manufacturing*. Caution: *forbidden* flours are used to *dust* conveyer belts, to keep foods from sticking. Question all food products processed on a conveyer belt. (See *dust.*)

Cook: Cooking food is a method of *preparing food* with heat. This process does not render *food* GF. Methods of cooking include *bake, boil, broil, grill, steam, fry, deep fry, microwave, roast* and *toast.* [Look up each different cooking method individually.] (See *cookware.*)

Cookies: Cookies are individual *confection baked-goods* generally made with *wheat flour*. Avoid. You can *home make* cookies with GF *ingredients. Commercially prepared* GF cookies and cookie *mixes* are available through *specialty companies*. There are many superior *recipe books* available to *home bake*

GF *cookies*. (See *baked-goods* and *special resources*.)

Cooking Spray: (See *nonstick spray*.)

Cooking Wine: Cooking wine is basically, inferior *wine* reserved for *cooking*. Quality drinkable wine can substitute cooking *wine*. Verify GF. (See *wine* for details and specifics.)

Cookware: Cookware are *culinary* tools used to *cook* of *foods*. Choose heavy-duty *stainless steel* cookware. *Stainless steel* is non-reactive to *acid* and *alkaline food*. Stainless steel cookware is easy to clean and resists corrosion and scratching. The best type of cookware is *stainless steel* with a layer of *aluminum* or copper in the middle for better heat conducting.

Coriander Seed: A type of *seed*. *Pure whole* are GF. (See *seed*.)

Corn: Corn is a type of GF *cereal grain* from the *grass plant family*. Other names for corn include maize, zia, zia maize and Indian corn. Although corn contains a certain type of gluten protein, corn is GF according to *celiac disease* standards. Different types of corn include *dent*, *flint*, *flour*, *sweet* and *popcorn*. Corn is a *base ingredient* in making *alcohol*, *starch*, *flour*, *dextrose* and many other corn *byproducts*. [Look up each corn product individually.] There is a type of *sweet corn* that is GF and eaten as a *vegetable*. (See *sweet corn* and all the other corn products.)

Corn Bran: Corn bran is the outer layer of *corn*. GF. (See *bran* and *corn*.)

Cornbread: Cornbread is a type of *bread*-like *baked-good*, made with *cornmeal* and added *flour*. Question the source of flour (*rice*, *bean* or *wheat*). Cornbread is easy to *home-make*. *Commercially prepared* GF cornbread and cornbread *mixes* are available through *specialty companies*. (See *baked-goods* and *cornmeal*.)

Corn Dextrin: Dextrimaltose. GF. (See *dextrin*.)

Corn Dhokla: Corn dhokla is a type of *corn* and *wheat* balls. Avoid.

Corn Dog: Corn dogs are a type of *batter dipped frankfurter* served on a stick. Corn dogs are usually not GF. Question the type of *frankfurter* and source of *batter*. (See *batter*.)

Corn Flour: Corn flour is a type of *grain flour* typically *milled* from soft *flour corn kernels*. Corn flour will *mill* from *popcorn kernels*. [Corn flour is not the same as *cornstarch* and corn flour cannot *substitute cornstarch*.] Corn flour is *milled* fine as opposed to coarse milled corn like *cornmeal* or *corn grits*. Check for GF purity. *Commercially prepared* GF corn flour is available through *special resources*. (See *flour*.)

Corn Gluten: Corn gluten is a certain type of *protein component* of *corn*. Corn gluten is considered safe for *celiacs*. (See *corn* and *protein*.)

Corn Grits: Corn grits are a type of coarsely *ground corn kernels* used as a coarse-*flour*. Corn grits are used to make *porridge*. [Corn grits are a coarser *milled corn* than *cornmeal*.] You can *home mill* corn grits with *popcorn kernels*. *Polenta* is also termed corn grits. *Commercially prepared* GF corn grits are available through *specialty companies*. Check for GF purity. (See *corn flour*.)

Corn Husk: The *edible* leafy outer *plant part* of *corn on the cob*.

Cornhusk is used to wrap around some *foods* before *cooking* (e.g. *tamale*). GF.

Corn Kernel: Corn kernel is the core (*nucleus*) part of the *husk* (e.g. *corn*). GF. (See *corn.*)

Cornmeal: Cornmeal is coarsely *milled corn kernels*. Cornmeal is *milled* less coarse than *corn grits*, but more coarse than *corn flour*. Use cornmeal as a *breadcrumb* replacement in some recipes. Question some *commercially prepared cornmeal* for the addition of *wheat flour*. *Commercially prepared* GF cornmeal is available through *specialty companies*. Check for GF purity. (See *corn.*)

Corn Muffin: Corn muffins are a type of individual *cornbread baked-good,* made with *cornmeal* and added *flour*. Question the source of flour (*rice*, *bean* or *wheat*). Corn muffins are easy to *home-make*. *Commercially prepared* GF corn muffins and corn muffin *mixes* are available through *specialty companies*. (See *baked-goods* and *cornmeal.*)

Corn Oil: A type of *oil* obtained from *corn* kernels. Check for GF purity. (See *corn* and *oil*)

Corn On The Cob: A type of *fresh sweet corn cooked* on the cob and eaten as a *vegetable*. GF. (See *corn* and *vegetable.*)

Corn Pasta: Corn pasta is a type of *pasta* made from *corn*. Check for GF purity. (See *corn* and *pasta.*)

Corn Silk: Corn silk is the tuft part at the top of an ear of *fresh corn on the cob*. GF. Corn silk is used to make a type of *tea*. (See *corn.*)

Corn Silk Extract: Verify GF.

Corn Smut: Corn smut is a type of *fungal disease* that attacks *grains* including *corn*.

Cornstarch: Cornstarch is a type of highly *refined thickening agent* made from the *starchy* part of *corn*. [Cornstarch is not the same as *corn flour* and cannot *substitute* corn flour.] Caution. Verify GF.

Cornstarch Acid Modified: *Cornstarch chemically modified.* Caution. Verify GF. (See *cornstarch.*)

Cornstarch Oxidized: *Oxidized cornstarch*. Caution. Verify GF.

Corn Sugar: A type of highly *processed sugar* derived from *corn glucose*. Caution. GF. (See *sugar.*)

Corn Sweetener: A type of *sweetener* derived from *corn*. Caution. Verify GF. (See *sweetener*)

Corn Syrup: A type of highly refined *syrup* made from *corn*. {Corn syrup may contain added *flavorings*.} Questionable. Caution. Verify GF. (See *syrup.*)

Corn Syrup Solids: A certain type of *solid substance* derived from *corn syrup*. Verify GF. (See *corn syrup.*)

Cosmetic: Cosmetics are beautifying *substances* usually applied *topically* to the body. Some *sensitive CD* patients are concerned with *topically* applied *cosmetics* containing *gluten*. [You will ingest lipstick and foundation applied in the lip area.] Question added *oat gum* in lipsticks and *forbidden wheat flour* in foundation powders. Question all facial moisturizing lotions and any cosmetic applied to the facial area. Assure possible ingested facial makeup is GF. Patients with *DH* should avoid *topically* applied cosmetics and body care products containing *gluten*. (See *sensitive* and *topical*.)

Cottage Cheese: Cottage cheese is a type of *fresh cheese* made from cow's *milk*. {Cottage cheese may contain added *filler, flavorings, alcohols, enzymes, gums* and *coagulating* and *stabilizing agents*.} Question flavorings added to cottage cheese. Choose *plain* GF cottage cheese. Verify GF. (See *dairy*.)

Cotton Seed: A type of *seed*. Caution. GF. (See *seed*.)

Cotton Seed Oil: A type of *oil* obtained from *cotton seeds*. Caution. Verify GF. (See *cotton seeds*.)

Couscous: Coarse particles from processed *durum wheat* (*semolina*). Avoid. [*Quinoa* can substitute couscous in most *recipes*.]

Coush Coush: A type of *cornmeal* dish. Avoid unless all ingredients are verified GF. (See *cornmeal*.)

Cowpea: A type of *black-eyed pea bean*. GF. (See *bean*.)

Crab: A type of *shellfish*. Fresh and *plain* crabs are GF. (See *seafood* and *seafood seasonings*).

Cracked Flour: *Flour milled* from *cracked wheat grains*. Avoid.

Cracked Wheat: Cracked *whole-wheat grains*. Avoid.

Cracker: A type of *snack food* made with *grains* (e.g. typically *corn*, *rice* or *wheat*). Avoid crackers made with *forbidden grains* and/or *forbidden grain byproducts*. {Crackers may contain added *colorings, flavorings preservatives* and *dough conditioners*.} Question if the crackers were dried on a conveyer belt *dusted* with *forbidden flours*. Choose *pure* GF *rice* or *bean* crackers. Question all the ingredients in crackers. *Commercially prepared* GF crackers are available at *health food grocery stores* and *ethnic grocery food stores*. Some GF rice crackers are in the Chinese food section of the grocery food store. There are *commercially prepared* GF crackers available through *special resources*. (See *baked-good* and *rice crackers*.)

Cracker Flour: *Flour milled* from soft *wheat grains*. Avoid.

Cranberry: A type of *fruit*. Fresh and *plain* cranberries are GF.

Cranberry Bean: A type of mottled color *bean*. Cranberry beans *mill* well into an excellent *bean flour*. GF. (See bean *flour*.)

Cranberry Juice: A type of *juice* produced from *cranberries*. Fresh *pure* and *plain* is GF. (See *juice*)

Crappie: A type of *fish*. Fresh and *plain* are GF. (See *fish*.)

Crayfish: A type of *fish*. Fresh and *plain* are GF. (See *fish*.)

Cream: Cream is a *dairy* product obtained from the thick *liquid* forming on the top of *raw milk*. Cream is used to make *butter, ice cream* and *cheese*. {Cream may contain added *fillers, gums, flavorings, alcohol, enzymes* and *stabilizing agent*.} Avoid some non-dairy *creamers* and *dairy substitutes*. Choose *pure fresh plain* GF cream. Verify GF.

Cream Cheese: Cream cheese is a type of *fresh* soft *un-ripened cheese*. {Cream cheese may contain added *fillers, gums, flavorings, alcohol, enzymes* and *emulsifying, gelling, stabilizing* and *thickening agents*.} Choose *plain* regular or *plain Neufchatel* GF cream cheese. The majority of cream cheese are GF. Verify GF. (See *cream, double* cream cheese, triple cream cheese and dairy products.)

Creamer: Creamers are either natural or artificial substances used to flavor hot beverages (e.g. tea or coffee). Some nondairy creamers are GF. Question all. (See cream.)

Cream of Rice: Cream of rice is a type of breakfast cereal made from milled whole rice grains. You can home make cream of rice by briefly blending whole white or brown rice grains in a coffee mill. (See rice.)

Cream of Tartar: Cream of tartar is a type of fine white acidic powder (potassium bitartrate) obtained from the residue remaining on the inside of barrels after making wine. Cream of tartar is a baking powder ingredient. You can purchase cream of tartar at regular grocery food stores. GF. (See baking powder.)

Crema Dania Cheese: A type of double cream cheese made from cow's milk. Verify GF.

Creme Fraiche: Cream Fraiche is a type of thickened cream. Question the source of thickener. (See cream.)

Creole Cream Cheese: A type of tart flavored cream cheese. Question added flavorings. Risky. Verify GF.

Crepe: A type of very thin pancake customarily made with forbidden wheat flour. Avoid. (See pancake.)

Crescenza Cheese: A type of soft fresh cheese made from cow's milk. Verify GF. (See cheese.)

Cress: A type of vegetable. Fresh plain are GF. (See vegetable.)

Crisp Bread: Crisp bread is a type of crispy wheat bread baked-good. Avoid. Commercially prepared GF crisp bread is available through specialty companies. (See special resource.)

Crisps: A term for potato chips or crisp bread. [Look up each.]

Crock Pot: (See slow cooker.)

Croissant: A type of flaky wheat dough pastry baked-good. Avoid.

Croquette: Croquettes are a type of dish containing wheat filler and a breadcrumb coating. Avoid.

Cross Contamination: Cross contamination is contamination occurring during or after food production, but not necessarily within the composition of food. Gluten cross contamination is a concern for GF foods. (See contamination and prepared foods.)

Crouton: Croutons are stale wheat flour bread cubes. Avoid. Commercially prepared GF croutons are available through special resources. (See salad)

Crudités: Crudités are raw seasonal vegetables used with dips and spreads. All fresh and plain raw vegetables are GF. (See vegetables.)

Crumpets: Unsweetened yeast bread made with wheat flour. Avoid.

Crushed Tomatoes: (See tomatoes crushed.) Verify GF.

Crustacean: All fresh and plain crustaceans are GF. Types of crustaceans include barnacles, crabs, crayfish, lobsters and shrimp. [Look up each individually.] (See seafood)

Crystalline: A type of clear and crystal-like substances. Verify GF.

Crysta Sugar: Crystal sugar is a type of coarse granulated sugar cane sugar. Verify GF. (See sugar.)

Cucumber: A type of vegetable. Fresh and plain are GF.

Cuitlacoche: (See corn smut.)

Culinary: Culinary is a term relating to anything concerning food and/or cooking. (See cookware and kitchen)

Culinary Supplies: Culinary supplies are provisions used for *food* or *cooking*. (See *kitchen supplies*.)

Culture: *Material* (*bacteria*, *plants*, *microorganisms* and *tissue*) grown in specialty controlled conditions.

Cumin Seed: A type of *seed*. *Pure* and *fresh whole* cumin *seeds* are GF.

Cupcake: Cupcakes are individual *cakes*. Most cake batters can be poured into muffin pans to make cupcakes instead of a single cake pan. Most *commercially prepared* cupcakes are prepared with *forbidden grain*s and *forbidden grain byproducts*. (See *cake*.)

Cured: Curing is a method of *preserving food* (e.g. *smoking*, *drying* or *salting*; *meat*, *poultry* and *fish*). Look up each individually. {Cured food may contain added *sweeteners*, *enzymes* and *flavorings*.} Verify GF.

Currants: Currants are a type of *raisin*. Verify GF. (See *raisin*.)

Custard: A type of *pudding*. Avoid.

Cuttlefish: A type of *fish*. *Fresh* and *plain* are GF. (See *fish*.)

Cydonia Seed: (See *quince seed*.)

Dab: A type of *flounder*. *Fresh* and *plain fish* are GF. (See *fish*.)

Dahi: (See *yogurt*.)

Dairy and Dairy Products: Dairy products are any product made from or containing nearly all *milk*. Dairy comes from female *animals* (e.g. cows, sheep, goats, buffalos, reindeers, camels, mares or yaks). Types of dairy products include *butter*, *cream*, *cheese*, *milk*, *sour cream*, *whey powder* and *yogurt*. All dairy products need to be verified GF. [Look up each individually.] Dairy contains lactose. Some *celiacs* experience *lactose intolerance* in the beginning of diagnosis but for most it is temporary. *Dairy products* made from goat and sheep milk are easier to digest than *dairy products* made from cow *milk*. {Dairy products may contain added *fillers*, *alcohol*, *enzymes*, *flours*, *starch*, *emulsifiers*, *additives*, *flavorings*, *sweeteners*, *preservatives*, *gums*, *emulsifiers*, *stabilizers* and other *food agents*.} Although dairy itself is GF, cautions are necessary. Question all dairy products. Avoid dairy products made with *forbidden grains* and *forbidden grain byproducts*. Avoid all *veined cheese*. Avoid kefir, commercially prepared *flavored milk*, some non-*dairy creamers/substitutes* and *yogurt* with added *toppings*. All *processed cheese* and *cheese spreads* are risky. *Forbidden fillers* and *thickening* agents in dairy products are not always clearly listed as ingredients. *Flour* is sometimes used to *dust cheese* so it does not stick to the *package*. Most dairy products, list the manufacturers contact information. (See *lactose intolerance* and also see 'dairy' in A & F charts.)

Dal Bean: Any *split dried bean* or *split bean* dish. Other terms include dhal, dalh, urad and tur dal. Verify GF. (See *bean*.)

Dal Chinne: (See *cinnamon*.) GF.

Dalia: Cracked *wheat*. Avoid.

Dalmation Bean: A type of *heirloom pinto bean*. GF.

Danablu: A type of *veined cheese*. Avoid all veined cheese.

Danbo Cheese: A type of firm *aged* Swiss *cheese*. Verify GF.

Dandelion: A type of *spice/herb*. *Pure* are GF. (See *herbs* and *spices*)

Dandelion Greens: A type of *vegetable*. *Fresh* and *plain* are GF.

Danish: A type of *flour dough pastry baked-good*. Most danish *commercially prepared* are prepared with *forbidden grains* and *forbidden grain byproducts*. GF danish are available only through *specialty companies*. (See *baked-goods*)

Danish Agar: *Furcellaran gum*. GF.

Dapsone: Dapsone is a type of drug used to suppress a skin rash on the skin of patients with DH. The DH skin rash disappears on most patients following a strict GF diet. (See *DH*.)

Dashi: A type of *soup stock* made with *tuna* flakes and *kombu*. Question added *fillers* in the *powdered* form of dashi. Verify GF.

Date: Dates are a type of *dried fruit*. The best types of dates are Medjool and Khadrawy. Question dates *dusted* with *oat flour*. Check for GF purity. (See *dried fruit*)

Date Sugar: A type of *granulated sugar* made from heated *dried dates*. Verify GF. (See *dates* and *sugar*.)

Dating: Dating is a procedure during *manufacturing* where dates are printed somewhere on the *food* products. Types of dates indicate the *packaged date*, the *sell by date*, the *expiration date* or the *freshness date*. [Look up each term individually.]

Decaffeinated: Decaffeinated means most of the *caffeine* has been removed. The best-decaffeinated *tea* and *coffee* is *naturally* decaffeinated with water. (See *tea*, *coffee*, *carob* and *caffeine*.)

Decorating Sugar: *Sugar cane sugar* coarsely *granulated* and used for decorating *baked-goods*. Question added *colorings*. Verify GF. (See *sugar*.)

Deep Fry: Deep frying is a cooking method by which *food* is submersed into hot *fat* or *oil*. Verify the *fats* and *oils* are GF and do not contain gluten *residue* from previously deep fried *foods* containing *gluten*. Avoid deep fried *foods* with *forbidden coatings*. (See *coating*, *breaded* and *batter*.)

Deer: A type of *'game' meat*. Fresh and *plain* are GF. (See *game*.)

Defatted: *Foods* to which the *fats* or *oils* have been removed (e.g. defatted *nuts* and *beans*). (See *mill*.)

Degenerative Stage: The degenerative stage is the fourth stage of a *disease*. It is the point in a *disease* where the body starts to deteriorate and/or loose its ability to function normally. The degenerative stage can be the point of no return in some diseases, but with *celiac disease*, patients normally recover with a strict adherence to the GF diet. [With *active celiac disease* in the *degenerative stage*, a strict GF diet must be maintained or other diseases and even death are possible.] (See *four stages of disease*, *celiac* and *disease*.)

Degerminated: *Pollinated* with human intervention.

Deglaze: To use pan drippings. Caution: *thickener* is generally added to this *liquid mixture* of *residue* to create a *sauce* or *gravy*. Question the source of all added *ingredients*.

Dehydrate: A method of *preserving food naturally* by removing moisture with low heat, *sun dried* or air-dried. Question the source of dehydrated foods. Question *additives*. Caution: dehydrated *foods* may be *dusted*.

Deli Foods: Deli food is a term for *prepared* or *processed foods* served at the deli department of a *grocery food store*. Most prepared deli foods are not GF. *Contamination* is always an issue with deli foods. Question the preparation area and deli equipment for possible *contaminants* (e.g. food slicing machine, counters, cutting boards and utensils). [These must be free of *gluten*.] (See *cheese sliced* and *lunchmeat*).

Demerara Sugar: (See *raw sugar cane sugar*.) Verify GF.

Dent Corn: Dent corn is a variety of GF *dried* hard *corn kernels* with an indent on the top of the *corn kernel*. Dent corn is widely grown and used in *commercially prepared corn* products. Dent corn is hard to *mill* and most dent corn is GMO. [Choose *popcorn kernels* for *milling* corn products.] (See organic.)

Denatured: Denatured is a term for any *food* altered *chemically* or *physically*. [Chemically denatured *food* is unhealthy and unsuitable for consumption, because of the added *substances*.] (See *pure*.)

Deoxyribonucleic Acid (DNA): A type of *nucleic acid* molecule found in all living *organisms*. DNA is the major *component* of chromosomes. The DNA contains the *genetic* information and passes these *genetic* characteristics from one generation to the next. (See *genetic*.)

De Pug Lentil: (See *lentil bean*.) GF

Derby Cheese: A type of semi-firm *aged* cow's milk *cheese* similar to *cheddar cheese*. Verify GF.

Dermatitis Herpetiformis (DH): DH is a type of chronic *immune* disease of the skin. DH is common to have along with *celiac disease*. The majority of individuals with DH also have CD. Treatment for DH is a *diet* free of *gluten*. Individuals with DH should avoid *topical* skin products containing *gluten*. *Drug* treatment for the DH skin rash may include *dapsone*, which stops itching and clears the skin rash lesions. [The DH skin rash normally disappears from DH patients who follow a strict GF diet.] DH is diagnoased with a skin biopsy of a lesion. (See *dapsone, iodine, topical, cosmetic* and *gluten free*.)

Desiccated: To *preserve foods* by *drying*. (See *dehydrated*.)

Desserts: Desserts are a type of sweet dish, typically eaten at the end of a *meal*. Avoid desserts made with the *forbidden grains* and *forbidden grain byproducts*. {Desserts may contain added *fillers, emulsifiers, additives, acidifiers, gums, buffers, flavorings, colorings, sweeteners, preservatives, stabilizers* and other *food agents*.} Question all the ingredients in desserts especially added *thickeners*. Avoid desserts with *crusts, crumb toppings* and *breading* unless verified GF. *Commercially prepared* GF desserts are available through *specialty companies*. [Look up each dessert individually.] (See *pudding, baked-goods* and 'desserts' in A & F charts.)

Devan Sweet: (See *rice syrup*.)

Devonshire Cheese: A type of soft *cheese*. Verify GF.(See *cheese*.)

Dewberry: A type of *fruit*. Fresh and *plain* dewberries are GF.

Dextran: A type of *glucose* polymer produced from *bacteria* grown on *sucrose*. GF. (See *sucrose*.)

Dextrimaltose: (See *corn dextrin*.)

Dextrin: Dextrin is produced from a *starch* treated with *acids, alkalis,* or *enzymes* to form *maltose*. Dextrin is a *thickener, binder* and *stabilizer*. Dextrin may be from arrowroot powder, *corn, potato, rice, tapioca,* *sorghum*, *sago* or *wheat*. Question the source. (See *corn dextrin*.)

Dextrose: Dextrose is a type of *sweetener* derived from *fruits* (e.g. *grapes*), bees (e.g. *honey*) and *grains* (e.g. *corn*, *rice* or *wheat*). Dextrose is a major *component* of *honey* and *corn syrup*. Question the source. (See *sweeteners*.)

DH: (See *dermatitis herpetiformis*.)

Dhania: (See *coriander*.) GF.

Diacetyl: Diacetyl Tartaric Axid Ester of Mono and Diglycerides. (See *mono* and *diglycerides*.)

Diagnose: To diagnose is to identify an illness or *disease*. With a strong clinical suspicion of *celiac disease*, diagnosis can be done quickly through blood *tests* to screen for specific antibodies to *gluten* and most accurately by an *endoscope* used to examine the *small bowel* and obtain a *biopsy*. [The serum test will be negative if the patient is already on the GF diet.] *Symptoms* of *celiac disease* are variable in combinations and severity and vary from person to person. In all stages of CD, the disease is always present, but the body might not display visible *symptoms*. (See *celiac disease, blood test, biopsy, antibodies, self diagnose* and *gastroenterologist*.)

Diarrhea: Diarrhea is a type of *gastrointestinal* upset causing frequent and excessive bowel movements. It is quite common for patients with CD to experience abnormal bowel movements anywhere within 20 minutes to 24 hours after consuming *gluten*. Diarrhea may be one of the very few *symptoms* a patient with *active celiac disease* exhibits. (See *symptoms, constipation* and *digestion*.)

Diced Tomatoes: (See *tomatoes diced*.)

Dichlorvos: Dichlorvos are *pesticides* and *insecticides* used on *produce* and in *food packaging*. Both are harmful. Avoid if possible. Wash *fresh produce* well. [To avoid these harmful *substances*, buy *organic* produce.] (See *organic*.)

Diet: Diet is the intake of *food* consumed with or without control. Some people control their diet to improve and maintain their health and possibly body weight. Some *newly diagnosed celiacs* are concerned with the need to gain weight. [People increase their caloric intake to gain weight. People decrease their caloric intake, along with exercise to lose weight.] *Celiacs* need to eat a diet free of *gluten*. *Celiacs* generally gain weight normally on the GF diet, once the diarrhea stops and the *villi* start to grow back (typically within one to three months after maintaining a strict GF diet). Visiting a *nutritionist* or *dietitian* may help celiacs on the GF diet, but remember most deal with weight loss issues and few are actually familiar with the GF diet. *Celiacs* and others can receive additional health benefits by eating a diet rich in *whole foods* and avoiding as much *processed* and *prepared food* as possible. Choose *fresh*, *pure organic foods* whenever possible. (See *villi, digestive system, calorie, nutritionist* and *gluten free*.)

Dietitian: A dietitian is someone who is educated in the field of *food* and *nutrition* in relation to health. Dietitians generally specialize in helping individuals gain weight or loose weight and/or conform to a restricted *diet*. At present time, the *treatment* for *CD* and *DH* is to eliminate form the *diet*, all *grains* and grain *byproducts* containing the *toxic gluten proteins*. [Dietitians are commonly found in clinical settings, whereas *nutritionists* generally work more independently, in private practice.] Visiting a *dietitian* may help with the gluten free diet but remember most deal with weight issues and few actually specialize with the GF diet. It is important to receive help from a registered dietitian with experience in *gluten sensitivities*. To locate a registered dietitian in your area call the American Dietitian Association at 312-899-0040. (See *diet* and *nutritionist*.)

Digestion: Digestion is the process of breaking down *food* by the body's *digestive system*. *Food* is broke down during digestion into a form *absorbable* through the *intestinal tract*. [*Nutrients* are absorbed via the *villi* in the *intestinal tract*.] When people with *celiac disease* consume the offending *protein* from *gluten,* the *villi* in the *intestinal tract* may become damaged. (See *indigestible, villi, diarrhea, constipation, intestinal tract* and *protein*.)

Digestive Aids: Digestive aids are a type of *supplement* that aids and/or promotes *digestion*. Verify GF. (See *digestive enzymes*)

Digestive Disease: A digestive disease is a type of *health* condition in the *digestive tract* causing *medical* significant *symptoms*. (See *symptoms, celiac disease, digestion* and *digestive tract*.)

Digestive Enzyme: Digestive enzymes are a certain type of *enzyme* when consumed aiding *digestion* and reducing *flatulence*. Digestive enzymes can break down a variety of *food* molecules of the same general type. Living *cells* from *raw food* are *natural digestive enzymes*. There is also a *supplement* form of *digestive enzymes*. Verify GF. (See *enzyme, fruits* and *vegetables*.)

Diglycerides: (See *mono* and *diglycerides* and *monoglycerides*.)

Dill Seeds: A type of *spice*. *Pure* are GF. (See *spice*.)

Dill Weed: A type of *herb*. *Pure dried* and *fresh* are GF. (See *herb*.)

Dilute: To thin or make weaker by adding another *substance* (usually *liquid* and possibly water).

Dining Out: (See *restaurant*.)

Dinkel: A type of *forbidden grain*. Avoid. (See *spelt*.)

Dioctyl Sodium Sulfosuccinate: GF.

Dip: Dips are a type of side dish made for dipping *snack foods* (e.g. *vegetables, crackers* or *chips*). Dips are always risky. {Dips may contain added *fillers, gums, emulsifiers, additives, flavorings, colorings, sweeteners, preservatives, stabilizers* and other *food agents*.} Avoid dips with *forbidden grains* and *forbidden grain byproducts*. Question the source of all dips. Question dips for additives especially *thickeners*. There are a handful of *commercially prepared* GF dips. It's best to choose pure *natural* dips with basic GF *ingredients*. (See *spreads*.)

Diples: A type of *wheat flour dough pastry baked-good*. Avoid.

Diploid: A *wheat* relative. Avoid.

Disease: Diseases are *health* conditions that cause *medical* significant *symptoms*. Certain diseases have specific *symptoms* of recognizable signs often having a known cause. *Symptoms* of *celiac disease* are variable in combinations and severity and vary from person to person. In any stages of *celiac disease* the disease is always present but the body might not display visible *symptoms* especially in the early stages. Patients with celiac disease generally recover with a strict adherence to the GF diet. (See *four stages of disease, celiac disease, symptoms* and *gastroenterologist*.)

Dish: (See *meal* and *recipe*.)

Disodium Guanylate: Disodium guanylate is a certain type of *additive* that may be *yeast based*. Verify GF. (See *yeast*.)

Distillation: Distillation is the process of separation by heating (*boiling*) *liquids* to the point of evaporation then condensing the *liquid* vapors. This process is questionable for *vinegar*. (See *distilled vinegar*.)

Distilled Alcohol: Distilled alcohol is GF. Distilled alcohol in *topical medications* is GF. (See *alcohol*)

Distilled Vinegar: Distilled vinegar is *vinegar* prepared in a *distillation* process. Distilled *vinegar* is prepared from *diluted grain alcohol mixtures* (e.g. *distilled alcohol* from *grains* such as *barley*, *corn* or *rye grains*). Properly distilled vinegar does not contain the gluten peptides / prolamins. Distilled vinegars with additives are not gluten free. Malt vinegar is not distilled and therefore still needs to be questioned. Distilled *vinegars* may be synthetic ethanol. The source of vinegar as an ingredient is not always identified on the label. Question the source of vinegar. Distilled vinegar is largely used in *commercially prepared* products. Distilled vinegar is the least *nutritious* and least *flavorful vinegar* and contains the highest *acidity* levels. [Personal tolerance should dictate use.] (See *distillation* and *prolamins*.)

Distributor: The distributor is the company that sells and distributes *food* products to *stores*. *Distributors* are not typically the ones who *manufacture* the products, so it is sometimes of little use to call them for product information. Distributors are the ones who decide what they will carry and thus make available to local *grocery stores*. [Behold the power of buying!] Upon request, local food stores will ask their distributor to supply them with requested products. (See *grocery food stores* and *manufacturer*.)

Dixie Speckled Bean: A type of small *lima bean*. GF.

DNA: (See *deoxyribonucleic acid*.)

Dolcelatte Cheese: A type of *veined cheeses*. Avoid all veined cheese.

Dong Quai: A type of *spice/herb*. *Pure* are GF. (See *spices* and *herbs*.)

Doodh: (See *milk*.)

Dosa: A type of *rice pancake*. Avoid unless source is known.

Double Acting Baking Powder: This is a type of *baking powder* with a two stage *leavening* process. Double acting baking powders typically contain *aluminum*. (See *baking powder*.)

Double Cream Cheese: Double cream cheese is an extra-soft *fresh* or *ripened cream cheese enriched* with *cream*. Verify GF. (See *cream cheese* for details and specifics).)

Dough: Dough is a type of moist *flour* based *mixture* made with water and *flour*. Most dough is prepared with *forbidden wheat grain*s and *forbidden wheat grain byproducts*. You need several different GF *ingredients* mixed together to imitate the properties of *wheat dough*. Types of GF ingredients mixed together may include a certain few of the following are needed *amaranth flour, arrowroot powder, bean flour, buckwheat flour, corn flour, cornmeal, garbanzo bean flour, millet flour, potato starch-flour, quinoa flour, rice flour, sorghum flour, soybean flour, sweet rice flour, tapioca flour, seed flours, nut flours* and *dried vegetable flours*). *Commercially prepared* GF dough is available only through *specialty companies*. (See *special resources*.)

Dough Conditioners: Dough conditioners are a type of *yeast food* or blend of *minerals* (possibly *sodium* or *chemicals*) added to *dough*, to improve its texture and/or volume. Dough conditioners make *dough* easier to knead. Question all dough conditioners. Caution. Risky.

Dough Enhancer: Dough enhancers are *substances* used in *dough* to enhance its performance. Dough enhancers are always questionable. Caution. Risky.

Doughnut: Doughnuts are a type of dense *baked-good*. Most doughnuts *commercially prepared* are prepared with *forbidden grain*s and *forbidden grain byproducts*. GF doughnuts are available only through *specialty companies*. (See *baked-goods*)

Dough Pasta: Dough pasta is a type of *pasta* made from *dough* instead of *flour*. (See *dough* and *pasta*.)

Dough Strengthener: Dough strengtheners are *substances* added to *dough* to make it resilient. Question the source of all dough strengtheners. Caution. Risky.

Dove: A type of *fowl*. *Fresh* and *plain* are GF. (See *fowl*.)

Dredge: Dredge is a term meaning to *coat food* generally with *flour*. Question the coating source.

Dressing: Dressing is a term for *stuffing*. Avoid. Dressing is also a term for a hot or cold *salad sauce* used to dress *salads*. {Dressings may contain added *emulsifiers, vinegars, seasonings, oils/fats, sweeteners* and other *food agents*.} Question all the ingredients in dressings. Various *commercially prepared* dressings are GF. You can *home make* dressings easily with GF *ingredients*. Fresh squeezed *lemon juice* or GF *oil* and *vinegar* are safe alternatives.

Dried: Dried is a procedure and/or term for *food* that is ordinarily *fresh* and *whole* with most of the moisture removed. (See *sun dried, bean dried, dehydrated, dried fruit* and *spices*.)

Dried Corn: Dried corn is a type of hard *corn* kernel or *dried* out *sweet corn kernels*. Dried corn may be slaked in lime. GF. (See *corn*.)

Dried Field Corn: Dried field corn is *dried sweet corn*. GF.

Dried Fruit: Dried fruit is *dehydrated fruit*. Dried fruits are certain types of *fresh fruit* to which most of the moisture has been removed. Dried fruit are a healthy *natural snack food*. All *pure plain sun dried fruits* are *naturally* GF but there are concerns. Avoid dried fruit mixed with forbidden *grain cereals* (e.g. *trail mixes* and *granola bars*). Avoid dried fruit in *forbidden* *sauces*, *creams* and *gravies*. Avoid dried fruit dusted with *forbidden flours* and *polished* or *coated* with *forbidden sweeteners*. You should rinse dried fruit well before using and/or *soak* it in boiled water for about one minute to *re-hydrate* and/or reduce *mold* and *bacteria* growth. <u>Choose *pure* dried fruit</u> (*unsulfured* if possible). Extra fancy and fancy grades are the best dried fruits. (See *fruit* and also see 'dried fruit' in A & F charts.)

Dried Fruit Flour: Dried root flour is a type of *flour milled* from *dried fruit*. Check for GF purity. (See *dried fruit* and *flour*.)

Dried Peas: Dried pea is a term for dried *peas whole* or *split*. Dried pea is also a term for mung *beans*. GF.

Dried Root Flour: Dried root flour is a type of *flour milled* from *dried roots* (e.g., *dried potato*, *yam*, *arrowroot* and *tapioca*). Check for GF purity. (See *exotic flour*.)

Dried Sweet Corn: Dried sweet corn is *sweet corn dried* out. GF.

Dried Vegetable Flour: Not considering *grains* as *vegetables*, all *flour milled* from dried *vegetables* (e.g. <u>potatoes</u> and <u>artichokes</u>) are GF. Avoid dried vegetable flour containing *forbidden grain flours*. Check for GF purity. *Commercially prepared* GF vegetable flour is available through *special companies*.

Drizzle: Drizzle is a culinary term meaning to dribble *liquid* slowly into or on *foods*. (See *spritz*.)

Drug: Drugs are any *natural* or *artificial substance* given as *medication* for treatment of an illness or *disease*. The treatment for most *celiac* patients is non-medical (e.g., the lifelong strict avoidance of

foods containing *forbidden gluten*). (See *medication*.)

Drug Store: A drug store is a place were a broad-spectrum of drugs prescribed by a doctor are prepared by a *pharmacist* and sold to the general public. Not all *pharmacists* in drug stores *compound medication*. Drug stores commonly carry a large selection of *non-prescription medication*. A number of drug stores carry GF *meal replacement bars/drinks*. (See *drug*, *compound medication*, *meal replacement* and *pharmaceuticals*.)

Drum: A type of *fish*. Fresh and *plain* are GF. (See *fish*.)

Dry: Dry is a *culinary* term used mostly in *restaurants* to order *salads* without *dressing*. Celiacs must request the *salad* served without *dressings*, *croutons*, *bacon bits* and any other *forbidden topping*. (See *restaurant* and *dried*.)

Drying: A method of preserving. (See *preserve*.)

Dry Milk Powder: (See *milk powder*.)

Dry Roast: Dry roast is a method of cooking *whole foods* (whole *seeds*, *nuts*, *grains* and *beans*) in an oven generally at low temperatures for a long time. Question the addition of *seasonings*. (See *roast*.)

Dry Yeast: (See *yeast*.)

Duck: A type of *fowl*. Fresh and *plain* are GF. (See *fowl*.)

Dulse: *A type of seaweed. Fresh* and *plain* dulse is GF. (See *seaweed*.)

Dumplings: A type of *wheat flour* mixture bread-food. Avoid.

Dunlop Cheese: A type of mild *cheese* made from cow's *milk* similar to *cheddar cheese*. Verify GF.

Durian: A type of *fruit*. *Fresh* and *plain* are GF. (See *fruit*.)

Durkex Oil: A type of highly refined *partially hydrogenated vegetable oil*. Caution. Verify GF.

Durum: A type of *forbidden wheat*. Other forbidden durum foods include durum flour, durum semolina and durum *pasta*. Avoid.

Durum Wheat: A type of *wheat* high in *gluten*. Durum wheat produces glutinous *flour* and is most often used in *pasta making*. Avoid.

Dust: Dust is a term referring to *powder* lightly with *dry substances*. (See *dusting agent*)

Dusting Agent: Dusting agents are freeing *agents* used to preventing sticking. Caution. Risky. Question the source used for dusting.

Dye: Dyes are *natural* or *artificial coloring agents*. Question the source. Avoid all if possible. Caution. (See *sensitivities*)

Echinacea: A type of *herb*. *Fresh* and *dried pure* are GF. (See *herb*.)

Eclair: A type of cream *filled wheat dough pastry baked-good*. Avoid.

Edamame: A type of large green soybean. GF. (See *soybean*.)

Edam Cheese: An all-purpose *aged cheese* made from cow's *milk*. Verify GF. (See *cheese*.)

Edible: Edible refers to any *food* fit for human consumption.

Edible Starch: Edible starch refers to any edible *food starch ingredient* used in *foods*. Question the source. (See *starch*.)

Eel: A type of *fish*. *Pure fresh* and *plain* are GF. (See *fish*.)

Egg: Eggs are laid by *fowl*. Eggs are *naturally* GF. [No matter what the *fowl* ate, eggs are GF.] Choose *fresh* eggs. Eggs from free-range vegetarian feed *poultry* are the best choice. *Tofu* can replace eggs as a *binder* in some *recipes*. Types of prepared GF eggs include plain soft or hard-boiled eggs and fried eggs (e.g., fried over light or scrambled). Eggs fried in *butter* or *pure* GF *oil* are safe. Avoid eggs *fried* in *oil* previously used to cook *foods* containing *gluten*. *Omelets* and *frittatas* can be prepared with GF *ingredients* but verify all the *ingredients* are GF. (See 'eggs' in A & F charts.)

Eggnog: Eggnog is a Holiday *beverage* customarily made with *milk, eggs* and possibly *alcohol*. Caution. Question the source. (See *beverage* and *alcohol*.)

Egg Noodle: (See *noodle*.) Avoid.

Eggplant: A type of *vegetable*. *Fresh* and *plain* are GF.

Egg Replacer: Egg replacer is a type of *powdered substances* used to replace *eggs* in *recipes*. There are GF egg replacers available. Questionable. (See *egg substitutes*.)

Egg Roll: Egg rolls are a *deep fried* side dish *filled* with *vegetables* and *wrapped* in a *wheat-flour pastry* shell before *deep*-frying. Avoid.

Egg Slicer: Egg slicers are a type of *kitchen utensil* with several fine wires that cut hard-boiled *eggs* and *raw mushrooms* into thin even slices.

Egg Substitutes: Egg substitutes are *processed eggs* used in *substitution* of eggs. {Egg substitutes may contain added egg whites, *starch, milk, fats/oil, emulsifiers, colorings, flavorings, preservatives* and other *food agents*.} There are GF egg substitutes available. Questionable.

Einkorn: A *wheat* relative. Avoid.

Elbo Cheese: A type of mild *Swiss cheese* from cow's *milk*. Verify GF.

Elderberry: A type of *fruit*. *Fresh* and *plain* are GF. (See *fruit*.)

Elderflower: A type of *herb*. *Fresh* and *pure dried* are GF. (See *herb*.)

Electric Fish: A type of *fish*. *Fresh* and *plain* are GF. (See *fish*.)

Elk: A type of *meat*. *Pure fresh* and *plain* are GF. (See *meat*.)

Embryo: Embryo is a type of *plant* in its earliest stage of development. Embryo is the life force contained within the *seed/plant*. (See *grains*.)

Emmentaler Cheese: A type of *Swiss cheese* made from cow's *milk*. Verify GF. (See *Swiss cheese*.)

Emmer: A *wheat* relative. Avoid.

Emulsifier: Emulsifiers are *substances* used in foods to make two or more *liquids* stick together in an emulsion. Emulsifiers are stabilizers facilitating the combination of *ingredients* that otherwise would not combine (e.g. water and *oil*). Types of emulsifiers include *chemicals*, *yeast*, *cellulose*, *lecithin*, *gelatin*, *various gums*, *pectin*, *fats/oils* and *mono* and *diglycerides*. [Look up each individually.]

Enchilada: Enchiladas are a type of *filled* softened *tortilla meal*. Question if the *tortilla* is made with *forbidden wheat flour*. Question the *source* of all the *ingredients*. Varieties of frozen *commercially prepared* GF enchiladas are available through *specialty companies*. (See *specialty companies* and *special resources*.)

Endive: A type of *vegetable*. *Fresh* and *plain* are GF. (See *vegetable*.)

Endoscope: Endoscope is a procedure performed with an endoscope by a *gastroenterologist* to examine the *small bowel* and obtain a *biopsy* if there is a strong clinical suspicion of *celiac disease*. (See *biopsy* and *gastroenterologist*.)

Endosperm: Endosperm is the *tissue* inside a *seed* that surrounds the *embryo*. [The heart of the *wheat kernel* contains the *gluten*.] Endosperms are found in the grains of *rice*, *corn* or *wheat*.

English Mustard: English mustard is a type of *prepared mustard* with *wheat* flour. Avoid. (See *mustard*.)

English Pea: A type of *fresh pea*. GF. (See *pea*.)

Enhanced Food: Enhanced food is *food* to which substances (normally *vitamins* and *minerals*) are added to enrich its *nutritional* value. Foods enhanced need to be verified GF.

Enriched Bleach Flour: An enriched *bolted wheat flour*. Avoid.

Enriched Food: Enriched food is *food* to which substances (normally *vitamins* and *minerals*) are added to enhance its *nutritional* value. Foods enriched need to be verified GF.

Enriched Rice: Enriched rice is *rice* (generally *white rice*) to which *substances* (normally *vitamins* and *minerals*) are added to enhance its *nutritional* value. (See *rice* for details and specifics.)

Enteropathy Disease: (See *celiac disease*).

Entire Flour: *Flour milled* from *bolted wheat*. Avoid.

Envelopes: Non self-sticking envelopes are manufactured with an *edible* type of *glue* containing *gluten*. Avoid licking the glue on stamps and envelopes. (See *glue*.)

Enzyme: Enzymes are specialized *complete protein molecules* found and produced only in living things (e.g. *plants* or *animals*). Enzymes are essential to life and promote a specific biochemical reaction by acting as a *catalyst*. Types of enzymes include *maltose, chemicals, dairy* and *rennet*. [Look up each individually.](See *digestive enzyme*.)

Equipment: (See *kitchen supplies*.)

Escarole: A type of *vegetable. Fresh* and *plain* are GF. (See *vegetable*.)

Esrom Cheese: A semi-soft *aged* cow's *milk Swiss cheese*. Verify GF.

Essence: Essence is the concentrated constituent of a *plant*. [Essences are *substances* obtained from the *plants'* essential properties.] Essences are used for their *aromatic* and *flavoring* abilities. Question *substances* used to extract the *plants* essence. Verify GF. (See *extracts* and *plant*.)

Essential: Essential elements are necessary and fundamentally required in the *diet* for their *nutritional* purposes.

Ester: Ester is an *organic compound* formed in a reaction between an *acid* and *alcohol*. Verify GF.

Ethnic Grocery Food Store: Ethnic grocery food stores are specific types of grocery food store carrying products from other cultures. Ethnic grocery food stores typically carry unique GF *food* items (e.g. *rice noodles, rice pasta* and a variety of *whole grain rice, dried beans, bean flour, tapioca flour, rice crackers, potato starch flour, fine white rice flour, spices* and some *prepared gluten free foods*). Make sure the items you select are GF. Some food *labels* in ethnic grocery food stores are printed in a language other than English.(See *grocery food store* and *health food grocery store*.)

Ethyl Alcohol: A type of *alcohol* containing ethanol. Ethyl alcohol may contain spirits, grain alcohols and a variety of *fermented starches* and *sugars*. (See *alcohol*)

Ethyl Maltol: A type of *additive* with a possible *wheat* or *corn* base. Caution. (See *maltol*.)

Eugenol: A type of oily *liquid* obtained from *cloves*. Verify GF. (See *vanillin*.)

Evaporated Milk: Evaporated milk is a type of *unsweetened milk* to which water was evaporated. {Evaporated milk may contain added *emulsifying agents*.] Verify GF.

Excipient: (See *inert substance*.)

Exotic Flour: Exotic flours are any unusual *flour*. Exotic flours are uncommon. Exotic flours can be prepared from *fruits, nuts, seeds* and *vegetables*. Not considering *grains* as *vegetables*, exotic *flours* are GF. Check for GF purity. *Commercially prepared* GF exotic flours are available through *special companies*.

Exotic Starch: Exotic starch is any unusual *starch*. Exotic starches are uncommon. Exotic starches can be prepared from *fruits, nuts, seeds* and *vegetables*. Not considering *grains* as *vegetables* exotic *starches* are GF. Check for GF purity. *Commercially prepared* GF exotic starches are available through *special companies*.

Expiration Date: Expiration dates are the *date* indicating when *food* is no longer *edible*. (See *dating*.)

Explorateur Cheese: A type of *triple cream cheese*. Verify GF.

Extender: Extenders are food *substances* added to *food* to add body or to *modify* it. (See *filler*.)

Extract: Extracts are types of *concentrated flavorings*. Extracts are *substances* extracted from a *plant sources*. [Extracts are the *essences* derived from *plant parts* with a *liquid extracting agent*.] Extracts typically contain very little of the actual *plant* part and more of the extracting *solvent*. Question the *extracting solvent*. Avoid extracts extracted with *forbidden substances* (*forbidden vegetable glycerin*). [The best choice are *essences* because they are possibly more pure.] There are GF extracts available at *regular grocery food stores, health food grocery stores* and by *mail order*. (See *essence* and *alcohol*)

Extracting Agent: An extracting agent is any *liquid substance* used to *isolate* or *extract* the *essence* of *plant parts*. Types of extracting agents include *water, alcohol, glycerin, oil* and *chemical compounds*. [Look up each individually.] Question the source of the extracting agent. (See *carrier*.)

Extracting Solvent: (See *extracting agent*.)

Extra Virgin Olive Oil: This is a type of *olive oil* obtained only from the first pressing of the olives. Extra virgin olive oil is the best choice of *olive oil*. Check for GF purity.

Fajita: Fajitas are a type of steak *tortilla meal*. Question if the *tortilla* is made with *forbidden wheat flour*. Question the *source* of all the ingredients. Varieties of frozen *commercially prepared* GF fajitas are available through *specialty companies*. (See *specialty companies* and *special resources*.)

Family Flour: A type of *flour milled* from *soft* or *hard wheat*. Avoid.

FAO: (See *food* and *agricultural organization*.)

Far: (See *farina*.) Avoid.

Farina: Farina is a type of *flour* or *meal* made from <u>*nuts*</u>, <u>*vegetables*</u> or *grains* (e.g. <u>corn</u> or *wheat*). Questionable. Farina can also refer to *potato starch* or *potato flour*. [Look up each individually.]

Farmer Cheese: A type of *fresh* and pressed *cottage cheese*. Verify GF.

Farr: (See *farina*.) Avoid.

Farro: A *forbidden grain*. Avoid.

Fasnact: A type of *wheat flour potato pastry baked-good*. Avoid.

Fat: Fat is a water *insoluble* or semi-solid *chemical compound* derived from *animal* products (e.g. *butter* or *lard*) or *plants* (e.g. *coconut*). Fat is a *nutritional component* of *food*. Verify GF. (See *fat substitutes, fat free* and *fat replacers*.)

Fat & Oil: [Look up '*fat*' and '*oil*' separately.] Gluten free fats and oils include certain brands of *grain* oils (e.g. <u>corn</u>), *vegetable* oils (e.g. <u>avocado</u>), *animal fat* (e.g. <u>lard</u> and <u>butter</u>), *fruit* oils (e.g. <u>olive</u>), *bean* oils (e.g. <u>soy</u>), *seed* oils (e.g. <u>cotton</u>, <u>apricot kernel, pumpkin, canola, sesame, safflower, sunflower</u> and <u>grape seed</u>), *nut* oils (e.g. <u>almond, coconut, hazelnut, peanut</u> and <u>walnut</u>), some *margarines* and most *hydrogenated oils*. [Look up each individually.] Question the source of all fats and oils. {Fats and oils may contain added *preserving, enhancing, antifoaming, coloring, flavoring, emulsifying* and other *food agents*.} The *source* of fats and oils is not always specifically identified on a *label*. Question added *seasonings* and *flavorings* in fats and oils. Avoid oils made from *forbidden grains, wheat germ oil* and *hydrolyzed vegetable protein* (*HVP*) and *vegetable oils* from an unknown source. Avoid *oils* previously used to cook *gluten foods*, *margarines* with unknown *ingredients* and *wheatex*. Question *fat replacers olestra, olean* and *oatrim*. Choose *100*% *pure* GF *fats* and *oils*. (See *sensitivities* and see 'fats and oils' in A & F charts.)

Fat Free Food Products: Fat free food products are a type of *food* product produced without *fat*. [A person can still gain weight from fat free products because they contain *calories*.] Risky. Fat free products are always questionable for *forbidden ingredients*. (See *fat replacers* and *fat substitutes*.)

Fat Replacers: (See *fat substitutes*)

Fat Substitutes: Fat substitutes are *natural* or *artificial substances* (frequently *artificial*) used to replace *fat* in *food* products. {The fat may be replaced with *emulsifying*, *preserving*, *stabilizing*, *gelling* and other *food agents*.} Fat substitutes are commonly a combination of *substances*. There are some GF fat substitutes. Question the source of all fat substitutes. Caution. Risky.

Fatty Acids: Fatty acids are *liquid* or *solid fats* used in *food* products as *binders, emulsifiers, lubricants* and *stabilizers*. Question the source.

Fava Bean: Fava beans are a certain type of large *dried bean*. Fava beans are GF and *mill* well into *flour*. Some people react to fava beans (favism). (See *favism*.)

Favism: Favism is an acute *anemia* caused by an *allergic* reaction from consuming *fava beans*.

F & D: F & D is the abbreviated term for pertaining to *food* and *drug*.

FDA: (See *Food* and *Drug Administration*.)

FD & C: FD & C is the abbreviated term for pertaining to *foods, drugs* and *cosmetics*.

Fennel: A type of *vegetable. Fresh* and *plain* are GF. (See *vegetable*.)

Fennel Seed: A type of *seed. Raw* and *plain* are GF. (See *seed*.)

Fenugreek: A type of *seed. Raw* and *plain* are GF. (See *seed*.)

Fermented: Fermentation is the result of *fermenting agents* added to *ingredients* in a process (biochemical changes). [Fermentation is the creation of *alcohol* by the action of *yeast* on *sugar*.] Some *individuals* are *sensitive* to fermented *foods* (e.g. *miso, alcohol* and *vinegar*). Question all fermented food. [Look up each type of fermented food individually.] (See *fermenting agents* and *vinegar*.)

Fermenting Agents: Fermenting agents are *substances* (possibly *yeast* or *enzymes*) used in *ingredients* (possibly *liquids*) to initiate *fermentation*. [Look up each type of fermenting agent individually.] (See *yeast* and *fermentation*.)

Ferrous: Containing iron.

Feta Cheese: A semi-firm *cheese* made from sheep or goats *milk*. Verify GF. (See *dairy* and *cheese*)

Feverfew: A type of *herb. Fresh* and *pure dried* are GF. (See *herb*.)

Fiber: Fiber is roughage. Fiber is a type of dietary *fiber* from course fibrous *plant parts* not completely *digestible*. Fiber is found in *grains*, *fruits* and *vegetables*. Verify GF.

Field Corn: Field corn is a type of *dried corn*. Field corn is a term for *corn* grown as feed for livestock.

Field Trial: Field trial is a term for the testing of *plant* species grown in an agricultural setting.

Figs: Figs are a type of *dried fruit* *dried* from *fresh figs*. Check for GF purity. (See *dried fruit*)

Filbert Nut: A type of *tree nut* similar to the *hazelnut*. *Raw* and *plain* are GF. (See *nut* and *hazelnut*)

Filet Bean: A type of green *bean*. GF. (See *vegetable*.)

Filler: Fillers are *substances* used to increase the *bulk, volume* and weight of some foods. Fillers are also used to *dilute* and strengthening some *ingredients*. Types of filler include *flour* or *meal prepared* from *grains* (e.g. *rice, corn* or *wheat), roots* (*arrowroot flour), beans, vegetables, starch* (e.g. *wheat* or *corn*) or *chemical compounds* (caution). Fillers *thicken* thin clear *liquids* (e.g., fillers thicken *sauces, gravies* and broths). Fillers add *bulk* and pourability to *dried food* (e.g. *seasoning, spices* and *spice blends*). Question all *processed* and *prepared* food for the possibility of fillers. Caution: 'fillers' can be '*hidden*'. Avoid foods with fillers of any unknown source. [The listing of fillers as an *ingredient* is not required on *food labels*. Added filler makes reading labels difficult.] Fillers are what make a *food list* invaluable. (See *food list, hidden ingredients, extender* and *processed foods* and *prepared foods*.)

Fillet: Fillet is a culinary term for boneless. The bones of an animal have been removed (e.g., fillet of fish and fillet of meat).

Filling: The word filling defined in this definition statement means to fill. [Filling is not the same as *filler*.] Fillings are stuffed into *meat, poultry, vegetables* and *fish*. Question all the ingredients in the filling. Unless the filling is *homemade* with GF ingredients, it most likely is not GF. (See *stuffing, pesto, pie filling* and *filler*.)

Filtered: Filtration is a process where *substances* (usually *liquid*), have been *strained*. This process removes the larger particles. The filtration of *gluten byproducts* in foods does not render food GF. (See *strain* and *distillation*.)

Fine Rice Flour: Fine rice flour is a type of flour highly *refined* from *white rice*. Check for GF purity. (See *ethnic grocery store*.)

Fingerling Potato: A type of *heirloom potato* finger shaped. GF.

Fining: *Clarifying liquids*. This process does not remove *gluten*.

Finnish Yellow Wax: A type of *potato* with yellowish flesh. GF.

Firming Agent: Firming agents are *substance* (possibly *chemical compounds*) that cause *foods* to firm. Firming agents are used to control firmness and texture. (See *agent*)

Fish: Fish are any cold-blooded aquatic vertebrate *animal*. All *pure fresh* and *plain* fish are naturally GF. [Look up each type individually.] Choose *plain, blackened, baked, grilled, fried, roasted, broiled* or steamed fish lightly *seasoned* with GF *spices* or seasoned with *lemon* juice from a fresh squeezed *lemon*. Question added *seasonings* and/or *condiments*. Avoid *fresh, cooked* and *frozen* fish in *forbidden sauces, gravies* and *creams*, with *pasta, breaded, batter dipped, coated* or *pickled* in *vinegars,* unless all ingredients are verified GF. Avoid *imitation seafood*. [Fish *patties* and fish cakes are extremely risky.] Question prepared fish in jars and/or cans (e.g., *herring* and *sardines*). Question fish canned in vegetable *broth*. Question all fish *pickled, canned, preserved, fermented, smoked, pre-seasoned, dried, marinated, sweetened, flavored* and *treated* with *additives*. (See *tuna canned* and also see 'fish' in A & F charts.)

Fish Cake: A type of *fish patty* side made with cooked *fish* and *fillers* rolled in *breadcrumbs*. Avoid unless specially made with GF ingredients.

Fish Sauce: Fish sauce is a type of *condiment* made from *fermented* fish. Question all ingredients (e.g. added *soy sauce* and *sweetener*.) Verify GF. (See *condiment*.)

Fish, Shellfish & Seafood: All *pure fresh* and *plain fish, shellfish* and *seafood* are naturally GF. [Look up each type individually.] Question added *seasonings* and *condiments*. Some *seafood seasonings* and *condiments* are GF. (See 'fish, shellfish and seafood' in A & F charts.)

Fish Sticks: A type of side dish made from sticks of *fish, breaded* with a *crumb mixture*. Avoid unless specially made with GF ingredients.

Flan: A type of *filled pastry baked-good* made with *wheat flour*. Avoid.

Flap Jack: (See *pancake*.) Avoid.

Flatbread: Flatbread is a type of thin *unleavened bread baked-good*. Flatbread is commonly made with *forbidden wheat flour*. Flatbread is a term use for *tortillas*. Question if the *tortilla* is made with *forbidden wheat flour*. Flatbread is also a term for certain *batter-breads*. Questionable. (See *batter bread* and *tortilla*.)

Flat Fish: A type of *fish. Pure fresh* and *plain* are GF. (See *fish*.)

Flatulence: Flatulence is the medical term referring to gas produced in the *digestive system*. (See *intestinal tract*.)

Flavor: Flavor is a culinary term for adding flavorings to food. Question the flavor source. (See *flavor agent*.)

Flavor Agent: (See *flavoring agent*.)

Flavor Carrier: Flavor carriers are *natural* or *artificial substances* used to deliver *flavor* to *foods*. Question the source. (See *carrier*.)

Flavored Milk: (See *milk flavored*.)

Flavored Sugar: Flavored sugar is a type of *refined granulated white sugar* with added *flavorings*. Question the source of *flavoring agents*. Caution. (See *sugar* and *flavoring agents*.)

Flavored Vinegars: Flavored vinegars are *vinegars* with added *flavorings*. Risky. Question the source of *flavoring agents*. Caution. (See *vinegar* and *flavoring agent*.)

Flavored Wines: Question the source. (See *wine*.)

Flavor Enhancer: Flavor enhancers are *natural or artificial substances* added to *food* to intensify its flavor. Question the source. (See *flavoring agent*.)

Flavoring: Flavoring is a blanket term for a variety of *substances* used to *flavor* foods.(See *flavoring agent*.)

Flavoring Agent: Flavoring agents are *natural* or *artificial substances* used to impart flavor or enhance the *flavor* of other *foods*. All flavorings are questionable. The term flavoring listed as an 'ingredient' is not always *specifically defined*. Question the source of any flavoring agent. Caution. Question any *carrier* used to transport flavoring agents. GF flavoring agents are available through *specialty companies*. (See *extracts, sensitivities, artificial flavorings, carrier, seasoning, natural flavoring* and *sweeteners*.)

Flavor Solvents: Flavor solvents are *natural or artificial substances* (commonly *liquids*) able to dissolve *flavor substances*. (See *substances*)

Flax **Meal**: *Whole flax seeds* are coarsely *milled* into flax meal. Check for GF purity. (See *flax seed*.)

Flax **Seed**: A type of *seed*. *Raw* and *plain* are GF. Caution: contains *laxative* properties. (See *seed*.)

Flax **Seed** **Oil**: A type of *seed oil* obtained from *flax seeds*. Check for GF purity. (See *flax seed* and *oil*.)

Flint **Corn**: Flint corn is a type of field *corn kernel* containing hard *starch*. Flint *corn kernels* are very difficult to *mill* into *flour*. [Instead of flint corn *kernels* use *popcorn corn kernels* for home *milling flour*.] Flint *corn* is customarily used to make *posole* and *polenta*. GF. (See *corn*.)

Flora: Flora are a group of *good bacteria* in the *digestive system* that help maintain a *nutritional* balance in the body. *Acidophilus* is a type of *good bacteria* that will help restore *intestinal flora*. (See *good bacteria* and *acidophilus*.)

Flounder: A type of *fish*. *Pure fresh* and *plain* are GF. (See *fish*.)

Flour: Flour is a term used for a method of *dusting food*. Question the source of all flours used to dust foods. Flour is also a term for a type of dry *powder* based *mixture* made from any of a variety of finely ground *seeds*, *beans*, *nuts*, grains (e.g. *corn*, *rice*, oat, wheat, barley or rye) and *dried roots*, *tubers*, *legumes* and *vegetables*. Caution: the use of the term flour generally refers to

flour made from *forbidden grains*. [The word '*flour*' listed as an *ingredient* is typically *forbidden wheat flour* unless specifically identified.] Caution: flour may be a combination of one or more flours. Types of gluten free flours include certain brands of pure *amaranth flour*, *arrowroot powder*, *bean flour*, *buckwheat flour*, *root flours*, *corn flour*, *cornmeal*, *sago starch-flour*, *garbanzo bean flour*, *millet flour*, *potato starch-flour*, *quinoa flour*, *rice flour, sorghum flour*, *teff flour*, *job's tears flour*, *ragi flour*, *soybean flour*, *sweet rice flour*, *tapioca flour*, *seed flours*, *nut flours*, *dried vegetable flours* and possibly oat flour. [Look up each individually.] Several GF *ingredients* mixed together are needed to imitate the properties of *wheat flour*. Forbidden flours containing *gluten* that need to be avoided include flours made with *wheat, barley, rye, bulgur, diploid, durum, einkorn, emmer, far, farro, seitan, hexaploid, kamut, semolina, spelt, tsampa, tetraploid, triticale, triticum, mir, relatives of these grains* and possibly *oats*. Caution: *forbidden* flours are used to stretch the content of foods as *filler*, to *dust* conveyer belts, to *dust foods* to keep them separated and to *dust foods* to make them malleable. Choose *100*% *pure* GF flours. *Commercially prepared* GF flours are available through *specialty companies*. You can home *mill* GF flours with *whole beans*, *nuts*, *seeds* and GF *grains* (e.g. *rice*, *corn*, *millet*, *quinoa*, *amaranth*, *buckwheat*, *ragi*, *job's tear* and *teff*). [Look up each individually.] (See *contamination* and *special resources*)

Flour Corn: Flour corn is a type of corn kernel having a softer structure. Soft *corn kernels* are excellent for *milling corn flour*. GF. (See *corn* and *corn flour*.)

Flour Pasta: A type of *pasta* made from *flour* as opposed to *dough*. (See *pasta* and *flour*.)

Flour Treating Agents: Flour treating agents are *natural or artificial substances* added to *flour* to improve its abilities. (See *agent*.)

Flowers: Flowers are the scented and colored part of plants that contains its reproductive organs. Some types of flowers are *edible*. All *pure culinary edible*-flowers are GF.

Flummery: *Pudding* made from stewed *fruit* and various other *ingredients*. Question the source. (See *pudding*.)

Foaming Agent: Foaming agents are *natural* or *synthetic substances* preventing *food* from foaming and/or causing the removal of foam. (See *agent*)

Folacin: (See *folic acid*.) Verify GF.

Folic Acid: A type of B vitamin. Verify GF. (See *supplement*.)

Fontina Cheese: A type of semi-firm *cheese* made from cow's *milk*. Verify GF. (See *cheese*.)

Food: Food is any of a variety of *nourishing liquid* or *solid ingredients* eaten for their *nutritional* value. Not all *processed* or *prepared foods* and *beverages* are *nutritious*. All food must be verified GF. (See *bulk food, nutrition, gluten free, contamination, ingredients, label* and *manufacturing*.)

Food Agent: (See *agent* and *food*.)

Food & Agricultural Organization: The FAO is an *organization* developed with members of the food industry, food science community and government to evaluate food *additive* safety. The FAO does not test; they only rely on information given to them. (See FDA.)

Food Allergy & Anaphylaxis Network: The FAAN is a type of non-profit organization for people with food allergy and anaphylaxis disorders. Their phone number is 1-800-929-4040. (See *children and gluten free*.)

Food & Drug (F&D): Pertaining to *food* and *drug*. (See *FDA*)

Food & Drug Administration: The FDA is a type of organization pertaining to food and drug. The FDA does not require all *food components* listed on *labels*. [Not all *ingredients* or *components* of *ingredients* performing a function 'in' or has any effect 'on' *food* are defined.] If you would like these laws to change, write the FDA and let the FDA know you have a restricted diet, *label* reading is essential to your *health* and you would like everything going 'into' or 'on' a product listed in the *ingredient* section. The FDA allows *processors* the voluntarily *labeling* of products free of *gluten*. At present time, the FDA has no *allergenic labeling* regulations for the term '*gluten free*'. The FDA expects *processors* to abide to the policy on '*hypoallergenic foods*'. The FDA address is- 5600 Fishers Lane, Rockville MD 20857. Their phone number is- 1-888-SAFE FOOD (723-3366). For an emergency or to report about a product dial 1-888-463-6332. To order special documents by phone dial 1-800-332-4010. (See *allergenic* and *hypoallergenic foods*.)

Food Drug & Cosmetic (FD& C): F D & C pertains to *foods*, *drugs* and *cosmetics*.

Food Intolerance: Food intolerance is a condition where a persons system cannot tolerate a certain *food* (e.g., individuals with *celiac disease* cannot tolerate a specific type of *gluten protein* in certain *grains*). (See *celiac disease* and *gluten*.)

Food List: A food lists is a listing of food products for a specific purpose (e.g., a *gluten free food* list for individuals with *celiac disease*). Even with a food product list, it is imperative you read every *label* on every product, every time of purchase, along with avoiding any food questionable. Caution: not all foods on a food lists are updated or obtained through personal contact with *manufacturing* companies. [Read labels and call companies with questions.] A gluten free food product list is essential for anyone on the GF diet. Choose the most recent annual book of commercially *prepared* GF food products. [I have personally gathered information from manufactures and distributors through thousands of phone calls and letters, along with research on the internet in order to put together a food product list. For information about purchasing the *Gluten Free Food Product List 'the manufactures list of commercially prepared gluten free foods'* from *Guide Books Publication Company* write for details, visit the web site or use the order form; see pages 206 and 207. (See *Gluten Free Food Book* and *label reading*.)

Food Product List: (See *food list*)

Food Starch: In the USA, the term food starch is from the source of corn. GF. (See *starch*)

Food Store: There are a variety of common and unique *foods* available at different types of food stores. (See *grocery food store, ethnic grocery food store, regular grocery food store, health food grocery store* and *mail order companies*)

Food Yeast: Food yeast is a certain type of non-*leavening yeast*. Avoid.

Forbidden: Forbidden in this book is a term referring to *foods* and/or *ingredients* not fit for the *celiacs* on the *gluten free diet*.

Forbidden Grains: Forbidden grains in this book refers to *grains* and/or *grain byproducts* not fit for *celiacs* on the *gluten free diet*. The forbidden grains toxic to celiacs include *wheat, barley, rye, bulgur, diploid, durum, einkorn, emmer, far, farro, hexaploid, kamut, mir, seitan, semolina, spelt, tetraploid, tsampa, triticale, triticum, relatives of these grains* and possibly *oats*. [Look up each individually.] Patients with *celiac disease* and/or *dermatitis herpetiformis* disease are intolerant to the *gluten* in these *grains* and any *foods* prepared with these forbidden grains and *grain byproducts*. Avoid all forbidden grains, relatives of forbidden *grains, byproducts* of forbidden grains and foods made from forbidden grains and *grain byproducts*. (See *grain, gluten, CD, DH, byproduct* and *gluten free*.)

Fordhook Bean: A type of large *lima bean*. GF. (See *lima bean*.)

Formula: Infant formula. Call the infant formula companies you favor and request their *allergen/gluten free* product list. {Formulas may contain added *sweeteners, fillers, starch, flavorings* and other *food agents.*)

Fortified Food: Fortified food is *food* to which *vitamins* and *minerals* were added to improve its *nutritional* value. All fortified foods need to be verified GF. (See *additives.*)

Fortified Rice: *Rice* (customarily *white rice*) to which *vitamins* and *minerals* were added to improve its *nutritional* value. (See *rice.*)

Fortified Wines: Questionable. (See *wine, sherry* and *port wine.*)

Fortune Cookie: A type of *wheat cookie/cracker*. Avoid.

Four Stages of a Disease: There are *four stages of disease*. Listed in order of least severe the stages include *acute, subacute, chronic* and *degenerative*. [Look up each stage individually.] In all stages of *celiac disease*, the disease is always present but the body might not display visible *symptoms* especially in the early stages. Patients with celiac disease generally recover from every stage of celiac disease with a strict adherence to the GF diet. (See *celiac disease, symptoms* and *disease.*)

Fowl: Fowl are any type of *bird*. All *pure fresh* and *plain* fowl are GF. (See *poultry* for details and specifics and also see 'fowl' in A & F charts.)

Frankfurters: Frankfurters are *meat* or *beef* franks. Frankfurters are a type of *sausage*-like *hot dog* served on a *bun*. [Definitely avoid the *bun*.] You can eat frankfurters without the *bun*. In general *pure meat* franks do not contain *filler*, but may contain other *forbidden ingredients*. There are a variety of GF frankfurters. [*Kosher* franks are usually safer.] Choose *100% pure all meat* franks (free of *nitrates* if possible).

Question all *condiments* used on frankfurters. (See *bun* and *condiments.*)

Freeze: (See *frozen food* and *freezing.*)

Freeze Dried: Freeze dried is a method of *preserving foods*. Some foods are freeze dried and stored in airtight containers. Freeze-dried foods make convenient *travel foods*. Examine *preparation* instructions. Question the source of all freeze dried foods. (See *backpacking food, camping food* and *preserve.*)

Freezing: Freezing is a *natural* method of *preserving foods*. Frozen foods can be chemical free. Frozen foods still need to be verified GF. (See *preserve.*)

French Bean: (See *green bean.*) GF.

French Dressing: French dressing is a type of creamy textured *vinegar* and *oil dressing,* red-orange in color. {French dressing may contain added *thickeners, vinegar* and *seasonings.*] Creamy dressings are always questionable. Some companies label their dressings gluten free.

French Fries: French fries are sliced *potatoes* deep-fried in *oil*. You can *home-make* French-fries by slicing *potatoes fresh* and then frying them in GF *oils*. Avoid French fries *coated* with *gluten*. Avoid French fries *deep-fried* in *oil* used previously to fry *foods* containing *gluten*. Always question. Verify GF.

French Toast: French toast is a type of breakfast meal made with *bread* dipped in an *egg* and *milk batter* and then *fried*. *Commercially prepared* French toast is normally made with *wheat bread*. You can use GF *bread* to home-make French toast. *Fry* the French toast on a clean *grill*.

Commercially prepared GF French toast is available only through *specialty companies.*

Fresh: Fresh is a term routinely referring to foods that are *raw, natural,* wholesome and possible *pure. Fresh _fruits_, _vegetables_, _seeds_* and *_nuts_* are some of the safest GF foods. [Look up each fresh food individually.] The term fresh is also a term used for *food* not old, stale, *processed* or *prepared.* (See *pure, plain, organic* and *pesticides.*)

Fresh Beans: Fresh beans are a variety of *edible raw fresh beans.* Some fresh beans are eaten within their *pods.* GF. (See *vegetable.*)

Fresh Cheese: Fresh cheese is any of various *un-ripened immature cheeses,* as opposed to any *aged mature cheese.* (See *cheese.*)

Freshness Date: Freshness date is the *date* indicating when the *food* will no longer be *fresh.* (See *dating.*)

Fresh Peas: Fresh peas are a variety of *edible raw fresh peas.* Some fresh peas are eaten within their *pods.* GF. (See *vegetable.*)

Fresh Yeast: (See *compressed yeast.*) Verify GF.

Fried Food: Question the source of all the *foods* being fried. Question any *coatings* used on the *foods* to be fried. Question if the *oil* was previously used to fry *foods* containing *gluten.* (See *fry, breading* and *coatings.*)

Fried Rice: Fried rice is a type of *seasoned rice* dish usually made with *soy sauce, eggs, vegetables* and sometimes *MSG.* Question the *soy sauce, seasonings* and all other ingredients. Caution: the use of *MSG.* (See *Chinese food.*)

Frittata: Frittatas are a type of breakfast dish made with *eggs* and *filled* with a variety of *foods* (possibly *_cheese_, _meats_* and *_vegetables_*). Question the source of added *fillings* and *sauce.* (See *eggs.*)

Fritter: Fritter is a type of fried *wheat flour batter pancake.* Avoid.

Frost: To decorate with *icing* or *glaze.* (See *icing* and *glaze.*)

Frosting: Frostings are a spreadable *mixture* generally used on *baked-goods.* Frostings are typically made with *sweeteners.* {Frostings may also contain added *_cream_,* colorings, *flavorings, _butter_* and *thickeners.*} Some frostings are GF. Verify GF.

Frozen Desserts: Frozen desserts are a type of dessert kept frozen. All desserts including frozen desserts are questionable. {Frozen desserts may contain added *sweeteners, foaming agents, alkalis flavorings, colorings, thickeners, fillers, texturizers, fat substitutes* and other food *additives.*} (See *desserts* for details and specifics.)

Frozen Food: Frozen foods are *foods preserved* by the method of freezing. Most plain frozen fruits and vegetables are GF. Most frozen *meals* are not GF. Question added *sauces* and *gravies* on frozen *foods.* Freeze GF *leftovers* for convenience. (See *processed* and *prepared* foods for additional details and specifics.)

Frozen Meals: (See *frozen foods.*) Most frozen *meals* are not GF.

Frozen Yogurt: Frozen yogurt is a type of frozen *dessert* made from *yogurt.* Questionable. (See *frozen dessert* and *yogurt* for details.)

Fructooligosaccharides (FOS): FOS are an additive obtained from *fruit carbohydrates.* GF.

Fructose: Fructose is a fine *powdery sugar* granulate from certain *fruits* or *honey*. Fructose may be *corn* based. Verify GF. (See *sweetener*.)

Fruit: Fruits are the *edible* part of a *plant*. All *fresh, raw, pure* and *plain* fruits are naturally GF. Choose *fresh, raw* or *pure* plain *frozen* fruit. Choose canned fruit *unsweetened* if possible. Avoid *fresh, cooked* and *frozen* fruits in *forbidden sauces, gravies* and *creams*, with *pasta, breaded, batter dipped, coated* or *pickled* in *vinegars,* unless all ingredients are verified GF. Avoid some *pie fillings*. Question *commercially prepared fruit salads*. Avoid *sulfured* dried fruit if possible. Avoid *dried fruit dusted* with *forbidden flour*. (See 'fruit' and 'dried fruit' in A & F charts.)

Fruit Butter: (See *fruit spread*.)

Fruitcake: A type of holiday *baked-good* made with *candied fruit* and customarily a *forbidden wheat flour mixture*. Avoid.

Fruit Canned: Canned fruit is fresh *fruit* usually *cooked* and *preserved* in *sweeteners*. {Canned fruit may contain added *sweeteners* and other *food additives*.} Choose *pure plain* canned *fruit* (*unsweetened* or *naturally sweetened* if possible). Verify GF. (See *fruit* and *canned food*.)

Fruit Cocktail: (See *fruit cup*.)

Fruit Cup: Fruit cup is a type of *dessert* made with *preserved fruit*. An abundance of fruit cups are GF. {Fruit cup may contain added *sweeteners, flavorings* and *colorings*.} Verify GF. (See *fruit*.)

Fruit Dried: (See *dried fruit*.)

Fruit Drinks: Fruit drinks are a type of *beverage*. Question all *flavored* *fruit drinks, fruit drinks* made from concentrates and *fruit punch*. {Fruit drinks may contain added *artificial colorings* and *flavorings*.} Caution. Questionable. Verify GF.

Fruit Juice: Fruit juice is juice obtained from *fruits* or *artificial* sources. *Pure fresh* and *plain* juiced or squeezed *fruit* juices are *naturally* GF. Several fruit juices are GF. Choose *100% pure* GF fruit juice. Question *ingredients*. Verify GF. (See *juice* and *fruit drinks*)

Fruit Leather: Fruit leather is a type of *fruit snack* made with *dehydrated* fruit *puree*. {Fruit leather may contain added *flavorings, colorings, preservatives* and *other food agents*.} Many brands of fruit leather are GF. Choose *100% pure* fruit leather. Question all ingredients.

Fruit Preserves: Fruit preserves are a type of *fruit spread* made with *cooked* pieces of *fruit*. {Fruit preserves may contain added *sweeteners*.} Verify GF. (See *fruit spread*.)

Fruit Salad: Fruit salads are a type of salad (usually cold) made with a variety of *fresh* or *processed fruit*. Question all the ingredients in *prepared fruit salads*. Avoid *forbidden toppings* and *sauces*. (See *fruit* for details and specifics.)

Fruit Spread: Fruit spreads are any of various spreadable *fruit*. *Commercially prepared* GF fruit spreads include certain brands of *fruit preserves, jams, jellies* and *compote*. [Look up each individually.] The majority of fruit spreads are GF. {Fruit spreads may contain added *fillers, sugars, emulsifiers, pH additives, buffers, adjusting agents, antifoaming* *agents, acidifiers, antimycotic agents, humectants, thickeners, colorings, preservatives, flavorings, sweeteners, stabilizers* and *other food agents.*} Verify GF.

Fruit Sugar: (See *fructose*.)

Fruit Vinegar: Fruit vinegar is a type of *vinegar* made from soft *fruit* (usually *berries*) and *vinegar* (usually *wine vinegar*). Verify GF.

Fry: To cook in hot *oil*. The *oil* used to fry *foods* must be clean and not used previously to fry *foods* containing *gluten*. (See *fried food*)

Fryer: (See *grill*.)

Fu: *Dried wheat gluten*. Avoid.

Fudge: Fudge is a type of a dense *cake*-like candy made with *sweeteners*. {Fudge may contain added *sugar*, *corn syrup*, *flavorings* and *cream*.} Question all the ingredients in fudge. Verify GF.

Ful Medame Beans: An Egyptian brown *bean*. GF. (See *bean*.)

Fumaric Acid: A type of *leavening agent* derived from *plants*. Verify GF. (See *leavening agent*.)

Fungus: Fungus is an *organism* without *chlorophyll*. Types of fungus include *mildews, molds, mushrooms, smut* and *yeast*. [Look up each type of fungus individually.] (See *chlorophyll* and *sensitivities*.)

Funnel Cake: Funnel cake is a type of *deep-fried baked-good* type *dessert*. Funnel cakes are prepared by pouring a batter mix into hot oil. Most *commercially prepared* funnel cakes are prepared with *forbidden grain byproducts*. You can *home make* funnel cake with allowable GF *specialty ingredients*. *Commercially prepared* GF funnel cake mixes are available through *specialty*

companies. (See *fry, batter, baked-goods* and *recipes*.)

Furcellaran Gum: A certain type of gum derived from *seaweed*. Caution. GF. (See *gum*.)

Gajar: (See *carrot*.) GF.

Galactose: A type of white crystalline *milk sugar* derived from *lactose* or certain *plant gums*. GF.

Game: Game are wild *animals* hunted for *food*. *Pure fresh* and *plain* game are *naturally* GF. (See *meat* and *poultry*.)

Gandula: (See *pigeon pea*.) GF.

Garam Masala: A type of Asian *ground spice mix*. Verify GF.

Garbanzo Bean: A type of *dried bean* that looks like a baby chicks face and is tan in color. Garbanzo beans *mill* into an excellent *bean flour*. Garbanzo beans are also an excellent *sprouting bean*. *Cooked garbanzo beans* are good in *bean dip* (e.g. *hummus*). Garbanzo beans are available at most *health* and *ethnic grocery food stores*. GF. (See *bean*.)

Garbanzo Bean Flour: A type of *bean flour milled* from *garbanzo beans*. *Garbanzo beans* are hard to *mill* but do *mill* into an excellent *bean flour*. Garbanzo *bean flour* adds moisture and improves texture in *baked-goods*. [Garbanzo *bean flour* is one of the best *bean flours* for *baking* especially if there is *fruit* in the *recipe*.] *Garbanzo bean* flour works well as a portion of *corn flour* or *rice flour mixtures*. *Garbanzo beans* are sometimes too big for some *blade mill* shoots. Garbanzo *bean flour* is available at most *health* and *ethnic grocery food stores*. Check for GF purity. (See *garbanzo beans* and *blade mills*.)

Garbfava Bean Flour: A type of *bean flour* combination of *fava beans* and *garbanzo beans*. [Look up each bean individually.] Check for GF purity. (See *favism* for cautions.)

Garbure: (See *stew*.) Question.

Garden Pea: (See *fresh peas*.) GF.

Garlic: A type of *spice/bulb*. *Pure fresh* and *plain* are GF. (See *spices*, *bulbs* and *garlic powder*.)

Garlic Clove: A section of a *fresh garlic bulb*. (See *garlic*.)

Garlic Powder: A type of spice / *condiment* made with a *mixture* of *ground-dehydrated garlic* and added *filler*. Question the *filler* and possibly other *food agents*. Choose *100% pure* garlic powder or home-make with *milled dehydrated* garlic and *arrowroot powder* or *rice flour* as *filler*. Caution. Verify GF. (See *spices* and *condiments*.)

Garlic Press: A garlic press is a type of *kitchen utensil* used to press *fresh garlic cloves* or tiny pieces of *fresh ginger* root. You can leave the skin on both and then discard after pressing. The press extracts the juice and some *pulp*.

Gastroenterologist: A type of medical doctor studying and treating *diseases* of the stomach, *intestinal tract* and their associated organs. Gastroenterologist will examine the *small bowel* and obtain a *biopsy*, if there is a strong clinical suspicion of *celiac disease*. (See *blood test*, *biopsy*, *diagnose* and *endoscope*.)

Gastrointestinal Tract: (See *intestinal tract*.)

Gastronomist: Someone educated in the science of *gourmet beverage* and *food*. Gastronomists are also persons knowledgeable in the art of fine dining.

Gazpacho: A type of cold *vegetable soup*. {Gazpacho may contain added *flavorings* and *vinegar*.} Verify GF.

Gelatin: Gelatin is a type of fine white *powder* derived from *animal tissue*. *Plain unflavored* gelatin is GF. Gelatin is a *gelling agent*. [*Agar* can replace gelatin as a *natural gelling agent* in various *recipes*.] Gelatin is also a term for a type of *prepared dessert*. {Powdered flavored gelatin may contain added *sugar cane sugar*, *artificial flavorings, artificial colorings* and other *artificial ingredients*.} Question added *food* (e.g. *fruit*, *seed*, *nut* or *grain byproducts*) in prepared gelatin. Verify GF. (See *agar*.)

Gelatin Capsule: (See *gelatin*, *capsules* and *medication*.)

Gelatin Cups: Gelatin cups are *prepared gelatin* in individual serving sizes. Most gelatin cups are GF. Verify GF. (See *gelatin*.)

Gelling Agent: Gelling agents are *natural* or *artificial substances* used to form *food* (e.g., making food firm or malleable). Question the source. Types of gelling agents include *chemicals, mono* and *diglycerides, lecithin, gelatin, yeast*, various *gums, pectin, oil/fat* and *cellulose*. [Look up each individually.] (See *agent*)

Genera: The plural word for *genus*.

Generally Recognized as Safe: GRAS is a type of United States listing of *additives* used in the *food* industry considered 'generally recognized as safe'. (See *additives*.)

Genes: Genes are *basic* units containing *genetic* characteristics passed on from one generation to the next. Genes contain the *DNA* or *RNA*. (See *genetic*)

Genetic: Genetic refers to inherited, hereditary, inborn and/or resulting from *genes*. [Predetermined information is stored in the *genes*.] (See *genes, genus* and *GMO*.)
Genetically Engineered Food: (See *genetically modified organisms*.)
Genetically Modified Food: (See *genetically modified organisms*.)
Genetically Modified Organism: GMO is a term for a type of *microorganism, plant* or *animal* that has received *genetic material* from another. A compositional change takes place and its *DNA* is altered. This *modification* is *labeled* voluntarily and does not render a food GF. *Foods* most likely to be GMO may include certain types of *corn, canola seeds, potatoes, green peppers*, HVP, *lactose*, lecithin, *flax, papaya*, enzymes, dairy, *sunflower seeds, tomatoes, soybeans, cotton* and *squash*. *Foods* not GMO are labeled 'non-GMO'. Avoid GMO food if possible. Certified *organic* foods are the only foods guaranteed not to be GMO. (See *organic* and *heirloom*.)
Genoise: (See *sponge cake*.) Avoid.
Genotype: The *genetic* constitution of any of various *organisms*.
Generic Brand: The generic brand is a none-*brand name* or trademark name product that is a suitable replacement. Generic products may not contain the exact *ingredients*. If you purchase the generic equivalent, it needs to be verified GF.
Generic Medication: If you purchase the generic equivalent brand of medication, it also needs to be verified GF. (See generic and medication.)

Genus: Genus is a term for related organisms. A set of closely related *plant* and *animal* species. Grouped into families (e.g., the species '*wheat*' is included in the 'genus' *plant*). *Celiacs* must avoid all relatives of the *forbidden grains*. (See *common name* and *grains*.)
Germ: The *germ* part of any *seed / grain* contains the *essentials* for new life. (See *grains* and *byproducts*.)
Germinated: When a grain or seed germinates, it begins to sprout. [The *seeds* and *grains* that have started to grow.] The germinated *sprout* of wheat is harmless, but if the sprout has not *germinated*, then it still contains the *forbidden protein gluten* therefore all *commercially prepared* products made with sprouts are questionable. (See *sprout*.)
Gervais Cheese: Verify GF.
GF: GF is the abbreviation for *gluten free*. (See *gluten free* and CF.)
GF Food: (See *gluten free food*.)
GF Recipes: (See *gluten free recipes*.)
Ghatti Gum: A type of *gum* derived from a tree. Verify GF.
Ghee: Ghee is basically *clarified butter*. (See *clarified butter*.)
Gin: Gin is a type of *distilled alcohol*. GF. (See *alcohol*.)
Ginger: A type of *spice/root*. Fresh and *pure dried* are GF. (See *spice, root* and *garlic press*)
Gingerbread: Gingerbread is a type of ginger *flavored cookie baked-good* customarily made with *wheat flour*. Avoid (See *cookie*.)
Ginger Candied: Candied ginger is *cooked ginger* with added *sweetener* (possibly added *forbidden barley malt*). Question all ingredients.

Ginger Powder: Ginger powder is a type of spice / *condiment* made with a *mixture* of *ground-dehydrated ginger* and added *filler*. Question the *filler* and possibly other *food agents*. Choose *100% pure* ginger powder or *home-make* with milled *dehydrated ginger* and *arrowroot powder* or *rice flour* as *filler*. Caution. Verify GF. (See *spices* and *condiments*.)

Gjetost Cheese: A type of semi-firm *cheese* made from a combination of goats and cows *milk*. Verify GF.

Glace: (See *glaze*.)

Glaze: To *coat food* with a thin layer of *ingredients* (usually *liquid sweeteners*) to produce a shiny surface. {Glaze may contain added *chemical compounds, flavorings, gums, oil/fat, wax* and *starch*.} Question the source.

Gliadin: Gliadin is a type of *plant protein* (*prolamin*) found in *wheat*. Individuals with *celiac disease* have a genetic predisposition to the reaction from this *prolamin*. Therefore, celiacs must avoid *wheat* grains, relatives of wheat *grains* and *byproducts* of these *forbidden grains*. (See *wheat* and *prolamins*.)

Gloss: (See *polish* or *coat*.)

Gloucester Cheese: A type of *cheese* made from cow's *milk*. Verify GF. (See *cheese*.)

Glucose: Glucose is a type of *simple sugar* produced in *plants* and *animals* by conversion of *carbohydrates, proteins* and *fats*. Glucose is a type of *syrup* containing *dextrose, maltose* and *dextrin*. [Look up each type individually.] Question the source.

Glue: Certain types of *food* grade glues are prepared from specific *ingredients* in case of digestion.

Ingredients in *edible* glues can be *toxic* to *celiacs*. Food grade glues are a certain type of glue that may come in contact with your *food* or mouth. Glue is used on *tea bags, packaging material, stamps* and *envelopes*. Celiacs must avoid licking *stamps* and *envelopes*. Some packaging materials are question. You can use a *tea infuser* to eliminate possible concerns for glue on *tea bags*.

Glutamic Acid: (See *monosodium glutamate*.)

Glutelin: Glutelin is a type of *simple protein* intolerable to *celiacs*. Avoid. (See *gluten*.)

Gluten: Gluten is a *protein* (*prolamin*) found in certain types of *cereal grains* (e.g., gluten is found in corn, *barley, rye, wheat* and *oats*). Gluten referred to in this book is the gluten intolerable for individuals with *celiac disease* (e.g., the type of gluten found in *barley, rye* and *wheat* and relatives of these *grains*). The highest content of *forbidden* gluten is contained within the *wheat grain*, then in descending order *rye* and *barley*. It is the gluten prolamins (gliadins and glutenins) in wheat most toxic to celiacs. [The gluten in *wheat-flour* is what gives *baked-goods* their elasticity.] Gluten containing grains (intolerable for *celiacs*) include *wheat, rye, barley* and possibly *oats*. Advanced testing indicates 'pure' oats are not harmful to those who have *CD* and/or *DH*. (See oats for additional details.) Other forbidden grains include *bulgur, diploid, durum, einkorn, emmer, far, farro, hexaploid, kamut, mir, seitan, semolina, tetraploid, tsampa, triticale, spelt, triticum* and *relatives of these grains*. [Patients with *celiac disease* and/or *dermatitis herpetiformis* disease are intolerant to the *gluten* in these *grains* and any *foods* prepared with these *forbidden* grains and grain *byproducts*.] *Gluten free grains* (tolerable for *celiacs*) include <u>corn</u>, <u>rice</u>, <u>wild rice</u>, <u>amaranth</u>, <u>ragi</u>, <u>job's tears</u>, <u>teff</u>, <u>buckwheat</u>, <u>millet</u>, <u>quinoa</u> and possibly oats. (See oats for additional details.) *Tef*, *ragi* and *job's tear* are considered closely related to <u>corn</u>. [Look up each specific grain individually.] When choosing questionable *grains* individual tolerance should dictate use. Avoid gluten in all amounts. Avoid foods made with *forbidden gluten grains*, relatives of *forbidden grains* and *byproducts* of these *grains*. <u>Choose</u> <u>foods</u> <u>made</u> <u>with</u> <u>gluten</u> <u>free</u> <u>grains</u> <u>and</u> <u>byproducts</u> <u>of</u> <u>these</u> <u>grains</u>. (See *celiac disease, protein, prolamins, process, contaminated* and *byproduct* and see A & F charts.)

Gluten Byproducts: Gluten byproducts in this book refers to any type of gluten containing *substance* reproduced as a secondary result of the *manufacturing* of a *forbidden grain* containing the gluten toxic for celiacs (e.g. *wheat-starch, barley-malt* and *rye-flour*). [No matter how incidental the *byproduct* if produced from *grains* containing *toxic gluten*, the *byproduct* and any food prepared with these byproducts you should avoid them.] Avoid all byproducts of the toxic gluten grains and all foods made with *forbidden grains* and *byproducts* of these *grains*. (See *byproducts*.)

Gluten Flour: Gluten flours are a type of hard *wheat flour*. Types of flours containing gluten include any flour made from *wheat, barley, rye, bulgur, diploid, durum, einkorn, emmer, far, farro, hexaploid, kamut, mir, seitan, semolina, spelt, tetraploid, tsampa, triticale, triticum* and *relatives of these grains*. Avoid. (See *gluten free flour*)

Gluten Free: Gluten free (GF) in this book is a term meaning referring to free of the *toxic gluten* intolerable for people with *celiac disease*. [*Corn gluten* is safe for *celiacs*.] Gluten containing grains (intolerable for *celiacs*) include *wheat, rye, barley* and possibly *oats*. Advanced testing indicates 'pure' oats are not harmful to those who have *CD* and/or *DH*. (See oats for additional details.) Other forbidden gluten grains include *bulgur, diploid, durum, einkorn, emmer, far, farro, mir, hexaploid, kamut, seitan, semolina, spelt, tetraploid, tsampa, triticale, triticum* and *relatives of these grains*. <u>Gluten</u> <u>free</u> <u>grains</u> (tolerable for *celiacs*) include <u>corn</u>, <u>rice</u>, <u>wild rice</u>, <u>amaranth</u>, <u>ragi</u>, <u>job's tears</u>, <u>teff</u>, <u>buckwheat</u>, <u>millet</u> and <u>quinoa</u>. *Job's tear, tef,* and <u>ragi</u> are considered closely related to <u>corn</u>. When choosing questionable *grains* individual tolerance should dictate use. [Look up each specific grain individually.] Avoid gluten in all amounts. Avoid foods made with *forbidden gluten grains*, relatives of forbidden *grains* and *byproducts* of these *grains*. <u>Choose</u> <u>foods</u> <u>made</u> <u>with</u> <u>gluten</u> <u>free</u> <u>grains</u> <u>and</u> <u>byproducts</u> <u>of</u> <u>these</u> <u>grains</u>. (See *celiac disease, gluten, contaminated, byproducts, grains, children* and *gluten free, prolamins, proteins* and also see the A & F charts.)

Gluten Free Diet: This term refers to a 'diet' free of the toxic *gluten* intolerable for individuals with *celiac disease*. (See *diet, gluten free* and *celiac disease*.)

Gluten Free Flour: Gluten free flours in this book refers to a type of flour free from the *gluten* intolerable for people with *celiac disease*. Types of *gluten free* flours include *pure amaranth flour, arrowroot powder, bean flours, buckwheat flour, corn flour, cornmeal, garbanzo bean flour, millet flour, potato starch-flour, quinoa flour, rice flour, sago starch-flour, sorghum flour, soybean flour, sweet rice flour, tapioca flour, seed flours, nut flours teff flour, ragi flour, job's tears flour, dried vegetable flours* and possibly oat flour. [Look up each type individually.] Caution: *flours* may be a combination of one or more *flours*. Avoid flours containing gluten (see *gluten flour*). You can *home mill* GF flours with certain types of *dried roots, vegetables* and *tubers* and *dried whole grains, beans* and *seeds*. *Commercially prepared* GF flours are available at most ethnic and health food grocery stores, by mail order and at some regular grocery food stores. Check gluten free flours for GF purity. (See *specialty companies, gluten flour, gluten free, whole food* and *flour*.)

Gluten Free Food: Gluten free *foods* in this book, refers to *foods* free from the *toxic gluten* intolerable for people with *celiac disease*. Types of *gluten free* foods include *fresh raw fruits, vegetables, seeds* and *nuts*. All food must be verified GF. Question all *processed* and *prepared foods*. Avoid foods made with

forbidden gluten grains, relatives of these *grains* and *byproducts* of these *grains*. Choose foods made with gluten free grains and *byproducts* of GF *grains*. (See *whole foods, gluten free, processed foods, prepared foods* and see the A & F charts.)

Gluten Free Food Book: *Guide Books Publication Company* publishes an annual gluten free food list of *commercially prepared* GF *food products* in book format. The title is- *Gluten Free Food Product List 'the manufactures list of commercially prepared gluten free foods'*. To purchase this book see the order form on page 207. (See *Gluten Free Food List* for additional information.)

Gluten Free Food List: A gluten free food lists is a list of *commercially prepared gluten free food products*. Some *whole food grocery stores* hand out gluten free food lists, but these hand-out-lists are not considered accurate, nor are these lists comprehensive or complete. Always read the *labels* of *foods* on a GF food list. [Mistakes are made and *product ingredients* can change.] For a comprehensive commercial food product list I recommend the *Gluten Free Food List 'the manufactures list of commercially prepared gluten free* foods' by *Guide Books Publication Company*. This book is essential for *celiacs* and anyone following the *gluten free diet*. The *Gluten Free Food Product List* is a convenient, easy-to-use book of commercially prepared gluten free brand name foods. With this book, you can look up any particular food item and find a brand/trade name that is gluten free. All the foods entered in the book where obtained through personal contact through thousands of phone calls, e-mails and letters to processors, manufacturing companies and distributors. You can take the *Gluten Free Food Product List* with you shopping and discover the abundance and availability of gluten free foods. To purchase this book- see the ordering form on page 207.

Gluten Free Grains: *Gluten free* (GF) grains in this book refers to grains tolerable for individuals with *celiacs disease*. Types of GF grains (tolerable for *celiacs*) include *corn*, *rice*, *wild rice*, *amaranth*, *ragi*, *job's tears*, *teff*, *buckwheat*, *millet*, *quinoa* and possibly oats. (See oats for additional details.) *Tef, ragi* and *job's tear* are considered closely related to *corn*. [Look up each grain individually.] When choosing questionable *grains* individual tolerance should dictate use. Avoid foods made with *forbidden gluten grains*, relatives of these *grains* and *byproducts* of these *grains*. Choose foods made with gluten free grains and *byproducts* of these *grains*. (See *gluten free, forbidden grains* and also see A & F charts.)

Gluten Free Resource Guide: *Guide Books Publication Company* publishes an excellent resource book titled the *Gluten Free Resource Guide 'a consumers guide for living gluten free'*. This book is the ultimate guide to gluten free eating! It is the best and most recently updated compilation of information to help assist you with some of the challenges associated with the gluten free diet. It contains the names phone numbers and addresses of various resources that provide information about the *gluten free diet, celiac disease* and *dermatitis herpetiformis*. The book is praised for its creative design and usability. This book contains various must-have information (e.g., sample letters to manufactures and the food industry, the who, what, where, when and why's of the gluten free diet, menu planning ideas, charts, illustrations, book recommendations and reviews, practical information on how to shop, dine, travel and stock a pantry gluten free, and contact information to travel clubs dinning clubs, certain eateries, gluten free grocery food stores and specialty mail order companies. To purchase this book- see the order form on page 207. (See *books*)

Gluten Grains: Gluten grains referred to in this book are the gluten grains intolerable for individuals with *celiac disease* (e.g., *barley, rye* and *wheat* and relatives of these *grains*). (See *forbidden grains*.)

Glutenin: A type of *simple protein* found in *wheat* intolerable to *celiacs*. Avoid. (See *gluten* and *wheat*.)

Gluten Intolerance: A condition where a persons system cannot tolerate *gluten*. (See *celiac disease*.)

Gluten Sensitive: Gluten sensitive is a term used for anyone sensitive to gluten. Some patients with *celiac disease* are extremely sensitive to *gluten* and exhibit *symptoms* upon ingesting the smallest amounts of *gluten*. Individuals without a *diagnosis* of CD can also be sensitive to *gluten*. (See *gluten,* *celiac disease, celiac shock* and *sensitivities*.)

Gluten Sensitivity Disease: (See *celiac disease*.)

Gluten Testing: Gluten testing is a procedure done to test foods for a possible content of a specific *gluten*, using the *enzyme* immunoassay. To independently test the *gluten* content of small amounts of *commercially prepared foods* is time consuming and expensive. Individuals with CD need to rely on the *manufacturers* to prepare and *label* foods GF. Celiac patients also need stricter *labeling* laws. A gluten free food list is essential for anyone on the gluten free diet. (See *gluten free food product list, FDA, label reading* and *manufacture*.)

Glutinous: Glutinous is a term used for 'sticky' or 'gummy'. Glutinous means having a sticky consistency. [*Glutinous rice* is GF.] The term glutinous does not mean, containing gluten. Glutinous has a letter 'i' in its spelling, glutenous has a letter 'e' in its spelling. [The term *glutinous-wheat* describes both a type of *forbidden wheat* high in *gluten* content and a type of grain flour producing a gummy texture, which gives *baked-goods* their elasticity. Avoid *glutinous-wheat*.]

Glutinous Rice: Glutinous rice is a type of *sweet rice*. The term applies to a certain type of rice grain with a gummy / sticky consistency when *cooked*. GF. (See *sweet rice*.)

Glutinous Rice Flour: Glutinous rice flour is a type of *grain flour* milled from *sweet rice* grains. (See *glutinous rice* and *sweet rice flour*.)

Glutinous Rice Starch: Glutinous rice starch is produced from *sweet*

rice grains. (See *glutinous rice* and *sweet rice starch*.)

Glutinous Wheat: A type of *forbidden wheat* high in *gluten* content. (See *glutinous*.)

Glyceride: Glyceride is *synthetically* produced. Caution. GF.

Glycerin: Glycerin is a type of thick *liquid* obtained from *fats* and *oils*. {Glycerin may contain *animal byproducts, vegetable byproducts* (e.g. *coconut, corn,* peanut, *soy* or *wheat*) or *petroleum*.} Glycerin is a *carrier, extraction, coating* and *polishing* agent. Question if glycerin is 'in' *processed foods* or 'on' *whole foods*. Always question the source.

Glycerol: (See *glycerin*.)

Glycine: GF.

Glycogen: A *compound* stored in the body that converts to *glucose* as a source of energy. (See *glucose*.)

GMO: (See *genetically modified organisms*.)

GMP: (See good *manufacturing* practices.)

Gnocchi: Gnocchi is a type of *potato pasta* usually made with *potatoes* and a *forbidden flour*. *Commercially prepared* GF gnocchi are available only through *specialty companies*. (See *special resources*.)

Goa Bean: (See winged *bean*.) GF.

Goat: Goats are used in the food industry for there edible *meat* and *milk*. *Pure fresh* and *plain* goat meats are GF. Goat milk is GF. (See *meat* and *dairy* and *goat milk*.)

Goat Milk: Goat milk is a *naturally* GF *dairy product* and *beverage* obtained from female goats. Some celiacs are *lactose intolerant* but for most it is temporary. *Dairy products* made from goat and sheep milk are easier to digest than *dairy products* made from cow *milk*. (See *milk, dairy* and *dairy products*.)

Gobhi: (See *cauliflower*.) GF.

Gobo: A type of *vegetable*. *Fresh* and *plain* are GF. (See *vegetable*.)

Golden Apple Seed: (See *quince*.)

Golden Gram: (See *mung beans*.)

Golden Raisins: Avoid golden *raisins* if possible. (See *raisins*.)

Goldenrod: A type of *herb*. *Fresh* and *pure dried* are GF. (See *herb*.)

Goldenseal: A type of *herb*. *Fresh* and *pure dried* are GF. (See *herb*.)

Golden Syrup: A type of *syrup* made from evaporated *cane juice*. Caution. Verify GF. (See *syrup* and *sugar cane*.)

Good Bacteria: Good bacteria are beneficial parasitic *microorganisms* lining the *intestines*. Good bacteria are necessary in the *intestinal tract* to maintain good health. *Acidophilus* will help increase the good bacteria. (See *bacteria*, a*cidophilus*, *intestinal tract* and *villi*.)

Good Manufacturing Practices: GMP is a type of practice allowing *manufacturers* to use as much of any *additive* as they deem necessary to achieve a desired effect. (See *FDA*.)

Goose: A type of *fowl*. *Pure fresh* and *plain* are GF. (See *fowl*.)

Gooseberry: A type of *fruit*. *Fresh* and *plain* are GF. (See *fruit*.)

Gordita: A type of *wheat flour* pancake-like *tortilla*. Avoid.

Gorgonzola: A type of *veined cheeses*. Avoid all veined cheese.

Gouda Cheese: An *aged cheese* made from cow's *milk*. Verify GF.

Gourmandise Cheese: A type of soft *cheese* made from cow's *milk*. Verify GF. (See *cheese*.)

Gourmet Cooking: Gourmet cooking is a style of quality *cooking*. Gourmet cooking is the *preparation* of *exceptional food* by someone with refined taste and knowledge for *food*.

Gourmet Food: Gourmet food are a particular type of *food* that is rare unique, expensive and/or of high quality. Gourmet *food* is usually *prepared* in a meticulous way by an epicurean. (See *gourmet cooking*.)

Goya Bean: (See *flat bean*.) GF.

Graham Cracker: A *sweetened wheat flour cracker*. Avoid.

Graham Flour: A type of *coarse ground whole-wheat flour*. Avoid.

Grain: Grains are any tiny hard *seed / fruit* of the *grass plant family*. Grains are a major source of *carbohydrates* in the *diet*. Some *seeds* are considered grains because of their grain-like similarities and uses but are actually seeds (e.g., *millet, amaranth, buckwheat* and *quinoa*). [Grains are not, referred to as seeds in this book and seeds in this book are not referred to as *grains* with the exception of *quinoa, amaranth* and *buckwheat*.] There always seems to be controversy about which grains are safe for *celiacs* on the GF *diet*. According to my research the *gluten* containing grains intolerable for *celiacs* include *wheat, rye, barley* and possibly *oats*. Advanced testing indicates pure oats are not harmful to those who have *CD* and/or *DH*. (See oats for details.) Other forbidden grains include *bulgur, diploid, durum, einkorn, emmer, far, farro, hexaploid, kamut, mir, seitan, semolina, tetraploid, tsampa, triticale, spelt, triticum* and *relatives of these grains*. Patients with *CD* and/or *DH* disease are intolerant to the *gluten* in these *grains* and any *foods* prepared with

these *forbidden grains* and *grain byproducts*. *Gluten free grains* tolerable for *celiacs* include <u>corn</u>, <u>rice</u>, <u>wild rice</u>, <u>amaranth</u>, <u>ragi</u>, <u>job's tears</u>, <u>teff</u>, <u>buckwheat</u>, <u>millet</u>, <u>quinoa</u> and possibly oats. *Tef, ragi* and *job's tear* are considered closely related to <u>corn</u>. [Look up each type of grain individually.] When choosing questionable *grains* individual tolerance should dictate use. [Foods consumed frequently are far more likely to cause food *intolerances*. Therefore, vary grains as not to overdue the same grains and thus making it necessary to give up additional foods.] Question polished and/or coated grains. Avoid gluten in all amounts. Avoid foods made with *forbidden gluten grains*, relatives of these *grains* and *byproducts* of these *grains*. <u>Choose</u> <u>foods</u> <u>made</u> <u>with</u> <u>gluten</u> <u>free</u> <u>grains</u> <u>and</u> <u>byproducts</u> <u>of</u> <u>these</u> <u>grains</u>. For more information about grains write to *The U.S. Department of Agricultural* and ask for their free literature about grains and their relationship to *celiac disease* and the *gluten free* diet. *Whole* GF grains are available at most ethnic and health food grocery stores, by mail order and at some regular grocery food stores. (See *gluten free, grain byproducts* and also see 'grains' in A & F charts.)
Grain Alcohol: Grain alcohol is a type of *alcohol* produced from *fermented cereal grains*: <u>corn</u>, *barley, rye* and *wheat*. (See *alcohol*.)
Grain Byproduct: Grain byproducts refer to *food* reproduced as a secondary result of the *manufacturing* of grains (e.g. *wheat-starch*, *corn* <u>syrup</u>, *barley-malt*, *rice* <u>flour</u> and *rye-flakes*). Byproducts of

gluten free grains are acceptable. Avoid all byproducts of *forbidden gluten grains* and all foods made with *forbidden grains byproducts*. (See *gluten byproducts*.)
Grain Cereal: Grain cereal is *cereal* made from *cereal grains*. Quetion the source. (See *cereal grains*.)
Grain Flour: Grain *flour* is a type of *flour milled* from *whole grains*. Types of gluten free grain *flours* include pure <u>corn flour</u>, <u>cornmeal</u>, <u>rice flour</u>, <u>sorghum flour</u>, <u>sweet rice flour</u>, <u>teff flour</u>, <u>job's tears flour</u>, <u>ragi flour</u> and possibly oat flour. (See oats for details.) Grain *flour* is also a term used for some flours *milled* from *seeds* with grain-like similarities (e.g. <u>amaranth flour</u>, <u>buckwheat flour</u>, <u>millet flour</u> and <u>quinoa flour</u>). Forbidden grain flours include flours made with *wheat, barley, rye, bulgur, diploid, durum, einkorn, emmer, far, farro, seitan, hexaploid, kamut, semolina, spelt, tsampa, tetraploid, triticale, triticum, mir, relatives of these grains* and possibly *oats*. [Look up each individually.] Question the source of all flours. Caution: flour may be a combination of one or more flours. <u>Choose *100%* pure GF grain flours</u>. *Commercially prepared* GF grain flours are available from *specialty companies*. You can home *mill* GF grain flours with *whole* GF *grains* (e.g. <u>rice</u>, <u>corn</u>, <u>millet</u>, <u>quinoa</u>, <u>amaranth</u>, <u>buckwheat</u>, <u>ragi</u>, <u>job's tear</u> and <u>teff</u>). (See *flour, grain* and *special resources*.)
Grain Foods: Grain foods are *foods* prepared from *grains* and/or *grain byproducts*. Types of grain foods include *breads, crackers, cookies, cereals* and *pasta*. [Look up each

type individually.] Avoid all grain food made with *forbidden grains* and forbidden grain *byproducts*. Choose grain foods made with gluten free grains and gluten free grains byproducts. (See *grain, gluten free* and *prepared* and *processed foods*.)

Grain Mill: (See *mill*.)

Grain Sorghum: (See *sorghum*.)

Grain Sprout: (See *sprouted grains*.)

Grain Vinegar: Grain vinegar is a type of *vinegar* produced from *cereal grains*: *corn, barley, rye* and *wheat*. (See *vinegar*.)

Gram Bean: Gram bean is a term for any of various edible *beans* (e.g. *garbanzo, lentil* and *mung*). GF. [Caution: the word *graham* is a type of *forbidden wheat grain*.]

Gram Flour: Gram bean flour is a term for any of various *bean* flours (e.g. *garbanzo, lentil* and *mung*). GF. [Caution: the word *graham flour* is a type of *forbidden wheat grain*.]

Granary Flour: A type of *flour* milled from miscellaneous *grains*. Avoid. (See *grain flour*.)

Grandma's Bean: A type of large *lima bean*. GF. (See *lima bean*.)

Granola: Granola is a type of dry *snack* food *mixture*. Granola typically contains *dried fruit, seeds* and *grains* (usually *oats*). Commercially prepared granola is generally not GF. You can *home-make* granola with GF *ingredients*.

Granulated Sugar: Granulated sugar is the common table sugar used in most recipes. It is a highly *refined cane sugar*. Verify GF.

Grape: A type of *fruit*. Fresh and *plain* are GF. (See *fruit*.)

Grapefruit: Grapefruit is a type of *citrus fruit. Fresh* and *plain* are GF. (See *citrus, rind* and *fruit*.)

Grape Juice: Grape juice is a type of *fruit juice* obtained from *raw* grapes. Choose *100% pure naturally sweetened* or unsweetened grape juice. Verify GF. (See *juice*.)

Grape Leaves: Considered a *vegetable. Fresh* and *plain* are GF.

Grape Seeds: *A type of seed. Raw* and *plain* are GF. (See *seed*.)

Grape Seed Oil: A type of *oil* obtained from *grape seeds*. Verify GF. (See *grape seeds* and *oil*.)

GRAS: (See *generally recognized as safe*.)

Grass Family: (See *grass plant family*.)

Grass Plant: (See *grass plant family*.)

Grass Plant Family: Grass plants are plants of the grass family. Species of the grass family are cultivated for their *seed/fruit* used as *food. Grains* are the *common name* for the *seed/fruit* of the grass family. [Grains are not referred to as seeds in this book and seeds in this book are not referred to as *grains,* with the exception of *millet, quinoa, amaranth* and *buckwheat* (e.g., these non-grass plant *seeds/fruits* are considered *grains* because of their grain-like similarities but are actually *seeds*).] The leading *grains* of the grass plant family include *barley, corn,* oats, *rice, rye* and *wheat.* (See *grains* for addition details and specifics.)

Grate: To *shred* into small or thin pieces. Clean the grater well between uses. (See *shred*.)

Grated Cheese: Grated cheese is *cheese grated* and packaged for convenience. Question all *commercially* pre-grated *cheeses*. {Grated cheese may contain added *flavoring, preservatives* and *anti-caking agents.*} You can hand grate and refrigerate a container of hand grated GF *cheeses*. (See *cheese.*)

Gravy: Gravy is a type of *sauce mixture* usually made with *cooked food* remains (e.g. *residue* and/or drippings of *cooked meat* or *poultry*). Gravy contains a *thickening agent*. Question the *source* of *thickener. Forbidden wheat flour* is frequently used to thicken gravies. {Gravy may contain added *seasonings* and *emulsifiers.*} You can *home-make* gravy with GF thickening agents (e.g. <u>arrowroot powder</u>, <u>cornstarch</u> and <u>rice flour</u>). Question the source of all ingredients in gravies. (See *gravy mix, residue* and *deglaze.*)

Gravy Mix: Gravy mixes is a type of *dry* packaged powdery *seasoning mix* added to meat *residue* or water to make gravy. Most gravy-mixes are not GF. A limited amount of *commercially prepared* GF gravy mixes are available. (See *seasoning mixes, gravy* and *special companies.*)

Grayling: A type of *fish. Pure fresh* and *plain* are GF. (See *fish.*)

Grease: To *coat* a pan with a *fat* or *oil* to prevent *foods* (usually *baked-goods*) from sticking. <u>Most pure butters</u> and <u>vegetable shortenings</u> <u>are GF</u>. Clean baking pans well between uses. (See *nonstick spray.*)

Great Northern Bean: A certain type of white bean. Great Northern beans are an extremely versatile type of white *bean*. GF. (See *bean.*)

Green Bean: Green beans are a *fresh* immature *bean* eaten in its pod

stage. Types of green beans include *string, filet, French* and *snap beans.* GF. (See *vegetable.*)

Green Gram: (See *mung bean.*) GF.

Green Lentil: Green or brown colored *lentils*. GF. (See *lentil bean.*)

Green Pea: A type of *fresh pea.* GF.

Greens: (See *leafy greens.*) GF.

Green Split Pea: Brown or green *dried split peas.* GF. (See *split pea.*)

Grenadine: A type of *syrup* made from *pomegranates.* {Grenadine may contain added *alcohol, fruit-juice* concentrates and *flavorings.*} Caution. Verify GF.

Griddle Cake: (See *pancake.*)

Grill: To cook *food* on a grill over heat. You need to *cook* GF *food* on a 'clean' grill or put '*aluminum foil*' under the *food* to avoid *cross contamination.* (See *aluminum foil.*)

Grind: (See *ground* and *mill.*)

Grinder: (See *coffee mill, ground* and *mill.*)

Grissini: (See *breadsticks.*) Avoid.

Grits: Grits are any coarsely *ground seeds* or *grains.* Types include <u>buckwheat, corn</u> or *barley*. Grits are coarser than *ground meal.* Question the source.

Groats: Groats are a type of *seed/kernel* having had its *hull* removed. Types include <u>buckwheat</u> and <u>corn</u> groats. Question the source.

Grocery Food Store: Grocery food stores are any type of store carrying a large variety of *foods*, especially *processed* or *prepared food.* Some grocery food stores are large enough to carry a variety of *foods* with more of a selection and some carry *specialty food items.* Grocery food stores commonly carry a variety of *fresh perishable foods* (e.g. <u>fruits</u>, <u>vegetables</u>, <u>some</u> <u>dairy</u>, <u>eggs</u> and *yogurt*). Some *produce* may be *organic*. Some degree of *processed prepared meals* will be GF. You can talk to your local grocery food store manager and request GF items you would like the store to carry. The store will generally stock these items or order them specifically for you. [You might find shopping at *health food grocery stores* easier and with more of a GF selection.] (See *ethnic grocery store, health food grocery store* and *mail order*.)

Ground: To *grind food*. Question the purity and source of ground food. (See *mill, filler* and *bulking agent*.)

Ground Meat or Poultry: Meat and poultry freshly ground in the *deli* section of the *grocery food store* or at the butchers. *Fresh ground 100% pure meat* or *poultry* is GF. Question ground meat loaf for added *filler*, *seasoning* and other food *additives*. (See *patties* and *deli*.)

Ground Spices or Seeds: (See *spice, seasoning* and *spice blends*.)

Grouper: A type of *fish. Fresh pure* and *plain* are GF. (See *fish*.)

Gruviera Cheese: A type of semi-firm *cheese* similar to *Swiss cheese* made from cow's *milk*. Verify GF.

Gruyere Cheese: A type of semi-firm *cheese* made from cow's *milk*. Verify GF. (See *cheese*.)

Guacamole: Guacamole is a type of *dip*. {Fresh avocado dip may contain added *avocadoes, lemon* juice and *seasonings*.} Question all prepared *dips*. (See *dip* for cautions.)

Guaiac Gum: *Gum* obtained from the guaiacum tree. Caution. GF.

Guaran: (See *guar gum*.) GF.

Guar Gum: A type of *gum* derived from the guar *plant*. Guar gum is a *thickener* and *stabilizer*. Caution:

guar gum contains *laxative* properties. GF. (See *gum*.)

Guava: A type of *fruit. Fresh* and *plain* are GF. (See *fruit*.)

Guide Books Publishing Co: To purchase gluten free books and/or gluten free material; write for details or visit the web site. The mailing address is 2113 Washington Lane, Bensalem PA 19020   USA. The web address is www.GlutenFreeCentral.com (See pages 206 and 207.)

Guinea: A type of *fowl. Pure* and *fresh plain* are GF. (See *fowl*.)

Gum: Gums are *natural* or *synthetic substance* used in *food* as a *gelling agent, thickener, stabilizer* or *emulsifier. Natural* gums are obtained from various *plants*/trees. [Look up each type individually.] Question the source.

Gum Arabic: (See *arabic gum*.)

Gum Base: Gum base refers to *natural* or *synthetic substance* used as a *base* for *gum*. Question the source. (See *gum*.)

Gumbo: (See *stew*.) Question.

Gum Gluten: *Wheat gluten*. Avoid.

Guna: (See *pigeon pea*.) GF.

Gunja: *Wheat pastry*. Avoid.

Gyro: Gyros are a type of Greek style *sandwich* served on a *pancake* like *forbidden wheat flour bread*. Avoid. The gyro *sauce* is also questionable. (See *sandwich*.)

Haddock: A type of *fish. Pure fresh* and *plain* are GF. (See *fish*.)

Hake: A type of *fish. Pure fresh* and *plain* are GF. (See *fish*.)

Haldi: (See *turmeric*.)

Halibut: A type of *fish. Pure fresh* and *plain* are GF. (See *fish*.)

Halva: (See *pudding*.) Avoid.

Ham: Ham is *cured pork. Canned* ham contains *gelatin*. {Hams commonly contain added *sweeteners* (e.g. injected *barley malt*).} Avoid *ham flavored* with *forbidden additives*. Question all ham. Choose *pure GF* ham. Some brands of GF ham are labeled. Check for GF purity. (See *pork*.)

Hamburger: Hamburgers are a type of sand*wich* made with a *meat patty* placed in a *bun*. [You can eat the hamburger without the *bun*.] {Hamburger meat *patties* may contain added *seasonings* and *filler*.} Choose 100% pure ground beef patties. Question added *condiments*. (See *burger* and *condiment*.)

Hand Held Mixer: *Kitchen appliance*. A portable mixer held in one hand used to *blend* wet *ingredients*. Clean the attachments well in between uses. (See *mixer*.)

Handkase Cheese: A type of sharp *cheese* from cow's *milk*. Verify GF.

Handvo: A type of *bean* and *wheat flour* cake *baked-good*. Avoid.

Hara Dhania: (See *cilantro*.) GF.

Hard Candy: Solid candy (not soft). A variety of hard candy is GF. (See *candy* for details and specifics.)

Hard Flour: A type of *flour* milled from *hard wheat grains*. Avoid.

Hard Wheat: *Wheat grains* yielding a high content of *gluten*. Avoid.

Haricot Beans: *White beans*. GF.

Hash: Hash is a type of side dish containing beef, potatoes and *seasonings*. Question all ingredients. {Hash may contain added *filler*.} (See *canned foods*.)

Hash Browns: Hash browns are *fried* chopped or sliced *potatoes* sometimes in *patty* form. Avoid hash browns *fried* in *oil* previously used to cook *gluten-containing* foods. Verify GF.

Hato Mugi: (See *Job's tears*.)

Havarti Cheese: A type of semi-soft *cheese* made cow's *milk*. Verify GF.

Hawthorne: A type of *herb*. Fresh and *pure dried* are GF. (See *herb*.)

Hazelnut: *A type of nut. Raw* and *plain* are GF. (See *nut*.)

Hazelnut Butter: *Nut butter ground* from *hazelnuts*. Verify GF.

Hazelnut Oil: A type of *oil* obtained from *hazelnuts*. Verify GF. (See *oil*.)

Health: The term health relates to your well-being (e.g., the condition of your body and mind. (See *health food, diet* and *nutrition*.)

Health Food: Health food is a type of *food* considered more beneficial for your health than ordinary *food* (e.g. *healthy nutritious* food). Types of healthy foods include *natural food*, *organic* food, non-*irradiated food*, non-*genetically modified* food and food without added *chemicals*. [Look up each type individually.] All health food needs to be verified GF. (See *health food grocery store*.)

Health Food Grocery Store: Health food grocery stores are a variety of stores offering healthy *food*. You can find *specialty* GF items at most health food grocery stores not readily available at most regular grocery food stores. Most health food grocery stores will carry *foods* upon a customer request, especially *specialty food items* (e.g. *gluten free foods*). Some health food grocery stores offer discounts on cases or *bulk* buying. There are plenty of privately owned health food grocery stores and many chains of very large health food grocery stores across the United States. To locate a health food store in your area, look in the yellow pages of your local phone book. In my area, there is an abundance of *ethnic* and *healthy food stores*. If this is not the case for you, I suggest mail order, especially for the main staples (e.g. GF *bread*, GF *pasta*, GF *cereal*, GF *crackers*, GF *baking mixes,* GF *supplies* and GF *cookies*). If you travel, I suggest purchasing a book that lists the location of independent, corporate and coop natural food stores across the United States offering specialty food items. (See *resource guide, health food, manufacturer, specialty foods, distributor* and *mail order*.)

Heavy Cream: Heavy cream is a type of *cream* used for whipping. GF. Question the source of any added *gum*. (See *cream*.)

Heirloom: Heirloom is a term meaning original, a type of non-*hybrid*. These ancient varieties have been around for centuries. Heirloom varieties are not GMO.

Hemp: A type of *seed. Raw* and *plain* are GF. Hemp seeds in the United States are irradiated so they will not sprout. (See *seed*.)

Herbal Tea: (See *tea herbal*.)

Herbs: Herb is an umbrella term for various *fresh* or *dried plant parts* used as *seasoning*. All *'fresh'* and *'pure-dried'* herbs are GF. {*Dried* herbs may contain added *filler*.} Always question the least-expensive *dried*-herbs because they most likely contain *filler*. The word herb listed as an *ingredient* is not specific and this makes all *seasoned* foods questionable. Choose *fresh* herbs or *100%* pure *dried* herbs. Good *fresh culinary* herbs include *parsley*, *basil*, *rosemary* and *thyme*. [Look up each

herb individually.] Verify GF. (See *spices* and *seasoning* and see 'herbs in A & F charts.)

Herbs & Spices: *Herbs* and *spices* are various *fresh* or dried *plant parts* used as *seasoning*. All *'fresh'* or *'dried-pure'* herbs and *spices* are *naturally* GF. Question all *powdered* and dried herbs and spices for added *filler* especially *spice blends* (e.g. *curry powder, taco seasoning* and *chili seasoning*). The word 'spice' or 'herb' listed as an *ingredient* is not specific and this makes all seasoned foods questionable. Choose *fresh* herbs and *spices* or *100% pure dried* herbs and spice. Always question inexpensive brands for the possibility of *filler*. [Look up each individually.] Verify GF. (See 'herbs and spices' in A & F charts.)

Herb Vinegar: Herb vinegar is a type of *vinegar* made with *fresh herbs steeped* in warmed *vinegar*. Types of herbs often used in herbed vinegar may include *basil, mint, oregano, rosemary, thyme, tarragon* and *garlic*. The type of *vinegar* is customarily *wine vinegar*. Question the source of *vinegar*. You can home make herb vinegar easily with GF ingredients. (See *vinegar*.)

Herkimer Cheese: A type of semi-firm *cheddar cheese* from cow's *milk*. Verify GF. (See *cheese*.)

Herring: A type of *fish. Pure fresh* and *plain* are GF. Question herring in *brine, marinated* or *seasoned*. Verify GF. (See *fish*.)

Herve Cheese: A type of soft, *bacteria* grown *cheese* from cow's *milk*. Verify GF. (See *cheese*.)

Hexaploid: A *wheat* relative. Avoid.

Hickory Nut: A type of *tree nut. Raw* and *plain* are GF.(See *tree nut*.)

Hidden Ingredient: Hidden ingredients include *ingredients* not visibly listed on a *label*. Question all products for hidden *ingredients* (e.g. *wheat flour* as *filler* or to keep food separated.) [Law does not require the listing of all *food components* on *labels*.] Gluten *byproducts* may be hidden in *sauces, seasonings, dressings, condiments, soups, candy, gravy, broth, self-basting fowl, thickeners, marinades, colorings* and *additives*. (See *contaminated*.)

High Fructose Corn Syrup: (See *fructose* and *corn syrup*.)

Hing: (See *asafetida*.) Caution.

Hi Oleic Acid: *Oleic acid* high in *fat*. (See *oleic acid*.)

Hiyamugi: *Wheat noodles*. Avoid.

Hiziki: A type of *seaweed*. Fresh *pure* and *plain* are GF.

Hogie: (See *sandwich*.) Avoid.

Home Fries: Home fries are *fried* chopped or sliced cooked *potatoes*. Avoid home fries *fried* in *oil* used previously to cook *foods* containing *gluten*. Verify GF.

Homemade: Homemade is a term meaning to make or *prepare* at home or by hand, as opposed to *manufactured commercially*. Homemade foods *prepared* with GF *ingredients*, in a contaminant free environment are generally safer. There are many superior GF *recipe books* available to home-make GF foods. (See *recipe book*.)

Home-Make: (See *homemade*.)

Homeopath: A homeopath is someone who is educated in the treatment-system in which a *patient* is given a minute dose of *natural* drugs that in large doses would produce symptoms of the *disease* itself (e.g., the assumption, like can be cured by like). This type of treatment is not appropriate for *celiac disease* because *celiacs'* need to avoid gluten in all amounts. (See *naturopath* and *nutritionist*.)

Hominy: Hominy is hulled *puffed* and *dried corn kernels*. Hominy is used to make *posole*. Verify GF.

Hominy Grits: Hominy grits is *dried hominy* coarsely *milled*. Verify GF. (See *hominy*.)

Honey: Honey is a type of *natural sweetener* produced by bees from the nectar of *flowers*. This type of *condiment* needs no *refrigeration*. Honey's *natural flavor* depends on the *flowers* to which the bees gathered the nectar. Always question honey with added *flavorings, honey butter* and *honey spread*. Choose *100% GF pure* and *plain* honey.

Honeydew: A type of *melon*. Fresh and *plain* are GF. (See *fruit*.)

Hopfenkase Cheese: A type of medium firm *cheese* made from cow's *milk* sometimes *flavored*. Question added flavorings. Verify GF. (See *cheese* and *flavoring*.)

Hopi Corn: Hopi corn is a type of hard *corn* kernels with multi colors. Hopi *corn* is usually used for Halloween decorations or *popping*. GF. (See *corn* for specifics.)

Hops: A type of *herb*. Fresh *plain* and pure *dried* are GF. (See *herb*.)

Horedin: Horedin is a type of *plant protein (prolamin)* found in *barley*. Individuals suffering from *celiac disease* have a genetic predisposition to the reaction from this *prolamin*. Therefore, avoid barley grains and all relatives of barley *grains*. Also, avoid all *byproducts* of barley grains and barley grain relatives. (See *barley* and *prolamins*.)

Horehound: A type of *spice/herb*. *Fresh* and *pure dried* are GF.

Horno: (See *dried sweet corn*.) GF.

Hors D'oeuvre: Hors d'oeuvres are tiny finger *food* (usually *cooked*) served as *appetizers*. Most hors d'oeuvres are not GF. *Crudités* with GF *dips* are safe. Avoid unless source is known. (See *appetizers* and *special occasion*.)

Horse Bean: (See *fava bean*.) GF.

Horseradish: Horseradish is a type of *spice* and *root*. *Fresh* horseradish *root* is GF. Question *prepared* horseradish *sauce*. (See *sauce*.)

Horsetail: A type of *spice/herb*. *Fresh* and *pure dried* are GF.

Hot Cake: (See *pancake*.) Avoid.

Hot Dog: Sometimes referred to as dogs, hot dogs are a type of *sandwich* made with a *cooked frankfurter* or dog placed in a *bun*. [You can eat the dog without the bun.] {*Meat* hot dogs may contain *fillers* and *additives*.} *Kosher* franks are usually safer. Choose 100% pure all meat GF dogs (free of *nitrates* if possible). Question *condiments* used to dress the dog. (See *frankfurter*).

Hot Peppers: (See *jalapeno pepper*.)

HPP: (See *hydrolyzed plant protein*.)

Huckleberry: A type of *fruit*. Fresh and *plain* are GF. (See *fruit*.)

Huitlacoche: (See *corn smut*.)

Hull: Hulls are the indigestible outer *coating* of *seeds/grains*. Question the source. (See *bran*.)

Hulled: Hulling is a process where the *hull* of *seeds/grains* are removed. [Hulling a *gluten grain* does not render it GF.] (See *hull*.)

Humectant: Humectants are *substances* helping *food* absorb or retain *moisture*. Question the source.

Hummus: A type of bean *dip* made with cooked *garbanzo beans*, *oil*, *garlic* and *lemon* juice. Question the source of all ingredients. Verify GF. (See *dip* for details and specifics.)

Hushpuppies: A type of *cornmeal batter dumpling*. Question the possibility of a combination of *wheat flour* and *cornmeal* mixture. Avoid unless source is known. (See *batter*.)

Husk: Husk is the outer *coating* or layer of a *plant*. (See corn husk.)

HVP: (See *hydrolyzed vegetable protein*.)

Hyacinth: A type of *spice/herb*. *Fresh* and *pure dried* are GF.

Hyacinth Bean: A type of *bean*. GF.

Hybrid: Hybrids are any *plant* resulting from a crossing of two *plants* with different *genetic* constituents. This also applies to *animals* (cross species). Question the source. (See *heirloom*.)

Hydrate: To add *liquid* (usually *water*). Some *instant* and *dehydrated foods* need to be re-hydrated. Foods expand when hydrated.

Hydrocolloids: *Natural* or *synthetic substances* used in *food* as *gelling*, *stabilizing* and *emulsifying* agents. Question the source.

Hydrogenated: A process where hydrogen gas is added to a *food* (usually *oil*) in a *chemical* reaction to prevent rancidity. [Hydrogenated *food is* not *digestible*.] Caution. Question the source. (See *hydrogenated oil*.)

Hydrogenated Oil: A type of *oil hydrogenated*. Hydrogenated oil is used to make *margarine*. The majority of hydrogenated oils are GF. Caution. Verify GF. (See *hydrogenated*.)

Hydrolysis: The breaking down of *proteins* by *acid* or *enzyme*. Question the *plant source*. (See *protein* and *hydrolyzed plant protein*.)

Hydrolyzed Plant Protein (HPP): A type of *protein* obtained from *plants* (e.g. *corn*, *soy*, *peanuts* or *wheat*). HPP is usually defined. HPP is used as a flavoring agent. Question the source.

Hydrolyzed Vegetable Protein (HVP): A type of *protein* obtained from *vegetables* (e.g. *corn*, *soy*, *peanuts* or *wheat*). Question the source. (See *hydrolysis*.)

Hydroxpropylmethyl Cellulose: A type of *gum* derived from *cellulose*. GF. (See *cellulose*.)

Hydroxylated: Hydroxyl is introduced into a *food* to make it more *soluble*. Caution. Verify GF.

Hypoallergenic: Any *product* not likely to cause an *allergic* reaction. Caution: hypoallergenic does not guarantee 'free of all allergenic *substances* and/or the product will not cause an allergic reaction'. (See *hypoallergenic food*.)

Hypoallergenic Food: Hypoallergenic foods are *foods* not likely to cause an *allergic* reaction. Hypoallergenic foods must list the *allergenic substance* for which they purport absent in the food. Hypoallergenic foods must reveal the *common name* or *unusual name* and quantity or proportion of each *synthetic*, *plant* or *animal ingredient* source. Hypoallergenic foods must also list any treatment or *processing* that would change the *ingredient* and/or *foods allergenic* properties. Some food *ingredients* are exempt from a documentation of their *components* except for *hypoallergenic foods*. Certain *ingredients* not necessarily defined in regular foods are defined in hypoallergenic foods (e.g. *spices*, *seasoning*, *sweeteners*, *flavoring* and *coloring*). At present time, the FDA has no specific *labeling* regulations for the term '*gluten free*'. The FDA expects processors to abide to the policy on 'hypoallergenic foods'. If you would like the labeling laws for processors to change, write the *Food* and *Drug Administration 5600 Fishers Lane, Rockville MD 20857*. Let them know you would like '*gluten*' listed as a hypoallergenic food. [Foods *labeled* made without gluten, do not mean the *food* was prepared without the possibility of *gluten contamination*.] (See *label reading* and *FDA*.)

Hyssop: A type of *spice/herb*. Fresh and *pure dried* are GF.

Ice Cream: A type of *frozen dairy* product made with *milk* and *sweetening agents*. {Ice cream may contain added *grain byproducts*, *fillers*, *sweeteners*, *gums*, *flavorings*, *stabilizers*, *colorings*, *alcohol* or *enzymes*.} Several ice creams are GF. Always question ice cream. Question added *toppings*. Choose ice cream made with the *purest ingredients*. (See *ice cream cones* and *dairy* and also see 'desserts' in A & F charts.)

Ice Cream Cones: Ice cream cones are *edible* cones used to hold scoops of *ice cream*. Ice cream cones are typically made with *forbidden wheat flour*. *Commercially prepared* GF *ice cream* cones are available only through *specialty companies*. (See *special resources*.)

Ice Milk: Ice milk is a type of *dessert* similar to *ice cream*, but with less *fat* and *milk* solids. {Ice milk may contain added *filler, sweeteners, flavorings, gums, stabilizers* and *colorings*.} Several ice milks are GF. Question the source of all ingredients. (See *ice cream*.)

Icing: (See *frosting*.)

Icing Sugar: (See *powdered sugar*.)

Idaho Potato: A type of *russet potato*. GF. (See *russet potato*.)

Identified Ingredients: Identified ingredients are *ingredients* listed in the *ingredient* section. Not all labeled *ingredients* are clearly identifiable (e.g. *starch, flavoring, coloring* and *sweetener*). Question the source of all ingredients. (See *ingredients, unidentified ingredients* and *hidden ingredients*.)

Ideopathic Steatorrhea Disease: (See *celiac* disease.)

Illness: (See *disease*.)

Imitation: Imitation is a blanket term for a variety of *substances* made with *natural* or *synthetic chemicals*. Imitation *substances* can also be *natural substances*, but derived from sources other than the *food* it is *imitating*. [Imitation *substances* are from sources other than the *plant* part it names.] Imitation *substances* are generally *unnatural*. Caution: anything imitation is still questionable. Question all imitation foods and/or ingredients. Risky. (See *sensitive*.)

Imitation Bacon: A type of fake *bacon*. Avoid. (See *bacon* and *imitation*.)

Imitation Cheese: A type of fake *cheese*. Imitation cheese is sometimes referred to as a *dairy product*. Question all imitation cheeses. Risky. (See *cheese, imitation* and *cheese spreads*.)

Imitation Coloring: Imitation colorings are derived from sources other than the *color* it names. {Imitation colors may contain added *sweeteners, colorings, preservatives, alcohols, oils* and *emulsifiers*.} Question the source. Caution. (See *imitation* and *colorings*.)

Imitation Flavoring: Imitation flavorings are derived from sources other than the *flavor* it names. [*Flavorings* derived from sources other than the *aromatic plant* part *flavor* it names.] {Imitation flavors may contain added *sweeteners, colorings, preservatives, alcohols, oils* and *emulsifiers*.} Question the source. Caution. (See *imitation* and *extract*.)

Imitation Food: Imitation foods are *foods* derived from sources other than the food named (e.g. *imitation bacon, imitation meat* and *imitation seafood*). Imitation *foods* are very risky. {Imitation foods may contain filler.} Question all imitation foods. Risky. (See *imitation* and *food*.)

Imitation Ingredient: (See *imitation, artificial* and *ingredient*.)

Imitation Meat: A type of fake *meat. Imitation* meat is very risky. Question. (See *meat* and *imitation*.)

Imitation Seafood: A type of fake *seafood. Imitation* seafood is very risky. Question all. (See *imitation* and *seafood*.)

Imitation Sweetener: (See *artificial sweetener* and *imitation flavoring*.)

Imitation Vanilla: A type of *vanilla flavoring* composed of *artificial substances*. Question the source. Caution.

Imli: (See *tamarind*.) GF.

Immature Cheese: Fresh, *un-ripened cheese*, as opposed to *aged mature cheese*. Verify GF.

Immersion Blender: A convenient *blender* that immerses into a beaker to mix a small amount (usually one serving) of *food* rather quickly. This hand held electronic *kitchen appliance* is one of the best travel tools. Clean well between uses. (See *blender*.)

Immune System: The immune system is the body's interactive system initiating the response to fight off sickness and *disease*. One of the major concerns for *celiacs* is a *weakened immune system*. For *celiacs*, the body's immune system rebuilds by avoiding the offending *protein* from *gluten*. *Celiacs* should always be concerned with their immune system. The immune system of certain *celiacs* must constantly be monitored (e.g. especially infants and the elderly). Some *celiacs supplement* their *diet* to help rebuild their immune system, from *nutrients* lost from prior damage to the *villi* in the *intestinal tract*. *Celiacs* must avoid *gluten* to maintain a healthy immune system. (See *autoimmune disorder, weaken immune system, disease, supplement* and *nutrition*.)

Impurities: *Foods* that are *contaminated* with *gluten* are considered impure not *pure*. Impurities are *substances* that *contaminate* something else. (See *adulterated* and *contaminated*.)

Inactive Ingredient: (See *inert substance*.)

Indian Corn: (See *flour corn*.) GF.

Indian Pudding: *Pudding* made with *cornmeal*. {Indian pudding may contain added *sweeteners, spices* and seasonings.} Question the cornmeal's purity. Verify GF.

Indigestible: Any *edible ingredient* and/or *food* the *digestive system* is unable to *metabolize* and/or absorb *nutrients* from is considered indigestible. Some *ingredients* put in *foods* are indigestible (e.g. *paraffin*). Celiacs cannot properly digest *forbidden gluten grains* and their grain *byproducts*. Caution. Avoid indigestible ingredients if possible. (See *digestive system*.)

Inert Ingredients: (See *inert substance*.)

Inert Substance: Inert substances are *inactive ingredients*. Inert substances are non-reactive and frequently used in, *medications*. Inert substances may include *binders, disintegrates, preservatives, antioxidants, starch, fillers, colorings, dilutents, coatings, sweeteners, stabilizers, dextrates, dextrin* and other *food agents*. Question the source.

Infant Formula: Call the infant formula companies you favor and request their *allergen/gluten free* product list. {Formulas may contain added *sweeteners, fillers, starch, flavorings* and other *food agents*.)

Infuser: (See *tea infuser*.)

Ingredient: Ingredient is an umbrella term for various *edible food substances* used in *recipes* and/or as a *component* part of a *mixture*. Ingredients may be *natural* or *artificial* and living or non-living. Not all ingredients used in *foods* are beneficial to your health. *Labeled* ingredients are listed in descending order of their proportion by weight. Ingredients may be a combination of one or more ingredients (e.g., an ingredient combined to form a unit of food). Not all ingredients or components of ingredients performing a function 'in' or has any effect 'on' a *food* are defined. [Law does not require the listing of all *food components* on *labels*.] Not all listed *ingredients* are clearly identifiable (e.g. *starch, flavorings, colorings* and *sweeteners*). Question all ingredients. Avoid all ingredients containing *forbidden gluten* and *gluten byproducts*. Choose *100*% *pure* GF *ingredients*. Verify all ingredients are GF. Some specialty GF ingredients used in *recipes* are available only through *specialty companies*. (See *hypoallergenic foods, label* and *specialty foods*.)

Ingredient Section: The ingredient section is the area of a food *label* listing *ingredient* information about the food product. Not all ingredients or components of ingredients performing a function 'in' or has any effect 'on' a food are listed. (See *ingredients* and *label*.)

Inherited: Inherited refers to genetically resulting from the *genes* of biological *relatives*. Relatives of gluten free patients may be more adversely affected than others when introduced to *gluten*. (See *genetic*.)

Inhibitor: Inhibitors are *substances* reducing the action of another. Question the source.

Inorganic: Inorganic substances are composed of *minerals* as opposed to living *material* (e.g. *animal* or *plant*) and also a *chemical compound* not containing *carbon*. (See *organic*.)

Insecticide: Insecticides are *natural* or *chemical substance* used to kill insects. *Chemical* insecticides are harmful to the *immune system*.

Avoid if possible. Wash fresh produce well. Buy *organic* produce to avoid harmful insecticides. (See *immune system* and *organic*.)

Insoluble: A term for any *substance* that will not dissolve in *liquid*.

Instant: Instant food and drinks are *food* and *drinks precooked, premixed* or *powdered* that can be *prepared* quickly. Instant food lack the *nutritional* value of fresh foods. Instant foods are risky. Question carefully. (See *processed foods* and *prepared* foods.)

Instant Coffee: Instant coffee is a type of coffee in a *powdered* form, prepared to add to hot water to make a hat *beverage* quickly. Question added *wheat flour* in instant coffee. The safest *coffee* is *fresh-milled* from *plain* GF *coffee beans*. Some brands of instant coffee are GF.(See *coffee*.)

Instant Flour: Highly *processed wheat flour*. Avoid. (See *flour*.)

Instantized Flour: A type of readily pourable *wheat flour*. Avoid.

Instant Potatoes: (See *potatoes instant*.)

Instant Rice: *Precooked* white or brown *rice*. Instant rice lacks nutrition. Verify GF. (See *rice*.)

Intestinal Flora: (See *flora*.)

Intestine: The *intestines* are one of the major parts of the *digestive system*, absorbing *nutrients* from *food*, via the *villi*. The *villi* become damaged when people with *celiac disease* consume the offending *gluten proteins* (e.g., the prolamins *gliadin* found in *wheat*, *horedin* found in *barley* and *secalin* found in *rye*). Celiac disease has a specific response to gluten (e.g., *gluten* provokes an *autoimmune* response by the body, which then damages the lining of the intestines. *Acidophilus* (good *bacteria*) will help restore intestinal *flora*. Various *unnatural, synthetic, artificial* and *chemical substances* adversely affect the gastrointestinal tract. Choose *fresh, pure organic GF foods* whenever possible. (See *fresh, pure, organic, villi, flora, celiac disease, gastroenterologist* and *acidophilus*.)

Intoxicant: Intoxicant *substances* cause a person to become intoxicated. (See *alcohol*.)

Invert Sugar: Invert sugar is a type of *sugar* produced from *glucose, fructose* and *sucrose* by a visible inversion of *sucrose*. Invert sugar is produced *synthetically* and occurs *naturally*. Caution. Question *additives*. Verify GF. (See *sugar*.)

Invert Syrup: A type of *sugar* broken down with an *acid* while being heated into *syrup*. Caution. Question *additives*. Verify GF. (See *syrup*.)

Iodine: Iodine is a type of nonmetallic *crystalline* halogen element. Iodine is a germicide and antiseptic. Iodine is in the preparation of *dyes, medicines* and *alcohol* solutions (e.g., *tincture of iodine*). Iodine is a concern for those with *dermatitis herpetiformis* (DH). Individuals with *DH* are advised to avoid iodine. Caution. (See *sea salt*.)

Iodized Salt: Iodized salt is a type of refined table salt with *iodine* added. {Iodized salt may contain potassium iodine, *dextrose, stabilizers* and a *bleaching agent*.} Individuals with *DH* are advised to avoid iodine and must choose un-iodized *salt*. [*Natural sea salt* contains *a natural organic form of iodine* that may not affect individuals who may react to the *synthetic iodine* frequently added to *refined table salt*.] Caution. Verify GF. (See *sea salt* and *iodine*.)

Irish Moss: A type of *seaweed*. *Carrageen gum* is derived from Irish moss. GF. (See *carrageen gum*.)

Irradiated: Irradiated foods and/or ingredients are treated with the exposure of ionizing *radiation* (e.g. gamma radiation, x-rays or electrons). Irradiation *inhibits sprouting* and insect infestation and reduces the *natural* process of *mold* or *bacterial* growth. Irradiation does not render gluten containing food gluten free. Choose *organic* non-irradiated food if possible. Irradiated *seeds, beans* and *grains* will not sprout. (See *organic*.)

Isoascorbic Acid: (See *ascorbic acid*.) GF

Isolate: I*solates are substances* that separate themselves or other *substances*. Isolate are also biological *materials* or *chemical microorganisms* grown in a laboratory. Question the source.

Italian Dressing: Italian dressing is a *seasoned oil* and *vinegar mixture*. {Italian dressing may contain added *thickeners* and *gums*.} Question all ingredients and if the *vinegar* is GF. (See *dressing*.)

Italian Ice: Italian ice is a type of *frozen dessert* made with finely ground ice and added *flavorings*. Most Italian ice are GF. Verify GF. (See *colorings* and *flavorings*.)

Italian Rice: (See *risotto rice*.) GF.

Jack Cheese: (See Monterey Jack *cheese*.) Verify GF.

Jackfruit: A type of *fruit*. *Fresh* and *plain* are GF. (See *fruit*.)

Jacobs Cattle Bean: A *heirloom bean* similar to the *pinto bean*. GF.

Jaggery: A type of *unrefined sugar*. Verify GF. (See *unrefined sugar*.)
Jalapeno Peppers: A type of *vegetable. Fresh* and *plain* are GF. If preserved; question the preserving *brine, vinegar* and *seasonings*.
Jam: Jam is a type of *fruit spread* made with *cooked fruit puree*. Question added *sweeteners* and *food agents*. A variety of jams are GF. Verify GF. (See *fruit spread*.)
Jambalaya: A Creole type of *stew* served with *rice*. {Jambalaya may contain added *seasonings* and *thickeners*.} Question all ingredients. If *ham* is in the *recipe*, verify its GF.
Jarisberg Cheese: A *Swiss* style *cheese* from cow's *milk*. Verify GF.
Jeera: (See *cumin*.)
Jejunum: The jejunum is the section of the *intestines* situated between the duodenum and the ileum, whose main function is the *absorption* of *nutrients* from *digested foods*. (See *intestines, absorption, nutrients, villi* and *digestion*.)
Jelly: Jelly is a type of clear *fruit spread* made with *fruit juice* and sometimes *pectin*. Question added *sweeteners* and *food agents*. A variety of jelly are GF. Verify GF. (See *fruit spread*.)
Jellybeans: Jellybeans are a type of *candy* in small size pieces. {Jellybeans may contain added *sweeteners, flavorings* and *colorings*.} All are questionable. Verify GF. (See *candy* for specifics.)
Jerky: Jerky is a type of *dehydrated meat* and *poultry*. Question added *flavorings* and *food agents*. Choose *pure plain* GF *jerky*. [*Vegetarian* jerky frequently contains *forbidden wheat*.] Verify GF. Several *commercially prepared* jerky is GF.

Jicama: A sweet tasting *starchy tuber vegetable*. Jicama must be peeled before consumed. *Fresh* and *plain* are GF. (See *vegetable*.)
Jinengo: A sweet tasting starchy *tuber* vegetable. Jinengo must be, peeled before consumed. *Fresh* and *plain* are GF. (See *vegetable*.)
Job's Tears: A type of *heirloom grain*, closely related to *corn* considered safe. GF. (See *grains*.)
Johnny Cake: (See *pancake*.) Avoid
Juice: Juice is a type of *beverage* prepared from *fresh fruits* or *vegetables* or from *artificial* sources. Freshly juiced *pure fruit* and *vegetable* juices are GF. {Commercially prepared juice may contain added *sweeteners, caramel, preservatives, invert sugar, pH adjusting agents, antifoaming agents, flavorings* and *colorings*.} Many commercially *prepared* juices are obtainable GF. Choose *100*% *pure commercially prepared* GF juice or *home-make*. Verify GF. (See *fruit juice* and *vegetable juice*.)
Juicer: A juicer is a type of *kitchen appliance* that *mechanically produces juice* from *raw fruits* and *vegetables*. Choose a quality juicer that gives you the option of adding the remaining *pulp* (the *pulp* is beneficial to your health, especially because of its ability of removing *toxins* from the body). Choose a juicer that will juice solid foods such as carrots and delicate leafy greens such as *parsley* and *spinach*.
Julienne: To easily slice *fresh fruits* and/or *vegetables* into thin matchstick type strips with a *mandoline* or other *kitchen utensil*.
Juniper Berry: A type of *spice*. *Pure* are GF. (See *spice*.)

Kachori: *Wheat pastry.* Avoid.
Kaju: (See *cashew*.)
Kakri: (See *cucumber*.) GF.
Kalakand: (See *pudding*.) Avoid.
Kale: A type of *vegetable*. *Fresh* and *plain* are GF. (See *vegetable*.)
Kalonji: (See *nigella*.) GF.
Kamut: *Durum wheat*. Avoid.
Kanteen: (See *agar*.) GF.
Karaya Gum: A type of *gum* from the stericulia urens tree in India. Caution. GF. (See *gum*.)
Karela: (See bitter *melon*.) GF.
Karhi Patta: (See *curry* leaves.) GF.
Kasa: This type of *food* containing *forbidden grains*. Avoid.
Kasha: Toasted *buckwheat* whole or buckwheat *porridge*. Check for GF purity. (See *buckwheat*.)
Kasha Grits: *Ground* toasted *buckwheat*. Check for GF purity.
Kashi: A *trademark* name for a blend of several *whole grains*. Avoid. (See *grains*.)
Kasseri Cheese: A semi-firm *cheese* from goats or cows *milk*. Verify GF.
Katcha: A term meaning *raw*.
Kau Fu: (See *seitan*.) Avoid.
Kefir: A *fermented* type of sour *milk* *dairy* product typically containing *alcohol*. Caution. Risky. Verify GF.
Kela: (See *banana*.) GF.
Kelp: A certain type of *seaweed*. Kelp is available *fresh* or *dried*. Choose *100*% *pure dried* kelp without *filler*. Check for GF purity.
Keri: (See *mango*.) GF.
Kernel: The core (*nucleus*) part of any *nut*, *fruit*, grain, *seed* or husk (e.g. *corn*). [Look up each individually.] Question the source.
Kesar: (See *saffron*.) GF.
Ketchup: Ketchup is a type of *condiment* made with *tomato puree*. {Ketchup may contain added

vinegar, sweeteners, *spices* and possibly *filler*.} Choose ketchup using *apple cider vinegar*. Verify GF. (See *condiment*.)
Khas: (See *poppy seeds*.) GF.
Kheer: (See *pudding*.)Avoid.
Khichadi: *Rice* and *lentils*.
Khopra: (See *shredded coconut*.)
Kidney: Kidney is a particular *animal* organ, classified as *meat*. *Pure plain kidney* is GF. (See *meat*.)
Kidney Beans: A type of red or white colored *bean* in a kidney shape. GF. (See *bean*)
Kielbasa: A type of *smoked sausage*. Question. (See *sausage*.)
Kippers: A type of *fish*. *Pure fresh* and *plain* are GF. (See *fish*.)
Kishmish: (See *raisin*.) GF.
Kitchen: The kitchen is the place where *foods* are *prepared* and *cooked*. The kitchen must be *contaminant* free. Areas of most concern are *gluten crumbs* on the counter and in the *toasters* and *condiments*. It helps to stay organized. This includes keeping a GF grocery food list. (See *kitchen supplies* and *special resources*.)
Kitchen Supplies: There is special equipment available that makes GF food preparation and *cooking* safer and more efficient. Useful kitchen tools for GF food preparation include the following: *coffee mill, tea infuser, grain mill*, GF *recipe books* and an extra *toaster* and *flour sifter*. If your new to cooking, the following is a list of all the kitchen supplies you will need to home cook GF foods: can opener, immersion blender, colander, citrus juicer, garlic press, mortar and pestle, nutcracker, pastry brush, potato peeler, sieve, spatula, scraper,

strainer, vegetable brush, cheese grater, nutmeg grater, knives, measuring cups and spoons, utensils, sandwich bags, plastic wrap, coffee mill, cutting board, dish cloth, extension cord, food processor, hand grain grinder, mandaline, muffin pan, nutcracker, thermometer, paper bags, storage bags, sponge, toaster oven, wax paper, glass baking dishes with storage lids, aluminum foil, dish soap, muffin papers, paper towels, parchment paper, produce wash, dish soap and a pan and pot (both with lids). (See *kitchen*.)

Kitchen Utensils: (See *utensils*.)

Kiwi: A type of *fruit*. *Fresh* and *plain* are GF. (See *fruit*.)

Knish: *Wheat dough pastry*. Avoid.

Kofta: *Vegetable* balls. Question the source of all ingredients.

Kohlrabi: A type of *vegetable*. *Fresh* and *plain* are GF.

Koji: An *ingredient* used in *rice malt*.

Kombu: *A type of seaweed*. Kombu is a *natural flavoring*. *Fresh* and *plain* are GF. (See *seaweed*.)

Korma: A type of thick *sauce*. Question the source of all ingredients. (See *sauce*.)

Kosher: Kosher is a term meaning acceptable for *Passover*. To prepared *pure* under Jewish law for a religious ritual. Kosher <u>*dairy*</u> and <u>*meats*</u> are never combined.

Kosher Salt: A certain type of *salt* that is *kosher* and *additive* free. GF. (See *sea salt* and *kosher*.)

Kraut: A type of *vegetable*. *Fresh* and *plain* are GF. (See *sauerkraut*.)

Kudzu: Kudzu is a type of tasteless *dried nutritious starch root* used as a *natural thickening* and *stabilizing agent*. You can *substitute* kudzu for

cornstarch as a *thickener* in a good number of *recipes*. Kudzu is available at *health food grocery stores* and by *mail order*. GF.

Kuminost Cheese: A semi-firm *cheese* from cow's *milk*. Question added *seasoning*. Verify GF.

Kumquat: A type of *fruit*. Fresh and *plain* are GF. (See *fruit*.)

Kuzu: (See *kudzu*.) GF.

Label: A label is a gummy type of sticker sometimes moistened before applied. Avoid licking the *glue* on labels. Labels are also a piece of paper attached to a food product identifying the food and/or listing certain food and *manufacturing* information. Labels sometimes contain *preparation* instructions. Labels do not always list *gluten*. (See *glue* and *label reading*.)

Label Reading: Individuals with a *gluten-intolerance* must read *labels* carefully. Some companies *label* potential *allergens* not included in their *products*. [Gluten is not considered an allergen.] Labels do not always list the possibility of *gluten* foods. Not a lot of GF food products are labeled. Make sure the label states *gluten free* (GF) not just *wheat free* (*WF*). A good number of GF *labeled*-foods are available at *health food grocery stores* and through *specialty mail order companies*. *Labels* are not always marked clearly. Some GF *foods* not labeled GF are actually themselves GF. Some products may appear GF according to their *label*, but are not. This is confusing and difficult especially to the newly diagnosed *celiac* and/or extremely *gluten sensitive*. [This is where a GF *food product list* comes in handy.] Some *manufacturers* list *manufacturing* information (e.g., the companies name, phone number, web site and mailing address). *Manufactures* suggest calling them with product questions. If you call a *manufacturer* about a certain product, have as much information as possible on hand (e.g., product name, bar code and *manufacturing date*). Most *manufacturers* will tell you plenty about a particular product and others may need to get back to you. Sometimes calling a company may not be of any help at all. If after calling a *manufacturer*, you still feel unsure or questionable about a particular food product, then avoid that product until certain. A *manufacturer* may claim a product is GF, but the food may contain *gluten*. [Mistakes are made!] A food may be GF during production, at the time you call, but then next months batch, may contain different *ingredients* or a different method of production. [*Ingredients* can change as much as from batch to batch.] Manufacturers change ingredients, so always read labels even on your favorite GF foods. This *diet* is very complex and you cannot expect people to understand the diets' complexities or that a food is absolutely GF. Unless a product *label* states GF, you cannot be positively sure. Remember how difficult understanding the GF *diet* was for you. You must always read the *ingredients*. Even read the *ingredients* on products *labeled* GF. [I have personally, on a rare occasion seen *gluten* (e.g. *barley malt*) listed as an *ingredient* in a food labeled GF.] You may find reading labels on *healthier foods* that contain *basic ingredients* easier. Foods in *health food grocery stores* seem to have fewer *ingredients* and most of these *ingredients* are common and recognizable. Look for the words '*pure*' on *labels*. [Only the word '*pure*' means *pure*. The term *100%* does not mean *pure*.] Read *labels* carefully and look for 'red-flag' items (e.g. *gluten grains, gluten grain byproducts* and *forbidden flavorings, colorings, excipients, fillers, emulsifiers, stabilizers, vinegars, cereal protein, sweeteners, preservatives, binders, food starch, certain fats/oils, additives* and other *food agents*). The safety of every *food* item is impossible to check with *label* reading alone. Law does not require the listing of all *food components* on *labels* and then there is the possibility of *cross contamination*. Some *food* stores hand out lists of in-store GF foods. You must still read *labels*, because these lists are not accurate. Nor are these lists complete or comprehensive. [I frequently come across items printed on GF hand out lists that I know are not GF.] Learn to recognize the names of ingredients you 'do not' want in your food. An abundance of *labeled* GF foods are available from *specialty companies*. The majority of foods labeled GF are available through *specialty companies*. *DH* and *CD* patients must read the *ingredients* on every *label*, on every product, every time. [*Foods labeled* 'made without *gluten*', do not mean the *food* was prepared without the possibility of *gluten contamination*.] Verify all foods and food ingredients are GF. Avoid all food questionable.

(See *100%*, *pure*, *natural*, *basic*, *gluten free*, *hypoallergenic food*, *special resources*, *special companies* and *contamination*.)

Lactalbumin: Lactalbumin is obtained from milk. (See *dairy*.)

Lactase: Lactase is a *substance* obtained from *yeast*. Verify GF.

Lactic Acid: A *substance* obtained from the *fermentation* of certain *plants* and *dairy products* (*corn* or *milk* based). GF. (See *aid*)

Lactose: Lactose is a type of *sweetener*. Lactose is *sugar* obtained from *milk* and *whey*. Some *celiacs* are *intolerant* to lactose (this is commonly temporary). *Dairy products* made from goats and sheep are easier to digest than *dairy products* made from cow's *milk*. GF. (See *lactose intolerant*.)

Lactose Intolerant: A condition where someone has insufficient *lactose enzymes* responsible for *digesting* lactose (*milk sugar*). Lactose intolerance is usually temporary for the *newly diagnosed celiac* (e.g., until the *digestive system* heals). Healing can be between three-six months. (See *lactose*.)

Laddu: *Wheat flour* balls. Avoid.

Lady Fingers: Individual size *sponge cake* usually made with *wheat flour*. Avoid. (See *baked-goods*.)

Lager: (See *beer*.) Avoid.

Lal Mirch: (See jalapeno *peppers*.)

Lamb: A type of *meat*. *Pure fresh* and *plain* are GF. (See *meat*.)

Lancashire Cheese: A type of medium-firm cows *milk cheese*. Verify GF. (See *cheese*.)

Larch Gum: A type of *gum* from larch trees. GF. (See *gum*.)

Lard: *Clarified fat* from *pork*. {Lard may contain *bleaching* and *emulsifying agents*.} Verify GF.

Lasagna: Lasagna is a layered dish usually made with *forbidden pasta*. {Lasagna may contain added *sauce*, *egg*, *fillings* and *ricotta cheese*.} You can *home make* lasagna with GF *ingredients*. [Look up each ingredient individually.]

Lassi: A type of *beverage* yogurt *drink*. Question the source.

Latka: A type of *potato pankake* made with *unleavened wheat flour* (*matzo meal*). Avoid. (See *potato pancake*.)

Laurel: A type of *herb*. *Fresh* and *dried pure* are GF. (See *herb*.)

Lavender: A type of *herb*. *Fresh* and *dried pure* are GF. (See *herb*.)

Laxative: Any *substance* with the ability to facilitate bowel movements via the *intestines*. (See diarrhea.)

Leaf Lettuce: A type of *vegetable*. *Fresh* and *plain* leaf lettuce is GF.

Leafy Greens: The *edible* fresh leaves of certain green *plants* with green leaves. GF. (See *vegetable*.)

Leavening Agent: Leavening agents are *acid* and/or *alkali substances* used to increase the volume of *baked-goods*. Leavening agents give *baked-goods* the ability to rise. Types of leavening agents include *baking soda*, *baking powder* and *yeast*. [Look up each individually.] Use GF leavening agents. (See *yeast substitutes* and *batter*.)

Lecithin: Lecithin is a *substance* obtained from either *animal* or *plant* sources (*eggs*, *corn* or *soy*). Lecithin is an *emulsifier* and *texturizer* in *baked-goods*. Verify GF.

Lecithinated Soy Flour: (See *soy flour lecithinated*.) Verify GF.

Leek: A type of *vegetable. Fresh* and *plain* are GF. (See *vegetable*.)

Leftovers: Leftovers are pre-prepared *food* served again for another *meal*. Leftovers are convenient and timesaving. *Mold* grows quickly on leftovers. Leftover food should be *refrigerated* immediately, to prevent *bacteria* growth. Question leftovers for possible *gluten contamination* (e.g., serving *utensils* used for both *gluten* and *gluten free* dishes). Prepare a GF leftover dish before serving the original meal to prevent contamination. (See *sensitivities*.)

Legume: Legumes are *peas* or *beans*. Legume is a term used for over a thousand *species* of *seeds* from the *pods* of a certain *plant*. GF. (See *bean, pea* and *vegetable*.)

Leguminosae: The *botanical* name for *legume*. GF. (See *bean*.)

Leicester Cheese: A type of semi-firm *cheese* made from cow's *milk*. Verify GF. (See *cheese*.)

Lemon: A type of *citrus fruit. Pure fresh* and *plain* are GF. (See *citrus fruit* and *fruit*.)

Lemon Balm: A type of *herb. Fresh* and *pure dried* are GF. (See *herb*.)

Lemon Grass: A type of *herb. Fresh* and *pure dried* are GF.

Lentil: Lentils are a certain type of *bean*, green, orange, yellow, brown or red in color. Lentil *beans* are either whole or *split*. (Neither needs soaking.) Lentil beans will *mill* into *bean flour*. GF. (See *bean*.)

Lettuce: A type of *vegetable. Fresh* and *plain* are GF. (See *vegetable*.)

Leyden Cheese: A type of semi-soft *cheese* made from cow's *milk*, *seasoned* with *spices*. Question added *seasonings*. Verify GF.

Licorice: A type of *candy. Forbidden wheat flour* is routinely used in making licorice. Avoid. *Commercially prepared* GF licorice is available only through *specialty companies*. (See *licorice root*.)

Licorice Root: A type of *spice/herb* and *root. Pure* licorice root is GF.

Lieder Kranz Cheese: A type of semi-soft *cheese* from cow's *milk*. Verify GF. (See *cheese*.)

Light: Light is a term referring to reduced *calories*. Question the *source* used to replace the *calories*. If possible, avoid any product labeled 'lite' or 'light'.

Lima Bean: A type of *vegetable*. Lima beans are *fresh* and/or *dried beans*, less fatty, but more *starchy* than other *beans*. GF. (See *bean*.)

Limburger Cheese: A type of soft *ripened cheese* from cow's *milk*. Verify GF. (See *cheese*.)

Lime: A type of *citrus fruit. Pure fresh* and *plain* are GF. (See *fruit* and *citrus fruit*.)

Limpet: A type of *shellfish. Pure fresh* and *plain* limpets are GF.

Linguine: A type of flat style *spaghetti* generally made with *forbidden flour*. Avoid. (See *pasta*.)

Linoleic Acid: It may be *corn peanut* or *soy* based. Verify. GF.

Liptauer Cheese: A type of soft *cheese* made from goat's *milk*. Verify GF. (See *cheese*.)

Liqueurs: Liqueurs are sweet *flavored alcoholic* after-meal *beverage*. Choose pure GF liqueurs. Verify GF. (See *alcohol*.)

Liquid: Liquids are *fluid substances*. Liquids are either thin (e.g. *broth*) or thick (e.g. *gravy*). The *peptides* in *gluten* are too small to strain, therefore straining does not render *gluten*-containing food GF. (See *thickener*.)

Liquid Aminos: Liquid aminos is an all-*natural* non-*fermented* liquid *vegetable protein*. Liquid aminos is customarily produced from a *vegetable protein* of *pure soybeans* and purified water. This type of *flavoring agent* is high in *naturally* occurring *sodium*. The best liquid aminos does not contain *alcohol*, *preservatives*, *coloring agents*, *additives* or *chemicals*. Liquid aminos' *flavor* is similar to *tamari sauce*, but with a slightly lower *sodium* content. Liquid aminos can *substitute tamari sauce* or *soy sauce* in most recipes. Liquid aminos stores up to 3 years in a cool dark place or refrigerated. Liquid aminos is available at *health food grocery stores* and by *mail order*. GF.

Liquid Medication: Medication is often prepared into a liquid form. Liquids are one of the many forms in which medication and/or supplements are concentrated for ingestion. Some non-gluten free tablet medications are available GF in the liquid form. (See *medication*.)

Liquor: (See *alcohol*.)

Litchi Nut: A type of *fruit*. Fresh and *plain* are GF. (See *fruit*.)

Lite: (See *light*.)

Liver: A type of *animal* organ, classified as *meat*. *Pure fresh* and *plain* liver is GF. (See *meat*.)

Liverwurst: A type of spreadable *seasoned sausage*. Verify GF. (See *sausage* and *lunchmeat*.)

Lobelia: A type of *spice/herb*. *Pure* are GF. (See *spices* and *herbs*.)

Lobster: A type of *seafood*. *Pure fresh* and *plain* lobsters are GF. (See *seafood* and *seafood seasonings*).

Locust Bean Gum: A type of *gum* derived from *carob beans*. GF.

Loganberry: A type of *fruit*. Fresh and *plain* are GF. (See *fruit*.)

Long Grain Brown Rice: *Long grain rice* with the *bran* still intact. (See *brown rice* and *long grain rice*.)

Long Grain Rice: Long grain rice is a term used for *rice* characteristically four times longer than it is wide. Long grain *rice* is either *brown* or *white* in color. [Look up each individually.] Long grain *rice* cooks up light and fluffy, as opposed to *short grain rice,* which cooks up sticky. Cooked long grain *rice* is a great accompaniment to many dishes. Long grain *rice* will *mill* into *flour*, but *short grain rice mills* better into *rice flour*. Question *polished rice*. Verify GF. (See *rice*.)

Long Grain Rice Flour: Long grain rice flour is a type of *grain flour* *milled* from *long grain brown or white rice* grains. [Short grain rice *mills* into a better rice flour.] Check for GF purity. (See *rice flour*.)

Long Grain White Rice: Long grain white rice is a type of *long grain* rice with the *bran* removed. (See *white rice* and *long grain rice*.)

Longhorn Cheese: A type of semi-firm *cheddar cheese* from cow's *milk*. Verify GF. (See *cheese*.)

Long Patent Flour: A type of *flour* *milled* from hard *wheat*. Avoid.

Long Potato: (See *jinengo*.) GF.

Loquat: A type of *fruit*. Fresh and *plain* are GF. (See *fruit*.)

Lotus Root: A *root* type of *vegetable. Fresh* and *plain* are GF.

Louki: (See *zucchini*.) GF.

Low Fat Food: Low fat *food* is a type of food containing less *calories*. Question the *source*. If possible, avoid any product *labeled* low fat. (See *light*.)

Low Methoxyl Pectin: A type of *gum* derived from *pectinic acid*. Caution. Verify GF.

Lunchmeat: Lunchmeat is a type of convenient *meat*. The source of lunchmeat may be *pure meat, meat byproducts* or a combination of both. {Lunchmeats may contain added *preservatives, fillers, starch, flour* and *sweeteners*.} Question the possibility of *contamination* by deli equipment (food slicing machines) and in the preparation area. Choose 'pure' GF lunchmeats. Certain prepackaged pure lunchmeats are GF. Question the source. (See *meat*.)

Lupine Bean: Lupine beans are a type of high *protein bean* used frequently to make bean *pasta*. GF. (See *bean* and *bean pasta*.)

Lutein: A *powdery substance* obtained from algae, egg yolks or certain *plant parts*. Verify GF.

Mac & Cheese: (See *macaroni and cheese*.)

Macadamia Nut: *A type of nut. Raw* and *plain* macadamia *nuts* are GF.

Macadamia Nut Butter: *Nut butter ground* from *macadamia nuts*. Verify GF. (See *nut butter*.)

Macaroni: A type of tube-shaped *pasta* customarily made with *forbidden flour*. Avoid. (See *pasta*.)

Macaroni & Cheese: Mac and cheese is a type of *meal* made with cheese and generally *wheat pasta*. Avoid. You can *home make* macaroni and cheese with GF *ingredients. Commercially prepared* GF macaroni and cheese is available through *specialty companies*. (See *special resources*.)

Macaroons: A type of moist *cookie* typically made with *sugar, eggs* and *almonds* or coconut. A good number of macaroons are GF. Verify GF.

Mace: Mace is a type of *spice. Pure* is GF. (See *spice*.)

Mackerel: A type of *fish. Pure fresh* and plain are GF. (See *fish*.)

Madagascar Bean: A type of large *lima bean*. GF. (See *lima bean*.)

Madeira Cake: *Pound cake*. Avoid.

Madeleine: Individual *sponge cakes*. Avoid. (See *baked goods*.)

Magdalena: Individual *sponge cakes*. Avoid. (See *baked-goods*.)

Magnesium Hydroxide: A type of *additive*. Caution. Verify GF.

Maida: A type of *all-purpose flour*. Avoid. (See *all-purpose flour*.)

Mail Order: You can purchase *specialty gluten free foods* through the mail. Mail order shopping is more convenient but sometimes more costly then local shopping. Many GF mail order suppliers make their own line of GF *foods*. Some GF mail order companies have retail stores convenient for local shoppers. You can call GF mail order companies and request a free catalog. [Get several catalogs from various mail order companies, to compare prices, S & H fees and product selections.] You might want to divide your order between different mail order companies. Various GF mail order companies carry a complete line of GF *ingredients, baking* supplies, *flours, cereals, main dishes, snacks, baking mixes, baked-goods, recipe books* and *kitchen supplies*. A few GF mail order companies also carry *frozen foods*. The *Gluten Free Resource Guide 'a consumers guide for living* *gluten free'* provides a list of GF mail order companies that will deliver gluten free food. Most of the GF *specialty* items are available through mail order companies. (See *health and grocery food stores*.)

Mail Order Company / Supplier: (See *mail order*.)

Maisoor Pak: A *bean dessert*. Avoid unless source is known.

Maize: Maize is a term used for <u>corn</u>. Maize is also a term for *wheat* in foreign countries. Question the source. (See *corn*.)

Maize Meal: A term for <u>cornmeal</u>. Maize meal is also, a term for coarsely ground *barley*, *wheat* or a blend of *grains* in foreign countries Question the source.

Maize Starch: Maize starch is a term used for <u>cornstarch</u>, *barley starch* or *wheat starch*. Question the source. (See *starch*.)

Malabsorption: Malabsorption is the inability of the *digestion system* to absorb *nutrients*. [When consumed, *food* does not *metabolize* through the *digestive system*, nor does it transform into energy.] Individuals with *active CD* generally have trouble absorbing *nutrients*, because of damaged *villi*. (See *villi, active celiac disease, digestion* and *malnutrition*.)

Malabsorption Syndrome: (See *malabsorption* and *celiac disease*.)

<u>Malango</u>: A type of *vegetable*. *Fresh plain* is GF. (See *vegetable*.)

<u>Malic</u> <u>Acid</u>: A type of *flavoring agent* derived from *fruit*. Verify GF.

<u>Mallow</u>: Mallow is a type of *spice/herb*. *Pure* and *fresh* are GF. (See *herbs* and *spices*.)

Malnutrition: Malnutrition is a condition of physical harm (undernourishment) caused by a sickness, *disease (celiac disease)* or the lack of healthy *food*. For *celiacs*, malnutrition is from damage to the *villi* in the *intestinal tract*. Those suffering with *active celiac disease* are actually suffering from malnutrition. Malnourishment is one of the major concerns for *celiacs* (e.g., causing a *weakened immune system*). Some individuals suffering from malnutrition *supplement* their *diet*, to help rebuild their body from lost *nutrients*. *Celiacs* must avoid *gluten* to stay *nourished*. (See *villi, supplement, immune system* and *nutrition*.)

Malpua: A type of *pancake*. Avoid.

Malt: Malt is *hydrolyzed starch* into *sugar*. The source of malt may be from various *germinated cereal grains* (e.g. *barley*, *wheat* or <u>corn</u>). [Look up each individually.] Question the source.

Malted Milk: Malted milk is a type of *milk* with added *malt*. Risky. Question the source. (See *malted milk powder* and *malt*.)

Malted Milk Powder: Malted milk powder is a concentrated form of *powdered malt* and *milk powder* mixture. {Malted milk powder is frequently from *barley*.} Risky. Avoid unless source is known.

Malt Extract: An *extract* obtained from *germinated cereal grains*. Question the source. (See *malt*.)

Malt Flour: A type of *flour milled* from *malted cereal grains*. Question the source. (See *malt*.)

Maltodextrin: Maltodextrin is a type of *malted grain* obtained by hydrolyzing starch or combining *maltol* and *dextrin*. Question the source. (See *malt* and *starch*.)

Maltol: A type of *synthetically* produced *food enhancer*. Maltol may be <u>corn</u> or *wheat* based. Caution. Question the source.

Maltose: A type of *sweetener* produced from a *malt sugar starch*. Maltose may contain a base of *barley*, <u>corn</u>, <u>potato</u>, <u>rice</u>, <u>tapioca</u> or *wheat*. Question the source.

Malt Sugar: (See *maltose*.) Avoid.

Malt Syrup: A type of *syrup* made from *malted cereal grains* (e.g. *barley*, <u>corn</u> or *wheat*). Avoid unless source is known. (See *malt*.)

Malt Vinegar: Malt vinegar is an *vinegar* made from *malted barley* (sour *beer*) or fermented <u>millet</u>, *wheat* or <u>sorghum</u>. {Malt vinegar may contain added *caramel* color.} Although *distilled vinegar* is GF, malt vinegar is not *distilled* and therefore not GF. Avoid.

Malt Wines: Avoid. (See *wine*.)

Manchego Cheese: A type of semi-firm *cheese* made from sheep's *milk*. Verify GF. (See *cheese*.)

Mandoline: This *kitchen utensil* is a hand-held slicing tool for various *raw vegetables* and *fruits*. The mandoline is great for *travel*.

Mango: A type of *fruit*. *Fresh* and *plain* are GF. (See *fruit*.)

Manicotti: A type of large tube-shaped *pasta* customarily made with *forbidden flour*. Avoid. (See *pasta*.)

<u>**Mannitol**</u>: A type of *sugar substitute* good for diabetics. Mannitol may be *corn* or *seaweed* based. Verify GF.

<u>**Manomin**</u>: (See *wild rice*.) GF.

Manteca Cheese: A semi-soft type of *mozzarella cheese* made from cow's *milk*. Verify GF.

Manufacturer: Manufactures are the company that manufactures *food products* for specific companies.

[The company that distributes the manufactured-food is referred to as a distributor.] The manufacture is the company that produces the finished *food/product* from *raw ingredients*. *Raw ingredients* are not always *pure*. *Raw ingredients* need to be verified GF (e.g. *spice blends*, *flavorings*, *fillers*, *stabilizers*, *preservatives*, *additives*, *excipients*, *emulsifiers*, *colorings*, *vinegars*, *starch*, *binders* *oils/fats* and *sweeteners*). Some *specialty-companies* manufacture their own *food/products*. [One manufacturer may manufacturer the same *food* carrying the label of several different companies (e.g. *br*and labels form several different trademark brands).] Not all manufactures are knowledgeable in the area of GF, nor are most receptionists. I, personally, spend countless hours on the phone with people willing to learn about the GF diet. This is one of the reasons why putting a product list together takes time. I also try to encourage producers to consider the GF *diet* when *labeling* products and in designing new *recipes*. I have found their response very optimistic and encouraging. Address all product concerns, questions and ideas directly to the manufacturer. (See *distributor*, *label reading*, *food list*, *raw ingredients* and *compound ingredient*.)

<u>**Maple**</u> <u>**Butter**</u>: A thicker form of *maple syrup*. <u>Choose</u> <u>*pure*</u> <u>*unflavored*</u> maple <u>butter</u>. Verify GF.

Maple Flavored Sugar: Avoid. (See *maple sugar* and *flavoring*.)

Maple Flavored Syrup: Avoid. (See *maple syrup* and *flavoring*.)

Maple Granules: (See *maple sugar*.)

Maple Spread: A thick form of *maple syrup*. Avoid maple spread with unknown added *ingredients*. Verify GF. (See *spreads*.)

Maple Sugar: Maple sugar is a type of *sweetener*. The maple granulates result from *evaporated maple syrup*. Avoid maple-flavored sugar. Choose *pure* maple sugar. Verify GF. (See *maple syrup*.)

Maple Syrup: Maple syrup is a thick liquid *sweetener* obtained from the *sap* of *maple trees*. [The *sap* is boiled until most of the moisture is removed.] This type of *condiment* needs no *refrigeration* unless exposed to intense heat and humidity. The best maple syrup is AA grade. Choose *pure* maple syrup. Avoid maple-flavored syrup. Check for GF purity.

Maple Syrup Flavored: *Maple syrup* with added *flavorings*. Avoid.

Margarine: Margarine is a type of *butter substitute* made with *hydrogenated vegetable oils*. A good number of margarines are GF. {Margarines may contain added *flavors, colors, sweeteners, oils/fats, emulsifiers* and *preservatives*.} Choose margarines made with *100% corn oil*. Avoid margarines with an unknown *vegetable* source and *filler*.

Marigold: A type of *herb*. *Fresh* and *pure dried* are GF. (See *herb*.)

Marinade: A type of *liquid* to which *food* is soaked (*marinated*). {Marinades may contain *vinegar, seasoning, colorings, flavorings* and *gums*.} Question the source of all ingredients. (See *dressings*.)

Marinara: Marinara is type of seasoned *tomato sauce*. Question all ingredients. (See *tomato sauce* and *seasonings*.)

Marinate: To soak *foods* in a *liquid* or *marinade*. (See *marinade*.)

Marine Algae: A type of aquatic *organisms* obtained from fresh or saltwater *sources*. Check for GF purity. (See *agar* and *algae*.)

Marjoram: A type of *herb*. *Fresh* and *pure dried* are GF. (See *herb*.)

Market: (See *grocery food stores*.)

Marlin: A type of *fish*. *Pure fresh* and *plain* are GF. (See *fish*.)

Marmalade: A type of *citrus fruit spread* containing fruit *rinds*. Verify GF. (See *fruit spread* and *rind*.)

Marshmallow: A type of *candy snack food* generally made with *corn syrup*. {Marshmallows may contain added *color, dye, gum* and *flavor*.} Always question. Verify GF.

Marshmallow Creme: A type of spreadable *marshmallow food product*. Questionable. Risky. Verify GF. (See *marshmallow* and *spread*.)

Marshmallow Root: A type of *spice/root*. *Pure* are GF. (See *root*.)

Marzipan: A type of *paste mixture* of *almonds* and *sweeteners*. {Marzipan may contain added *thickeners, colorings, sweeteners* and a *forbidden base*.} Risky. Avoid unless source is known. (See *paste*.)

Masa: Masa is a type of wet *cornmeal mixture* made from *hominy* or *slaked corn*. Verify GF.

Masa Harina: A *cornmeal mixture* used to make *tortillas*. Masa harina is typically made from *dried masa* or *posole*. Verify GF.

Masala: A type of *spice mix*. Questionable. (See *spice blends*.)

Mascarpone Cheese: A semi-soft *triple cream cheese* from cows *milk*. Verify GF. (See *triple cream cheese*)

Mash: *Ground germinated grains* (*corn*, *wheat or barley*) used as a starter. Question the source of the mash and all foods using a mash starter (e.g. *vinegars*).

Matar: (See *peas*.) GF.

Material: Material is any *substance* used in making something. [Look up all material *substances* individually.]

Mathari: (See *crackers*.) Avoid.

Matter: Matter is any *material substance* used in making something. (See *material*.)

Mature Cheese: Any *ripened aged cheese*, as opposed to any *fresh immature* cheese. Verify GF. (See *cheese* and *aged cheese*.)

Maturing Agent: Maturing agents are any *substance* causing food to fully develop (e.g. *sodium* or *chemical*). Maturing *agents* are also considered *bleaching agents*. Verify GF. (See *bleach* and *age*.)

Matzo: *Unleavened bread* made with *wheat flour*. Avoid.

Matzo Balls: *Unleavened dumplings* made with *wheat flour*. Avoid.

Matzo Meal: A type of *unleavened wheat flour/meal*. Avoid.

Mayonnaise: Mayonnaise is a type of *condiment* and/or rich creamy *dressing*. {Mayonnaise may contain added *sweeteners*, *oils*, *vinegars*, *seasonings*, *spices* and other *food agents*.} Mayo is generally not GF, but a few common name *brands* are. Question the source. (See *condiment*.)

Meal: Meal is a term for course-textured *flour* made from any *ground* whole *seed*, *bean*, *nut* or *grain*. Types of meal include *almond*, *corn*, *rice*, *oat*, *wheat*, *barley* or *rye*. Question the source. Meal is also a term for *food* usually eaten at one

time. Most *commercially prepared* meals are not GF. Question the source of all *commercially prepared meals*. {Prepared meals may contain added *thickener*, *preserves*, *flavors*, *colors* and *filler*.} There are very few *commercially prepared* GF meals *labeled* GF. Most labeled GF prepared meals are available through *specialty companies*. A variety of GF labeled meals are sold at *health food grocery stores* and by *mail order*. (See *special resources*.)

Meal Replacement Bar: A meal replacement bar is a type of *nutritional bar* usually eaten to replace one *meal* a day. Meal replacement bars are extremely convenient and a must-have in every *travel bag*. A limited amount of meal replacement bars are GF. Various GF meal replacement *bars* are available at *drug stores*, *grocery food stores*, *health food grocery stores* and by *mail order*. Verify GF.

Meal Replacement Drink: Meal replacement drinks are a type of *nutritional drink* usually consumed to replace one *meal* a day. Meal replacement drinks are convenient. Meal replacement drinks will help you gain *weight*. Meal replacement drinks are typically high in *protein*. A handful of meal replacement drinks are GF. Some *commercially prepared* GF meal replacement *drinks* are available at *drug stores*, *grocery food stores*, *health food grocery stores* and by *mail order*.) Verify GF. (See *protein*.)

Meat: Meat is an umbrella term used for any *edible* mammal. All *pure*, *fresh* and *plain* meats are naturally GF. Question all *prepared* and *processed* meats. {Meats may contain added *color, dyes, sweetener* and *preservatives.*} Avoid *fresh, cooked* and *frozen* meats in *forbidden sauces, gravies* and *creams,* with *pasta, breaded, batter dipped, coated* or *pickled* in *vinegars,* unless all ingredients are verified GF. Question all meat *patties* and *meat loaf.* Avoid most *canned meats.* You are generally safer choosing fresh meats from the *fresh meat* department of the grocery food store. You can talk with a butcher about the *source* of all *ingredients,* meat processing and the possibility of contamination. Choose *100% pure* GF meats. [Look up each type of meat and/or meat organ individually.] (See 'meat' in A & F charts.)

Meat Analog: (See *textured vegetable protein.*) Avoid.

Meatballs: Meatballs are ground *meat* or *poultry* combined with *bread filler, eggs, seasoning* and then shaped into little balls for easy *cooking.* Meatballs are usually made with *forbidden bread filler.* Instead, you can home-make meatballs with *pure fresh ground meat* and GF *ingredients* or *substitute* the meatballs with *homemade meat-sauce.* (See *meat.*)

Meat Binders: Meat binders are *binding agents* for *meat.* Types of include *sweeteners, eggs, gelling* and other *food agents.* Question the source. (See *binder.*)

Meat Extender: (See *textured vegetable protein.*) Avoid.

Meatloaf: Meatloaf is *ground meat* or *poultry* combined with *bread filler, eggs* and *seasonings* and then shaped into a loaf for easy *baking.* Meatloaf is usually made with

forbidden bread filler. Instead, you can home-make meatloaf with *pure fresh ground meat* and GF *ingredients.* (See *meat* and *bread.*)

Meat Tenderizer: Meat tenderizers are *substances* used on *meat* to make meat tender by breaking the meats *fibers.* Meat tenderizers are made with *chemicals* or *natural substances* (e.g., *natural papain* derived from *papaya*). You can tenderize *meat mechanically* with a hand-held pounder. Verify GF.

Mechanically: Mechanically describes a technique performed by hand or with a machine, as opposed to using *substances* or *chemicals.*

Medical Distilled Alcohol: Considered GF. (See *alcohol.*)

Medication: Medications are *pharmaceutical* products. *Gluten* is a minor problem in *pharmaceutical* products. Nevertheless, gluten must be avoided even in relatively small amounts. Gluten is problematic most commonly in tablets and capsules. The concerns are commonly in *inert substances* (e.g. *disintegrates, filler, starch, preservatives, antioxidants, colorings, diluents, dextrin, binders, sweeteners, dextrates, coatings, stabilizers, pregelatinized* and all other *agents*). Question all ingredients in all medication. Question if tablets are coated with forbidden substances. *Prescription drugs free from allergens/gluten are available through the* majority of pharmaceutical companies. You and/or your pharmacist may need to call each pharmaceutical company whenever you get a *prescription* filled to find out if a *prescription* is GF, because a medications *inactive ingredient* can change and the pharmacist may not have this information on hand. [The word *gluten* may not be listed therefore you need to ask what the medication contains and then from that information determine if the medication is GF.] You may need your doctor to call in an alternative *prescription*. If you purchase the generic equivalent, it also needs to be verified GF. There are pharmaceutical companies that will *compound prescription* and *non-prescription* medication, according to your needs thus eliminating potential *intolerances* and/or *allergens*. *Compounding* pharmacists can properly combine any medicine into any required form or preparation free of gluten. To obtain a referred compounding pharmacy call *The International Academy of Compounding Pharmacists* at 1-800-927-4227 and ask for a compounding pharmacy in your area. [Areas include all of the USA and Canada.] You should keep some GF *prescription* and *non-prescription* medications on hand for emergencies (e.g. antibiotics, antihistamines, cold and flu formulas, anti diarrhea medication and acetaminophen). *Topical medications* are considered *nontoxic*. *Medical distilled alcohol* is considered GF. Verify all medication you ingest is GF. (See *compounded medication, prescription medication, drug* and *topical medication*.)

Medium Grain Rice: Medium grain rice is a type of *brown* or *white rice* grain medium in size. Medium size rice grains are closer in size and performance to *short grain rice*, as opposed to *long grain rice*. (See *short grain rice* for characteristics.)

Melba Toast: Melba toast is small pieces of thin dry *cracker*-like *bread* typically made with *wheat flour*. Avoid. Commercially prepared GF melba toast is available only through *specialty companies*.

Melissa: Melissa is a type of *herb*. *Pure fresh* are GF. (See *herb*.)

Melons: Melons are a type of *fruit*. *Fresh* and *plain* are GF. (See *fruit*.)

Menhaden: A type of *fish*. *Pure fresh* are GF. (See *fish*.)

Mesclun: A type of fancy *salad mixture*. Verify GF. (See *salad*.)

Metabolized: Metabolize is a type of biochemical process (e.g., the *chemical* interactions in living *organisms*). When *food* is consumed it metabolizes through the *digestive system* and is transformed into energy. Individuals with active *celiac disease* may have trouble metabolizing their *food* because of damage to the *villi*. (See *villi* and *malabsorption*.)

Methi: (See *fenugreek seed*.) GF.

Methylcellulose: Methylcellulose is obtained from *wood pulp*. Caution. Avoid if possible. (See *wood pulp*.)

Methyl Ethyl Cellulose: (See *carboxymethylcellulose*.)

Mexican Bean: A type of red *kidney bean*. GF. (See *bean*.)

Micci Bread: A type of spiced / *seasoned wheat bread*. Avoid.

Microcrystallinecellulose: A type of *gum* derived from *cellulose*. Question the source. (See *cellulose*.)

Micronizer Mill: This is a type of *mill* used to *grind foods* such as *whole dried beans*, *seeds*, *nuts* and *grains*. The micronizer is a quality *mill* for *flour*, because the pieces of *food* are whirled at high speed, then shattered apart by air pressure, thus, very little heat is created. The result is an extended shelf life for the *milled* product and an increase in its *nutritional* value. (See *mill*.)

Microorganism: Living things (virus, protozoan or bacterium) visible only under a microscope.

Microwave Oven: A type of *kitchen appliance* that *cooks food* with high frequency radio waves. (See *cook*.)

Mictrocrystallincellulose: A type of *additive* derived from *cellulose*. GF.

Mildew: Mildew is a type of *fungi* that occurs *naturally*. Mildew causes *organic* matter to decay. Caution: mildew helps break down the *immune system*. Mildew in *food* and the air should be avoided as much as possible. Prevent mold on *foods* by *refrigerating leftovers* as soon as possible. Prevent mildew in the home environment by cleaning with *natural* cleaning products (e.g. *baking soda, pure glycerin, washing soda* and *apple cider vinegar*) and installing a good air filtration system. [Most *commercially* sold cleaners are flammable, caustic, explosive, harmful to humans, pollute the environment and many of these products sold and used as common household cleaners are not even necessary.] Natural cleaners are safer for humans, the environment and are easy to purchase or prepare. Most ingredients needed to home-make *natural* cleaners are available at regular *grocery food stores*. A variety of *commercially prepared natural* cleaners are available at *health food grocery stores*.] (See *weakened immune system* and *sensitivities*.)

Milk: Milk is a *naturally* GF *dairy product* and *beverage* obtained from female *animals* (e.g. cow, sheep, goat, buffalo, reindeer, camel, mare or yak). Milk is also prepared from *nondairy ingredients* (see *milk nondairy*). *Pure* unflavored dairy milk is GF. Question *fiber* added to some brands of milk (e.g. *oat fiber* or *barley fiber*). Avoid *malted milk* and *commercially prepared flavored milks*. Question *nondairy creamers* and *milk substitutes*. Question if the milk is pasteurized especially for the elderly, very young and individuals with a *weakened immune system*. Verify GF. (See *casein, nondairy milk, milk flavored* and also see 'dairy' in A & F charts.)

Milk Dairy: (See *milk*.)

Milk Flavored: Flavored milk is *dairy* or *nondairy milk* with added *flavorings*. {*Commercially prepared* flavored milk may contain added *sweetener, colors, stabilizers, flavors* and *starch*.} Risky. Avoid unless source is known. You can *home make* flavored-milk with acceptable GF *ingredients*. (See *milk*.)

Milk Nondairy: Nondairy milk is a type of *milk* made without *milk* or *dairy*. Nondairy *milk* is made from *beans, nut, seeds* and *grains* (*barley* and *rice*). Types of GF nondairy *milks* include certain brands of *almond, coconut, cashew, soybean, sunflower seed* and *rice milks*. {Nondairy milk may contain added *filler, gum, flavors, alcohol* or *enzymes*.} Question low amounts of gluten in nondairy milks, including some *barley* in *rice milks*. Several nondairy milks are GF. Verify GF.

Milk Powder: Milk powder is *milk* from which almost all the moisture has been removed. Types of dry *powdered milks* include *regular* and *nonfat*. {Milk powders may contain added *emulsifying agents*.} [*Nonfat milk powder* does not need *refrigeration*.] Several nondairy milk powders are GF. Verify GF.

Milk Protein: Milk protein is a type of *protein* derived from *milk*. Verify GF. (See *protein* and *milk*.)

Milkshake: Milkshakes are a type of *beverage* usually made with *ice cream*, *milk* and *sweeteners*. Many *commercially prepared* milkshakes are GF. {Milkshakes may contain added *chemicals, flavorings, lactose, sweeteners* and other *additives*.} You can *home make* milkshakes with acceptable GF *ingredients*. [Look up each ingredient individually.] Verify GF. (See *ice cream*.)

Milk Sugar: Milk sugar is a type of *sugar* obtained from *milk*. GF.

Milk Toast: Milk toast is *toasted bread flavored* soaked in *milk* and with *sweeteners*. Question all ingredients. (See *bread*).

Mill: Mill is a term used for a mechanical method of *grinding whole foods* into fine or coarse *powdery substances*. *Foods* that will home mill easily include *whole dried beans*, *seeds*, *nuts* and *grains* (e.g. *rice, corn, millet, quinoa, buckwheat* and *amaranth*). These *whole foods* are available at some *grocery food stores*, most *health food grocery stores* and *ethnic grocery food stores* and by *mail order*. Check with each mills *manufactures*-suggestion on what their equipment will *mill*. Some mills will not mill *foods* with a high *oil* content (e.g. *peanuts* and *soybeans*). Although these mills generally mill *defatted ingredients*

(e.g. *defatted peanuts* and *soybeans*). It is very important to sort out any stones, dirt and debris from the foods prior to milling. Types of mills include *blade mills, micronizer mills, stone mills* (considered the best) and *coffee mills* (a must-have for small amounts of soft *ingredients*). You must cool milled *foods* before storing them to prevent moisture build up and possibly *mold*, especially with corn products. [The recommendation is to mill all food *fresh* as needed.] Store milled *beans* and *grains* in the refrigerator up to three months and store milled *seeds* and *nuts* in the refrigerator up to one month. Store milled *beans* and *grains* in the freezer up to six months and store milled *seeds* and *nuts* in the freezer up to three months. Avoid *cross contamination* by milling acceptable GF *ingredients* only in the same mill (e.g., do not mill *forbidden grains* in the same mill used to mill *acceptable grains*). [Look up each type of food you intend to mill individually.]

Millet: Millet is a type of GF *seed*. Millet is not a *grain*, but considered a *grain* because of its *grain*-like similarities. You can *prepare* millet in many dishes. Millet is a nutritious *seed* that will *mill* easily into *flour*. You can purchase *whole* millet seeds at *health food grocery stores* and by *mail order*. (See *millet flour*.)

Millet Flour: Millet flour is a type of *seed flour milled* form *whole millet seeds*. Check for GF purity. (See *millet, flour* and *coffee mill*.)

Milo: A variety of *sorghum*. GF.

Milt: The seminal *fluid* of the male *fish*. GF . (See *roe*.)

Mincemeat: Mincemeat is a type of *condiment* prepared with chopped *ingredients*. Question all *ingredients*.

Mineral: An *essential inorganic substance* for human existence. GF.

Mineral Oil: Mineral oil is a certain type of oil *distilled* from *petroleum*. Caution. GF.

Mineral Water: Mineral water is a type of *pure water* containing a high *mineral* content. GF.

Minnow: A type of *fish*. *Pure fresh* and *plain* are GF. (See *fish*.)

Mint: A type of *herb*. *Fresh plain* and *pure dried* are GF. (See *herb*.)

Mir: Mir is a term used for *cereal grains* (possibly *wheat*). Avoid.

Mirch: (See *jalapeno*.)

Mirin: A type of *fermented condiment* used to *flavor* dishes. Mirin is a *rice wine* slow *brewed* from *sweet rice grains*. Choose unsweetened GF mirin. Verify GF.

Miscellaneous: An assortment of *gluten*-cautions not necessary connected include *communion wafers*, *packaging materials* and *glue* on *packaging material*, *tea* bags, *stamps* and *envelope paste*. [Look up each individually.]

Miso: Miso is a type of *soy* paste *fermented food* used as a *condiment* or *soup* base. Miso is traditionally made with *forbidden barley*. There are types of miso prepared with pure rice or bean based miso. Question the source. *Commercially prepared* dry packaged GF miso is available at *health food stores* and by *mail order*. (See *sensitivities*.)

Mixer: Mixers are any type of hand held or stationary kitchen *appliance* that mixes, beat, whisks and possibly kneads. Clean mixers and all attachments well between uses.

Mixes: Mixes in this book refers to *prepared dry* packages of a blend of *dry ingredients* used to make *baked-goods* (e.g. *bread, muffins, cakes, brownies, pancakes* and *waffles*). [Look up each type individually.] Mixes are added to *moist ingredients* before *cooking*. Most commercially prepared mixes contain *forbidden grain byproducts*. Mixes truly GF will most likely will be labeled. *Commercially prepared* GF mixes are available through *specialty companies*. You can home-*prepare* GF *baked-good* mixes and then store them in individual containers in the *freezer* until needed (adding the moist ingredients before baking).

Mixture: A *mixture* is two or more various *ingredients* combined. [Law does not require the listing of all *food component* mixtures on *labels*.] Question all source of all ingredients in a mixture. (See *mixes*.)

Mochi: A type of *cooked sweet rice*. Verify GF. (See *sweet rice*.)

Modified: (See *modifier*.)

Modified Food Starch: Modified food starches are various *starches* (e.g. corn, potato, rice, tapioca or *wheat starch*) that have been modified. Avoid modified food starch listed as an *ingredient* made from *wheat*. Question the source.

Modified Maltodextrin: (See *modified* and *dextrin*.)

Modified Starch: (See *modified food starch*.)

Modifier: Modifiers are *substances* that (slightly improve or change) *foods*. Modifiers are used to modify *starch*. Modifiers may be *chemical substances*. Question the source. Caution. (See *modified starch*.)

Modifying Agent: (See *modifier*.)

Moisture Controlling Agent: Any *substance* controlling moisture in *food*. Question the source.

Molasses: Molasses is a type of *sweetener* produce by *boiling* the *liquid* obtained from *sugar cane* or *sorghum grains*. Types of molasses include light, dark, black strap and sorghum molasses. Molasses contains small amounts of *minerals*. Choose *pure* molasses (*un-sulfured* if possible.) Verify GF.

Mold: Mold is a type of *fungi* occurring *naturally*, causing *organic* matter to decay. Molds are in *fermented foods, baked-goods, olives* (green), *peanuts, wines, vinegars, teas, dry roasted nuts, xanthan gum, mushrooms, yeast*, some *cheeses, alcoholic beverages* and *supplements*. To avoid mold: soak *dried fruit* in *boiled* water at least one minute, *refrigerate leftovers* immediately and avoid *fermented foods, yeast* and *sweeteners* as much as possible. Avoid mold if possible. (See *sensitivities*.)

Molecules: Molecules are the smallest physical unit of a *chemical compound* existing independently and consisting of one or more atoms held together by chemical forces. (See *enzymes*.)

Mollusk: A type of *fish. Pure fresh* and *plain* are GF. (See *fish*.)

Monihot: (See *tapioca*.) GF.

Monioc: (See *tapioca*.) GF.

Mono & Diglycerides: *Synthetically* produced *fatty acids* used as *binders* and *emulsifiers*. The source may be *corn, soy, wheat* or *peanut* based. Caution. Question the source.

Monocalcium Phosphate: A type of *leavening agent*. Verify GF.

Monoglycerides: *Synthetically* produced. Caution. Verify GF.

Monosodium Glutamate (MSG): MSG is glutamic acid. MSG is a type of *flavor enhancer* obtained from *seaweed, corn, soybeans* or *wheat* or *manufactured* from *sugar beets*. The *sodium salt* of glutamic acid, which is an *amino acid* is also found in *mushrooms*. MSG is found *naturally* in some *fermented foods*, such as *miso* and *soy sauce*. MSG has no *flavor* of its own but enhances the *flavors* of other *foods*. MSG (glutamic acid) may be *specifically identified* as an *ingredient* on a label. MSG is used generously in the restaurant and take-out food industry without mention. Caution. Avoid MSG if possible. Question the source. (See *sensitivities*.)

Monterey Jack: An un-*aged* semi-soft *cheese* from cow's *milk*. Verify GF. (See *cheese*.)

Montrachet Cheese: A type of semi-soft *chevre cheese*. Verify GF.

Mooli: (See *radish*.) GF.

Moong Dal: A type of *dried mung bean* pulse. Verify GF.

Moose: A type of *meat. Pure fresh* and *plain* are GF. (See *meat*.)

Mortar & Pestle: A mortar and pestle is a set of a specific type of bowl (mortar) and pestle (round pummel type handle) made of glass, marble stone or wood. [A mortar and pestle made with stone is one of the best.] This kitchen tool pulverizes *herbs* and *spices* (e.g. *garlic, cori*ander, *seeds, roots*, grains and other *plant parts*). Clean the mortar with a dry *pastry brush* or damp cloth between uses.

Mother of Vinegar: In the process of making *vinegar*, the 'mother' is a layer of *yeast cells* and *bacteria* that converts the *alcohol* into a *natural acetic acid*. *Pure vinegars* such as *unfiltered apple cider vinegar* still contain the mother. (See *apple cider vinegar*.)

Mountain Yam: (See *jinengo*.) GF.

Mousse: A type of *pudding*. Avoid.

Mozzarella Cheese: A type of *stretched-curd cheese*. *Fresh* mozzarella is packed in *whey* or water. Verify GF. (See *stretch curd cheese* and *pizza cheese*.)

MSG: (See *monosodium glutamate*.)

Mucosa: Mucosa is the moist tissue lining of the bodies passages.

Muenster Cheese: A type of semi-soft aged *cheese*. Verify GF.

Muesli: Muesli is a cereal combination typically made with *cereal* flakes (*oats*), *seeds* and *dried fruit*. Muesli is generally not GF. Avoid unless source is known or home-make with GF *ingredients*.

Muffins: Muffins are individual *cake*-like *bread baked-goods*. Most *commercially prepared* muffins are prepared with *forbidden grain byproducts*. *Commercially prepared* GF muffins are available through *specialty companies*. You can *home make* GF muffins with allowable GF *ingredients*. There are many superior *recipe books* available to *home bake* GF *muffins*. (See *baked-goods*.)

Mulberry: A type of *fruit*. *Fresh* and *plain* are GF. (See *fruit*.)

Mullein: A type of *herb*. *Fresh* and *pure dried* are GF. (See *herb*.)

Mullet: A type of *fish*. *Pure fresh* and *plain* are GF. (See *fish*.)

Multi Grain: Multi grain is a term referring to more than one *grain*. Multi grain *foods* most always include *forbidden gluten grains*.

Mung Bean: Small *dried* green or yellow *peas / beans*. GF. (See *bean*.)

Mung Bean Flour: Mung bean flour is a type of *bean flour milled* from dried *mung beans*. It is great for *bean pasta*. Check for GF purity. (See *bean flour* and *bean pasta*.)

Mung Bean Pasta: Mung bean pasta is a type of *bean pasta* made from *mung bean flour*. Verify GF. (See *bean pasta* and *mung bean flour*.)

Mush: Mush is a hot *breakfast* dish (*porridge*) customarily prepared with *cornmeal*. Question the cornmeal purity. Verify GF. (See *cornmeal*.)

Mushrooms: A type of *fungus*. *Fresh* and *plain* mushrooms are GF. (See *fungus* and *sensitivities*.)

Muskellunge: A type of *fish*. *Pure fresh* and *plain* are GF. (See *fish*.)

Muskie: A type of *fish*. *Pure fresh* and *plain* are GF. (See *fish*.)

Mussel: A type of *shellfish*. *Pure fresh* and *plain* are GF. (See *fish*.)

Mustard: Mustard is a type of *condiment* containing *vinegar* and possibly *filler*. {Mustards may contain added *coloring, flavoring* and *filler*.} Avoid *English mustard* because it is prepared with *wheat flour*. *Vinegar* listed as an *ingredient* in mustard is usually *distilled white vinegar* unless specified. *Apple cider vinegar* in prepared mustard is GF. The best types of mustards include German, Creole, Meaux, French Dijon, Chinese and American mustard. Question the ingredients in prepared mustard. (See *vinegar*.)

Mustard Greens: A type of *vegetable*. *Fresh* and *plain* are GF.

Mustard Powder: Mustard powder is a type of *ground spice, ground* from *mustard seeds*. Question the addition of *wheat flour*. You can *home mill whole mustard seeds* easily into powdered mustard and add of rice flour. Verify GF. (See *spices* and *seasonings*.)

Mustard **Seeds**: A certain type of *seed*. *Raw* and *plain* are GF. (See *mustard powder*.)

Mutton: A type of *meat*. *Pure fresh* and *plain meats* are GF. (See *meat*.)

Naan: *Wheat bread*. Avoid.

Naan Khatai: *Wheat cookie*. Avoid.

Nacho: Nachos are a type of Mexican *pizza* made with *tortillas*, *vegetables*, *cheese* and *seasonings*. Question all ingredients. Question that the *tortilla* is *100*% *corn*. (See *nacho seasoning*.)

Nacho Seasoning: Nacho seasoning is a type of *seasoning mix*. Question the source. Risky. (See *seasoning mix* and *nacho*.)

Nama Shoyo: This type of *food* contains *wheat*. Avoid.

Namkin Baati: *Flour balls*. Avoid.

Namkin Shakerpera: (See *cracker*.)

Nan Bread: Nan bread is a type of *wheat flour bread*. Avoid.

Napoleon: A type of cream filled *dough* (typically *forbidden*) *pastry* puff *baked-good*. (See *baked-goods*.)

Nasturtium: A type of *vegetable*. *Fresh* and *plain* are GF.

Natta: A type of Japanese *seasoning / condiment* made from *fermented soybeans*. Question the *soy sauce* source. Verify GF. (See *condiments*.)

Natural: (See *Natural Food*.)

Natural Color: Natural coloring agents are a type of *food coloring* from *natural* sources, but this does not mean it is without *artificial substances*. Natural colors can be either *plant* or *animal* sources. Caution. Question the source. (See *color*.)

Natural Flavor: Natural coloring agents are a type of *flavoring* from *natural* sources, but this does not mean it is without *artificial substances*. Natural flavorings can be either *plant* or *animal* sources. Some *flavorings* are *extracted* with *chemicals* or *alcohol*. Caution. Question the source. Choose *natural* food ingredients for added flavoring (e.g. *applesauce, crushed pineapple, dried fruits, spices, herbs, nuts, seeds, yogurt, sugar, fruit spreads, molasses, maple syrup* and *honey*).

Natural Food: Natural *food* is present in or produced by nature. The term natural is not defined. Natural *ingredients* are not *artificial* or *synthetic*, but this does not mean natural products are without *artificial substances*, nor does it mean the product is *pure*. All natural foods need to be questioned and verified GF. Natural is also a term for minimally *processed food*. Certain *ingredients* not defined are sometimes defined in natural *foods*. The majority of GF natural foods are available at *health food grocery stores*. A variety of GF natural foods are available at *regular grocery food stores* and by *mail order*.

Natural Food Source: Natural food sources are the food source from which an *ingredient* or *food* was derived. The ingredient source of all foods and/or ingredients need to be questioned and/or verified GF. (See *ingredient, component* and *artificial*)

Natural Food Store: (See *health food grocery store*.)

Natural Gum Systems: Natural gum systems are from a combination of several *gums*. {Natural gums may

contain *artificial substances*.}
Question the source.

Naturalist: A naturalist is someone who is educated in the field of natural history (e.g. botany). (See *naturopath* and *nutritionist*.)

Naturally Decaffeinated: Naturally decaffeinated is a term for *food* without *caffeine naturally* (e.g. <u>carob</u>) or *food* to which the *caffeine* has been removed *naturally*, as opposed to using *chemicals* or other *substances* or methods (e.g., <u>coffee beans</u> decaffeinated naturally using pure water). (See *coffee* and *carob*.)

<u>Natural</u> **Salt**: (See *sea salt*.)

<u>Natural</u> **Sea** <u>Salt</u>: (See *sea salt*.)

Natural Sweetener: Natural sweeteners are *natural substances* used to *sweeten food*. The sources of natural sweeteners include <u>fruit</u>, <u>tree sap</u>, <u>plants</u>, <u>bees</u> and *grains*). Specific types of natural sweeteners include <u>sugar</u>, <u>fruit spreads</u>, <u>molasses</u>, <u>maple syrup</u>, <u>honey</u> and *malt syrups*. Always question the source. (See *sweeteners* and also see 'sweeteners' in A & F charts.)

Naturopath: A naturopath is someone who is educated in the field of *natural medicine* (e.g., the belief that *diet*, exercise and other *natural* factors contribute to good *health* and the treatment of *disease*). At present time, the *treatment* for *CD* and *DH* is to eliminate all *forbidden grains* and grain *byproducts* containing the *toxic gluten proteins* from the diet. (See *diet, nutritionist, celiac disease* and *dermatitis herpetiformis disease*.)

<u>Navy</u> **Bean**: A type of small white *kidney bean*. GF. (See *bean*.)

<u>Nectarine</u>: A type of *fruit*. *Fresh* and *plain* are GF. (See *fruit*.)

Neufchatel Cheese: A type of soft *cream cheese*, slightly moister and with less fat than *regular cream cheese*. Verify GF.

Neutralizing Agent: Neutralizing agents are types of *adjusting agents*. Neutralizing agents are *substances* (usually *chemical*) rendering *food* ineffective. [Neutralizing agents adjusts the *acidity* and *alkalinity* balance in *food* by making *food* neither *acid* nor *alkaline*.] Question the source. (See *acidic* and *alkali*.)

Newly Diagnosed Celiacs: Newly diagnosed is a term for a recently diagnosed patient. [Celiac disease can be diagnosed at any *stage* in the *disease*.] There are special concerns for newly diagnosed *celiacs* patients diagnosed in the *chronic* or *degenerative* stage. {Concerns may include *weight gain, malnutrition, yeast, mold, fungus, digestion, xanthan gum, sensitivities, gluten sensitive* and *nutrient deficiencies*.} [Look up each concern individually.]

<u>New</u> **Potato**: A type of GF *tuber*. An *immature potato* with a thin skin. To cook; steam or boil. (See *potato*.)

<u>Niacin</u>: A type of B *vitamin*. *Nicotinic acid. Nicotinamide*. GF.

Nigari: Nigari is GF magnesium chloride used as a *coagulant* in making a superior *tofu*. (See *tofu*.)

<u>Nitric</u> **Acid**: GF

<u>Nitrogen</u>: GF

Nondairy: Nondairy is a term for not containing *dairy*. [Nondairy does not mean *casein free*.] {Nondairy products may contain added *oils/fats, sweeteners, preservatives* and other *food agents*.} Question the source of all nondairy foods. (See *dairy*.)

Nondairy Creamer: Nondairy creamer is a type of *cream*

substitute. Nondairy creamer is available in *liquid* or *powdered* forms and may still contain *casein.* {Nondairy creamer may contain added *oils/fats, sweeteners, emulsifiers, preservatives,* other *food agents* and *chemical compounds.*} Avoid *fat free* or *reduced fat* nondairy creamer if possible. Several GF nondairy creamers are available at *regular grocery food stores.* Question the source.

Nondairy Milk: (See *milk nondairy*)

Nonfat: Nonfat food is a type of *food* that contains less and/or no fat. Nonfat *foods* are always questionable. Risky. (See *low fat, fat free* and *fat substitutes.*)

Non-Gluten: Non-gluten is a term meaning without *gluten.* (See *gluten* and *gluten free.*)

Non-GMO: Non-GMO is a term used for foods produced with *microorganism, plant* or *animal* byproducts that have not received *genetic material* from another. No compositional changes were performed and its *DNA* has not been altered. *Foods* not GMO are labeled 'Non-GMO'. Avoid GMO food if possible. Certified *organic* foods are the only foods guaranteed not to be GMO. (See *GMO.*)

Non-Leavening Yeast: (See *yeast substitute.*)

Nonnutritive: Nonnutritive is a term for *foods* that do not provide *nourishment. Processed instant* and *artificial foods* are the least *nutritious.* (See *nutritive.*)

Nonprescription Medication: Nonprescription medications are types of *medication* purchased without a prescription, as opposed to prescription medications prescribed by a doctor. Verify all medication is GF. You should have some GF *nonprescription* medications on hand for emergencies (e.g. cold and flu formulas, antihistamines, anti diarrhea medication and acetaminophen). (See *medication.*)

Nonspecific Ingredient: Nonspecific ingredients are any non-specified *ingredient.* Types of nonspecific ingredients may include *spices, herbs, seasonings, flavorings* and other food *additives.* Not all *ingredients* or *components* of *ingredients* are *specifically identified.* [Law does not require the listing of all *food components* on labels.] All *ingredients* in a *food* product need to be 'identified'. (See *ingredients* and *FDA.*)

Nonstick Spray: Nonstick spray is a type of cooking spray, 'sprayed' on as opposed to 'applied' on manually. A number of nonstick sprays are GF. Question the source. Caution. (See *butter substitutes, shortenings* and *fats & oils.*)

Nontoxic: Nontoxic is a term used for any *substance* that does not cause injury or harm. Nontoxic is a term for celiacs meaning safe. (See *toxic.*)

Nontropical Sprue Disease: (See *celiac disease*).

Non Yeast Leavening Agents: (See *yeast substitutes.*)

Noodles: Noodles are a type of *pasta* customarily long, thin and usually flat. Caution: the use of the term noodle generally refers to noodles made from *forbidden wheat* and usually *eggs.* Noodles can be made from _beans_, _rice_, _potato_, _cornstarch_ or *wheat.* Always question the source of noodles. *Commercially prepared* GF noodles are available at *ethnic* and *health food grocery stores* and by *mail order*. (See *pasta*.)

Nopales: A type of *vegetable*. *Fresh* and *plain* are GF. (See *vegetable*.)

Nori: A type of *seaweed*. *Fresh pure* and *plain* are GF. (See *seaweed*.)

Nori Sheets: Nori sheets are a type of *seaweed* wrappers used in traditional Asian cooking. Verify GF. (See *seaweed*.)

Nourishment: Nourishment is required for *health* and obtained from valuable *substances* found in *whole foods*. (See *nutrition*.)

Nuclei: Nuclei is the center membrane within a *cell* containing the *DNA*. (See *DNA*)

Nuna Bean: Nuna beans are GF *popping beans*. (See *popping bean*.)

Nut: Nuts are a type of hard *edible kernel* (*fruit/seed*) with a hard outer shell. Nuts grow on *plants* and in *trees*. *Raw fresh* and *plain* nuts are naturally GF. [Look up each type individually.] *Mechanically hulled* nuts are the best. Question *flavored*, *processed* and *roasted* nuts. Check for GF purity. (See nut butter, nut oil and also see 'nut' in A & F charts.)

Nut Butter: Nut butter is a type of thick creamy *paste* produced from *ground nuts*. Types of nut butters include *almond, cashew, hazelnut, macadamia* or *peanut* nut butters. *Plain pure* un-roasted nut butters are the best choice. A variety of nut butters are GF. Check for GF purity. (See *nut*.)

Nutmeg: Nutmeg is a type of *seed* ground into a *spice*. *Whole* nutmeg seeds and *pure ground* nutmeg are GF. Verify GF. (See *spice* and *seed*.)

Nutmeg Grater: A nutmeg grater is a type of flat *kitchen utensil* with a rough surface to which *nutmeg seeds* are rubbed against to create a fine *powder. Pure grated nutmeg* is GF.

Nut Oil: Nut oil is a certain type of *liquid* oil obtained from nuts. Pure nut oils are naturally GF. The best choices of GF nut oils include *walnut, hazelnut, pistachio* and *almond* oil. [Look up each individually.] A variety of *pure* GF nut oils, are available at *regular* and *health food grocery stores* and by *mail order*. Check for GF purity. (See *oil* and *nut* and also see 'fats and oils' in A & F charts.)

Nutrasweet: (See *aspartame*.) GF.

Nutrient: Nutrients are *substances* providing *nourishment* to the body. (See *nutrition*.)

Nutrition: Nutrition is the science of *food*. Nutrition refers to receiving *nourishment* through *food*. *Nutrients* absorb through the *digestive system*. Those suffering with *active celiac disease* are actually suffering from *malnutrition*. (See *malnutrition, immune system* and *digestive system*)

Nutritional Bars: (See *meal replacement bars*.)

Nutritional Drinks: (See *meal replacement bars drinks*.)

Nutritional Yeast: Nutritional yeast is a type of *non-leavening yeast* and popular *health food*. Avoid unless source is known.

Nutritionist: A nutritionist is someone who is an expert in the field of *food* and *nutrition* in relation to health. At present time the *treatment* for *CD* and *DH* is to eliminate form the *diet*, all *grains* and grain *byproducts* containing the *toxic gluten proteins*. [Dietitians are usually found in a clinical setting, where as nutritionist work more independently in private practice.]

Visiting a nutritionist may help with the gluten free diet but remember most deal with weight issues and few actually specialize with the GF diet. It is important to receive help from a nutritionist with experience in *gluten sensitivities*. (See *celiac disease* and *gluten free*.)

Nutritive: Nutritive is a term used to describe *foods* that provide *nourishment*. *Whole raw fresh foods* are the most *nutritious*. (See *whole foods, raw, fresh* and *nutrition*.)

Oat: Oats are a certain type of *cereal grain* from the *grass plant family*. Oats contain the *gluten prolamin avenin*. Advanced testing indicates pure oats are not harmful to those who have *CD* and/or *DH*. Oats are considered non-toxic, however due to the possibility of contamination all oats and oat byproducts should be cautioned. [Oats used in test studies are pure and uncontaminated.] If you choose to eat oats, know that although oats appear to be safe, perhaps the oats are contaminated by *wheat* (e.g., in the field or during processing). [This is cause for concern.] When choosing questionable *grains* individual tolerance should dictate use. Question all oats. Question all foods made with oats and *byproducts* of oats. Avoid contaminated oats. (See *avenin, grains* and *byproducts*.)

Oat Bran: The outer layer of *oat*. Questionable. (See *oats*.)

Oat Flour: Oat flour is a type of *grain flour milled* from *oats*. Questionable. (See *oat*.)

Oat Gum: A type of *gum* derived from *oats*. Questionable. (See *oat*.)

Oatmeal: Oatmeal is a type of breakfast *cereal* made from *oats* crushed or rolled with their *husk* removed and *customarily precooked*. Questionable. (See *oat*.)

Oatrim: Fake *fat* containing an *oat byproduct*. Questionable. (See *oat*.)

Oat Straw: Oat straw is a type of *spice/herb*. *Pure* is GF. [Oat straw is not the same as *oats*.]

Octopus: A type of *seafood*. *Pure fresh* and *plain* is GF. (See *seafood*.)

Oil: Oils are specific types of *liquids* obtained from *plants*, *beans*, *mineral deposits*, *nuts*, *seeds*, *fruits* and *grains* (*corn* or *wheat*). Oil is fluid at room temperature, as opposed to fat, which is solid at room temperature. The best choices of GF oils include *flax seed*, *extra virgin olive*, *grape seed*, *walnut*, *pumpkin seed*, *hazelnut*, *pistachio*, *almond* and *hemp seed* oils. Use different types of oils at different temperatures for different culinary uses. [Look on the label of a bottle of brand name oils, for phone numbers, then call and ask for their free chart on selecting, storing and using the appropriate oil.] A variety of *pure* GF oils are available at *regular* and *health food grocery stores* and by *mail order*. Check for GF purity. (See *oils & fats* and also see 'fats and oils' in A & F charts.)

Oils & Fats: Look up *fats & oils* separately. (Also see 'fats and oils' in A & F charts.)

Okara: (See *soy okara*.) GF.

Okra: A type of *vegetable*. *Fresh* and *plain* are GF. (See *vegetable*.)

Olean: A type of *fat substitute*. Questionable. (See *fat substitutes*.)

Oleic Acid: Oleic acid is a type of unsaturated fatty acid found in *plant* and *animal* fats. Oleic acid is used as a *binder* and *flavoring*. Caution.

Olestra: Olestra is a type of *fat substitute* containing an *oat byproduct*. Combining *sucrose* and a *vegetable oil* produces olestra. Caution. Questionable (See *oats*.)

Olive: Olives are a type *fruit* used as a *condiment* and to produce *olive oil*. Olives are *black* or *green* in color. [Look up each individually.] Organic black olives appear brown. {*Preserved* olives may contain added *sweeteners, preservatives, brine, vinegar* and *seasonings*.} Question the source of *stuffed olives*. Verify GF. (See *olive oil*.)

Olive Oil: Olive oil is a type of *oil* obtained from *olives*. *Extra virgin olive oil* is the first pressing. *Extra virgin olive oil* is the best choice. Check for GF purity. (See *extra virgin olive oil*.)

Olives Black: Black olives are a specific type of *olive* black in color. Organic black olives appear brown. Question the *preserving* solution (e.g. *brine* or *vinegar* and any added *seasonings*). The best black olives are Kalamata and Nicoise. Verify GF. (See *olive*.)

Olives Greek: (See *olives black*.)

Olives Green: Green olives are a specific type of *olives* green in color. Green *olives* are first soaked in lye and then *fermented* in *brine*. Question the *preserving* solution (e.g. *brine* or *vinegar* and any added *seasonings*). Verify GF. (See *olive*.)

Olives Stuffed: Stuffed olives are a type of *condiment* made with *black* or *green* olives *filled* with *seasonings* (usually *garlic* or *pimentos*) and soaked in a *brine* or *vinegar* solution. Question the *preserving* solution (e.g. *brine* or

vinegar. Verify the *filling* is GF. (See *olives* and *fillings*.)

Omelet: Omelets are a type of breakfast dish made with beaten *eggs* cooked and *filled* with a variety of foods (e.g., typically <u>cheese</u>, <u>meats</u> and <u>vegetables</u>). [Look up each ingredient.] Cook omelets on a clean *grill*. Omelets are sometimes covered with *sauce*. Verify all ingredients in or on the omelet are GF. (See *eggs*.)

Onion: A type of *vegetable*. *Fresh* and *plain* are GF. (See *vegetable*.)

Onion Powder: Onion powder is a type of *spice / condiment* made with a *mixture* of *ground-dehydrated onions* and added *filler*. Question the *filler* and possibly other *food agents*. Choose <u>100%</u> <u>pure</u> onion powder or *home-make* with *milled* <u>dehydrated</u> onions and <u>arrowroot powder</u> or <u>rice flour</u> as *filler*. Caution. Verify GF. (See *spices* and *condiments*.)

Open Dating: (See *dating*.)

Open Pollinated: Open pollination is the action of pollinated *naturally* without human intervention.

Orange: A type of *fruit*. Fresh and *plain* are GF. (See *fruit*.)

Ordinary: Ordinary *foods* are common foods to which people are familiar. Ordinary *foods* need to be verified GF. (See *natural, simple, plain, pure, basic* and *regular*.)

Oregano: A type of *herb*. Fresh and *pure dried* are GF. (See *herb*.)

Organic: Organic refers to living things and/or derived *naturally* from living things. Organic refers to living things free of *synthetic chemicals* and cultivated and/or *processed* without *chemicals*. Each State has their individual definition of organic. [California organic standards are strict. Look for foods labeled 'organic by California standards'.] Organic foods are not; *polished, gassed, parched* or *colored* or *preserved* or *treated* with harmful substance and have been grown without the use of *toxic pesticides* or *fertilizers*. Organic *foods* are generally richer in *nutrients* and therefore better for your health and immune system. Organic *foods* are free from most harmful *residue*. The best foods are organic. Favor organic GF foods that are *whole, fresh, unprocessed* and *additive* free, to support optimum health. Especially favor organic *fat foods* to avoid harmful *substances* concentrated in *fatty acids* (e.g. *meats, dairy, oils, nuts, seeds* and *grains*). Certified *organic* foods are the only foods guaranteed not GMO. Certain *ingredients* not necessarily defined are defined in organic foods. [Laws are continuously being proposed for the use of harmful substances on crops. To change these laws, write the FDA.] All organic foods need to be questioned and verified GF. Some organic GF foods are available at *regular grocery food stores*. Most organic GF foods are available at *health food grocery stores* and by *mail order*.

Organic Chemicals: Organic chemicals are chemicals of living things, chemically made in a laboratory. [This is a relatively misleading term.] (See *chemicals*.)

Organism: Organisms are living things (e.g., *animal, bacteria, plant* and virus). [Look up individually.]

Orzo: Tiny size *wheat pasta*. Avoid.

Ovaltine: Ovaltine is a type of *drink mix* made with *wheat*. Avoid.

Oven: Ovens are kitchen *appliances* that *cook* (*bakes, roasts* or *broils*) foods using heat elements (electric or gas). You need to *cook* GF *food* in separate dishes and/or separately on a piece of *aluminum foil* to avoid *gluten contamination*. (See *aluminum foil* and *cooking*.)

Oxalic Acid: Oxalic acid is a type of *toxic acid* found in *plants* such as buckwheat. Buckwheat contains high levels of *oxalic acid*. Oxalic acid can be used as a *bleaching agent*. GF. (See *buckwheat*.)

Oxidizing Agent: Oxidizing agents are *substances* that combine oxygen with another *substance*. (See *agent*.)

Oyster: Oysters are a type of *seafood. Pure fresh* and *plain* are GF. (See *seafood*.)

Oyster Plant: A type of *spice/herb. Pure* is GF. (See *herbs* and *spices*.)

Pablum: Pablum is a type of food contains *wheat*. Avoid.

Packaged Date: The packaging date is the *date* that indicates when the *food* was packaged. (See *dating*.)

Packaging Material: Packaging materials are typically non-edible paper, metal, plastic or cardboard materials used to protect, store and/or preserve *foods*. There seems to be little concern about packaging material. (See *wrappers, glue* and *sensitivities*.)

Paella: Paella is a type of Spanish *dish* made with chicken or shellfish and saffron *seasoned rice*. Question all ingredients.

Pain: A term for *bread*. Avoid.

Pakoras: *Fritters/pancakes*. Avoid.

Palak: (See *spinach*.) GF.

Pancake: Pancakes are a *bread* type breakfast *meal cooked* in rounds on a skillet from *batter mixes*. Pancake batter is normally made with *forbidden wheat flour.* You can *home make* GF pancakes with *special ingredients. Commercially prepared* GF pancakes and pancake *mixes* are available through *specialty companies.* (See *baked-goods.*)

Pancake Syrup: Pancake syrup is a general term for *syrup* made with a combination of *corn syrup* and added *flavorings.* {Pancake syrup may contain added *sweeteners* and *colorings.*} Risky. Question the source. Pure *corn* and/or *maple syrup* are GF. [Look up both kinds.]

Paneer: Paneer is a term for firm *tofu* and also *fresh ricotta cheese.* [Look up each individually.]

Panir Cheese: Panir cheese is a type of *fresh un-ripened ricotta cheese.* Questionable. (See *ricotta cheese.*)

Panko: (See *breadcrumbs.*) Avoid.

Papain: A type of *enzyme* derived from *papaya seeds.* GF.

Papaya: A type of *fruit. Fresh* and *plain* are GF. (See *fruit* and *papain.*)

Pappadam: A type of *bean bread.* Avoid unless all ingredients are GF.

Paprika: A type of *spice. Pure* is GF. (See *spice.*)

Paraffin: Paraffin wax is a type of indigestible *wax mixture* obtained from *petroleum.* Paraffin is used in and on *food* (e.g., as a *coating* or *preservative*). Caution. Avoid if possible. GF. (See *wax.*)

Paratha: *Fried bread.* Avoid.

Parboil: Parboiled is a term used for food *partially cooked.* (See *parboiled food.*)

Parboiled Bran: *Partially cooked bran.* Question the source.

Parboiled Food: Parboiled foods are *dried food* (typically *grains* and *beans*) *partially cooked.* Parboiled

foods lack *nutrition.* Question the source of parboiled foods. (See *instant foods* and *dehydrated.*)

Parboiled Rice: *Partially cooked rice.* Check for GF purity. (See *rice.*)

Pareve: Pareve foods are specific *foods* made without *animal* or *dairy* products. (See *kosher.*)

Parfait: Parfaits are a type of *frozen dessert* prepared with *ice cream* and layered with *sauce* and *syrup.* Question all *ingredients.*

Parmesan Cheese: Parmesan cheese is a type of hard, dry, *aged cheese.* Parmesan cheese is good for *grating.* {*Commercially prepared* grated parmesan cheese may contain added *filler* and *additives.*} Verify GF. (See *cheese* and *grated cheese.*)

Parsley: A type of *herb. Fresh* and *pure dried* are GF. (See *herb.*)

Parsnip: A type of *vegetable. Fresh* and *plain* are GF. (See *vegetable.*)

Partially Cooked: (See *parboiled.*)

Partially Hydrogenated Oil: A type of *oil, hydrogenated.* The majority of partially hydrogenated oils are GF. Caution. Verify GF. (See *hydrogenated* and *oil.*)

Partially Hydrolyzed Plant Protein: A type of *hydrolyzed plant protein* used in *pharmaceuticals.* (See *hydrolyzed plant protein.*)

Partridge: A type of *fowl. Pure fresh* and *plain fowl* are GF.

Parts Per Million (PPM): PPM is a specific type of measuring system (e.g. measurement by weight). This type of measuring system measures the amount of a *substance* in *food. Labeled* ingredients list in descending order of their proportion by weight. (See *ingredients.*)

Parve: Parve is a specific term for *animal* and *dairy* free. (See *kosher.*)

Passion Fruit: A type of *fruit*. *Fresh* and *plain* are GF. (See *fruit*.)

Pasta: Pasta is a type of *food* made from *flour* or *dough* available *fresh* or *dried*. [The word *pasta* listed as an *ingredient* is usually made with *forbidden wheat flour* unless specifically identified.] Pasta can be made from beans (e.g. *bean thread pasta*), grains (e.g. buckwheat, rice, corn, *wheat* or a *wheat blend*) and vegetables (e.g. *potato*). Avoid pasta made with *forbidden wheat, barley, rye*, possibly *oats, bulgur, diploid, durum, einkorn, emmer, far, farro, hexaploid, kamut, mir, seitan, semolina, spelt, tetraploid, tsampa, triticale* and *triticum* and *relatives of these grains*. Choose pure GF pasta made with acceptable *amaranth, buckwheat, corn, millet, quinoa, potato, beans, tapioca, rice, job's tear, ragi* and *tef*. Caution: pasta may be prepared with a combination of *ingredients* and/or *flours*. Avoid pasta made with a *mixture* of both *gluten* and *non-gluten* containing *ingredients*. Question the source of all pasta. Most GF pasta is labeled. *Commercially prepared* GF pasta is available at some regular *grocery food stores* and most *ethnic* and *health food grocery stores* and by mail order. (See 'processed and prepared foods' in A & F charts.)

Pasta Filata Cheese: A type of *stretched-curd cheese*. Types include *mozzarella* or *provolone*. Verify GF.

Pasta Salad: Pasta salad is a type of *salad* made with *cooked pasta*. *Commercially prepared* pasta salads are generally made with *forbidden wheat pasta*. Avoid. [You can *home make* pasta salads with GF pasta and other GF ingredients.] (See *pasta*.)

Pasta Sauce: Pasta sauces are various *seasoned sauces* used on *pasta*. [Pasta sauce is not the same as *spaghetti sauce*.] A variety of pasta sauces are GF. Question the source of all ingredients in pasta sauces. (See *sauce* for cautions.)

Pasta Wheat: *Durum wheat*. Avoid.

Paste: Pastes are semi-*solid* spreadable *mixtures*. Pastes generally contain *filler*. Question the source of all ingredients in pastes and the source of *filler*. [Pure *tomato paste* is GF.] Pastes are risky. [Look up each type of paste individually.] You can *home make* pastes with GF ingredients. (See *spread*.)

Pastina: Tiny pieces of *dough pasta* typically made from *wheat*. Avoid.

Pastry: Pastries are types of *baked goods* made from *unleavened pastry dough*. If pastry is truly GF, it will be labeled. (See *baked goods* and *specialty companies*.)

Pastry Brush: Pastry brushes are a type of *kitchen utensil* similar to a paintbrush, but made for and used on *foods*. Use a different pastry brush for wet *ingredients* (e.g. buttering *baked-goods*) and a separate pastry for dry *spices* (e.g. cleaning out a *coffee mill* or *mortar* and *pestle*). Do not use the same pastry brush for both *gluten* and *gluten free foods*.

Pastry Dough: A type of moist *unleavened dough* used to make *pastry*, generally made with *wheat pastry flour*. Avoid. (See *dough*.)

Pastry Flour: A type of dry *unleavened flour* used to make *pastry* generally *milled* from soft *wheat*. Avoid. (See *flour*.)

Pate: Pate is a side dish made from pureed *meat, fish* or *vegetables*. {Pate may contain added *seasonings* and *filler*.} Question all *ingredients*. Pate is also a term for *dough*. Avoid. (See *spread*.)

Patent Flour: A type of *flour* made from a *wheat blend*. Avoid.

Pathogen: Pathogens are *organisms* (e.g., usually *bacteria* or viruses) capable of causing a *disease* in another *organism*. (See *disease*.)

Patta: A type of leaves/*greens*. *Pure* and *plain* are GF. (See *vegetable*.)

Patta Gobhi: (See *cabbage*.) GF.

Patties: Patties are flat round-shaped *burgers* generally made with *ground meats* or *poultry* and sometimes cooked *beans* and *vegetables*. {Patties may contain added *fillers* and *seasonings*.} Choose *fresh pure* and *plain* GF patties. You can home-make patties with *pure* GF *ingredients* and freeze until needed. Question the source of all ingredients. *Commercially prepared* GF patties are available through *specialty companies*. (See *burger*.)

Pawpaw: A type of *fruit*. *Fresh* and *plain* are GF. (See *fruit*.)

PB & J: (See *peanut butter* and *jelly* sand*wich*.)

PDR: (See *physicians desk reference*.)

Pea: Peas are a certain type of *legume* that usually grow in a *pod* and are eaten as a *vegetable*. GF. (See *bean* and *vegetable*.)

Pea Bean: A small type of *Navy bean*. GF. (See *bean*.)

Peach: A type of *fruit*. *Fresh* and *plain* are GF. (See *fruit*.)

Peaches Dried: Dried peaches are a type of *dried fruit* made from *dehydrated peaches*. Check for GF purity. (See *dried fruit*.)

Pea Flour: A type of *bean flour* milled from *dried peas*. Check for GF purity. (See *bean flour*.)

Peanut: Peanuts are considered a *legume* and n*ut*. *Raw* and *plain* are GF. Peanut are severely *allergenic* food for some individuals. Because of this, peanuts are usually *labeled* when used as *ingredients* and/or used in the environment when producing other foods. GF. (See *legume, beans* and *allergens*.)

Peanut Butter: Peanut butter is a type of *nut butter ground* from *peanuts*. Verify GF. (See *peanut* and *nut butters*.)

Peanut Butter & Jelly Sandwich: A type of sand*wich* generally made on *forbidden bread*. Avoid, or home-make with GF *bread*. You can serve PB and J on GF *crackers*.

Peanut Oil: Peanut oil is a type of *oil* extracted from *peanuts*. Caution. Check for GF purity. (See *peanuts*.)

Pear: A type of *fruit*. *Fresh* and *plain* are GF. (See *fruit*.)

Pear Dried: Dried pears are a type of *dried fruit* made from *dehydrated pears*. Check for GF purity. (See *dried fruit*.)

Pearl Barley: A type of *polished barley*. Avoid.

Pearled Barley: *Barley*. Avoid.

Pearl Millet: A type of *millet*. GF.

Pearl Starch: (See *cornstarch*.)

Pecan: *A type of nut. Raw* and *plain* pecans are GF. (See *nut*.)

Pecorino Cheese: An *aged* firm *Romano cheese* made from sheep's milk. Pecorino cheese makes an excellent *grated* cheese. Verify GF. (See *cheese* and *grated cheese*.)

Pecorino Romano Cheese: (See *pecorino cheese*.)

Pectin: Pectin is a GF *gelling* and *thickening agent* obtained from ripened *fruits* and *vegetables*. (See *pectin gum*.)

Pectin Gum: A type of *gum* derived from plant extracts (usually *citrus peels* and *apple pomace*). Verify GF.
Peel: Peels are the skin or outer layer of *plants* (e.g. *fruits*, *vegetables*, *bulbs* and *tubers*). Peels are not the same as the outer layer of *seeds* and *grains* (e.g., the outer *bran* or *hull*).
Penne: A type of tubular shaped *pasta* customarily made with *forbidden flour*. Avoid. (See *pasta*.)
Pepita: Pepitas are *pumpkin seeds* from *pumpkins,* as opposed to *squash seeds* sometimes termed pumpkin seeds but are actually from *squash. Raw* and *plain* are GF. (See *seeds* and *pumpkins*)
Pepper: Pepper is a term for *ground peppercorns* as a rule ground from untreated *whole* black peppercorns. Pepper is hard on the stomach. Check for GF purity. (See *spices*.)
Peppercorn: A type of *spice. Pure plain* are GF. Whole peppercorns are *ground* into *pepper*. (See *pepper*.)
Peppermint: A type of *herb. Fresh* and *pure dried* are GF. (See *herb*.)
Pepperoni: Pepperoni is a type of *salami*. Pepperoni is a ready-to-eat *food* made with *beef* and/or *pork*. {Pepperoni may contain added *seasonings* and *filler*.} Question all ingredients. Some pepperoni are GF.
Peppers: A type of *vegetable. Fresh* and *plain* are GF. (See vegetable and *jalapeno pepper*.)
Pepsin: GF
Peptides: Peptides are a type of molecular *compound* with *amino acid* bonds. Avoid *gluten* peptides. [The *peptides* in *gluten* are too small to strain.] (See *gluten*, *strain* and *distilled*.)
Perch: A type of *fish. Pure fresh* and *plain* are GF. (See *fish*.)

Perishable: Perishable foods are foods liable to decay, rot or spoilage. Types of perishable foods include *eggs*, *dairy products* and *fresh fruits*, *vegetables* and *herbs*. Prepared perishable foods spoil without *refrigeration*. (See *grocery food store*, *produce* and *organic*.)
Persimmon: A type of *fruit. Fresh* and *plain* are GF. (See *fruit*.)
Pesticide: Pesticides are *natural* or *chemical substances* used to kill pests. *Chemical* pesticides are harmful to the *immune system*. Avoid if possible. Wash fresh produce well before consuming. Buy *organic* produce to avoid harmful pesticides as much as possible. (See *organic* and *immune system*.)
Pesto: Pesto is a type of uncooked *sauce* or *filling* used on *pasta*, *meat*, *fish*, *poultry* or *vegetables*. Verify all ingredients in the pesto are GF. Verify the food the pesto is used with is GF, especially the pasta.
Petite Suisse Cheese: A type of soft *triple cream cheese*. Verify GF.
Petrolatum: (See *petroleum*.)
Petroleum: Petroleum is *naturally* occurring crude oil used to make petrochemicals and in *food*. Caution. Avoid if possible. GF.
PH: Measuring a *substances acidity* or *alkalinity*. (See *alkali* and *acid*.)
PH Adjusting Agents: PH adjusting agents are *substances* used to control the *acidity* or *alkalinity* in *food*. Types include *acids*, baking soda, citric acid, lactic acid, tartaric acid and *chemical compounds*. [Look up each individually.] Verify GF.
Pharmaceuticals: Involved in the *manufacturing*, dispensing and sale of *medication prescribed* by physicians. *Gluten* free medication

can be *compounded* through special resources. To get a referred *compounding pharmacy* in your area, call *The International Academy of Compounding Pharmacists* at 1-800-927-4227. Areas include all of the USA and Canada. (See *compounding* and *medication*.)

Pharmacy: (See *pharmaceuticals* and *drug store*.)

Pheasant: A type of *fowl. Pure fresh* and *plain* are GF. (See *fowl*.)

Phosphate: Any *Salt* or *ester* formed with phosphoric acid and metal or *alcohol*. Verify GF.

Phosphated Flour: Phosphated flour is a type of *forbidden flour* with added salt of phosphoric acid.

Phsyllium: (See *psyllium*.)

Physically: To alter *food* by *mechanical* means as opposed to using *chemicals*. (See *denatured, chemically* and *mechanically*.)

Physicians Desk Reference (PDR): The PDR is updated annually. You can research one at your doctors office, local library or pharmacy.

Pickled: Pickled foods are *foods* (generally *fruits* and *vegetables*, but may be meat, fish or flour-balls) *preserved* in a *solution* of *brine* or *vinegar* and *seasonings*. {Pickles may contain added *seasonings, sweeteners, coloring* and other *food agents*.} Question the source of *solutions*. Question if the *food* being-pickled is GF.

Pickles: Pickles are a type of *condiment* made from *pickled cucumbers*. Questionable. Verify GF. (See *pickled*.)

Pickling Salt: Pickling salt is a type of a finely refined *salt* without *additives*. GF. (See *salt* and *sea salt*.)

Pie: Pies are a type of *baked good*. Pies are any *piecrust filled* with a variety of *pie fillings*. Pies are customarily prepared with *forbidden grain byproducts*. Pie truly GF will be labeled. You can *home make* GF *pie* with *specialty ingredients*. There are many superior *recipe books* available to *home bake* GF *pie*. *Commercially prepared* GF pies are available through *specialty companies* only. (See *baked-goods, recipes, pie filling* and *piecrust*.)

Piecrusts: Piecrusts are the outer shell of *pies* customarily made with a *forbidden wheat flour based* of *cookie crumbs* or a wheat flour *dough*. Piecrust truly GF will be labeled. You can *home make* GF *piecrust* with allowable *specialty ingredients*. There are many superior *recipe books* available to *home bake* GF *piecrust. Commercially prepared* GF piecrusts are available through *specialty companies* only. (See *baked-goods, recipes* and *pie*.)

Pie Filling: Pie fillings are a type of *pudding dessert mixture* used to fill *piecrusts*. {Pie fillings may contain added *preservatives, thickeners, emulsifiers, sweeteners, stabilizers* and *artificial ingredients*.} There are several GF pie fillings. Question the source. (See *piecrust* and *pudding*.)

Pie Shell: (See *piecrust*.)

Pigeon: A type of *fowl. Pure fresh* and *plain* are GF. (See *fowl*.)

Pigeon Peas: A type of tropical yellowish *bean*, related to the *cowpea*. GF. (See *peas*.)

Pike: A type of *fish. Pure fresh* and *plain* are GF. (See *fish*.)

Pilaf: Pilaf refers to a type of *seasoned rice* or *wheat* based side dish. Avoid unless source is known. (See *seasoned rice*.)

Pilot: A type of *fish. Pure fresh* and *plain* are GF. (See *fish*.)

Pimento: Pimentos are a type of *condiment* made from *pickled* sweet *peppers*. Question the *pickling* solution and added *seasonings*.

Pinch: Pinch is a term referring to a tiny amount of any dry *ingredient* (e.g., whatever fits between your forefinger and thumb, about 1/16 tsp. or less). (See *season to taste*.)

Pineapple: A type of *fruit. Fresh* and *plain* are GF. (See *fruit*.)

Pineapples **Canned**: Canned pineapples are *pineapples preserved* in their own *juice* or in other *food agents*. {Canned pineapples may contain added *sweeteners* and *preservatives*). Choose *plain unsweetened pineapples* crushed or in rings, canned in their own juice.

Pineapples **Dried**: Dried pineapples are a type of *dried fruit* made with *dehydrated pineapples*. Check for GF purity. (See *dried fruit*.)

Pine **Nuts**: Pine nuts are termed *nuts*, but are actually *seeds* from the pinon tree. *Raw* and *plain* are GF. (See *seeds* and *trees*.)

Pink **Bean**: A type of small *pinto bean heirloom*. GF. (See *bean*.)

Pinole: Pinole is a term for *milled* soft *corn* kernels (gluten free). Pinole is also a type of *flour* made with a *mixture* of *corn*, *beans* and maybe *sugar*, spices and *vanilla* (question all *ingredients*).

Pinon: (See *pine nut*.) GF.

Pinquito: (See *pink bean*.) GF.

Pinto **Bean**: A type of *kidney bean* variety, mottled brown and pink in color. GF. (See *bean*.)

Pista: (See *pistachio*.) GF.

Pistachio: *A type of nut. Raw* and *plain nuts* are GF. (See *nut*.)

Pita: Pita is a term used for a type of *filled sandwich* made with *pita bread*. (See *pita bread* and *sandwich* for cautions.)

Pita Bread: A type of *wheat flour flatbread* with a center pocket. Avoid. (See *bread*.)

Pith: The soft white layer between the *citrus fruit peel* and its *flesh*. GF.

Pitorh: *Bean flour* balls. Make sure all *ingredients* used are GF.

Pitted: The *foods, stone* or *seed* has been removed (e.g. pitted *olives*).

Pizza: Pizza is a crispy *dough* pie topped with *sauce* and a variety of *toppings*. The pizza crust is normally made with *forbidden wheat flour*. You can *home make* GF pizza with *specialty ingredients*. But you must still make sure the *cheese* and *other toppings* (e.g. *pepperoni*, *sausage* or *anchovies*) are GF. *Commercially prepared* pizza truly GF will be labeled. *Commercially prepared* GF pizza is available only through *specialty companies*. (See *specialty ingredients, pizza crust* and *specialty resources*.)

Pizza Cheese: Pizza cheese is a type of *stretch curd cheese* with elastic properties (e.g. *mozzarella*). Pizza cheese stretches when heated. Verify GF. (See *pizza* and *mozzarella*.)

Pizza Crust: Pizza crust is the shell of *pizza*. Pizza crusts are customarily made with *forbidden wheat flour*. You can *home make* GF pizza crust with *specialty ingredients*. There are many superior recipe books available to home bake GF pizza crust. Any *commercially prepared* pizza crust truly GF will be labeled. *Commercially prepared* GF pizza crust is available only through *specialty companies*. (See *pizza, specialty ingredients* and *specialty resources*.)

Pizza Sauce: Pizza sauce is a specific type of *sauce* used on *pizza*. Several pizza sauces are GF. Verify GF. (See *sauce*.)

Pizza Sauce: Pizza sauce is a specific type of *sauce* used on *pizza*. Several pizza sauces are GF. Verify GF. (See *sauce*.)

Pizza Shell: (See *pizza crust*.)

Plain: Plain is a term referring to foods that are *simple, ordinary, basic* and sometimes *natural*. Plain foods are without accompaniments (e.g., without added extras such as *sauce, gravy, breading, seasoning, filler, sweetener* or *flavoring*). Eating or ordering *foods* plain is by and large safer (e.g., plain *broiled poultry*, plain steamed *vegetables* or plain *yogurt*). You can *season* plain GF *food* with GF *seasonings* or *condiments*. Still check the source of all plain foods for GF purity. Question the possibility of *contamination* and the possibility of *hidden ingredients*. (See *dry, whole foods, pure* and *contamination*.)

Plant: Plants are any living non-*animal organism* without independent movement. Most plants rely on water and soil for *nutrition*. Types of plants include *trees, root, tuber, bulb, fruits* and *vegetables*. [Look up each type individually.] The grains of some plants contain *gluten* (e.g. *wheat, rye* and *barley*). (See *gluten* and *plant parts*.)

Plantain: A type of *fruit*. Fresh and *plain* are GF. (See *fruit*.)

Plant Food: (See *plants* and *plant parts*.)

Plant Novel Trait (PNT): PNT is a term for *genetically* altered *plants*. PNT plants are characteristically different from other plants of its type. Avoid *foods* made with PNT plants if possible. (See *GMO* and *genetic*.)

Plant Parts: Plant parts are parts of plants. Types of plant parts include bark, berries, flowers, gums, leaves, needles, resins and stems, along with vegetables, fruits, roots, bulbs, seeds, nuts and grains. [Look up each plant part individually.] Avoid plant parts containing *gluten* (e.g., the *forbidden grains* of some plants). (See *plant, organisms* and *forbidden grains*.)

Plant Protein: Plant protein is a type of *protein* from a *plant* source as opposed to an *animal* source. Question the plant source. (See *protein* and *vegetable protein*.)

Plum: A type of *fruit*. *Fresh* and *plain* are GF. (See *fruit*.)

PNT: (See *plant novel trait*.)

Pod: Pods are the outer *shell* of certain *fresh beans* and *peas*. *Fresh* and *plain* pods are GF. [The outer shell of *grains* are not termed pod.]

Podina: (See *mint* leaves.) GF.

Poi: A type of *tuber*. *Fresh* and *plain* are GF. (See *tubers*.)

Polenta: Polenta is a type of fine yellow moist *cornmeal food* usually *milled* from *flint corn*. This type of *cornmeal* is *cooked* into a *mush*, set and then sliced and *cooked* (*baked* or *fried*). {Polenta may contain added *forbidden wheat flour*.} Polenta is always questionable. Choose GF polenta made with 100% pure cornmeal without added flavorings. Some *commercially prepared* GF polentas, are labeled. *Commercially prepared* GF polenta is available at *health food grocery stores* and some regular *grocery food stores*.

Polish: Polish is a food term meaning to *gloss, coat* or shine *food* (usually *beans* or *grains*) with *natural* or *artificial ingredients* (e.g. *glycerin, gluten* or *silicate*) to create a glossy shine. Rinsing does not remove polishing *material*. Question the source of all polishing material. Caution. Risky. *Organic* foods are not polished. (See *organic*.)

Polished Rice: Polished rice is generally *cargo rice, polished*. Question the source of polishing material. Risky. Avoid unless source is known. (See *polish* and *rice*.)

Polishing Agents: Polishing agents are *substances* used to *coat food* for a glossy shine. Polishing *agents* include *glycerin, gluten* or *silicate*. Caution. Risky. Question the source of all polishing material. (See *polish*.)

Pollock: A type of *fish. Pure fresh* and *plain* are GF. (See *fish*.)

Polyglycerol: A *substance* derived from *plant oils*. Verify GF.

Polymer: *Natural* or *synthetic compounds* such as *starch*. Question the source.

Polysorbate: Polysorbates are *acids* used as *emulsifiers, stabilizers* and *dispersing agents* in *foods*. Caution. Verify GF.

Pomace: Pomace is *ground dried fruit* or the *pulpy* mass remaining from pressed *fruits* (e.g. *apples*). Verify GF.

Pomegranate: A type of *fruit. Fresh* and *plain* are GF. (See *fruit*.)

Pomegranate Syrup: (See *grenadine*.) Questionable.

Pomelo: A type of *fruit. Fresh* and *plain* are GF. (See *fruit*.)

Pompano: A type of *fish. Pure fresh* and *plain* are GF. (See *fish*.)

Poori: A type of deep-fried *wheat bread*. Avoid.

Popcorn: Popcorn is a variety of GF *corn* with a hard *kernel* and an *endosperm* in which moisture is trapped. [The moisture is what makes the *kernel* explode when heated.] Popcorn *corn kernels* will *mill* into *flour*. You can *home make* popcorn in a microwave or with hot air, by using *whole* popcorn *corn kernels*. {Commercially prepared popped corn may contain added *flavorings* and *seasonings*.} Avoid *caramel* coated popcorn. Popped corn is a convenient GF *snack food*. Verify GF. (See *popcorn cakes, popcorn flour* and *snack foods*.)

Popcorn Cakes: Popcorn cakes are a type of *commercially* prepared *snack food* made from popped corn. {Popcorn cakes may contain added *flavorings, sweeteners,* coated *nuts* or *seeds* and *forbidden grains*.} Avoid *caramel flavored* popcorn cakes. Many popcorn cakes are GF. Choose *plain unflavored* popcorn cakes. Verify GF.

Popcorn Flour: Popcorn flour is a type *grain flour milled* from *popcorn corn kernels*. Whole *popcorn kernels mill* into an excellent *corn flour*. Check for GF purity. (See *popcorn* and *corn flour*.)

Popcorn Kernels: (See *popcorn*.)

Popover: Popovers are a breakfast *snack* made with a *forbidden flour* crust, *filled* with various moist *ingredients*. Avoid.

Poppandum: A type of *bean bread*. Make sure all *ingredients* used are GF. Question added *wheat flour*.

Popped Corn: (See *popcorn*.)

Popping Bean: A type of *bean* that pops when heated. [The popping beans are similar to the *popcorn corn kernel*.] GF. (See *popcorn*.)

Poppy Seed: A type of *seed*. Raw and *plain* are GF. (See *seed*.)

Poran Poli: Sweet *filled wheat bread*. Avoid.

Porgy: A type of *fish*. *Pure fresh* and *plain* are GF. (See *fish*.)

Pork: Pork is considered a type of *meat* from a hog/pig. *Pure fresh* and *plain* are GF. Pork is *cured* to make *bacon* or *ham*. {Look up bacon and ham individually.] Choose *fresh pure* and *plain pork*. Verify GF. (See *cured, bacon* and *ham*.)

Pork Cured: (See *bacon* and *ham*.)

Pork Sausage: Pork sausage is a type of uncooked *seasoned ground pork*. {Pork sausage may contain added *seasonings, spices, sweeteners, flavorings* and possible *filler*.} Question the source of all ingredients. (See *sausage*.)

Porridge: Porridge is a type of breakfast *meal* or side dish made from *oats* or *corn*. Question the source. (See *oats* for acceptability.)

Port Salut Cheese: A type of semi-soft *cheese*. Verify GF.

Port Wine: Question. (See *wine*.)

Posole: Posole is a type of *slaked corn*. Verify GF. Posole is also a term used for a type of *soup* made with *hominy, chicken, chilies* and *cilantro*. Question the source of all *ingredients* are GF. (See *soup*.)

Postum: A type of drink mix made with *wheat byproducts*. Avoid.

Potassium Acid Tartrate: (See *cream of tartar*.)

Potassium Bicarbonate: An *alkali leavening agent* in *baking powder*.

Potassium Bitartrate: (See *cream of tartar*.) GF.

Potassium Chloride: It is usually *specifically identified* as an *ingredient*. Caution. Verify GF.

Potassium Citrate: A type of *citrate* used as a buffering *agent* in *foods*. Verify GF.

Potassium Glysol Monostearate: Caution. GF.

Potassium Iodide: A type of *potassium salt* used as a *bleaching* and *dough conditioning agent*. GF.

Potato: Potatoes are various types of starchy *tubers* eaten as *vegetables*. *Fresh* and *plain* potatoes are *naturally* GF. You can cook various potatoes using several methods (e.g., *boil, fry, bake* or *roast*). Varieties of potatoes include *all purpose potato* (to *cook*: bake, *fry*, boil or steam), *fingerling, new potato* (to *cook*: steam or boil), *Idaho potato* (to *cook*: bake or *fry*), *purple potato* (to *cook*: steam, boil or bake), *red potato* (to *cook*: roasted, *fry* or boil), *russet potato* (to *cook*: bake or *fry*), *white potato* (to *cook*: bake, boil, steam or fry) and *yellow Finn potato* (to cook: *boil*). Question all *toppings* or *flavorings* used on potatoes. A special type of *starch* and *flour* is made from certain potatoes. (See *instant potatoes, potato starch* and *potato starch flour* and also see 'roots and tubers' in A & F charts.)

Potato Chips: Potato chips are a type of *snack food* made by *deep frying* thin *potato slices* into crunchy chips. Avoid chips made with *forbidden grains* and *forbidden grain byproducts*. Question the source of all ingredients in batter made potato chips. Several brands of *commercially prepared* potato chips are GF. Choose 100% *pure* GF *potato* chips. Verify the chips and any added seasonings are GF. (See *chips* for additional details.)

Potato Flour: Potato flour is a type of *flour* made from *dried cooked potatoes*. [Potato flour is not the same as *potato starch flour* and you cannot substitute potato flour with potato starch flour.] Potato flour is used as a *thickening agent*. [*Instant potatoes* can replace potato flour in most recipes.] Check for GF purity. (See *instant potatoes* and *potato starch flour*.)

Potato Instant: (See *instant potatoes*.) Verify GF.

Potato Pancake: Potato pancakes are a special type of *pancake* made from a *mixture* of *potatoes* and *flour* (*wheat flour* or *corn flour*). Question the source of flour. (See *latka*.)

Potato Ricer: (See *ricer*.)

Potato Salad: Potato salad is a type of cold or hot side dish made with *cooked potatoes*, chopped *vegetables* and possibly *eggs*. {Potato salad may contain added *seasonings*, *spices*, *mayonnaise*, *vinegar* and *pickles*). You can *home make* potato salad with GF *ingredients*. *Commercially prepared* potato salads are questionable. (See *salad*.)

Potato Starch: (See potato starch flour.)

Potato Starch Flour: Potato starch flour is a type of potato *starch* produced from *dried raw potatoes*. [Potato starch flour is not the same as *potato flour* and you cannot substitute potato starch flour with potato flour.] Use potato starch flour as a *baking ingredient*. Check for GF purity. Potato starch flour is available at *ethnic grocery stores*,

health food grocery stores or by *mail order*. (See *potato flour*.)

Potato Sticks: Potato sticks are a type of *commercially prepared snack food* made from *potato* slices *deep-fried* in oil. Avoid potato sticks fried in *forbidden oils* (e.g. *oils* previously used for *foods* containing *gluten*). Question all *flavored* potato sticks. Several pure plain potato sticks are GF. Verify GF. (See *chips*.)

Pot Cheese: A type of *fresh* soft *cheese* produced by draining *cottage cheese*. Verify GF. (See *cottage cheese*.)

Pot Pie: A type of *stew baked* with a *dough piecrust* top. Customarily the dough is made with *forbidden flour*.

Pot Stickers: *Dumplings* made with *wheat flour*. Avoid.

Poultry: Poultry are domestically raised *fowl* (e.g. *chicken*, *turkey*, *duck* and *geese*). [Look up each individually.] *Pure fresh* and *plain poultry* are GF. Avoid *fresh*, *cooked* and *frozen* poultry in *forbidden sauces*, *gravies* and *creams*, with *pasta*, *breaded*, *batter dipped*, *coated* or *pickled* in *vinegars*, unless all ingredients are verified GF. (See 'poultry' in A & F charts.)

Pound Cake: Pound cake is a type of dense *cake* traditionally made with *forbidden wheat flour*. *Commercially prepared* GF pound cake is available through *specialty companies*. (See *cake*.)

Powder: Powder is a term meaning to *dust*. Question the source of powder. Powder is also a term for any dry *substances* in the form of tiny particles. {Powders may contain added *bulking agents* and other *additives*.} Some solid foods are rolled on a powdery substances to make them more malleable. Always question the source of powders. Avoid unless source is known. (See *additives, dust* and *contamination*.)

Powdered Sugar: Powdered sugar is a type of *cane sugar* finely *granulated* with added *cornstarch*. Question added *wheat flour*. Verify GF. (See *sugar*.)

Powdered Vinegar: Powdered vinegar is a specially prepared *powdered* form of *vinegar* that is reconstituted with water before using. Powdered vinegar is great if *yeast* and *fermented foods* are a problem. Powdered vinegar is obtainable through specialty resources. Verify GF.

PPM: (See *parts per million*.)

Prawn: A type of *fish*. *Pure fresh* and *plain* are GF. (See *fish*.)

Preparation: (See *mixture*.)

Prepared Food: Prepared foods are *foods* made ready-to-cook and/or eat. All prepared *foods* are questionable. Question prepared foods for *forbidden gluten containing grains* and *forbidden grain byproducts*. Question prepared foods for *hidden gluten ingredients*. The majority of prepared foods are risky. {Prepared foods may contain added *preservatives, colorings, flavorings, stabilizers, filler, binders, modifiers, chemicals, gelling agents, sweetener, additives* and other *food agents*.} To make *homemade food* with *pure simple* and *basic* GF *ingredients*, in a contaminant free environment is one of the safest methods of preparing GF foods. A variety of prepared GF foods are available at local *grocery food stores* and *health food grocery food stores* and by *mail order*. (See *gluten, processed food, specialty*

companies, contamination, label reading, hidden ingredients and also see 'processed and prepared food' in A & F charts.)

Prescription Medication: Prescription medications are types of *medication* prescribed by a doctor, as opposed to *non-prescription medication* purchased without a prescription. You should have some GF prescription medications on hand for emergencies (e.g. antibiotics). (See *medication*.)

Preseason: Preseason is a term used for any *food* and/or *ingredient* that has been previously seasoned. Seasonings are added to nearly all *commercially prepared* foods to impart *flavor* (e.g. *burgers, sauce* and *prepared meals*.) {Preseason foods may contain added *spices, herbs, seasonings; flavorings, spice blends, vinegar* and other food *seasoning agents*.} Question any food that is preseason for the source of the *seasoning*. (See *seasoning*.)

Pre-Seasoned Food: (See *preseason*.)

Preservatives: Preservatives are *natural* or *artificial substances* added to *foods* to prevent the growth of or retard or delay spoilage due to *mold, yeast, bacteria* and *oxidation*. Types of preservatives may include *acids, sodium, lecithin, gums* and *chemical compounds*. Question any *substance* used in the preserving process. Question the source of all preservatives. *Vinegar, sweeteners, seasonings, salts, alcohol, flavorings* and other *food agents* are commonly used as a preservative. Caution.

Preserve: Preserved foods are protected with either *substances* or by a method, to prevent spoilage.

Foods are preserved using several methods (e.g. *canning, drying, freezing, salting* and *smoking*). [Look up each individually.] Question all *substances* used in the preserving process. (See *preservatives*.)

Preserved Meat: Preserved meats are *meats preserved* by either a process or with a *substance*. Question any *substance* used in the preserving process. (See *preserve* and *preservatives*.)

Preserves: (See *fruit spread*.)

Pressure Cooker: A pressure cooker is a pressurized pot that *cooks food* with high heat in a short amount of time. Pressure cooking helps food retain more of its *nutrients*. This type of *kitchen appliance*, especially useful for cooking *whole foods* (e.g. *whole beans* and *grains*).

Pretzels: Pretzels are a type of hard *snack food* customarily prepared with *forbidden flours* (e.g. *spelt, rye* and *wheat*). *Commercially prepared* GF pretzels are available only through *specialty companies*. (See *snack foods* and *special resources*.)

Prickly Ash: A type of *spice/herb*. *Fresh* and *pure dried* are GF.

Primary Grown Yeast: A type of *non-leavening nutritional yeast*. Question. (See *nutritional yeast*.)

Process: To date there has been no research indicating any process rendering *gluten* containing *plants* and/or *grains gluten free*. (See *processed food*.)

Processed Cheese: Processed cheese is a type of treated *pasteurized cheese*. {Processed cheese may contain added *emulsifiers, gums, preservatives, colorings, powdered milk, gelling agents, stabilizers,* *vinegars, sweeteners* and *various* other *food agents* used to lengthen its shelf life.} Caution. Verify GF. (See *processed cheese spread*.)

Processed Cheese Spread: Processed cheese spread is a type of spreadable *processed cheese*. Processed cheese spreads contain an added *liquid* (usually *fat/oil*) for spread-ability. A good number of processed cheese spreads are not GF. Caution. Risky. All ingredients need to be verified GF. (See *processed cheese* and *spreads*.)

Processed Food: Processed foods are *foods treated* by a process or with *food agents* or *chemicals*. To date there has been no research indicating any process rendering *gluten* containing plants and/or grains *gluten free*. The majority of processed foods are risky. All processed *foods* are questionable. {Processed foods may contain added *preservatives, colorings, flavorings, stabilizers, filler, binders, modifiers, chemicals, gelling agents, sweetener, additives* and other *food agents*.} Question processed foods for *forbidden gluten grains* and *forbidden gluten grain byproducts*. Question prepared foods for *hidden ingredients*. [To *home-make food* with *pure simple* and *basic* GF *ingredients,* in a contaminant free environment is generally the safest.] A variety of processed GF foods are available at *local grocery stores* and *health food grocery stores*. (See *gluten, prepared food, label reading, contamination, hidden ingredients, specialty companies* and also see 'processed and prepared food' in A & F charts.)

Processed Meat: (See *lunchmeat* and *preserved meat*.)

Produce: Produce are any *food* of a farm or garden (e.g. *fresh fruits, vegetables* and *herbs*). *Fresh* and *plain* produce are GF. *Fresh* produce are some of the safest *foods* for *celiacs*. (See *organic* and *whole foods*.)

Product List: (See *food list*.)

Prolamin: Prolamins are a certain type of *plant protein* found in *gluten*. Specific types of prolamins are *toxic* to people with *celiac disease*. *Celiac disease* is an adverse reaction to prolamins involving the *immune system*. Individuals suffering from *celiac disease* have a *genetic* predisposition to the reaction from certain prolamins (*gliadin* found in *wheat, horedin* found in *barley* and *secalin* found in *rye*). Prolamins are also found in oats, *corn* and *rice*, but these do not have the same *toxic* effect to individuals with *celiac disease*. [Look up each type of grain individually.] Prolamins are too small to be *filtered* and/or *strained* therefore *filtration* and/or straining does not render *food* containing gluten, gluten free. Avoid all forbidden grains and grain byproducts containing the toxic prolamins. (See *forbidden grains* and *grain byproducts*.)

Propellant: Propellants are a type of compressed inert gas used in aerosols. Caution. Verify GF. (See *aerosol*.)

Propygallate: An *additive* in *food*. Caution. Verify GF.

Propylene Glycol Alginate: A type of *gum* derived from *kelp*. GF.

Protein: Proteins are a complex *natural compound* essential to the structure and function of all living things. Proteins are from either *plant* or *animal* sources. There are certain types of *plant proteins* in *grains, toxic* to individuals with *celiac disease*. Individuals suffering from *celiac disease* have a *genetic* predisposition to the reaction from certain *proteins*. These proteins are *gluten*. The protein *gluten* is found in specific *cereal grains (e.g. corn, rice, barley, rye, wheat* and *oats*). The *gluten* proteins found in oats, *corn* and *rice* do not have the same *toxic* effect to individuals with *celiac disease*. *Gluten protein* referred to in this book is the *gluten protein* that is intolerable for people with *celiac disease* (e.g., *gliadin* found in *wheat, horedin* found in *barley* and *secalin* found in *rye*). [Look up each grain individually.] Individuals with celiac disease must avoid all forbidden grains and grain byproducts containing the toxic protein in all forms and in all amounts. (See *forbidden grains, grain byproducts, gluten, gluten free, protein powder* and *whey*.)

Protein Drink: (See *meal replacement drink*.)

Protein Powder: Protein powders are a type of *powder mix* composed of various *ingredients* added to *liquid* to create a *meal*. *Protein* powders are usually eaten for energy or weight gain. Question the source of all ingredients in protein powders. [Question the *protein* source and check for *filler*.] The occasional GF protein powders are available at *regular* and *health food grocery stores* and by *mail order*. (See meal replacement drinks.)

Provolone Cheese: A type of *stretched-curd aged cheese*. Verify GF. (See *cheese*.)

Prunes: A type of *dried fruit* made from *dehydrated plumbs*. Check for GF purity. (See *dried fruit*.)

Pryidoxine Hydrochloride: A type of *additive* used in *food*. Caution. Verify GF.

Psyllium: A type of *husk* and/or *seed* considered a *spice/herb*. *Pure* and *plain* are GF. The *plant* (*husk*) and *seeds* are used as a source of *fiber* and mild *laxative*. Question added *filler*. Check for GF purity. (See *laxative*.)

Psyllium Gum: A type of *gum* derived from *psyllium seeds*. GF. (See *psyllium*.)

Psyllium Husk: (See *psyllium*.)

Psyllium Seed: (See *psyllium*.)

Pudding: Pudding is a type of various *cooked desserts* with a smooth consistency. {Puddings may contain added *starch* and *thickening agents*.} *Commercially prepared* puddings generally contain *artificial ingredients*. Question the source of all the ingredients in puddings. You can *home make* pudding with *acceptable ingredients*. Risky. Avoid unless source is known. [Look up each type individually.]

Pudding Rice: Pudding rice is a term used for *short grain rice*. *Short grain rice* is the type of *rice* used in making *pudding* because it cooks up sticky as opposed to *long grain rice*, which *cooks* up light and fluffy. Verify GF. (See *risotto rice, short grain rice* and *rice*.)

Puff Pastry: A type of flaky layered *pastry* customarily made with *forbidden wheat dough*. (See *pastry*.)

Puffs: Puffs are a term used for specific types of light and fluffy *snack foods* made with a variety of *food ingredients*. Choose puffs with a base of *potato, corn, millet* or *rice*. Question the source of all ingredients included added *colors, flavors* and *preservatives*). (See *snack foods*.)

Pulav: (See *rice pilaf*.)

Pulp: Pulp is *plant tissue*. Pulp is the soft fleshy part of *fruits* and/or *vegetables* remaining after *juicing*. [If the food juiced is GF, then the pulp would also be GF.] (See *juicer*.)

Pulse: Pulse is a term for *edible fresh* and/or *dried seeds* from a *pod* (e.g. *beans* and *peas*). GF. (See *beans* and *peas*.)

Pumpkin: A type of *fruit*. Fresh and *plain* are GF. (See *fruit*.)

Pumpkin Seed: Pumpkin seeds are the *edible seeds* from a *pumpkin* or *squash*. *Raw* and *plain* are GF. (See *pepito*.)

Pumpkin Seed Oil: Pumpkin oil is a type of *oil* obtained from *pumpkin seeds*. Check for GF purity. (See *oil*.)

Punch: Punch is a type of *beverage*. Risky. Caution. Avoid most punch. [Instead, choose *pure fruit* or *vegetable juice*.] (See *beverage*.)

Pur Chevre: Pur chevre is a term ensures the product contains the *milk* of goats only as opposed to cows or cows and goats *milk* combined.

Pure: Pure is a term referring to foods sometimes *plain, basic* and *natural*. Pure foods and/or ingredients are generally not *mixed* with other *substances*. In its purest form that ingredient and/or food only is pure. [Pure is also a term for *contaminant* free.] Check pure foods for GF purity. Question the possibility of *contamination* and the possibility of *hidden ingredients*. (See *plain, basic, natural* and *contamination*.)

Puree: To purify *food* into a *paste*.

Purple Potato: Purple potatoes are a type of *tuber* similar to a *russet potato*, but with purple skin and white flesh. To *cook*: boil, steam or bake. GF. (See *potato*.)

Pyaz: (See *onion*.) GF.

Pyramide Cheese: A soft *cheese* made from cow's *milk*. Verify GF.

Pyrethrum: Pyrethrum is a type of *spice/herb*. *Pure* and *plain* are GF. (See *spices* and *herbs*.)

Quail: A type of *fowl*. *Pure fresh* and *plain* are GF. (See *fowl*.)

Quark Cheese: A type of soft *un-ripened cheese*. Verify GF.

Quesadilla: Quesadillas are a type of *filled tortilla meal*. Question if the *tortilla* is made with *forbidden wheat flour*. Question the *seasoning* and all other *ingredients*. Varieties of frozen *commercially prepared* GF quesadillas are available through *specialty companies*. (See *specialty companies* and *special resources*.)

Queso Fresco Cheese: A type of *fresh cottage cheese*. Verify GF. (See *cottage cheese*.)

Quiche: Quiche is a type of *egg-pie* customarily made with a *forbidden wheat piecrust*. You can *home make* quiche with GF *ingredients*. *Commercially prepared* GF quiche is available only through *specialty companies*. (See *piecrust*.)

Quick Bread: (See *batter bread*.)

Quick Cooked: Quick cooked foods are certain types of *foods* (usually beans, grains and pasta) precooked (usually *parboiled*) and re-dried.

Quick *cooked food* lacks *nutrition*. (See *whole foods*.)

Quillaia Extract: A type of *foaming agent* obtained from tree *bark*. GF.

Quince: A type of *fruit*. Fresh and *plain* are GF. (See *fruit*.)

Quince Gum: A type of *gum* derived from the *quince fruit*. GF.

Quinoa: Quinoa is a type of GF *seed* from a *plant* of the Goosefoot family. Quinoa is not a *grain*, but is considered a *grain* because of its grain-like similarities and uses. Unlike grains, quinoa is a *complete protein*. Quinoa is more versatile than *rice*. Quinoa *cooks* up quick. Quinoa makes a great breakfast cereal. Whole quinoa *mills* easily into *flour*. Whole quinoa seeds are available at *health food grocery stores* and by *mail order*. (See *quinoa flour*.)

Quinoa Flour: Quinoa flour is a type of *seed flour* easily *milled* from whole *quinoa* seeds. *Whole* quinoa seeds are soft and therefore *mill* easily with a *coffee mill*. Quinoa flour is excellent as part of a *flour combination* in *baked-goods*. Check for GF purity. Quinoa flour is available at *health food grocery stores* and by *mail order*. (See *coffee mill*.)

Rabbit: A type of *meat*. *Pure fresh* and *plain* are GF. (See *meat*.)

Raclette Cheese: A type of semi-firm *cheese* Verify GF.

Radish: A type of *vegetable*. Fresh and *plain* are GF. (See *vegetable*.)

Ragi: Ragi is a type of *cereal grain* closely related to *corn* considered safe. GF. (See *grains*.)

Rai: (See *mustard* seeds.) GF.

Raisins: A type of *dried fruit* made from *dehydrated grapes*. [Avoid golden raisins. if possible] The best types of raisins are Thompson or Monukka. Check for GF purity.

Raita: Raita is a type of *yogurt dressing/salad*. Question the source of all ingredients. (See *dressing*.)

Ram Mung Bean: (See *mung bean*.)

Rangoon Bean: A type of large *lima bean*. GF. (See lima *bean*.)

Rapadura Sugar: A trade name for a *sugar* cane *sweetener* less *refined* than *unrefined sugar* and it also contains more *nutrients*. GF.

Raspberry: A type of *fruit*. Fresh and *plain* are GF. (See *fruit*.)

Rattlesnake Bean: A type of *hybrid bean*. GF. (See *bean*.)

Ravioli: Ravioli is a type of *cheese* or *meat filled* pillows customarily made with *forbidden wheat dough pasta*. Avoid.

Raw Food: Raw foods are *foods* that are *fresh* and not *processed, refined* or *cooked*. Raw *food* (e.g. *fruits* and *vegetables*) still contain *natural enzymes*. Verify GF. (See *fresh, pure, plain, vegetables, fruits, whole foods* and *raw ingredients*.)

Raw Ingredients: A manufacturer produces finished *food/products* from *raw ingredients*. Although the term raw means unprocessed, raw ingredients in the *food industry* may refer to *compounded ingredients* (e.g. *spice blends, flavorings, colorings, filler, excipients, emulsifiers, binders, stabilizers, preservatives, additives, vinegars, starch, sweeteners, oils/fats* and other *food agents*). All *raw ingredients* need to be verified GF. (See *raw food, compound ingredient* and *manufacturer*.)

Raw Sugar: Raw sugar is a type of *sugar* derived from the remains of *processing sugar cane*. Verify GF. (See *sugar*.)

RDA: (See *recommended dietary allowance*.)

Real: Real is a term used for a *food* product containing at least a portion of the *food* named. The term real does not mean the food is pure. (See *100%* and *pure*.)

Reblochon Cheese: A type of soft *cheese*. Verify GF. (See *cheese*.)

Recipe: Recipes are a list of *ingredients* along with preparation instructions in order for you to create a *dish/meal*. You can design gluten free recipes using *whole* GF *foods* (e.g. *fresh fruits* and *vegetables, raw nuts, seeds, milk* and *cheese*). You can also design recipes using *prepared* GF *foods* (e.g. *canned meats and fish, sauces, creamed soups* and *icing*). It is healthier, sometimes safer and possibly easier to *prepare* GF recipes with *whole food ingredients*. [Simple *whole foods* are less complicated, although some *whole* food recipes require longer preparation time.] There are excellent *recipe books* available to *home-make* prepared-foods with GF *ingredients*. It is important to purchase a few good GF recipe books that provide easy to make GF recipes especially baked-goods with a variety of *substitutions* and alternative *cooking* suggestions. There are many GF recipes books in public libraries you can borrow free. [GF recipe books in libraries may be in the food allergy section.] After learning the GF *diet* well, you can go through your old favorite recipes and convert them to GF. On the internet, type in the words 'gluten free,' and see what comes up. Go from there!

Some *specialty GF ingredients* needed for GF recipes are available only through *special resources* (e.g., available at *health food grocery stores* or by *mail order*). (See *special resources, whole foods* and *scratch*.)

Recipe Book: (See *recipe*.)

Recommended Dietary Allowance: *Nutritional* dietary recommendations created by the United States government.

Red Bean: A type of small red *bean*. Red beans are also a type of red *kidney* or *lentil bean*. GF.(See *bean*.)

Red Lentil: A type of *lentil bean* red in color. GF. (See *bean*.)

Red Potato: Red rice is a type of *tuber potato* with red skin and white flesh. To *cook*: *boil*, *steam* or *roast*. GF. (See *potato*.)

Red Rice: Red rice is a certain type of *rice* (usually *hulled*) with a red *bran* and possibly a red *endosperm*. GF. (See *rice*.)

Red Scarlet Runner Bean: A certain type of *bean*. GF.

Reduced Calories: Reduced calories is a term referring to a reduced amount of *calories* in a food product. [Reduced calorie products, reduce a person's *caloric* intake.] Question what is being used as a *calorie* replacement. Verify the GF purity of all reduced calorie foods.

Red Wine: (See *wine*.)

Refined: Refined is a term referring to *ingredients* and/or *foods* that are highly *processed*. Refined foods are *processed foods* to which *impurities* or *nutrients* are removed and possibly *artificial substances* added. Verify the GF purity of all refined foods. (See *unrefined*.)

Refined Rice: A term for *white rice*. Verify GF. (See *white rice*.)

Refined Sugar: Refined sugar is a type of *sugar* commonly derived from highly refined *sugar cane*. Verify GF. (See *refined*.)

Refractory Sprue: Refractory sprue is a term for individuals with *celiac disease* (*celiac sprue disease*) in which the *villi* does not grow back. [The patient is resistant to the *gluten free diet*.] This happens in a small percentage of *celiacs*. Refractory sprue is unlikely to happen to a *celiac* following a strict *GF diet*. Celiacs with refractory sprue must still maintain a GF diet. (See *villi*.)

Refried Beans: Refried beans are *cooked beans* mashed and then *fried*. Question added *seasonings* and *filler*. Several refried beans are GF. Verify GF. (See *bean*.)

Refrigerate: To keep cool in an ice box or refrigerator. Cooked *food* should be refrigerated immediately after serving to prevent *bacteria* growth. Mold grow quickly on *leftovers*. Perishable foods also need refrigerating. (See *mold*.)

Refrigerator Cookie: A type of *wheat flour dough mixture, frozen* or *refrigerated* before *baking*. Avoid.

Regular: Regular is a term generally referring to usual things with which people are most familiar. (See *natural, standard, simple, pure, plain, basic* and *regular grocery food store*.)

Regular Grocery Food Store: Regular grocery food stores are the type of grocery food store where the majority of people shop and with which most people are familiar. Regular grocery food stores carry a large selection of *GF foods*. You will not find some *specialty* GF items at regular grocery foods stores. Instead these specialty GF food items must be obtainable at *health food grocery stores* or by *mail order*. (See *health food grocery stores, ethnic grocery food store* and *by mail order*.)

Rehydrated: Foods (usually *instant*) to which the moisture has been removed are rehydrated (usually with boiling water) before consuming. (See *hydrate*.)

Releasing Agent: (See *dusting agent*.) Question the source.

Relish: Relishes are types of *condiments* made with chopped *vegetables* (commonly *pickles*) and sometimes *fruits*. {Relishes may contain added *seasonings, vinegar, preservatives, sweeteners,* possibly *thickeners* and *firming agents*.} Question all ingredients in relish. Certain relish are GF. (See *pickles*.)

Rennet: Rennet is a type of *food enzyme* obtained from the stomach lining of *animals* (e.g. calves, kids or lambs). Rennet can also be made from *plants* (this type is usually used in *cheese*). GF.

Rennin: Rennin is a type of *coagulating enzyme* found in *rennet* from *animals*. GF.

Replace: A type of *fat substitute* containing *oats*. Question. (See *oat*.)

Residue: Residue is any *substances* remaining from previously *prepared food*. Types of residue include residue in a wok or *pan* after *cooking stir-fries* or *sautés*, in a *blender* from making *batter*, on a *grill* from other *barbequed food* or in *oil* from deep *frying breaded foods*. Avoid all residual *foods* containing gluten. (See *contamination*.)

Resource Guide: (See *gluten free resource guide*)

Restaurant: Going to public places where *meals* and *drinks* are prepared and served can be quite risky. More and more restaurants are making *allergen/gluten free food lists* available. A few restaurants have GF menu handouts. [Always be prepared for accidental *gluten contamination*.] Dining out can be challenging, especially in the early stages of the GF *diet*. Call your favorite eateries ahead of time to make any necessary arrangements for dining out. Visit restaurants you previously patronized and talk to food staff with whom you are already familiar. The chef will usually work with you to make your favorite dishes gluten free. Keep the phone numbers on hand of restaurants that make GF *foods*. Safe GF dining includes ordering the least *processed* foods and ordering with clear and specific *preparation instructions*, especially if there is a language barrier. Safe restaurant *foods* may include <u>*fresh fruit*</u>, *plain* <u>*vegetable salads*</u>, <u>*steamed vegetables*</u>, <u>*plain baked*</u> or <u>*broiled fish*</u>, <u>*poultry*</u> or <u>*meat*</u>, *plain* <u>*rice*</u>, <u>*soft-boiled eggs*</u>, <u>*pure fruit juice*</u>, <u>*lemon water*</u> and <u>*plain baked potatoes*</u>. Of course, these foods need to be *plain* (e.g., without *dressings, sauces, flavorings, croutons* and *gravies*). You can fill a stylish personal travel container with GF *seasonings, spices, dressings, condiments* and/or other essentials for dining out. Pack the travel container (lunch box or small bag) with your choice of any *condiment* not needing *refrigeration* Condiments not needing refrigeration may include *dried herbs* and *spices, coffee, instant* *creamer, bouillon cubes, liquid aminos, carob* or *chocolate powder, shredded coconut, dried fruits, arrowroot powder, potato starch, rice flour, tapioca starch, gelatin powder, vinegar, honey, kudzu, rice syrup, marshmallows, low-fat milk powder, nut butters, coconut oil, extra virgin olive oil, salt, sugar, tea, hot chocolate* packets and/or *vanilla flavoring.* All of course, verified GF. There are convenient individual sized travel *condiment* packets available (e.g. individual *mustards, mayonnaise, seasoning mixes, dressings* and *sauce* packets). [Taking your own condiments to a restaurant makes dining out safe and *food* taste better.] You can also, bring your own GF *bread, pasta* and *dessert.* This is smart and acceptable, especially if you call ahead and talk to management. Call the restaurant ahead of time and talk with the preparation chef/cook and or food staff. Preorder *foods* you know are safe. Even if you explained your *diet* to the wait-staff, cook or chef you cannot expect them to understand your *diets* complexities, nor can you expect them to recommend a *meal* that is absolutely GF. [You may accept a cook or chefs recommendation, but never rely on someone else to know your *diet*.] As you learn the GF *diet*, you will become better able to order-out. Remember in the beginning how difficult it was, understanding the GF diet. [Its human nature to help others and most people are supportive, but people do not know what you need unless you tell them.] If you feel the least bit concerned about what the wait-staff or chef

suggested, politely say "thank you for your suggestions" and then make a decision in private. Even if you do not order what the wait-staff or chef suggests, you have somewhat of an idea of how they understand the GF *diet.* Be clear and specific with your *food* request. Clear instructions may include instructing the chef to *broil* your *chicken* on a separate plate thus avoiding cross contamination, or to prepare your *salad* dry without *croutons* or *dressing.* The majority of cooks and chefs will make a special plate. Just do not expect this during rush hour. Avoid GF *foods fried* in oil previously used to *fry* foods containing *gluten.* Order foods you know are safe and GF. Restaurants do not generally deal with lots of gluten free food request, although restaurants do get specific plate request from people with many restricted dietary needs. [Some people with severe allergies dine out regularly.] If you want to learn more about dining out GF, I suggest contacting a guided club that helps people with special GF dietary needs. (See *special resources, travel, special occasion* and *caterers.*)
Rhizome: The underground *root* of a *plant. Fresh* and *plain* are GF. (See *root* and *vegetable.*)
Rhodigums: A type of *gum* made from a combination of several *gums.* Avoid unless the source of every type of gum is known.
Riboflavon: Riboflavon is a type of *vitamin.* Verify GF.
Rice: Rice is a particular type of GF starchy *grain* from a *plant* of the *grass plant family.* Rice *grains* are termed: *long, medium* or *short* in size and *brown* or *white* in color.

[*Glutinous* rice, which is also GF, means *sticky rice*. *Glutinous* rice is *sweet* rice. Look up sweet rice.] Choose *short grain rice* for *recipes* calling for a *sticky* and/or *sushi'* rice. [*Short grain* rice *cooks* up sticky, but not as sticky as *sweet grain* rice.] Choose *long grain* rice for *recipes* calling for rice that *cooks* up light and fluffy. You can *soak* the *whole* rice *grains* before *cooking*. To cook rice you can *boil* or *steam* it. Rice is used to make certain kinds of *pasta, flour, starch, bran, vinegar, milk* and *syrup*. *Whole uncooked* rice *grains* will *mill* into *flour*. Brown rice is more nutritious than white rice. Choose *pure plain* brown *unpolished* rice. Check for GF purity. Always question *polished* rice. Question polished rice listed as an *ingredient* in *foods*. [Individually look up *short, long, sweet, brown* and *white* rice.] (See *rice flour, polished rice, converted rice, fortified rice, enriched rice* and *enhanced rice* and also, see 'grains' in A & F charts.)

Rice Bran: Rice bran is the outer layer of *rice* plus some of the rice germ. Verify GF. (See *bran*.)

Rice Bran Syrup: Rice bran syrup is a type of thick *syrup* made from *malted (germinated) rice grains*. {Rice bran syrup may contain *forbidden barley malt*.} Rice bran syrup is a type of *condiment* that needs no *refrigeration*. [Rice bran syrup is better tolerated by people with blood sugar disorders.] Avoid rice bran syrup containing *barley malt*. Question its GF purity. *Commercially prepared* GF rice bran syrup is available at *health food grocery stores* and by *mail order*.

Rice Cakes: Rice cakes are a type of *commercially* prepared *snack food* made from puffed *rice*. Rice cakes make an excellent bread or cracker substitution for some recipes. {Rice cakes may contain added *flavorings, sweeteners,* coated *nuts* or *seeds* and *forbidden grains*.} Avoid *caramel flavored* rice cakes. Many *rice cakes are* GF. Choose *plain unflavored* rice cakes. Verify GF.

Rice Crackers: Rice crackers are a type of *prepared snack food* made from *rice* and commonly *forbidden flour*. {Rice crackers may contain added *flavorings, colorings, seasonings* and *sweeteners*.} There may be a small choice of GF rice crackers in the Chinese food section of any grocery food store. There are a variety of *commercially prepared* GF rice crackers available through specialty companies. Question the source of all ingredients in rice crackers. (See *crackers*.)

Rice Flakes: Rice flakes are *parboiled rice grains* flattened. Check for GF purity.

Rice Flour: Rice flour is a type of *grain flour* milled from *brown* or *white rice grains* that are either *long* or *short* in size. *Short rice grains mill* into the best rice flour. Both white and brown rice *flour* works well in most *recipes*. *Brown rice flour* is also more *nutritious* than *white rice flour*. You need to use rice flour with other *specialty ingredients* to replace *forbidden wheat flour* in *recipes*. [It takes several GF *ingredients mixed* together to *substitute* the affects of *forbidden wheat gluten* in a *baked-good recipes*.] Rice flour makes an excellent *thickening agent* in heated *foods. Sweet rice flour* has excellent freeze thaw ability when used as a thickener in *sauces* and/or *gravies*. Caution: *commercially* made rice flour may have been *milled* from *forbidden polished rice*. Avoid rice flour *milled* from *forbidden polished* rice. Choose *pure* GF rice flour or *home-mill* rice flour from the *whole grains* of *short grain brown* or *short grain white* rice *grains*. Check rice flour for GF purity. *Commercially prepared* GF rice flour is available at *health food grocery stores, ethnic markets* and by *mail order*. (See *flour, sweet rice flour* and *specialty ingredients*.)

Rice Flour Noodles: Rice flour noodles are thin translucent *noodles* made from *rice flour*. Rice flour noodles are *deep-fried* in oil. Avoid *oil* used previously to *fry* foods containing *gluten*. Verify GF.

Rice Germ: Rice germ is the *germ* part of *rice grains*. Verify GF. (See *germ* and *rice bran*.)

Rice Malt: Rice malt is a specific type of *malt* derived from *germinated rice grains*. Rice *malt* sometimes contains *barley* or *koji*. Question the GF purity. (See *malt*.)

Rice Milk: Rice *milk* is a certain type of *nondairy milk* made from *cooked rice*. {Rice milk may contain added *filler, gums, flavorings, grain byproducts, alcohol* or *enzymes*.} Always question rice milks. Low amounts of *gluten* are in some *rice milks*. Question the GF purity. (See *rice* and *nondairy milk*.)

Rice Noodles: Rice noodles are a specific type of *pasta* made from *cooked rice*. The *noodles* are long, thin and sometimes flat. *Commercially prepared* GF rice

noodles are available at *ethnic grocery stores, health food grocery stores* and by *mail order*. Verify GF. (See *rice flour noodles*).

Rice Paper: Rice paper is made from *rice flour*. Verify GF. This type of rice paper is not the same as the edible thin paper made from the rice paper *plant* used in *baking*. Verify GF. Rice paper is also a term for a *spring roll wrapper* made from *forbidden wheat flour*. Avoid.

Rice Pasta: Rice pasta is a type of *pasta* made from *brown* or *white rice grains*. Rice pasta comes in many shapes and sizes (e.g. *shells, spaghetti, penne, vermicelli* and *linguini*). You can purchase rice pasta at *ethnic, regular* and *health food grocery stores* and by *mail order*. Verify GF. (See *pasta, rice noodles* and *rice vermicelli*.)

Rice Polish: (See *rice bran*.) GF.

Rice Powder: (See *rice flour*.) GF.

Ricer: A ricer is a type of *kitchen utensil* resembling a large *garlic press*. It presses *cooked foods* into rice-grain-like morsels (e.g., cooked potatoes, vegetables, carrots, tubers, taros, yams and sweet potatoes).

Rice Starch: Rice starch is a certain type of *starch* obtained from *starchy rice grains*. GF. (See *sticky rice*.)

Rice Sticks: Rice sticks is a term for rice noodles. Verify GF. Rice sticks are also a type of *bread stick* made from *rice flour*. Question the GF purity.

Rice Syrup: (See *rice bran syrup*.) Question.

Rice Syrup Powder: (See *rice bran syrup*.) Risky. Question the GF purity.

Rice Vermicelli: Rice vermicelli is a type of extremely thin translucent *rice noodles*. Rice vermicelli resembles a birds-nest. [Rice vermicelli is not the same as GF *bean thread pasta*.] Verify GF. (See *rice pasta*.)

Rice Vinegar: Rice vinegar is a *condiment*. This type of *vinegar* is made from soured and *fermented rice wines*. Avoid black *Chinese rice vinegar* made from *sorghum*, *millet* and *forbidden wheat*, instead of *rice*. Question *flavored western rice vinegar*. Choose *brown rice vinegar* traditionally brewed and imported from Japan. *Commercially prepared* GF rice vinegar is available at ethnic and *health food grocery stores*. Question the GF purity.

Rice Wine: Rice wine is *mirin*. This type of *fermented condiment* is used to *flavor* dishes. Rice wine is slow *brewed* from *sweet rice grains*. Question the GF purity.

Ricotta Cheese: Ricotta cheese is a type of *fresh cheese byproduct* made from the *whey* from cheese making. Question added *vinegar*. Verify GF. (See *dairy*.)

Rigatoni: A short, wide tubular shaped *pasta* customarily made with *forbidden flour*. Avoid. (See *pasta*.)

Rind: The skin or outer-most layer of *citrus fruit*. The rind is the *peel* of citrus fruit. GF. (See *citrus fruit*.)

Rinse: To clean gently with any type of *liquid* (usually water). Rinsing *foods* contaminated with *gluten* will not remove the gluten.

Ripened Cheese: Ripened cheese is a type of *aged mature cheese*, as opposed to *un-ripened immature fresh cheese*. Ripened cheese matures from a variety of processes including subjection to *bacteria*. Question the GF purity. Numerous ripened cheeses are GF. (See *cheese* and *bacteria ripened cheese*.)

Riso: Riso is a type of *pasta* in tiny size pieces generally made with *forbidden flour*. Avoid. (See *pasta*.)

Risotto: Risotto is a type of *rice* dish prepared with cooked sweet rice (*starchy rice*) and a *mixture* of *meat*, *vegetables*, *fish* and *sauce*. This dish is renowned, because of how the rice absorbs *liquids*. Verify all the *ingredients* including the *sauce* are GF. (See *risotto rice*.)

Risotto Rice: Risotto rice is a type of *short grain rice* that *absorb liquid* without becoming soft or mushy. Risotto rice is the type of rice used in *risotto recipes*. Brands include arborio (easy to over *cook*), carnaroli (*cooks* firm) and vialone (retains a firm center when *cooked*). Verify GF. (See *rice*.)

Rissole: A term referring to a *fried* or *baked wheat pasta*. Avoid. Rissole is also a term for a type of *potato crisp*. Question the GF purity.

Rizcous: Rizcous is a type of *cracked brown rice* cooked like *couscous*. Verify GF. (See *rice*.)

Rizotto: (See *risotto*.)

Roast: To cook in an oven or over a heat source. You must roast GF *food* in a separate dish to avoid contamination. *Plain roasted meats, poultry, fish* and *vegetable*s are GF.

Rock Salt: Rock salt is crystal rock salt. Rock salt is less *refined* retaining some *minerals*. You need a *salt mill* or *mortar & pestle* to *grind* rock salt. [Rock salt is not the same as the non-*edible* freezing rock salt used for making ice cream.] Rock salt is drier, lighter and a better digestive stimulant than regular *table salt*. GF. (See *sea salt*.)

Rock Sugar: Rock sugar is a type of *cooked cane sugar*. Verify GF.

Roe: Hard roe are female *fish eggs* and soft roe is male milt. *Plain* are GF. (See *fish*.)

Roll: (See *bun*.) Avoid.

Rolled Oats: Rolled oats are *hulled oats* flattened and used to make oatmeal. Questionable. (See *oats*.)

Romano Cheese: A type of firm *aged cheese* from sheep's, goats and cow's *milk*. Verify GF. (See *cheese*.)

Root: Roots are the *plant part* that grows underground. *Plain pure* roots are GF. (See *vegetable, root flour, tapioca* and *arrowroot*.)

Root Beer: Root beer is a type of *soda beverage*. {Root beers may contain *natural* and *artificial flavorings, sweeteners* and *colorings*.} Risky. Avoid unless source is known.

Root Flour: Root flours are a type of GF *flour milled* from *dried plant roots*. Types include pure *arrowroot powder* and *tapioca flour*. Check for GF purity. (See *root* and *flour*.)

Root Vegetable: Root vegetables are any *edible root* or *tuber*. Types include *carrot, turnip, tapioca, arrowroot, beet, yam* and *potato*). [Look up each individually.] *Fresh* and *plain* are GF.

Roquefort: A type of *veined cheese*. Avoid all *veined cheese*.

Roquefort Dressing: A type of *veined cheese* dressing Avoid all *veined cheeses*. (See *dressing*.)

Rose Hip: A type of *spice/herb*. *Pure* are GF. (See *spices* and *herbs*.)

Rosemary: A type of *herb*. *Fresh* and *pure dried* are GF. (See *herb*.)

Rosette: A type of *fried wheat pastry*. Avoid.

Roti: A *pan-fried unleavened wheat flour pancake*-type *flatbread*. Avoid.

Rotini: A type of spiral shaped *pasta* customarily made with *forbidden flour*. Avoid. (See *pasta*.)

Roux: A *wheat flour* and *oil/fat* mixture used as *thickener*. Avoid.

Rubber Spatula: (See *spatula*.)

Rue: A type of *spice/herb*. *Pure* are GF. (See *spices* and *herbs*.)

Rum: A type of *distilled alcohol*. Pure is GF. (See *alcohol*.)

Rusk: A type of sweet crisp *yeast bread* made with *wheat flour*. Avoid.

Russet Potato: A type of GF *tuber/potato*. Russet potatoes are excellent *cooked baked* or *fried*.

Rutabaga: A type of *vegetable*. *Fresh plain* are GF. (See *vegetable*.)

Rye: Rye is a type of *forbidden cereal grain* from the *grass plant family*. Rye has a *gluten prolamin* that is toxic to celiacs. *Secalin* is the *gluten prolamin* in rye. Other *forbidden* types of rye include rye flakes, rye buckwheat and rye berries. Avoid rye grains and rye grain relatives. Avoid *byproducts* of these *forbidden* grains. Avoid food made with these *forbidden* grains and *byproducts* of these *forbidden* grains. (See *grains, byproducts* and *horedin*.)

Sabji: A type of spicy *vegetable* dish. Avoid unless source is known.

Saccharin: An *unnatural* type of *sugar substitute*. Avoid this *artificial sweetener* if possible. [Saccharin is not good heated or used in *baked-goods*.] Caution. Verify GF. (See *artificial sweetener*.)

Safflower Seed: A type of *seed* from the safflower *plant*. GF. (See *seed*.)

Safflower Seed Oil: A type of *oil* obtained from *safflower seeds*.

Check for GF purity. (See *safflower seeds* and *oil*.)

Saffron: Saffron is a type of *seasoning* and *coloring* obtained from the crocus *plant*. Caution. GF.

Saga Blue Cheese: A type of soft *double cream cheese*. [Saga bleu cheese is not the same as *blue cheese*.] Verify GF.

Sage: Sage is a type of *spice/herb*. *Fresh* and *pure dried* are GF. (See *herbs* and *spices*.)

Sago: Sago is a type of GF *powdery starch-flour* obtained from the sago palm. [Sago is not the same as *sorghum*.] Sago *binds* well, thus making it great as part of a *flour mixture* used in GF *pizza dough*. (See *starch* and *special ingredients*.)

Sago Flour: (See *sago*.) GF.

Sago Palm: An Asian palm tree that yields *sago*. GF. (See *sago*.)

Sago Starch: (See *sago*.) GF.

Saifun: *Pasta* made from *beans* and possibly *forbidden flour*. Avoid unless source is known.

Sailfish: A type of *fish*. *Pure fresh* and *plain* are GF. (See *fish*.)

Saint Andre Cheese: A type of soft *triple cream cheese*. Verify GF.

Saint John's Bread: (See *locust bean gum*.) GF.

Saint John's Fruit: (See *carob*.) GF.

Saive: Saive is a type of *wheat noodle*. Avoid. (See *pasta*.)

Sake: A *fermented rice wine* used in Japanese *cooking*. Avoid unless source is known. Question *additives* especially *barley byproducts*.

Salad: Salads are various types of side dishes or main meals (usually cold) made with *fruits* or *vegetables* usually *raw* and *fresh*, but sometimes *cooked*. {*Pasta salads* are normally made with *forbidden wheat pasta*.} Question the source of all *commercially prepared* salads. Avoid most toppings including *imitation bacon bits* and *croutons* normally added in *vegetable* salads. Question all *ingredients* used 'in' or 'on' the salad especially *dressing*. Order *fruit* or *vegetable* salads *plain* and *dry*. Homemade salads are one of the safest GF meals. You can prepare countless salads with a variety of different foods. Verify GF. (See *dry*, *pasta salad* and *dressing*.)

Salad Greens: Salad greens are certain types of *vegetables*. This term is generally used for *leafy greens*. *Fresh*, *plain* and *dry* are GF. (See *salad*.)

Salad Spinner: A type of *kitchen tool* that spins *salad greens* dry by using centrifugal force. You can soak and/or clean *salad greens* in water in the salad spinner, before spinning dry. (See *salad*.)

Salami: Salami is a type of *cured* and *seasoned meat* (typically *beef* or *pork*). [*Kosher* salami is *beef* only.] {Salami may contain added *filler*, *flavorings*, *colorings*, *preservatives* and other *food agents*.} Avoid unless source is known.

Salmon: A type of *fish*. *Pure fresh* and *plain* are GF. (See *fish*.)

Salsa: Salsa is a type of *condiment / vegetable dip* made with chopped *vegetables* and/or *fruits*. Salsas are either *uncooked* (*fresh/crudo*) or *cooked*. [Verde is green salsa.] {Salsas may contain *tomatoes*, *peppers*, *cayenne* and *seasonings*.} Question all *ingredients*. Several salsas are GF. Verify GF. (See *dip*.)

Salt: Salt is *sodium*. Salt is a GF *essential* metallic *chemical* element.

Salt is used as a *condiment* and *flavoring agent*. The majority of *commercial salts* are *highly refined*. Question any added *seasonings* in *seasoning salts*. Instead, home-make *seasoning* salt with *ground spices* mixed with *natural sea salt*. {Salt may contain added *anti-caking agents*.} Salt is specifically identified when used as an *ingredient*. Salt may be listed as *sodium* on the *label*. Individuals with *DH* are advised to avoid iodinized salt and must choose <u>uniodized *salt*</u>. The best salt is <u>*unadulterated pure natural sea salt*</u>. (See *sea salt, sodium* and *iodized salt*.)

Salting: Salting foods is a method of *preserving*. (See *preserve*.)

<u>Salt</u> of <u>Carbonic</u> <u>Acid</u>: (See *sodium carbonate*.) Caution. GF.

<u>Salt</u> <u>Peter</u>: A type of *substance* harmful in large quantities. GF.

Salt Substitutes: Salt substitutes are fake *salt processed* with little or no *sodium*. Caution. Question the source. (See *salt, sea salt* and *seasoning salt*.)

Sambar: Sambar is a type of *stew* made with <u>*vegetables*</u>, <u>*lentils*</u> and *seasoning*. Question all ingredients.

Sambar Masala: Sambar masala is a type of *powdered seasoning* used in *sambar stew*. Verify GF. (See *seasonings* for cautions.)

Samosas: A type of *filled, fried potato, wheat flour pastry*. Avoid.

<u>Samp</u>: *Hominy grits. Dried hominy* coarsely *ground*. Verify GF.

Samsoe Cheese: A type of *semi-firm Swiss cheese*. Verify GF. (See *Swiss cheese* and *cheese*.)

Sandesh: A type of *cheese pudding dish. Ingredients* are not GF. Avoid.

Sandwich: Sandwiches are any of various side *dishes* and/or *meals* customarily made with *forbidden wheat bread* then *filled* with a variety of *ingredients* (e.g. *cheese, lunchmeat, tuna, vegetables* or PB & J). You can *home-make* sandwiches with GF *bread* and *fillings*. You must also use GF *dressings, condiments* and *seasonings* on the sandwiches. You can also serve the sandwich *ingredients* (e.g. *lettuce, tomatoes, tuna* and/or *lunchmeat*.) on a plate without *bread*. Sandwich fillings can also be served on GF *crackers* and *rice cakes*. You can bring your own GF *bread* while *traveling* or *dining* out. (See *bread, rice cakes* and *crackers*.)

Sandwich Spread: Sandwich spreads are various types of spreadable *vegetable* or *meat pastes spread* on *bread*. {Sandwich spreads may contain added *fillers*.} Question the source of all the ingredients. (See *sandwich* for additional cautions.)

<u>Sap</u>: Sap is *syrup* from *plant tissue liquid* obtained from trees. Pure sap is naturally GF and contains *sugar*, various *minerals* and other *nutrients*. (See *maple syrup* and SAP.)

<u>SAP</u>: (See *sodium acid pyrophosphate* and *sap*.) GF.

<u>Sapodilla</u>: A type of *fruit*. Fresh and *plain* are GF. (See *fruit*.)

Sapsago Cheese: A type of firm *cheese*. Verify GF. (See *cheese*.)

<u>Sardines</u>: Sardines are certain types of tiny fish. *Pure fresh* and *plain* are GF. Question sardines *smoked, salted* or *canned*. Canned sardines are frequently *canned* in oil, *tomato* or *mustard*. Lots of sardines are GF. <u>*Canned* sardines in *plain* olive oil are generally the safest</u>. Verify GF.

Sarsaparilla: A type of *spice/herb*. *Pure* are GF. (See *spices* and *herbs*.)

Sassafras: A type of *spice/herb*. *Pure* are GF. (See *spices* and *herbs*.)

Sauce: Sauce is an umbrella term used for various types of thickened *seasoned liquids*. A variety of sauces are used on an array of *foods* (e.g. *pasta, eggs* Benedict, *meat loaf* and *eggplant parmesan*). {Sauces may contain added *filler, gum, colors, emulsifiers, additives, flavorings, sweeteners, preservatives, stabilizers* and other *food agents*.} *Forbidden wheat flour* used as a *thickening agent* is always a question. Always question the source of added *seasonings, thickeners* and any other *food* source used to make the *sauce*. Avoid sauces with *forbidden grains* and *forbidden grain byproducts*. There are a number of *commercially prepared* GF sauces available at *regular* and *health food* grocery stores. It is best to choose *pure natural* sauces with *basic* GF ingredients. You can *home-make* GF sauce with *pure spices* and GF *thickeners*. Sauces in restaurants are generally not GF. Question all. Avoid unless source is known. (See *thickeners, pasta sauce, spaghetti sauce* and *gravy*.)

Saucepan: A type of shallow *pan* with a lid. A saucepan is used to make a variety of *foods* including sauces. (See *cookware*.)

Sauerkraut: Sauerkraut is a type of *condiment* made with *fermented cabbage*. {Sauerkraut may contain added *flavorings* and *seasonings* but does not usually contain *vinegar*} Choose *plain* GF sauerkraut. The best sauerkraut is bagged or in glass jars in the refrigerated section. Verify GF.

Sausage: Sausages are ground *meat* parts generally *seasoned* and customarily packed into a *casing*. {Sausages may contain added *seasonings, preservatives, fillers, sweeteners, binders, flavorings, colorings* and other *food agents*.} Choose *fresh plain* sausage or choose *seasoned* sausage with acceptable GF *seasonings*. Choose fresh sausage without *fillers* from the *fresh meat department* of the grocery food store. Always question. Avoid unless source is known.

Sauté: To cook slowly in a *skillet* or *sauté pan*. Sauté is also a *meal* prepared in a pan or skillet over low heat. Question the source of all ingredients in sautés. Clean the *pan* well between uses, to avoid *contamination* from *residue*. (See *sautés*.)

Sauté Pan: A sauté pan is a type of shallow pan with a lid and a long handle. Sauté pans are used to *sauté foods*. (See *cookware*.)

Sautés: Sautés are any of various types of *meals* prepared in a sauté pan or skillet over low heat. {Sautés may contain added *thickeners* and *seasonings*.} Sautés must be cooked in a clean *pan* free of *gluten residue*. (See *sauté* and *sauce*.)

Savory: A type of *spice/herb*. *Pure* are GF. (See *spices* and *herbs*.)

Sbrinz Cheese: A type of firm *cheese*. Verify GF. (See *cheese*.)

Scallion: A type of *vegetable*. *Fresh* and *plain* are GF. (See *vegetable*.)

Scalloped Potatoes: Scalloped potatoes are a type of dish made with *potatoes* and an added *thickening agent* that is usually from a

forbidden source. Scalloped potatoes are risky. You can *home make* GF scalloped potatoes using only GF ingredients. (See *potato* and *meals.*)
Scallops: A type of *seafood*. *Pure fresh* and *plain* is GF. (See *seafood.*)
Scamorze Cheese: A type of firm *cheese* made from goats, sheep's or cow's *milk*. Verify GF. (See *cheese.*)
Scarified Rice: Scarified rice is a type of *brown rice* with the outer portion scratched. This treatment shortens the rice's cooking time. Verify GF. (See *rice.*)
Scarlet Runner Bean: A certain type of *bean*. GF. (See *bean.*)
Scone: A type of *wheat dough quick-bread*. Avoid. (See *bread.*)
Scrapple: Scrapple is a firm type of *loaf* made with *pork* scraps. Scrapple is sliced and *deep fried* in *oil* or pan-fried. {Scrapple may contain added *seasonings* and *filler*.} Scrapple must be cooked in a clean *pan* free of *gluten residue*. Risky. Question the source of all ingredients. (See *meats.*)
Scratch: To *prepare foods* from *basic ingredients*, as opposed to *mixes*. *Recipes* call for either whole foods *ingredients* or ingredients from *processed foods*. Your healthiest and possibly safest method for GF cooking is to prepare *recipes* made from *basic ingredients* with minimally *processed foods*, especially if *newly diagnosed*. (See *basic, plain* and *recipes.*)
Seafood: Seafood is an umbrella term for a variety of *edible fish* and *shellfish* from the sea. All *plain fresh* seafood is naturally GF. You can cook seafood *plain* baked, grilled, *blackened, sautéed, roasted, broiled* or *steamed*. You can *lightly season* cooked seafood with GF *spices* or *lemon juice* from a *fresh* squeezed *lemon*. Some *seafood seasonings* are GF. Avoid *fresh, cooked* and *frozen* seafood in *forbidden sauces, gravies* and *creams*, with *pasta, breaded, batter dipped, coated* or *pickled* in *vinegars,* unless all ingredients are verified GF. [Look up *fish* and *shellfish* individually, along with each type of *cooking* method.] (See 'seafood' in A & F charts.)
Seafood Seasoning: Seafood seasonings are specifically prepared to season *seafood*. Certain *seafood seasonings* are GF. Avoid unless source is known. You can *lightly season* cooked seafood with GF *spices* or *lemon juice* from a *fresh* squeezed *lemon*. (See *seasoning.*)
Sea Plants: (See *sea vegetables.*)
Sea Salt: Sea salt is a *natural* type of *salt* containing trace minerals. Scores of *commercial* sea salts are *dry* and pure-white in color which, indicates *minerals* have been removed and/or *drying agents* have been used. *Natural* sea salt is gray in color and slightly moist. *Natural* sea salt contains trace amounts of a *natural* form of *organic iodine*. [Individuals with *DH* are advised to avoid iodine. *Natural sea salt* contains *a natural organic form of iodine* that may not affect individuals who may react to the *synthetic iodine* frequently added to *refined table salt*.] Choose *unadulterated pure natural* sea salt traditionally harvested from unpolluted water (e.g. Celtic *sea salt*). Look for the "biogaranite" label. Pure natural sea salt is GF. (See *solar evaporated.*)

Season: To add *flavoring agents* to impart *flavor* in *recipes* and/or on *foods*. Always question the source of added seasonings. (See *seasonings* and *flavor*.)

Seasoned Beans: Seasoned beans are generally *seasoned canned* or dry-packaged *precooked beans*. {Seasoned beans may contain added *seasonings, fillers, thickening agents, sweeteners, additives* and other *food agents*.} A limited amount of *seasoned* beans are GF. Always question seasoned beans as a side dish with a meal.

Seasoned Rice: Seasoned rice is generally dry-packaged *precooked rice seasoned*. {Seasoned rice may contain added *seasonings, fillers, thickening agents, sweeteners, additives* and other *food agents*.} A limited amount of *seasoned* rice is GF. (See *rice pilaf*.)

Seasoned Salt: (See *seasoning salt*.)

Seasoning Blend: (See *spice blend*.)

Seasoning Mix: (See *spice blend*.)

Seasonings: Seasonings are any of various *herbs, spices, spice blends* or *spice mixes* used to add *flavoring* to *foods* to impart *flavor*. {Seasonings may contain a blend of *natural* or *artificial flavoring agents, anti-caking agents* and *filler*.} Question the possibility of added *filler* in all seasonings. Inexpensive brands of seasonings most likely contain *filler*. Avoid seasonings with *forbidden carriers* or *filler*. The word seasoning listed as an *ingredient* is frequently a term for a combination of *spices*. Caution: the term seasoning is not specific when listed as an *ingredient* and always makes *food* questionable. Always question the source of seasonings listed as an

ingredient. You can *home-make* seasonings with a *mixture* of your own *freshly ground pure dried* GF *herbs* and *spice*. [Look up *herbs* and *spices* individually.] (See *carrier, filler, spice blends* and *flavoring agent*.)

Seasoning Salt: Seasoning salts are various types of a combination of *table salts* and added *flavors*. You can *home-make* seasoning salt with *ground pure spices mixed* with *natural sea salt*. Question the *salt* and source of *seasonings*. (See *sea salt* and *seasonings*.)

Season-To-Taste: Season to taste is a term used for the addition of any *seasoning* in an amount that is preferred according to personal taste. (See *seasoning* and *pinch*.)

Sea Vegetables: Sea vegetables are any of a variety of *seaweed*. *Pure* and *plain* sea *plants* are naturally GF. These *edible* non-*animal foods* grow in the sea. Choose *100%, pure, dried* or *fresh* sea vegetables from clean coastal areas. (See *seaweed*.)

Seaweed: Seaweed are any of a variety of *plants* grown in the sea. All *pure plain* seaweed is naturally GF. Types of *edible* seaweed include *algae, arame, chlorella, chlorophyll* (from *algae*), *dulse, hiziki, kelp, kombu, nori, spirulina* and *wakame*. [Look up each type individually.] You can eat seaweed *raw* or *cooked* (*steam, sauté* or *grill*). Seaweed is available at *health food grocery stores* and by *mail order*. (See 'seaweed' in A & F charts.)

Secalin: Secalin is the type of *plant protein* (*prolamin*) found *rye*. Individuals suffering from *celiac disease* have a genetic predisposition to the reaction from this *prolamin*.

Therefore, you must avoid *rye* grains and all *byproducts* of rye grains. (See *rye* and *prolamins*.)

Seed: Seed is the *plant part* containing the *embryo*. [Grains are not, referred to as seeds in this book and seeds in this book are not referred to as *grains* with the exception of *quinoa, amaranth* and *buckwheat*.] Not considering grains as seeds, all pure plain seeds are naturally GF. {Seeds may contain added *colors, dyes, seasonings, flavorings* and *polishing agents*.} Question the source of al *processing additives* on seeds. Irradiated seeds will not *sprout*. Choose pure and plain mechanically hulled seeds. *Whole* seeds are available at *ethnic* and *health food grocery stores* and some *regular grocery food stores* and by *mail order*. (See *sprout* and also see 'seeds' in A & F charts.)

Seed Oil: Seed oil is a type of *liquid* obtained from seeds. Oil is fluid at room temperature, as opposed to fat, which is solid at room temperature. Not considering grains as seeds, all pure plain seed oils are naturally GF. The best choices of GF seed oils include *flax seed, grape seed, pumpkin seed* and *hemp seed* oils. [Look up each individually.] A variety of *'pure'* GF oils are available at *regular* and *health food grocery stores* and by *mail order*. Check for GF purity. (See *oil, seed* and also see 'fats and oils' in A & F charts.)

Seed Sprout: (See *sprouted seeds*.)

Seitan: A type of *food* made from *forbidden wheat gluten*. Avoid.

Self-Basting: Self-basting is a treatment of injecting *fowl* with *fats* and/or *oils* to prevent drying during cooking. Avoid self-basted *fowl* (e.g. *poultry, chicken* and *turkey*).

Self Diagnosis: Personally diagnosing *celiac disease* (CD) is inconclusive. The most reliable test to *diagnose* CD is a *biopsy* from the *small intestines*. If there is strong clinical suspicion of *CD*, it can be diagnosis through *blood tests*. If eating the GF diet helps, then by all means stay on the diet as much as possible. Although the *serum test* will be negative, if the patient is already on the GF diet, prior to blood test. (See *blood test, biopsy* and *diagnose*.)

Self Rising Flour: *Wheat flour* with added *leavening agents*. Avoid.

Sell By Date: The sell by date indicates the date by which *foods* should have been sold. (See *dating*.)

Semen Cydonia: (See *quince gum*.)

Semolina: Coarsely *milled durum wheat*. [The main *ingredient* in most *pasta*.] Avoid. (See *pasta*.)

Senegal Gum: (See *acacia gum*.)

Sensitive: Sensitive individuals are easily irritated and they may react *acutely*. Sensitive individuals are generally affected by a stimuli more aggressively than most ordinary-individuals. (See *sensitivities* and *sensitive celiac*.)

Sensitive Celiac: Sensitive celiac is a term used to describe *celiacs* who are extremely *sensitive* to *gluten*, even in minute amounts. [Sensitive celiacs may react to minuscule amounts of *gluten*.] A sensitive celiac may also respond *acutely* to *gluten*. A sensitive celiac may have an *acute* reaction (*celiac shock*). (See *celiac shock, acute, supplement, sensitivities* and *gluten*.)

Sensitivities: Sensitivities is a term used to describe a type of *condition* where a person is overly *sensitive* to something *natural* or *synthetic*. A small percentage of people, have sensitivities. For more information about sensitivities I recommend further reading about food allergies and food intolerance. (See *resource guide, celiac* and *sensitive celiac*.)

Sequestering Agent: Sequestering agents are *substances* that create *physical* or *chemical* changes in *food*, usually by preventing, maintaining or separating their texture, color and/or flavor. Types include *acids*, *sodium* or *chemical compounds*. Question the source.

Serum Test: (See *blood test*.) [If a patient is eating GF prior to the serum test, then the test will be negative.]

Sesame Seed: A type of *seed. Raw* and *plain* are GF. (See *seeds*.)

Sesame Seed Oil: A type of *seed oil* obtained from *sesame seeds*. Check for GF purity. (See *sesame seeds*.)

Sevaiyan: Sevaiyan is a type of *wheat pasta*. Avoid. (See *pasta*.)

Shad: A type of *fish. Fresh pure* and *plain* are GF. (See *fish*.)

Shaker Dried: (See *dried sweet corn*.) GF.

Shakerpera: (See *cracker*.) Avoid.

Shallot: A type of *vegetable. Fresh* and *plain* are GF. (See *vegetable*.)

Shark: A type of *fish. Pure fresh* and *plain* are GF. (See *fish*.)

Shavegrass: A type of *herb. Pure* are GF. (See *herb*.)

Sheep: A type of *meat. Pure fresh* and *plain* are GF. (See *meat*.)

Shell: Shells is a term for the outer covering of *plants* and *animals* (e.g. *shellfish, nuts* and *seeds*). Shells are generally not eaten. [*Bran* is considered the shell of a *grain*, but in this book bran is referred to as *bran* only.] (See *shells* and *shelled*.)

Shelled: Shelled refers to the removal of the outer covering (shell). *Nuts* are shelled. (See *hulled* and *bran*.)

Shellfish: Shellfish is an umbrella term for any aquatic invertebrate *animal* with a *shell*. All *pure plain fresh shellfish* are naturally GF. (See *seafood* for cautions and additional details and specifications and also see 'shellfish' in A & F charts.)

Shells: Shells are a type of shell shaped *pasta* customarily made with *forbidden flour*. Avoid. (See *pasta*.)

Shepard's Pie: Shepard's pie is a type of *meal* customarily prepared with a *forbidden dough pie shell*. Avoid. (See *piecrust*.)

Sherbet: Sherbet is a particular type of *frozen fruit-juice dessert mixture* customarily made with *fruit juice*, *water* and *sweeteners*. {Sherbets may contain added *eggs*, *gelatin*, *milk*, *colors, stabilizers, flavorings, sequestering agents* and other *food agents*.} Several sherbets are GF. Verify all ingredients are GF.

Sherry: Sherry is a type of *fermented fortified wine* with added *distilled* brandy. Highly questionable. (See *wine*.)

Sherry Vinegar: Sherry vinegar is a type of *vinegar* made from *sweet sherry*. Highly questionable. (See *sherry* and *vinegar*.)

Shiso Vinegar: Shiso vinegar is not really *vinegar*, but more like a *soy sauce* or *tamari sauce* and used like *vinegar*. It is a *byproduct* of making *umeboshi*. Risky. Avoid unless source is known. (See *umeboshi*.)

Short Bread: A type of *cookie* customarily made with *wheat* flour. Avoid. (See *cookie*.)

Short Cake: A type of *wheat flour* sweet *biscuit* typically *filled* or *topped*. Avoid. (See *baked-goods*.)

Shortening: Shortening is a type of *fat* solid at room temperature that is derived from *animals* or *plants*. Shortening is commonly *hydrogenated soybean* or *cotton seed* oils. The majority of *vegetable shortenings* are GF. Verify GF. Question additives. (See *fats & oils*.)

Short Grain Brown Rice: Short grain brown rice is short grain *whole* rice. The *bran* is intact. (See *bran, brown rice* and *short grain rice*.)

Short Grain Rice: Short grain rice is a specific type of *brown* or *white* rice, as a rule, as wide as it is long. Short grain rice *cooks* up sticky and absorbs *liquids*, which makes it great for making *pudding* and any dish where *rice* needs to absorb *liquids*. Types include *sweet, risotto* and *sushi* rice grains. Short grain *brown* rice is more *nutritious* that short grain *white* rice. Both white and brown short rice grains *mill* into the best rice flour. Check for GF purity. (See *rice, short grain rice flour* and *brown rice*.)

Short Grain Rice Flour: Short grain rice flour is a certain type of rice flour milled from *brown* or *white short rice grains. Short rice grains* are the best types of grains to *mill* into *rice flour*, as opposed to *long rice grains. Brown rice flour* (milled from short grain brown rice) is more *nutritious* than *white rice flour* (milled from short grain white rice). Both white and brown short

rice grains *mill* into the best rice flour and work well in most *recipes*. Check for GF purity. (See *short grain rice* and *rice flour*.)

Short Grain White Rice: Short grain white rice is *refined short grain brown rice*. [*White rice* is *brown rice* with the *bran* removed.] Verify GF. (See *short grain rice* and *bran*.)

Short Patent Flour: (See *cake flour*.) Avoid.

Shred: To *grate* into small or thin pieces. (See *grate*.)

Shredded Cheese: (See *cheese shredded*.)

Shredded Coconut: Shredded coconut is *dried coconut shredded*. Pure shredded coconut is naturally GF. Several brands of shredded coconut are GF. Choose *unsulfured* and *unsweetened* types if possible.

Shrikhand: A type of *yogurt pudding*. Avoid unless source is known. (See *pudding*.)

Shrimp: Shrimp is a type of *shellfish seafood. Pure fresh* and *plain* are GF. (See *shellfish, seafood* and *seafood seasoning*.)

Sieve: To *strain liquid food* away from *solid food* through a mesh *kitchen utensil*. The *peptides* in *gluten* are too small to strain. Clean the strainer well between uses.

Sieve Bean: A type of small *lima bean*. GF. (See *bean*.)

Sift: To pass *dry powdered ingredients* (usually *flour*) through a mesh *kitchen utensil* to separate the large *particles* or *aerate*. Use separate sifters for both *gluten* and *gluten free foods* to prevent *contamination*. In a pinch, use a fine mesh colander for sifting.

Silicate: Silicate is a type of *substance* produced from pulverized rock dust. Silicate is an *anti-caking* and *dusting agent* and to coat *foods* as a *polishing agent*. Caution. GF.
Silicon: (See silicate.) Caution. GF.
Silicon Dioxide: (See silicate.)
Simmer: To heat *liquid food* on high heat until it bubbles, then turning the heat down and continuing to cook the food over low heat while it barely-bubbles.
Simple: Simple foods and/or ingredients are not *complex*. They consist of one part or *element*. (Also, see *basic*, *pure* and *plain*.)
Simulated Food: Simulated foods are *foods* that do not contain the actual *food*-product, but have the appearance of being that *food*. Simulated foods are commonly not GF. Question the source. (See *imitation food* and *vegetarian*.)
Sirimi: Avoid.
Skates: A type of *fish*. Pure fresh and *plain* are GF. (See *fish*.)
Skipjack: A type of *fish*. Pure fresh and *plain* are GF. (See *fish*.)
Skullcap: A type of *spice/herb*. Pure are GF. (See *spices* and *herbs*.)
Slaked Corn: *Dried corn boiled* with slaked lime. [The hull is cooked-off.] Verify GF. (See *hull*.)
Sliced Cheese: (See *cheese sliced*.)
Sliced Meat: (See *lunchmeat*).
Slippery Elm: A type of *spice/herb*. Pure are GF. (See *spices* and *herbs*.)
Sloppy Joe Mix: Sloppy Joe mixes are types of wet or dry *seasoning mixtures* used with *cooked ground meat*, then placed on a *bun*. The buns are generally not GF. A few canned sloppy Joe mixes are GF. Question the source of all ingredients. (See *sauce*, *seasoning mix* and *bun*.)

Slow Cooker: A type of *kitchen appliance*. This electric pot is used to *cook* foods slow on low heat over a long period-of-time.
Slug: *Pure fresh* and *plain* are GF.
Small Bowel: (See *small intestine*.)
Small Intestine: The small intestine is the part of the *digestive system* where a *biopsy* is done if there is a strong clinical suspicion of *celiac disease*. Consuming the toxic *gluten prolamins* causes a reaction that damages the *villi* in the small intestines (the *jejunum*), resulting in *malabsorption* of *nutrients*. (See *intestine*, *villi* and *biopsy*.)
Smelt: A type of *fish*. Pure fresh and *plain* are GF. (See *fish*.)
Smoked Food: Smoking food is a method of *preserving/curing food*. Types of smoked foods include *sardines*, *bacon*, *sausage*, *meat*, *poultry* and *fish*. {Smoked food may contain added *sweeteners*, *flavorings* and *enzymes*.} Question the source of the *food* and all *smoking agents*.
Smoking: A method of *preserving*. (See *smoked food* and *preserve*.)
Snack Foods: Snack food is an umbrella term for a variety of various types of generally small portioned easy to *prepare servings of food*. The majority of *commercially prepared* snack-foods contain *forbidden ingredients*. Choose snacks with an ingredient base of *beans*, *rice*, *corn*, *fruits*, *vegetables*, *nuts*, *seeds* and acceptable *grains*. [Look up each type of snack food individually.] Question the source of all the ingredients in snack foods. GF snack foods are available at *regular*, *ethnic* and *health food grocery stores* and by *mail order*. (See 'snacks' in A & F charts.)

Snail: *Pure fresh* and *plain* are GF.
Snap Bean: (See *green bean.*) GF.
Snapper: A type of *fish*. *Pure fresh* and *plain* are GF. (See *fish.*)
Snickerdoodle: A type of *wheat flour sugar cookie*. Avoid.
Snow Pea: A type of GF *pea* in a *pod*. Snow peas are *edible raw* or *cooked*. (See *bean* and *vegetable.*)
Soak: To immerse in *liquid* (usually water). You can soak certain *whole dried grains* overnight in cold water before *cooking* (e.g. *brown* or *sweet rice grains*). Certain *whole dried beans* must be soaked overnight in cold water before *cooking* (e.g. *adzuki, garbanzo* and *kidney*). *Lentil beans*, *split peas* and *instant beans* do not need soaking. (See *steep.*)
Soba: A type of *noodle* customarily prepared from a *mixture* of *buckwheat* and *wheat flour*. Avoid.
Sockeye: A type of *fish*. *Pure fresh* and *plain* are GF. (See *fish.*)
Soda: Soda is an umbrella term for a variety of *beverages,* which are *flavored carbonated soft drinks.* {Soda may contain added *acidifiers, colorings, buffers, clarifying agents, flavor carriers, flavor enhancers, humectants, sequestering agent, stimulants* and *thickeners.*} Always question the source of added *colors* and *flavors*. Especially question most *root beer* and *cream sodas*. Most soda is GF. Verify GF. (See *carbonated drinks* and *soft drinks* and see 'beverage' in A & F charts.)
Soda Bread: A type of quick *bread* made with *wheat flour*. Avoid.
Sodium: A metallic *chemical element* that occurs in *salt*. Salt is used generously as a *preservative* and *flavoring*. Sodium is usually

specifically-listed when used as an *ingredient*. Verify GF. (See *sea salt.*)
Sodium Acid Carbonate: (See *baking soda.*) GF.
Sodium Acid Pyrophosphate (SAP): A type of *additive*. Caution. GF.
Sodium Aluminum Sulfate: A type of *leavening agent* used in *baked-goods*. Caution. GF.
Sodium Ascorbate: (See *ascorbic acid.*) GF.
Sodium Ascorbic: (See *ascorbic acid.*) GF.
Sodium Benzoate: (See *baking soda.*) GF.
Sodium Bicarbonate: (See *baking soda.*) GF.
Sodium Carbonate: An *alkali* used in *baked-goods*. *Salt* of carbonic acid. Soda ash in the industrial form. Caution. GF.
Sodium Carboxymethylcellulose (CMC): (See *carboxymethylcellulose.*) GF.
Sodium Caseinate: Caution. GF.
Sodium Citrate: An *additive* used as an *emulsifier* in *food*. Caution.GF.
Sodium Hexametaphosphate: *Sodium* hexametaphosphate is used as an *emulsifier*. Caution. GF.
Sodium Isoascorbate: (See *ascorbic acid.*) GF.
Sodium Metabisulphite: A type of *additive*. Caution. GF.
Sodium Nitrate: Caution. GF.
Sodium Nitrite: Caution. GF.
Sodium Polymetaphosphate: Sodium *polymetaphosphate* used as an *emulsifier*. Caution. GF.
Sodium Potassium Tartrate: (See *cream of tartar.*) GF.
Sodium Silaco Aluminate: An *anti-caking agent*. Caution. GF.
Sodium Sulphite: A type of *additive*. Caution. GF.

Soft Drink: Soft drink is an umbrella term for a variety of *beverages,* which are *flavored carbonated beverages.* Most soft drinks are GF. (See *soda* for additional details and specifics.)

Softeners: Softeners are *substances* added to *food* to make them softer. Question the source.

Soft Serve: Soft serve is a term referring to a type of *frozen dessert* similar to *ice cream,* but softer in texture. It is termed soft serve ice cream, but is normally made with *artificial ingredients.* Some plain vanilla and plain chocolate flavored soft serves are GF. Verify GF. [Avoid the *cone* and question all *toppings.*] (See *cone.*)

Soft Wheat: A type of *wheat grain* containing less *gluten.* Avoid.

Soisson Bean: A certain type of white *bean.* GF. (See *bean.*)

Solar Evaporated Sea Salt: This is a type of *unrefined,* hand harvested, solar evaporated (sun dried) and *additive*-free *natural sea salt* still containing its *natural* trace *elements.* (See *sea salt.*)

Soldier Bean: A certain type of *heirloom bean.* GF. (See *bean.*)

Sole: A type of *fish. Pure fresh* and *plain* are GF. (See *fish.*)

Solid: Solids are substances that are not *liquid* but a more malleable material. Always question *prepared* solid *foods* for added *filler.* Some solid foods are rolled on a powdery substances to make them malleable. Always question the source of powders. (See *spread, filler* and *prepared foods.*)

Soluble: Soluble *foods* and/or *ingredients* are foods designed to dissolve in other foods (generally *liquids*). Question the source.

Solution: Solution is a term for any *liquid mixture* formed by a combination of *substances,* one of which needs to be *liquid.* [*Solid substances* are dissolved in *liquids* to form a solution.] Question the source of all *ingredients* used to form a solution. (See *mixture.*)

Solvent: Solvents are *substances* able to dissolve another. Solvents are usually *chemical* in *liquid* form. Caution. Question the source. (See *extracting solvent.*)

Sopaipilla: Sopaipilla is a type of *wheat flour pastry.* Avoid.

Sorbet: Sorbets are a type of *frozen fruit-juice dessert mixture* similar to *ice cream* and *sherbet,* but they do not contain *milk.* {Sorbet may contain added *sweeteners, colorings, flavorings* and other *food agents.*} Several varieties of sorbets are GF. Verify GF. (See *sherbet* and also see 'desserts' in A & F charts.)

Sorbitan: Sorbitan is a type of concentrated *sorbitol* to which the water has been removed. GF.

Sorbitol: A type of *diabetic sugar substitute* obtained from *natural* or *artificial ingredients.* The sweet *alcohol* may be derived from algae, fruit (e.g. berries) or seaweed. GF.

Sorghum: Sorghum is a type of GF *cereal grain.* You can use sorghum the same as *millet. Dried* sorghum will *mill* into *flour.* GF. (See *grains, flour* and *cereal grains.*)

Sorghum Flour: Sorghum flour is a type of *grain flour milled* from *dried sorghum.* Check for GF purity. (See *sorghum.*)

Sorghum Molasses: Sorghum molasses is a type of *molasses* made from *sorghum*. Check for GF purity. Avoid *sulfured* molasses if possible. (See *molasses* and *sorghum*.)

Soup: Soup is a term used for a variety of various hot or cold liquid *meals* customarily *prepared* with *broth*. Soups are made with a variety of *foods* in a *liquid base*. {Soups may contain added *thickeners*, *emulsifiers*, *flavorings*, *starches*, *additives*, *sweeteners*, *stabilizers*, *preservatives*, *colorings* and *forbidden gluten byproducts* (e.g. *pasta* or *noodles*).} The majority of soups are not GF, especially thickened soups. Soups at restaurants are rarely GF. You cannot strain soups to make them GF. Question the source of all the ingredients in soups. Some of *commercially prepared* GF soups are available at regular grocery food stores but the majority are available at *health food grocery stores*. You can *home-make* GF soups and freeze leftovers. (See *strain* and *broth* and also see 'soup' in A & F charts.)

Source: Source is the thing from which an *ingredient* and/or *food* was derived. Source is the specific *base* of which *components* are made. The source of all ingredients need to be questioned and/or verified GF. (See *ingredients* and *components*.)

Sour Cream: Sour cream is a type of *dairy* product made from cultured *milk* and *milk products*. {Sour creams usually contain <u>gelatin</u>, <u>rennin</u>, <u>eggs</u>, starch, thickeners, emulsifiers, stabilizers, gums, flavorings, additives and enzyme.} Some sour creams are GF. Sour creams are questionable. (See *dairy*.)

Sourdough Bread: A type of *yeast-bread* made with *wheat flour*. Avoid.

Sour Salt: Sour salt is *citric salt* derived from *acidic fruits*. GF.

Soy: Soy is a term used for *soybeans*. Soy is also a term for certain *foods* made from *soybeans*. Verify GF. (See *soybean*.)

Soya: Soya is a term for a finely *milled soy powder* used to make *soymilk*. Soya is also a term for a type of *soy protein isolate* made from soybeans. Some soya is labeled GF. Question the GF purity of both. (See *soybean*.)

Soya Powder: (See *soya*.)

Soybean: Soybean is a type of GF *bean* high in *oil* and *protein* content. Soybeans are tan to black in color. Soybeans are one of the most *nutritious* and versatile *beans* and they take on the *flavor* of other *food*. Soybeans are used to make soy *butter*, soy *yogurt*, soy*milk*, tempeh and *tofu*. Caution: most soybeans are GMO. Caution: some individuals are *sensitive* to soybean products. Choose *organic* soybeans. [Look up each type of soy product.] (See *soybean*, *organic* and *GMO*.)

Soybean Cheese: (See *soybean* and *tofu*.)

Soybean Concentrate: (See *soy protein*.) Avoid unless source is known.

Soybean Curd: (See *soybean* and *tofu*.) Verify GF.

Soybean Oil: Soybean oil is a type of *oil* obtained from *soybeans*. Check for GF purity. (See *soybeans*.)

Soy Bran: Soy bran is not the same as *soy flour*. Verify GF. (See *soybean*.)

Soy Curd: (See *soybean* and *tofu*.)

Soy Dal: (See *soy lentils*.) GF.

Soy Deli Foods: Soy deli foods are *foods* made from *soy isolate* and *textured vegetable protein*. Caution. Risky. Avoid unless source is known. (See *soybean, soy isolate* and *textured vegetable protein*.)

Soy Flakes: Soy flakes are *soybeans* partially *cooked* and then flattened. Check for GF purity. (See *soybean*.)

Soy Flour: Soy flour is a type of *bean flour milled* from *dried soybeans*. Soy flour adds moisture and improves the texture in *baked-goods*. Check for GF purity. Soy flour is also a term for *soy protein*. Avoid unless source is known. (See *soybean, soy protein* and *bean flour*.)

Soy Flour Lecithinated: A type of *soy flour* to which *lecithin* is added to contribute to its *emulsification*. Avoid unless source is known.

Soy Flour Textured: This is a type of *processed soy flour*. Soy flour textured expands when *hydrated*. Risky. Avoid unless source is known. (See *textured soy protein*.)

Soy Food: Soy foods are any of a variety of various *foods* made from *soybeans* or *soybean byproducts*. Types include *soy flour, soy butter, soy yogurt, soymilk, tempeh* and *tofu*. The majority of soy food is not GF & may contain *MSG*. Choose *organic* GF soy foods if possible. Question the source of all the ingredients in soy foods. (See *soybean* and *organic*.)

Soy Grits: Soy grits are an extremely coarsely *milled soy flour*. Check for GF purity. (See *soybean* and *soy flour*.)

Soy Isolate: Soy isolate is a type of *isolate* made from *soy flour* that is most likely processed with *chemicals* or *alcohols*. Question its GF purity. (See *soybean*.)

Soy Lecithin: Soy lecithin is a type of *lecithin* in a *liquid* or *powder* form obtained from *soybeans*. It is used as an *emulsifier*. Verify GF. (See *soybean*.)

Soy Lentils: (See *split soybeans*.)

Soymilk: Soymilk is a type of *nondairy milk* made from *cooked soybeans*. {Soymilk may contain added *filler, gum, flavorings, alcohol* and *enzymes*.} Always question soy milk. Low amounts of *gluten* are in some *soymilks*. Question the GF purity. (See *soy* and *nondairy milk*.)

Soy Okara: Soy okara is the fibrous *pulp* that remains after pressing *soy paste* when making *soymilk*. Check for GF purity. (See *soybean*.)

Soy Paste: Soy paste is the *soybean* and water *mixture* before draining when *cooking soymilk*. Soy paste is also a *fermented soybean mixture*. Question the source of all ingredients. (See *miso* and *soybean*.)

Soy Powder: Soy powder is a type of finely *milled* GF *soy flour*. Soy powder is also a *soy drink mix*. Question the source.

Soy Protein: Soy protein is a type of *protein* obtained from *soybeans*. Soy protein can refer to *soy flour, soy concentrate* and *soy protein isolate*. [Look up each individually.] Verify GF. (See *soybean* and *soya*.)

Soy Protein Concentrate: Soy protein concentrate is a type of *protein* obtained from *soybeans* and/or *soy flour*. Verify GF. (See *soybean* and *soy flour*.)

Soy Protein Flour: Soy protein flour is a type of *protein flour* obtained from *soybeans* and/or *soy flour*. Verify GF. (See *soybean* and *soy flour*.)

Soy Protein Isolate: Soy protein isolate is a type of *protein isolate* obtained from *soybeans* and/or *soy flour*. Verify GF. (See *soybean* and *soya* and *soy flour*.)

Soy Protein Textured: (See *textured soy protein*.)

Soy Sauce: Soy sauce is a type of *fermented soybean condiment* used as a seasoning. {Soy sauce may contain added *barley* or *wheat byproducts*.} Soy sauce is questionable. You can *substitute* soy sauce with GF *tamari sauce* or *liquid aminos*. Choose wheat-*free* and yeast free soy sauce. (See *soybean, Chinese food* and *condiments*.)

Spaghetti: Spaghetti is a type of long-thin *pasta* customarily made with *forbidden flour*. GF spaghetti is available through *specialty companies*. (See *pasta*.)

Spaghetti Sauce: Spaghetti sauce is a type of *seasoned tomato sauce* used on *spaghetti pasta*. [Spaghetti sauce is not the same as *pasta sauce*, but sometimes spaghetti sauce is termed *pasta* sauce.] A variety of spaghetti sauces are GF. Question the source of all ingredients. (See *sauce* for cautions.)

Spanish Bean: A type of red *kidney bean*. GF. (See *bean*.)

Spatula: A type of *kitchen utensil* with a flat flexible rubber end on a long wood or plastic handle. A spatula is used to scrap *foods* away from the sides of containers.

Spearmint: A type of *herb*. Fresh and *pure dried* are GF. (See *herb*.)

Special Ingredients: (See *specialty foods*.)

Special Occasion: You must eat prior to attending special occasion, social gatherings and formal affairs because there may be little if any GF *foods* there for you to eat. (See *hors D'oeuvres, appetizers, restaurant, travel* and *caterers*).

Special Resources: Special resources are special contact and information centers for you to learn more about the GF diet and/or *celiac disease* and other related *immunological diseases*. Special resources are also specific links to and/or for *specialty companies* that produce specialty *gluten free foods*. [The *Gluten Free Resource Guide 'a consumers guide for living gluten free'* is a book that contains a list of various resources along with other must-have information. This resource guide provides the names of gluten free mail order companies, defines the do's and don'ts of the gluten free diet, provides charts, illustrations, book recommendations and menu planning ideas along with practical information on how to shop, dine, travel and stock a pantry gluten free. To purchase this book write for details or visit the web site. See- pages 206 and 207.] Special resources may include *health food grocery stores, ethnic grocery food stores* and *gluten free mail order companies*. [Look up each resource individually] (See *specialty stores, specialty companies, specialty foods* and *specialty gluten free items*.)

Specialty Companies: Specialty companies are specific *companies* producing and/or selling *specialty-food*-items *manufactured* with and/or for special *gluten free food* requirements available through special resources. You can purchase a variety of *labeled* GF foods manufactured by *specialty* companies. (See *special resources, specialty foods, mail order, health food grocery stores, distributors* and *manufacturers*.)

Specialty Food: Specialty foods are unique and unusual foods (e.g. *gluten free food*) manufactured by specialty companies. Specialty foods are prepared specifically for certain dietary needs (e.g., the *gluten free diet*). You can obtain specialty foods labeled GF at *health food grocery stores* and through specialty *mail order companies*. [Both industries are known for carrying unique GF foods.] (See *specialty gluten free items* for additional specialty foods and see *special resources* and *specialty companies*).

Specialty Gluten Free Items: Although all food items need to be verified GF, there are specific GF food items necessary for GF recipes. There are also certain GF food items available only through special resources. [Special resources may include *health food grocery stores, ethnic grocery food stores* and *gluten free mail order companies*.] A list of these specialty food items may include but not be limited to *gluten free baked goods* (e.g. *breads, bagels, muffins, brownies, cakes, pies, pancakes* and *waffles*), *pasta* (*rice pasta, corn pasta, bean pasta* and *potato pasta*), *flours* (e.g. *rice flour, arrowroot flour, potato starch-flour, corn flour, cornmeal, bean flour* and *tapioca starch/flour*), *baking mixes* (e.g. *bread, bagel, muffin, brownie, cake, pie crust, pancake and waffle mixes*), *nutritional bars* and/or *drinks, cereals* (e.g. *whole grains*, or *prepared cereals*), *snacks* (e.g.

pretzels, taro or *potato sticks, crackers, puffs, rice cakes* and *cookies*) and certain *condiments* (e.g. *spreads, dips, flavorings, baking powder* and *bouillon*). [Look up each type of food and/or ingredient separately.] (See *specialty foods, specialty companies* and *specialty resources*.)

Specialty Stores: Specialty stores are certain type of grocery food stores carrying unique and special food items (e.g. *gluten free foods*). Types include *health food grocery stores, ethnic grocery food stores* and *gluten free mail order companies*. [Look up each type individually.] (See *special resources, specialty food* and *specialty companies*.)

Spelt: Spelt is a type of *cereal grain* related to *wheat*. [Spelt is a relative of *wheat* and therefore should be avoided.] Some individuals on a *wheat-free diet* can eat spelt, but *celiacs* on a *gluten-free diet* cannot eat spelt. Avoid spelt and avoid all *byproducts* of spelt. (See *grains*.)

Spelta: Spelta is a type of *wheat* relative. Avoid. (See *spelt*.)

Spice: Spice is an umbrella term used for various aromatic *plant parts* used to *flavor food*. All *pure* spices are *GF*. Spices contain many beneficial properties (e.g. *natural flavoring agents*), but spices lack the *nutritional* value of *fruits* and *vegetables*. The word spice listed as an *ingredient* is usually a term for a combination of *spices* or a *spice blend*. [Question all *spice blends*.] Because the term spice is not specific it always makes foods with added spices questionable. {Spices may contain *filler* for *bulk* or *pour* *ability.*} You can grind *pure, whole, dried* spices with a *mortar* and *pestle* or *coffee grinder* and use them as needed. Good culinary spices include *allspice, basil, bay leaf, caraway seeds, cardamom, cayenne, celery seeds, chamomile, chives, cilantro, cinnamon, clove, cori*ander *seeds, cumin seeds, dill weed, fennel seeds, fenugreek, ginger, marjoram, mustard seeds, nutmeg, oregano, paprika, parsley, peppermint, poppy seeds, rosemary, sage, tarragon, thyme* and *turmeric. Commercially prepared pure* GF spices are available at *grocery food stores* and by *mail order*. Check for GF purity. (See *spice blend, seasoning* and *filler* and also see 'herbs and spices' in A & F charts.)

Spice Blend: Spice blends are typically a combination of spices. The term spice blend listed as an *ingredient* is not specific and always makes foods questionable. {Spice blends may contain *forbidden flour base*.} Question the source of all spice blends. Types of *spice blends* include *chili mixes, taco seasoning, cheese-sauces, seasoning salt* and *curry powders*. You can *home-make* spice blends with a *mixture* of your own <u>freshly</u> <u>ground</u> <u>pure</u> GF <u>herbs</u> and *spices* with a *mortar* and *pestle* or *coffee grinder* and use them as needed. Spice blends are risky. A small number of spice blends are GF. Avoid unless source is known. (See *spice* and *seasoning*.)

Spiced Vinegar: Spice vinegar is a type of *vinegar* made with *herbs* and *spices*. Question the *spice* source and the type of *vinegar*. (See *vinegar* and *herbs and spices*.)

Spice Mice: (See *spice blend*.)

Spikenard: A type of *spice/herb. Pure* are GF. (See *spices* and *herbs*.)

Spinach: A type of *vegetable. Fresh* and *plain* are GF. (See *vegetable*.)

Spirit: Spirit is a term for a type of *diluted distilled alcohol*. Caution. Verify GF. (See *alcohol*.)

Spirit Vinegar: Spirit vinegar is a strong tasting type of *vinegar* made from *diluted distilled alcohol*. Spirit vinegar contains small amounts of *alcohol*. Caution. Verify GF. Avoid all if possible. (See *vinegar*.)

Spirulina: *A type of seaweed. Pure* and *plain* are GF. (See *seaweed*.)

Splenda: GF.

Split Lentils: Split lentils are *whole lentil beans* split in half. GF.

Split Pea: Split peas are any of a variety of *dried* red, yellow or green *peas* split in half. GF. (See *pea*.)

Split Pea Lentils: (See *split lentils*.)

Sponge Cake: A type of light and airy *cake* made with *wheat flour*. Avoid. (See *baked-goods*.)

Spoon Bread: A type of *bread mixture* spooned on *stews* and *casseroles* before *baking*. The *mixture* is traditionally <u>cornmeal</u> or a <u>cornmeal</u> and *wheat* blend. Avoid unless you verify all ingredients GF.

Spread: Spread is an umbrella term for a variety of *snack foods* made from various ingredients used for spreading and/or dipping (e.g., dipping into with *snack foods* such as <u>vegetables</u>, crackers or *chips*). Spreads are always risky. {Spreads may contain added *fillers, gums, emulsifiers, additives, flavorings, colorings, sweeteners, preservatives, stabilizers* and other *food agents*.} Avoid spreads with *forbidden grains* and *forbidden grain byproducts*. Question the source of all spreads.

Question spreads for additives especially *thickeners*. There are a handful of *commercially prepared* GF spreads. It is best to choose pure *natural* spreads with basic GF *ingredients*. (See *dips*.)

Spring Roll: (See *egg roll*). Avoid

Spritz: A type of shaped *dough* cookies customarily made with *forbidden flour*. Spritz is also a term for adding a quick-spray of a small amount of liquid (usually water).

Sprout: The sprout is the part of a *bean*, *seed*, grain or *vegetable* when moistened or soaked in water starts to grow. Sprouts are the tiny shoots before becoming *mature plants*. Individuals with *weakened immune systems* are advised to avoid *alfalfa sprouts*. *Irradiated* seeds will not sprout. Sprouts are GF, but see *sprouted grains* for details and cautions. (See *bean*, *seed*, *grain*, *vegetable* and *sprouted grains*.)

Sprouted Grains: Sprouted grains are a type of *sprout* grown from *grains* as opposed to *seeds*, *beans* or *vegetables*. The *sprouts* of all grains including *wheat sprouts* are harmless, but if the *sprout* has not *germinated*, then it still contains the *forbidden protein gluten*. Sprouted grain drinks or other *commercially prepared* sprouted *products* cannot guarantee that every sprout has *germinated*, therefore caution all *sprout* and sprout products grown from *gluten grains* (e.g. *wheat*, *barley*, *rye* and *relatives of these grains*). [Individual tolerance should dictate use.] Acceptable grain *sprouts* are grown from *gluten free grains* (e.g. *corn*, *rice*, *wild rice*, *amaranth*, *buckwheat*, *millet* and *quinoa*). (See *grains* and *sprout*.)

Sprouted Seeds: [Grains are not, referred to as seeds in this book and seeds in this book are not referred to as *grains* with the exception of *quinoa*, *amaranth* and *buckwheat*.] Not considering *grains* as seeds, all *pure plain* seed sprouts grown from seeds are naturally GF. Individuals with *weakened immune systems* are advised to avoid alfalfa sprouts. (See *seed* and *sprouts*.)

Sprouted Wheat: The sprouts of *wheat grains* are harmless, but if a sprout has not *germinated*, then it still contains the *forbidden protein gluten*. Sprouted wheat drinks or other *commercially prepared* sprouted wheat products cannot guarantee that every sprout has *germinated*, therefore caution all *sprout wheat* products. Individual tolerance should dictate use. (See *sprout* and *sprouted grains*.)

Spun Sugar: Spun sugar is a type of *cooked cane sugar* used for decorating *desserts*. {Spun sugar may contain added *flavorings* and *colorings*.} Verify GF.

Squab: A type of *fowl*. *Pure fresh* and *plain* are GF. (See *fowl*.)

Squash Seeds: *A type of seed. Raw and plain* are GF. [Some squash seeds are termed pumpkin seeds.] (See *pumpkin seeds*.)

Squid: A type of *seafood*. *Pure fresh* and *plain* are GF. (See *seafood*.)

St: This the abbreviation used for *Saint*. [Look up as 'Saint'.]

Stabilizer: Stabilizers are *natural* or *artificial substances* used to make *food* resistant to physical change by improving its consistency and/or helping it maintain structure. Stabilizing agents include *setting*, *gelling*, *bulking*, *suspending* and *emulsifying agents* and some *chemicals*, yeast, cellulose, lecithin, *mono* and *diglycerides*, *gelatin*, *various gums*, *pectin* and *oils/fats*. Acceptable GF stabilizers may include certain brands of some *gums*, *bean flours*, *arrowroot powder*, *corn flour*, *rice flour*, *cornstarch*, *cornmeal*, *gelatin*, *kudzu*, *nut flours*, *potato flour*, *sago starch*, *seed flours*, *dried fruit flours*, *tapioca flour*, *cream of tartar* and *xantham gum*. Always question the source.

Stainless Steel Cookware: The best type of *cookware* is *stainless steel* with a center layer of *aluminum* or copper for better heat conducting. *Stainless steel* is non-reactive to *acid* and *alkaline food*; it is easy to clean and resists corrosion and scratching. Choose heavy-duty *stainless steel* cookware. (See *ascorbic acid*, *aluminum cookware* and *cookware*.)

Stamps: An *edible* type of *glue* containing *gluten* is used on stamps. Avoid licking stamps and envelopes. (See *glue*.)

Standardized: Standardized foods are prepared with standard limits. They are *foods* to which certain *additives* in specific-amounts are used for specific purposes.

Stand Mixer: A type of stationary mixer, as opposed to a portable mixer. (See *mixer*.)

Starch: Starch is a certain type of powdery *carbohydrate substances* found in *beans*, grains (e.g. *rice*, *corn* or *wheat*), *legumes*, *roots*, *tubers*, *plants* and *vegetables*. Starch is used in *medication* as a *binding agent* and in *cooking* as an *anti-caking, absorbing, binding, filling, gelling, stabilizing* and *thickening agent*. Acceptable GF starches include certain brands of *arrowroot powder, cornstarch, potato starch, rice starch, sago starch, tapioca flour, waxy cornstarch* and *sorghum starch*. Always question the source of starch. The word starch alone listed as an *ingredient* generally refers to *cornstarch* unless otherwise naming the source (e.g. *potato starch, tapioca starch* or *wheat starch*). Question the source of *modified starch* and *food starch*. *Commercially prepared* GF starches are available at *ethnic, regular* and *health food grocery stores* and by *mail* order. [Look up each type.]

Starch Modified: (See *modified starch*.) Highly questionable.

Starch Modifying Agents: These agents are *acids*, *sodium* or *chemical compounds*. Caution. Avoid if possible. Verify GF.

Star Fruit: A type of *fruit*. Fresh and *plain* are GF. (See *fruit*.)

Steak: Steak is a select piece of *meat*. You can *grill* steak *plain* on a clean *grill* and then season it with GF *condiments*. Verify GF. (See *meat* and *steak sandwich*.)

Steak Sandwich: Steak sandwich is a type of *sandwich* made on a long *roll filled* with thin slices of *steak sandwich meat*. The roll is normally made from *forbidden flour*. Various steak sandwich meats are GF. Question all ingredients. (See *sandwich* and *meat*.)

Steak Sauce: Steak sauce is a type of *condiment* used to *season steaks*. Certain steak sauces are GF. Verify GF. (See *condiments* and *sauce*.)

Steam: To cook *food* (e.g. *raw fresh vegetables* and *seafood*) in a steamer basket over simmering water, with a lid on the pan/pot to hold in heat.

Steamed *foods cook* in less time than *foods cooked* in boiling water and they retain more *nutrients*.

Steamed Bread: A *wheat-batter bread mix steam cooked.* Avoid.

Stearic Acid: An *additive* made *naturally* or *synthetically* with certain *vegetable oils.* Caution. GF.

Steel Cut Oats: (See *oat.*) Question.

Steelhead: A type of *fish. Pure fresh* and *plain* are GF. (See *fish.*)

Steep: To soak *food ingredients* (e.g. *plant parts*) in *liquid* (usually water).

Stevia: Stevia is a type of *natural sweetener* in a *liquid* or *powdered* form. It is good for people with candida, diabetes or hypoglycemia. Stevia is derived from a certain type of *dried flower.* Check for GF purity.

Stew: Stew is a certain type of *soup meal,* generally containing pieces of *vegetables* and *meat* in a *thickened liquid broth.* Stew is usually slow cooked. The majority of stews are not GF. Stews at restaurants are rarely GF. Question the source of all the ingredients in soups especially the added *thickener.* Avoid stew with *forbidden pasta, noodles* and *grains.* Some of the *commercially prepared* GF stews are available at regular grocery food stores but the majority are available at *health food grocery stores.* You can *home-make* GF stews and freeze leftovers. Types of GF thickeners for *homemade* stew include *arrowroot powder, rice flour, tapioca flour* or *tapioca pearls.* Avoid stew unless the source of all ingredients is known. (See *starch, flour* and *soup* and also see 'stew' in A & F charts.)

Sticks: Sticks are a type of *deep fried snack* food made with *potatoes* cut into matchstick shapes. Question added *seasonings.* A variety of sticks are GF. Choose *plain potato sticks.* Verify GF. (See *chips.*)

Sticky: Sticky is a term used for *glutinous.* [Sticky is not the same as gluten.] The term sticky applies to a *glutinous* type of *rice grain.* GF. (See *sweet rice* and *glutinous.*)

Sticky Rice: Sticky rice is type of *sweet rice.* GF. (See *sweet rice.*)

Sticky Rice Flour: (See *sweet rice flour.*) Check for GF purity.

Sticky Rice Starch: (See *sweet rice starch.*) Check for GF purity.

Stilton: Stilton is a type of *veined cheese.* Avoid all veined cheese.

Stimulant Agent: Stimulant agents are *substances* that increase the function and/or activity of *food.* Question the source. (See *caffeine.*)

Stingray: A type of *fish. Pure fresh* and *plain* are GF. (See *fish.*)

Stir Fry: Stir-fry's are a type of *meal prepared* in a *wok* or *skillet* over high heat. Stir-fry's are usually *seasoned* with a *fermented sauce* (e.g. *soy sauce, wheat-free soy sauce, tamari sauce* or *liquid aminos*). {Stir-fry's may contain added *seasoning, sauces* and *thickener.*} Chinese *restaurants* commonly use *cornstarch* as a *thickener.* Always question the source of seasonings and thickeners. Serve stir-fry's over *rice* or *rice noodles* not *forbidden pasta* or *couscous.* Stir-fry's must be *fried* in a clean *pan/wok* free of *food residue* from previously cooked *foods* containing *gluten.* All ingredients must be verified GF.

Stock: Stock is an umbrella term for a type of *broth* strained from cooking *meats, fish* or *vegetables.* Most stocks have at least a little added *thickener*. {Stock may contain added *thickener*, *flavors*, *colors* and other *food agents*.} You can *home-make* stock with GF ingredients and freeze it in ice cube trays, then place the individual cubes in freezer containers, then use them as needed. The majority of stocks are not GF. Avoid unless source is known. (See *strain*, *broth* and *bullion*.)

Stone Ground: Stone ground is a type of *milling* process without the use of heat. (See *stone mill*.)

Stone Mill: A stone mill is a type of *mill* used to *grind food* (e.g. *whole dried beans*, *seeds*, *nuts* and *grains*). Do not stone mill *foods* with a high *oil* content (e.g. *peanuts* and *soybeans*). [You can *mill defatted peanuts* and *soybeans* with a stone mill.] The stone *mill* is considered the best mill because in the *milling* process it flakes layers, therefore retaining the *foods fatty acids*. The stone *milled* products are *milled* cool and this also helps retain *nutrients* and extends the products shelf life. (See *mill*, *whole* and *grains*.)

Store: (See *health food grocery store*, *regular grocery food store*, *ethnic grocery food store* and *mail order companies*.)

Stracchino Cheese: A type of soft *cream cheese*. Verify GF.

Straight Flour: Straight flour is a type of *flour milled* from a variety of *wheat grains*. Avoid.

Strain: To pour *liquid* through a strainer or *sieve* therefore separating *solids*. This process does not remove *gluten*. The *peptides* in *gluten* are too small to strain, therefore straining does not render *gluten*-containing food GF.

Strainer: A type of mesh kitchen *utensil* used to strain *food*. Clean well between uses. (See *strain*.)

Strawberry: A type of *fruit*. Fresh and *plain* are GF. (See *fruit*.)

Stretch Curd Cheese: A type of *cheese* that has elasticity. It stretches when heated. Types of stretch curd cheeses include *caciocavallo* and *mozzarella*. [Look up each type.] Verify GF. (See *pizza cheese*.)

String Bean: A type of *vegetable*. A slim green *bean* in its *pod*. Fresh and *plain* are GF. (See *vegetable*.)

Stroganoff: Stroganoff is a type of *meal* made with *beef*, *cooked* in a *thickened sauce* and served over *noodles* or *rice pilaf*. Avoid unless the source of all ingredients are known. You can *home make* stroganoff with GF ingredients.

Stromboli: A type of enclosed *pizza*. Avoid. (See *pizza*.)

Strong Flour: A type of *grain flour milled* from *hard wheat*. Avoid.

Strudel: A type of *pastry* made with *wheat flour dough*. Avoid.

Stuffing: Stuffing is a term for type of *filling*. Stuffing is typically made with *forbidden wheat byproducts*. Stuffing is used to stuff *meat*, *fish*, *poultry* or *vegetables*. You can *home make* stuffing with GF ingredients. There is a *commercially prepared* GF stuffing available only through *specialty companies*. (See *filling* and *specialty companies*.)

Sturgeon: A type of *fish*. Pure fresh and *plain* are GF. (See *fish*.)

Subacute Stage: The subacute stage is the second stage of a *disease*. The subacute stage is the point in a *disease* where the body begins to worsen and gradually loose the ability to fight off problems. Patients with CD might show signs of brief, severe and quick onsets from the consumption of *gluten*. Patients in the subacute stage of celiac disease normally recover with a strict adherence to the GF diet. (See *four stages of disease, celiac* and *disease*.)

Submarine: A type of *sandwich*. (See *sandwich*.) Avoid.

Substance: Substances are either living or non-living. Substances are considered individual types of *material*, from *natural* or *artificial* sources, but may be a combination of one or more substances. Not all substances used in *foods* are *nutritious* or *beneficial* to your *health*, nor are they always *labeled* as an *ingredient*. Question the source of every substance. (See *ingredient*.)

Substitute: You can substitute most any *ingredient* to take the place of another *ingredient* with similar characteristics. Question the source and its abilities. (See *specialty food items, artificial* and *imitation*.)

Sucanant: A certain type of GF *sweetener* made from *sugar cane*.

Sucralose: A type of *artificial sweetener*. Avoid if possible. GF.

Sucrose: Sucrose is a *crystalline carbohydrate* found *naturally* in *plants*. This type of sweetener is obtained from *sugar cane, sugar beets* or *sorghum*. Verify GF.

Suet: Suet is a type of *animal fat*. Question if the suet was *dusted* with *forbidden flour*. Verify GF. (See *fat*.)

Sugar: Sugar is a type of *refined carbohydrate sweetener* frequently made from *sugar cane*. Sugar is an *ingredient* in a lot of *processed foods*. Types of sugar may include *brown sugar, castor sugar, crystal sugar, confectioner sugar, invert sugar, decorating sugar, flavored sugar, granulated sugar, milk sugar, powdered sugar, raw sugar, refined sugar, table sugar, unrefined sugar, Turbinado sugar* and *white sugar*. Sugar *labeled* as an *ingredient* may also apply to *corn sugar, corn syrup*, dextrose, *fructose*, galactose, barley malt, *glucose, lactose*, maltose or *sucrose*. [Look up each sugar source individually.] Always question the source of sugar. Avoid sugar as much as possible or choose *natural sweeteners* or the least *refined sugar*. (See 'sweeteners' in A & F charts.)

Sugar Snap Pea: A type of GF *vegetable* that is a cross between a *snow pea* and *green pea*. Both *pea* and *pod* are edible. (See *vegetable*.)

Sugar Substitutes: (See *artificial sweetener*.) Caution.

Sulfate: A type of *salt* or *ester* of *sulfuric acid*. Avoid if possible. GF.

Sulfide: A type of *chemical compound* containing *sulfur* and one or more other *elements*. Caution. Avoid if possible. GF.

Sulfite: *Salt* or *ester* of *sulfur dioxide* in the form of gas or *solids*, used as a *preservative* to retard spoilage or discoloration and to prevent the growth of *bacteria mold* and *yeast*. Some *individuals* are *sensitive* to sulfites. Caution. Avoid if possible. GF. (See *sensitivities*.)

Sulfosuccinate: A type of GF *food additive*. Caution. Avoid if possible.

Sulfur: A type of nonmetallic *chemical* element occurring in nature. Sulfur may also be a combination of *sulfide* and *sulfate minerals*. Sulfur is used to make *sulfuric acid* and *fungicides*. Caution. Avoid if possible. GF.

Sulfur Dioxide: Gas *sulphite*. A *toxic* gas used in making *sulfuric acid*. Caution. Avoid if possible. GF.

Sulfured: Sulfured foods are *foods* treated with *sulfur, sulfuric acid* or *sulfate* as a preservative. Caution. Avoid sulfured food if possible.

Sulfuric Acid: A type of corrosive *acid* used in making *starch*. Caution. Avoid if possible. GF.

Sulphite: (See *sulfite*.)

Sulphite Dioxide: Caution. Avoid if possible. GF.

Sulphurous Acid: (See *sulfite*.) Caution. Avoid if possible. GF.

Summer Pudding: A *cooked fruit* baked in a *forbidden wheat bread*-lined baking dish. Avoid.

Sundae: Sundaes are a type of *dessert* made with *ice cream* and *topped* with *syrup, flavorings* and *whipped cream*. [Look up each type of ingredient individually.] Question the source of all the *ingredients*.

Sun Dried: Sun dried foods are *raw foods* customarily *dried* in the sun. Sun dried is also a term used for foods *dried* by *artificial methods*. Caution: various sun dried *foods* are *presoaked* in a *solution*. Caution: various sun dried *foods* are *preserved* or *treated* after they dry. Question the source. Question if the sun dried foods were *dusted* with *forbidden flour*. Quite a lot of sun dried foods are GF. Caution. Verify its GF purity. (See *organic*.)

Sun Dried Corn: Sun dried corn is *dried sweet corn dried* out. GF.

Sun Dried Fruit: Sun dried fruit is made from *raw fruit* possibly *sun dried*. (See *dried fruit* and *sun dried food*.)

Sun Dried Tomatoes: Sun dried tomatoes are *dehydrated tomatoes* possibly *sun dried*. Sun dried tomatoes are available dry packed or packaged in *oil* possibly with added *seasonings*. Verify GF.

Sunfish: A type of *fish*. *Pure fresh* and *plain* are GF. (See *fish*.)

Sunflower Seed: *A type of seed*. *Raw* and *plain* are GF. (See *seeds*.)

Sunflower Seed Milk: Sunflower seed *milk* is a certain type of *nondairy milk* made from raw *sunflower seeds*. {Sunflower seed milk may contain added *filler, gum, flavorings, grain byproducts, alcohol* or *enzymes*.} Low amounts of *gluten* are in some *nondairy milks*. Question the GF purity. (See *sunflower seeds* and *nondairy milk*.)

Sunflower Seed Oil: A type of *oil* obtained from *sunflower seeds*. Check for GF purity. (See *sunflower seeds* and *oil*.)

Supermarket: (See *grocery store*.)

Supplement: Supplements referred to in this book are certain *substances* added to your *diet* on a daily basis to enhance your nourishment. Certain amounts of a variety of supplements are frequently taken by individuals who are *malnourished* and/or deficient in certain *nutrients*. Taking extra *nutrients* in addition to a healthy *diet* is considered beneficial. Although you can obtain all the *nutrients* you need from a well-balanced *whole foods diet*. Some *celiacs* find it necessary to supplement their *diet*. Types of supplements *celiacs* might choose to take may include *acidophilus* (good *bacteria* to help restore *intestinal flora*), a good multivitamin and mineral complex, zinc to help boost the *immune system, digestive enzymes* to help break down *food*, vitamin B complex and calcium for the bones and possibly folic acid, additional vitamin 12, vitamin A, vitamin K, vitamin C and vitamin D. Visiting a *nutritionist* may help with a *malabsorption disease* such as *celiac disease.* *Gluten* is a minor problem in *vitamin* products nevertheless gluten must be avoided in even relatively small amounts. Avoid gluten in supplements. Supplements frequently contain a statement that lists substances not in their product. There are several GF supplements and several are labeled. GF supplements available at *drug stores, regular* and *health food grocery stores* and by *mail order.* (See *nutritionist* and *malabsorption.*)

Supplies: (See *kitchen supplies.*)

Sushi: Sushi is a type of *sweet rice* seasoned with *rice vinegar* (question the *rice vinegar*). Sushi is also a term for seasoned *raw fish* with *wasabi,* wrapped around *sushi rice* with *nori sheets,* then sliced and *seasoned* with *soy sauce* (question the *rice vinegar, wasabi, soy sauce* and any other *ingredient*).

Sushi Rice: Sushi rice is a type of *short grain glutinous rice.* Sushi rice is an unusual type of *rice* that becomes *sticky* when *cooked,* thus absorbing *liquids.* [Sticky is a term used for *glutinous.* Glutinous is not the same as *gluten.* The term *sticky* and/or *glutinous* applies to a specific type of *rice grain.*] Varieties of sushi rice include Japanese rose, cal rose, uruchimai, Japanese short grain, glutinous and Kokuku rose. Verify GF. (See *sushi, glutinous* and *rice.*)

Suspending Agent: Suspending agents are *natural* or *artificial* *substance* used to delay action in *foods.* Question the source.

Sweet Bean: A sweet type of *soybean.* GF. (See *soybean.*)

Sweet Bread: The glands of young *animals.* Sweet bread is commonly used in *gourmet cooking.* GF.

Sweet Corn: Sweet corn is a type of GF *corn* eaten as a *vegetable.* Sweet corn can be *dried* (chicos) and *milled* into a *grain-flour.* (See *corn* and *vegetables.*)

Sweetened Condensed Milk: Sweetened condensed milk is a *mixture* of whole *milk* and *sugar* heated until some of the moisture evaporates. Verify GF.

Sweeteners: Sweeteners are a variety of various *natural* or *artificial substance* used to sweeten *food.* Sweeteners are obtained from a variety of sources including *fruits, tree sap, plants, bees* and *grains.* Types of sweeteners include *glucose, honey, dextrose, sugar, molasses, maple syrup, caramel, brown sugar, invert sugar, malt syrup* and *barley malt.* The source of a sweetener is not always *specifically identified* on labels. Always question the source of a sweetener. (See *natural sweeteners* and also see 'sweeteners' in A & F charts.)

Sweetening Agents: Sweetening agents are *substances* used to sweeten *foods.* (See *sweetener.*)

Sweet N Low: A *brand name* of a type of *artificial sweetener.* Caution. GF. (See *artificial sweetener.*)

Sweet Potato: Sweet potatoes are a specific type of sweet tasting *tuber,* orange in color. [Sweet potatoes are not the same as *yams.*] Sweet potatoes can be *dried* and *milled* into *flour.* GF. (See *vegetable.*)

Sweet Rice: Sweet rice is a specific type of *short grain rice* that becomes *sticky* (*glutinous*) when *cooked*. Sweet rice does not contain *gluten*. Sweet rice has more *starch* than regular *rice*. The endosperm of sweet rice is either black or white in color. Sweet rice grains are best *soaked* over night in cold water before *cooking*. You can *mill whole* sweet rice grains into a rice *grain-flour*. Verify GF. (See *rice, sweet rice flour* and *ethnic grocery food store*.)

Sweet Rice Flour: Sweet rice flour is a specific type of *rice flour milled* from *whole sweet rice grains*. Sweet rice flour makes a great *thickening agent*, because of its excellent freeze thaw ability. Sweet rice flour is great in *baked-goods* because it helps them stick together and retaining moisture. Check for GF purity. (See *rice flour* and *sweet rice*.)

Sweet Rice Starch: Sweet rice starch is a *refined starch* made from *sweet rice grains*. Sweet rice is the starchiest rice grain. Check for GF purity. (See *sweet rice*.)

Sweet Sherry: Highly questionable. (See *sherry*.)

Swiss Chard: A type of *vegetable*. *Fresh* and *plain* are GF.

Swiss Cheese: Swiss cheese is a genetic term for an *aged cheese* with large holes. Verify GF. (See *cheese*.)

Swordfish: A type of *fish. Pure fresh* and *plain* are GF. (See *fish*.)

Symptom: Symptoms indicate the presence of an illness, disorder or disease (e.g. *celiac disease*). Symptoms are usually undesirable. Symptoms of celiac disease (CD) are variable in combination and severity. Symptoms of CD may include weight loss, bone pain, moodiness, lactose intolerance, brain fog, fatigue, nausea, vomiting, flatulence, diarrhea, anxiety, hyperactivity, depression, skin irritations, nutrient deficiencies and stomach bloating, pain, gurgling and cramping. Some *celiacs* in the early stages may have no obvious symptoms of *celiac disease*. Without the classic symptoms of *CD*, many cases go undiagnosed and/or missed *diagnosed*. With CD, *diarrhea* may be one of the few physical symptoms. [Even without symptoms, in all stages of celiac disease, the disease is always present but the body might not display visible symptoms.] (See *four stages of disease, disease* and *celiac disease*.)

Synthetic Chemical: Synthetic chemicals are *manufactured chemicals* not occurring in nature, or only occurring *naturally* in small quantities, but are *manufactured* in large quantities. Although their basic chemistry is much the same, there are individualities. (See *chemical* and *synthetic ingredients*.)

Synthetic Flavoring: Synthetic flavorings are *chemically* made *nonnutritive flavor substitutes* added to *food* to impart *flavor*. Caution. Question the source. (See *synthetic ingredients*.)

Synthetic Ingredient: Synthetic ingredients are *chemically* made *nonnutritive substances* from *natural ingredients*, but have no counterpart in nature. These *substances* are produced by a *chemical process* (synthesis). Caution. Some individuals do not do well with synthetic ingredients. Avoid if possible. Question the source. Verify GF. (See *sensitive celiac*.)

Syrup: Syrup is a type of thick *liquid substance* generally obtained from *plants*. Syrup may be a *mixture* of a combination of *sweeteners*. {Syrups may contain added *flavor*, *sweeteners*, *coloring* and other *food agents*.} Avoid flavored syrups. Choose <u>pure</u> <u>syrups</u> <u>such</u> <u>as</u> <u>pure</u> <u>maple</u> <u>syrup</u> or <u>molasses</u> *unsulfured* if possible. Quite a few syrups are GF. Verify GF. (See *maple syrup* and *molasses*.)

Tabasco Sauce: Tabasco sauce is a *fermented* type of *condiment*. {Tabasco sauce may contain added *jalapeno peppers*, *vinegar* and *seasonings*.} Some are GF. Question all *ingredients*. (See *condiment*.)

Table <u>Salt</u>: Table salt is a type of highly *refined* and frequently *chemically processed* salt, usually kiln dried and obtained from an unknown source. [The source can be polluted waters.] {Table salt may contain added *chemicals*, *magnesium carbonate*, *aluminum* and *anti-caking*, *free flowing* and *anti drying agents*.} Individuals with *DH* are advised to avoid iodine and should choose <u>uniodized</u> <u>salt</u>. Plain table salts are generally GF. The best salt is <u>pure</u> <u>natural</u> <u>Celtic</u> <u>sea</u> <u>salt</u>. (See *sea salt* and *iodine*.)

Table <u>Sugar</u>: Table sugar is a type of *granulated sugar cane*. *White sugar*. Caution. GF. (See *sugar*.)

Tablets: *Medication* is often prepared into tablet form. Tablets are one of the many form in which medication and/or supplements are concentrated for ingestion. *Gluten* is a minor problem in tablets nevertheless gluten must be avoided in even relatively small amounts.

(See *compounded medication* and *medication* for details and specifics.)

Taco: Tacos are a type of *meal* made with a *taco shell filled* with *meat*, <u>lettuce</u>, <u>tomatoes</u>, *cheese*, *seasoning*, *taco sauce* and sometimes *refried beans*. Question if the *taco shell* (*tortilla*) is either <u>corn</u>, *wheat* or a <u>corn</u> and *wheat mixture*. Question the source of the *seasoning* on the meat, other *seasonings*, *taco sauce* and *refried beans*. Tacos can be made with GF ingredients.

Taco Seasoning: A type of *season mix* used for tacos. Questionable. (See *spice blends* and *seasonings*.)

Taffy: Taffy is a type of chewy candy made with *sweeteners*. {Taffy may contain added *flavorings* and *colorings*.} Question the source of all taffy. Question if the taffy was *dusted* with *forbidden powders* for *molding* or to prevent the candy from sticking to the wrapper. Verify GF. (See *candy*.)

Tagliatelle: Tagliatelle is a type of *pasta* customarily made with *forbidden flour*. Avoid. (See *pasta*.)

Tahini: Tahini is a type of *seed butter* made with *sesame seeds* and *oil*. Verify GF. (See *spreads*.)

Talc: Talc is a type of *substance* used to *coat foods* as a *polishing agent*. Caution. GF.

Taleggio Cheese: A type of semi-soft *cheese*. Verify GF. (See *cheese*.)

Tallow <u>Flakes</u>: Tallow flakes are a type of *food agent* obtained from sheep and cattle *fat*. Caution. GF.

Tamale: Tamale's are a type of *baked meal* made with *cheese*, *meat* and *seasoning* wrapped in *cornhusk*. The meat is usually *seasoned*. Question the source of *seasoning* and all other *ingredients*. (See *meal*.)

Tamarind: A type of *fruit*. *Fresh* and *plain* are GF. (See *fruit*.)

Tamarind Gum: A type of *gum* obtained from *tamarind seeds*. Caution: it contains *laxative* properties. GF. (See *gum*.)

Tamari Sauce: Tamari sauce is a *seasoning* high in *sodium*. This type of *condiment* is similar to *soy sauce*. [Liquid aminos contains a little-less *sodium* and can replace tamari sauce in most recipes.] If possible, avoid low sodium tamari sauce because of the added *preservatives*. Avoid tamari sauce with *wheat*. Choose traditionally fermented slow brewed wheat-free tamari sauce made from soybeans. *Commercially prepared* GF tamari sauce is available at *regular, ethnic* and *health food* grocery stores.

Tamatar: (See *tomatoes*.) GF.

Tangerine: A type of *fruit*. *Fresh* and *plain* are GF. (See *fruit*.)

Tannic Acid: A type of *acid* obtained from trees, *plants* and shrubs. Very GF.

Tapenade: Tapenade is a type of *condiment paste* made with pureed *anchovies, capers, olives, tuna* and *seasonings*. Question the source of all the *ingredients* including added *filler*. Avoid unless GF. (See *paste*.)

Tapioca: (See *tapioca pearls*.) GF.

Tapioca Flour: Tapioca flour is a specific type of fine white *flour* milled from *tapioca pearls*. You can use tapioca flour in *baked-goods* where a chewy-texture is desired. Tapioca flour is excellent as *thickener*. You can *substitute* tapioca flour for *cornstarch* or *wheat flour* as a *thickener* in *recipes*. Check for GF purity. *Commercially prepared* GF tapioca flour is available at *ethnic grocery stores, health food grocery stores* and by *mail order*.

Tapioca Pearls: Tapioca pearls are the white pearls formed by the *dried root* of the *cassava (tapioca) plant*. You can add tapioca pearls in *stews* and *soups* for an *excellent thickener*. Tapioca pearls *mill* into *tapioca flour*. Tapioca pearls are available at *regular, ethnic* and *health food* grocery stores and by *mail order*.

Tapioca Starch: (See *tapioca flour*.)

Tapioca Starch Flour: (See *tapioca flour*.) GF.

Taro: Taro is a type of *tuber*. *Fresh* and *plain* are GF. Taros are excellent in place of *potatoes*. (See *potato*.)

Tarragon: A type of *spice*. *Fresh* and *pure dried* are GF. (See *spices*.)

Tart: Tarts are small individual *crust baked-goods* customarily made with *forbidden pastry flour*. Tarts are obtainable GF only through specialty resources.

Tartaric Acid: Tartaric acid is a type of *acid* that occurs from *fruit*. It is an *acid base* for *cream of tartar*. GF. (See *cream of tartar*.)

Tartar Sauce: Tartar sauce is a type of *condiment* customarily made with *mayonnaise, pickles, seasonings* and *vinegar*. Question the source of all the ingredients. Risky. Tartar sauce is easy to home make.

Tartrazine: A type of *additive*. Caution. GF.

Tea: Tea is a type of hot or cold *beverage* made from various *dried mature* or *immature* tealeaves. Types of tea include regular, green and herbal). Black tealeaves are from *fermented* tealeaves. Instant and flavored teas are risky. Avoid herbal tea with *barley*. Choose pure 100% pure tealeaves. *Decaffeinated* tea should be *naturally decaffeinated*. Tea may contain *mold*. There is an abundance of GF tea. Pure loose GF tea is available at *regular, ethnic* and *health food grocery stores* and by *mail order*. (See *tea bags, herbal tea* and *naturally decaffeinated*.)

Tea Bags: The common tea bag contains a type of edible glue. Caution. Question the source. Choose *100% pure* loose tealeaves and use a tea *infuser*. (See *tea, infuser* and *glue*.)

Tea Herbal: Herbal tea is made from *dried* or *fresh herbs*. *Instant* and *flavored* herbal-teas are risky. Avoid herbal tea with *barley*. Choose *100% pure* GF herbal tea. Verify GF. Pure loose GF herbal tea is available at *ethnic, health food grocery stores* and by *mail order*. (See *tea* and *tea bags*.)

Tea Infuser: A tea infuser is a type of *kitchen utensil* used to make tea without using tea bags. Choose a *stainless steel* infuser. Using an infuser will eliminate concerns for possible *contamination* from the glue on tea bags. (See *tea bags*.)

Tef: (See *teff*.)

Teff: Teff is a type of *cereal grain*, closely related to *corn* considered safe. GF. (See *grains*.)

Teff Flour: Teff flour is a type of *grain flour milled* from *teff*. Do not use teff flour with *yeast*. (See *teff*.)

Tej Patta: *Cassia* leaves. GF.

Teleme Cheese: A type of soft *cheese*. Verify GF.

Tempeh: Tempeh is a type of *bean food* made from *fermented beans* (e.g. *soybeans, mung beans* or *winged beans*) and sometimes *grains*. Tempeh like *tofu* is versatile. Do not eat tempeh *raw*. To cook

tempeh, *bake, grill, steam* or *broil*, as you would chicken. Tempeh can be *seasoned* and used like *chicken* in recipes. Choose *pure unflavored bean tempeh*. Not all tempeh is GF. *Commercially prepared* GF tempeh is available at some *regular, ethnic* and *health food grocery stores*.

Tempura: Tempura is a *deep fried fish* or *vegetable* dish customarily *pre-dipped* in a *forbidden batter*.

Tentsuyu: Tentsuyu is a type of *condiment* made with *mirin* and *soy sauce*. Risky. Question the source of all the *ingredients*.

Tepary Bean: Tepary beans are a certain type of *bean*. GF. (See *bean*.)

Teriyaki Sauce: Teriyaki sauce is a type of *condiment*. Teriyaki sauce is a *marinated mixture* of *seasonings, sake* and *soy sauce*. Few are GF. Question the source of *ingredients*. (See *condiment* and *sauce*.)

Tetraploid: Tetraploid is a type of *wheat* relative. Avoid.

Texmati Rice: This type of *rice* is created from a cross between an American *long grain rice* and a *basmati long grain rice*. GF.

Textured Soy Flour: *Soy flour* textured. Avoid unless source is known. (See *soy flour textured*.)

Textured Soy Protein (TSP): TSP is a type of high-*protein food* made from *soybeans*. Textured soy protein is formed into chunk-like croutons. It expands when hydrated. Textured soy protein is *flavored* to taste like meat. Caution. Risky. Avoid unless source is known.

Textured Vegetable Protein (TVP): TVP is a type of *chemically modified soy protein flour* or *mixture* made from *corn* or *forbidden wheat*. TVP is a type of high-*protein food* commonly made from *soybeans*. TVP is formed into chunk-like croutons. It expands when *hydrated*. TVP is *flavored* to taste like meat. Caution. Risky. Avoid unless source is known.

Thandai: A type of spicy *beverage*. Avoid unless source is known.

Thiamin Hydrochloride: A type of coenzyme of B vitamin. Verify GF.

Thickener: Thickeners are *natural* or *artificial substances* used to improve the consistency of *foods* by *setting, gelling, bulking, suspending* or *emulsifying*. Types of thickeners include chemicals, yeast, mono and diglycerides, cellulose, lecithin, gelatin, various *gums*, pectin and oils/fats. Acceptable GF thickeners include certain brands of some *gums*, bean flours, arrowroot powder, corn flour, rice flours, cornstarch, cornmeal, gelatin, kudzu, nut flours, potato flour, sago starch, seed flours, dried fruit flours, tapioca flour, cream of tartar and xanthan gum. [Look up each individually.] *Forbidden wheat* and *barley byproducts* or various *gums* are widely used thickeners added to *prepared*-foods. You need to question most *prepared foods* for thickeners, especially *sauces*, *gravies* and *foods* stable or with a thick consistency. Question the source of all thickening agents.

Thin Boiling Starch: (See *cornstarch acid modified*.)

Thistle: A type of *spice*. *Pure* are GF. (See *spice*.)

Thousand Island Dressing: This is a type of *mayonnaise* based *dressing* mixed with *pickles*, *seasonings* and *vinegar*. Some are GF. Question all ingredients. (See *dressings*.)

Thyme: Thyme is a type of *spice*. *Pure* are GF. (See *spice*.)

Ticci: (See *patties*.) Avoid.

Tiger Bean: Tiger beans are a type of *black bean*. GF. (See *bean*.)

Til: (See *sesame seeds*.) GF.

Tillamook Cheese: A quality type of firm *cheddar cheese*. Verify GF. (See *cheddar cheese* and *cheese*.)

Tilsit Cheese: A type of medium firm *cheese*. Verify GF.

Tissue: Tissues are *organic* multi cellular *organisms* from either *animals* or *plants*. (See *organisms*.)

Titanium Dioxide: A type of *additive*. Caution. GF.

Toast: Toast is sliced *bread*, toasted. Unless specified toast is normally from a *forbidden* source. (See *bread* and *toaster*.)

Toaster: A toaster is a *kitchen appliance* used to toast breads, bagels, tarts and some muffins. Foods toasted in toasters are generally not GF. You need to toast GF *bread* in its own toaster so that tiny amounts of *forbidden* toaster *crumbs* from other foods do not contaminate the GF foods. One *wheat bread crumb* is enough to cause *gluten contamination*. To prevent *gluten contamination* use a separate toaster for GF toast or toast GF *bread* in a toaster oven on a piece of *aluminum foil*. (See *toast*.)

Toaster Oven: Toaster ovens are a type of kitchen *appliance* that *cook foods* with electrical heat elements (e.g. *bakes* or *broils*). Toaster ovens are mini ovens. [In a pinch you can use toaster ovens to toast GF *bread*, instead of using a *contaminated* toaster.] You need to cook GF foods separate from gluten containing foods. (See *oven* and *cook*.)

Tobacco: Tobacco is a type of *plant*. The *leaves* are dried and used in cigarettes. *Pure* are GF.

Toffee: Toffee is a certain type of *candy* commonly made with *forbidden ingredients*. Risky. Avoid unless source is known. (See *candy*.)

Tofu: Tofu is a type of bean *food* made from *unfermented* curdled *bean milk* (e.g. *soybean, mung bean,* or *winged bean milk*). Tofu is one of the most versatile *vegetarian foods*. Tofu is excellent *raw* in *salads* and *dips*. You can *cook* and *season* tofu just like *chicken*. You can use tofu as a *binder* in place of *eggs* in some *recipes*. You can use tofu in place of *cheese* in some recipes or as part of a cheese *mixture*. The best tofu is firm or extra firm tofu, water packed with a *nigari coagulant*. Verify GF.

Tomatill: A type of *vegetable*. Fresh and *plain* are GF. (See *vegetable*.)

Tomato: A type of *fruit*. Fresh and *plain* are GF. (See *fruit*.)

Tomatoes: Tomatoes can be a general term for *prepared cooked tomatoes*. (See *tomato products*.)

Tomatoes Crushed: Crushed tomatoes are a type of *prepared cooked tomatoes* crushed. *Choose plain* and *unseasoned*. Verify GF. (See *tomato products*.)

Tomatoes Diced: Diced tomatoes are a type of *prepared cooked tomatoes* diced. *Choose plain* and *unseasoned*. Verify GF. (See *tomato products*.)

Tomato Paste: Tomato paste made from *prepared tomatoes*, cooked until most of the liquids have evaporated. Question tomato paste for added *thickener*. *Choose plain* and *unseasoned*. Verify GF. (See *tomato products*.)

Tomato Products: Tomato products are various types of *processed tomatoes* used as a base in *recipes*. The majority of *plain stewed, whole, pureed, sauce, diced* and *crushed prepared tomatoes* are GF. [Look up each type individually.] All of these tomato products are used as a single-*ingredient* in *recipes*. Question the source of all tomato products. Verify GF. *Choose plain* and *unseasoned* whenever possible. (See *tomato, canned foods* and *prepared foods*.)

Tomato Puree: Tomato puree is made from strained *cooked tomatoes*. Verify GF. *Choose plain* and *unseasoned*. (See *tomato products*.)

Tomato Sauce: Tomato sauce is a type of thin *tomato puree*. [Tomato sauce is not the same as *pasta sauce* or *spaghetti sauce*.] *Choose plain* and *unseasoned*. Verify GF. (See *tomato puree, tomato products* and *sauce*.)

Tomato Stewed: Stewed tomatoes are *cooked whole* skinless *tomatoes*. The whole tomatoes are *cooked* into a sauce-like chunky consistency. *Choose plain* and *unseasoned*. Verify GF. (See *tomato products*.)

Tomato Whole: Whole tomatoes are *cooked whole* skinless *tomatoes*. *Choose plain* and *unseasoned*. Verify GF. (See *tomato products*.)

Tools: (See *kitchen supplies*.)

Topical: Topical products are *substances* (*cosmetic* or *medication*) used 'on' the skin, as opposed to 'ingested' internally. Individuals with DH disease are advised to avoid topical products containing *gluten*. Anecdotal reports indicate individuals with DH have been known to be affected by *gluten* in external products. CD patients can use caution with topically applied *substances* that contain *gluten*. (See *topical medication, label reading, cosmetics* and *sensitive celiac*.)

Topical Ingredients: (See *topical*.)

Topically: (See *topical*.)

Topical Medications: Topical medication is *medication* used *topically* as apposed to ingesting it internally. Topical medication is considered *nontoxic*. [*Medical distilled alcohol* is considered GF.] (See *medication* and *topical*.)

Topping: Toppings are typically one or more *unspecified ingredient*. Toppings are risky. Question all toppings especially on *yogurt*. Avoid unless source is known. (See *dry*.)

Tortellini: A type of stuffed *dough* pasta specifically shaped customarily made with *forbidden wheat*. Avoid. (See *pasta*.)

Tortia: Tortia's are an *unleavened flatbread* traditionally made with *corn* or both *corn* and *wheat*. Question the source. (See *tortilla*.)

Tortilla: Tortillas are a type of *unleavened flatbread* customarily made from *corn* or with both *corn* and *bean* or with both *corn* and *wheat*. {Tortillas may contain added *colorings, flavorings, preservatives* and *dough conditioners*.} Choose *100*% *pure corn* or pure *corn* and *bean* tortillas. Question the source. A variety of tortillas are GF. (See *tortilla chips*.)

Tortilla Chips: Tortilla chips are a certain type of *chip* made from *corn* or with both *corn* and *bean* or with both *corn* and *wheat*. {Tortilla chips may contain added *colorings, flavorings, preservatives* and *dough conditioners*.} Choose *100*% *pure corn* or pure *corn* and *bean* tortilla chips. Question the source. A good number are GF. (See *tortilla*.)

Tortilla Shell: Tortilla shells are a type of *edible* soft *shell* made from *corn* or with both *corn* and *bean* or with both *corn* and *wheat*. Tortilla shells are traditionally *filled* with *taco ingredients*. {Tortilla shells may contain added *colorings, flavorings, preservatives* and *dough conditioners*.} Choose *100*% *pure corn* or pure *corn* and *bean* tortilla shells. Question the source. Several are GF. (See *taco* and *tortilla chips*.)

Tostada: Tostada's are a type of a *bean filled* crispy *tortilla*. Question the source of *seasoning* and all other *ingredients* including the tortilla. Avoid unless source is known.

Tovar Dal: A type of *split peas*. GF.

Toxic: Toxic refers to any *substance* causing injury or harm. Toxic is also a term for poisonous. In this book the word toxic refers to *gluten contamination* for celiacs.

Trace Minerals: Tiny amounts of *essential inorganic substance* for human existence. (See *minerals*.)

Traditionally Prepared: Traditionally prepared *foods* and/or *ingredients* are prepared in a conventional manner. Traditionally prepared methods of preparation are possibly based on natural processes as opposed to nontraditionally prepared products with quicker methods that possibly use *chemicals*. Traditional methods of preparation may take longer but are generally of better quality. Traditionally prepared food items frequently contain less-*substances*. (See *processed* and *prepared*.)

Tragacanth Gum: A type of *gum* obtained from a bush *plant*. Caution. Avoid if possible. GF.

Trail Mix: Trail mixes are a type of dry *mixture* of various *dried ingredients*. {Trail mixes may contain added *dried fruits, nuts, seeds, cereals, c*andy, *pretzels*, other *ingredients* and frequently *seasonings* or *sweeteners*). *Commercially prepared* trail mixes are often not GF. Few *commercially prepared* GF trail mixes are available through *special resources*. You can *home make* trail mixes with GF *ingredients*. Avoid unless source is known.

Transgenic: Transgenic is a term for *organisms* introduced to *genetic matter* from sexually incompatible *organisms*.

Transglutaminase: Transglutaminase is a specific type of enzyme. A blood test for the diagnosis of celiac disease looks for *antibodies* to this *enzyme*, if there is a strong clinical suspicion of CD. (See *blood test*.)

Travel: To travel on any journey or while visiting other places (e.g., vacation, work, school, friends or relatives), it is a good idea to keep a small travel bag on hand packed, of course, with a few of your favorite GF *snacks* and *condiments*. Always have convenient GF *snacks* (e.g. *nutritional bars*) on hand for emergencies while touring on your trip. When traveling for long periods, packing the favorite most convenient difficult-to-get GF *food* items is the safest and easiest way to travel. Let traveling companions know about your *dietary needs*. If you are staying with friends or family and they want to prepare a big dinner for your visit, you may want to suggest that everyone go out to eat. [You feel more comfortable eating GF at a *restaurant* and no one gets offended and you have fun.] If traveling for a significant length of time, take along some *basic* hard-to-find GF *food* items (e.g. GF *pasta*, GF *cereal*, GF *bread* and *bread mixes*, GF *baking mixes*, GF *cookies* and GF *crackers*). It is always safest when traveling to bring the essentials. You can have special GF food items shipped ahead. Today there is an abundance of GF travel *foods* and places to purchase them. If your traveling, I recommend purchasing a guide book to help you locate independent, corporate and coop *natural food stores* across the United States that offer some GF food items. Gluten free foods that travel well and take up very little suitcase space include *nutritional bars, nutritional drink packets, freeze-dried foods* and *foods* sold for *backpacking* or *camping*. [Look up each type individually.] Do not experiment with new/untried GF foods on vacation. If you want to travel with a new fun GF food, test it prior to your trip! Ask a travel agency or touring company to help you plan your vacation GF, but do not expect this to be easy or quick. If traveling extensively you may want to book a hotel room with a kitchen and bring your own *kitchen supplies*. I always keep two travel boxes with basic kitchen supplies packed in order to prepare foods on lengthy trips (e.g., a small container and a large container). When I travel, I take both-boxes or just the smaller one, depending on the trips length and location. Types of culinary supplies to fill the containers may include any of the following: can opener, immersion blender, citrus juicer, garlic press, mortar and pestle, nutcracker, pastry brush, potato peeler, sieve, spatula, scraper, strainer, vegetable brush, cheese grater, nutmeg grater, knives, measuring cups and spoons, utensils, sandwich bags, colander, coffee mill, cutting board, dish cloth, extension cord, food processor, hand grain grinder, hot plate, mandaline, muffin pan, thermometer (for the cold travel food container), sponge, toaster oven, wax paper, glass baking dishes with storage lids, aluminum foil, dish soap, muffin papers, paper towels, parchment paper, produce wash, dish soap, cloth towels and a pan and pot each with a lid. [These supplies are convenient travel size.] If you want to learn more about traveling GF, I suggest contacting a guided club. (See *children* and *gluten free, special resources, restaurant* and *uncooked*.)

Travel Food: Finding GF food convenient for travel can be quite challenging. For emergencies, always pack a few of your favorite GF *snacks* (e.g. *nutritional bars*). If traveling for a significant length of time, take along some *basic* hard-to-find GF *food* items (e.g. GF *pasta*, GF *cereal*, GF *bread* and *baking mixes*, GF *baking mixes*, GF *cookies* and GF *crackers*). Gluten free foods that travel well and take up very little suitcase space include *nutritional bars, nutritional drink packets, freeze dried foods* and *foods* sold for *back packing* or *camping*. [Look up each individually.] (See

travel for more details about traveling GF and also see *uncooked*.)

Treating Agents: Treating agents are *chemical* or *natural substances* used to treat *food*. Question the source of all treating agents. Organic foods are not treated with harmful treating agents. Caution. Risky. Avoid treated *foods* if possible. (See *organic* and *polished*.)

Treatment: To date there has been no research indicating any treatment rendering *gluten* containing plants, foods and/or ingredients *gluten free*. (See *treating agents* and *process*.)

Tree: Trees are a type of large perennial plant. Wood, sap and tree nuts are obtained from trees. *Pure plain* foods from trees are naturally GF. (See *plants* and *wood pulp*.)

Tree Nut: Tree nuts are any of various types of *nuts* that grow on trees. *Raw* and *plain* are GF.

Tree Sap: (See sap.) *Pure* are GF.

Tricalcium Phosphate: A type of calcium *salt* of phosphate used as an *anti-caking agent*. Caution. GF.

Trinticale: A type of *wheat*. Avoid.

Triple Cream Cheese: Triple cream cheese is a type of soft *fresh/ripened cream cheese* extra *enriched* with *cream*. Verify GF. (See *dairy* and *cream cheese* for additional details.)

Tripolini: A type of bowtie shaped *pasta* customarily made with *forbidden flour*. Avoid. (See *pasta*.)

Triticale: A type of *hybrid wheat* and *rye grain*. Avoid. (See *grains*.)

Triticum: A type of *forbidden grain*. *Wheat* makes up the *genus* triticum. Avoid.

Trout: A type of *fish*. *Pure fresh* and *plain* are GF. (See *fish*.)

Trout Bean: A type of *heirloom* variety of the *pinto bean*. GF.

Truffle: Truffles are a type of *fungus*. *Fresh plain* are GF. Caution. (See *fungus*.)

Tsampa: (See *barley*.) Avoid.

TSP: (See *textured soy protein*.) Avoid unless source is known.

Tuber: Tubers are any of various fleshy swollen parts of a *root* that grow underground. *Potatoes* and *yams* are considered tubers. All *fresh* *pure* and *plain* tubers are naturally GF. (See *rhizome*, *vegetable* and also see 'tuber' in A & F charts.)

Tuber Flour: A type of GF *flour* milled from *dried tubers*. GF tuber flours include certain brands of *potato starch-flour* and *yam flour*. (See *tuber* and *flour*.)

Tumbleweed: A type of *spice/herb*. *Pure* is GF. (See *herbs* and *spices*.)

Tuna: Tuna is a type of *fish*. *Pure* *fresh* and *plain* tuna is GF. (See *fish* and *tuna canned*.)

Tuna Canned: Canned tuna is a type of precooked tuna preserved in cans. Several brands of canned tunas are GF. Choose canned tuna without *seasonings* or vegetable *broth*. Verify GF. (See *canned foods*.)

Tuna Salad: Tuna salad is a type of cold *salad* commonly made with canned *tuna* and chopped *vegetables*, *seasonings* and possibly *eggs*. {Tuna salad may contain added *seasonings*, *mayonnaise*, *vinegar* and *pickles*.} Question the source of all ingredients. (See *tuna*.)

Turbinado Sugar: A type of *raw* *sugar*. Verify GF. (See *sugar*.)

Turbot: A type of *fish*. *Pure fresh* and *plain* are GF. (See *fish*.)

Turkey: Turkey is an American bird domesticated and raised for *food*. Avoid *self-basting* turkey. Check for GF purity. (See *fowl* and *self-basting*.)

Turmeric: Turmeric is a type of *spice*. *Pure* are GF. (See *spice*.)

Turnip: A type of *vegetable*. *Fresh* and *plain* are GF. (See *vegetable*.)

Turnip Greens: A type of vegetable. *Fresh* and *plain* are GF. (See *vegetable*.)

Turnover: Turnovers are a type of *baked-good pastry* customarily made with *forbidden dough*. Avoid.

Turtle Bean: (See *black bean*.) GF.

TVP: (See *textured vegetable protein*.) Question the source.

Tybo Vacherin Cheese: A type of *cheese*. Verify GF. (See *cheese*.)

Udon: *Wheat flour noodles*. Avoid.

Umeboshi Plumbs: Umeboshi plumbs are *pickled plumbs*. Purchase additive free *traditionally fermented* umeboshi plumbs available at *health food grocery stores* and *ethnic grocery stores*.) Verify GF.

Umeboshi Vinegar: Umeboshi vinegar is not really *vinegar*, but more like *soy sauce* or *tamari sauce* and used like *vinegar*. Umeboshi vinegar is a *byproduct* of making *umeboshi*. Avoid unless source is known. (See *umeboshi plumbs*.)

Unadulterated: Unadulterated *foods* are food products *pure* and *unmodified* (e.g., foods without added *substance*s, *filler*, *artificial ingredients*, *chemical compounds*, *food agents* and *waxes*). Unadulterated *food* still needs to be questioned and verified GF. (See *pure*, *fresh*, *plain* and *organic*.)

Unbleached Flour: Generally a type of *wheat flour*. Avoid.

Unbleached White Flour: Usually type of *wheat flour*. Avoid.

Unbolted Flour: Generally *unbolted wheat flour*. Avoid.

Uncooked: Uncooked foods are either *raw foods* or *processed foods* not yet cooked. Countless varieties of foods are *edible* uncooked. Types of uncooked foods include; *raw fruits* and *vegetables*, *salads*, *yogurt*, *nuts*, *seeds*, *cereal*, c*andy*, *frozen bars*, *cottage cheese*, *mozzarella cheese*, *crackers*, *nut butters*, *fruit spreads*, *chips* and other *snack foods*. [Look up each type individually.] Scores of uncooked GF foods are available at *grocery food stores*. (See *travel* and *cook*.)

Undon: *Wheat noodles*. Avoid.

Unfiltered: Unfiltered *substances* (usually *liquid*) are not *strained*. [The larger particles are still within.] Filtering does not remove *gluten*. The *peptides* in *gluten* are too small to strain, therefore filtration does not render foods containing gluten, GF. (See *mother of vinegar* and *distilled*.)

Unflavored Gelatin: Unflavored gelatin is *gelatin powder*, without added *flavorings* or *sweeteners*. Verify GF. (See *gelatin*.)

Unidentified Ingredients: Unidentified ingredients are not recognized as an *ingredient*. [Unidentified ingredients are *ingredients* in or on *foods,* not *labeled* as an *ingredient*.] Question the source. (See *ingredients* and *hidden ingredients*.)

United States Dept of Agriculture: The USDA is an organization that oversees agriculture. The United States Department of Agriculture contact phone number is 1-800-535-4555. For information about grains write to *The US Department of Agricultural Research Service,* Western Regional Research Center, Albany CA 94710. Ask for their free literature about grains and their relationship to celiac disease and the gluten free diet. [You can also, write the USDA and let them know you have a restricted diet, *label* reading is essential to your *health* and you would like everything going 'into' or 'on' a product listed in the *ingredient* section.]

United States Pharmacopoeia: The USP is a publication in the United States about *ingredients* with *medical* usages. The USP lists a potential *medical ingredients chemistry*, composition and *source*. The USP contact phone number is 1-877-633-6279.

Unleavened Bread: A type of *flatbread* that is *yeast* and *leavening* agent free and generally made with *forbidden wheat flour*. Avoid. (See *leavening, bread* and *batter bread*.)

Unmodified: Not *modified*. (See *modified* and *unadulterated*.)

Unmodified Starch: Unmodified starch is a type of *cornstarch* not *modified*. Check for GF purity. (See *cornstarch* and *modified starch*.)

Unnatural: Not *natural*. Not *pure*. *Artificial*. (See *natural* and *pure*.)

Unrefined Sugar: Unrefined sugar is a type of *processed sugar* derived from *sugar cane* to which 'some' of the *nutrients* remain. Verify GF. (See *sugar*.)

Unripened Cheese: Un-ripened cheese is *fresh immature cheese*, as opposed to *aged mature ripened cheese*. Verify GF. (See *cheese*.)

Unstandardized: Unstandardized foods are *foods* to which various *additives* are used in a non-specific amount. [No *standard* limits.] (See *standardized*.)

Unsulfured: Not *sulfured*. (See *sulfured*.)

Unusual Name: The unusual name is the uncommon name. The unusual name is a 'specialized' name used by people with specific knowledge. Ocimum basilicum L is an unusual name for *basil*. (See *common name*.)

Urad **Bean**: A type of *bean* related to the *adzuki* and *mung* bean. GF.

Ura **Ursi**: Ura ursi is a type of *spice*. *Pure* are GF. (See *spice*.)

Urea: A certain *synthetic yeast food* agent. Caution. GF. (See *yeast food*.)

USDA: (See *United State Department of Agriculture*).

USP: (See *United States Pharmacopoeia*.)

Utensil: Various *culinary* tools. Clean all utensils well between uses. (See *culinary* and *kitchen supplies*.)

Vacchino Romano Cheese: A type of firm *Romano cheese*. Verify GF.

Vacherin Cheese: A type of soft *cheese*. Verify GF.

Vanilla: Vanilla is a type of *spice*. *Pure* are GF. (See *vanilla extract*.)

Vanilla **Bean**: Vanilla beans are a type of bean used for its *aromatic* properties. GF. (See *vanilla*.)

Vanilla Essence: (See *vanilla extract*.)

Vanilla Extract: Vanilla extract is a type of *flavoring extracted* from the *vanilla bean*. Vanilla is *extracted* with a *liquid substance* (e.g. typically with <u>*corn* *glycerin*</u> or *grain alcohol*). Question the *extracting solvent*. [You can home-make GF vanilla, easily.] Choose <u>*alcohol-free*</u> <u>*vanilla* *essence*</u>, <u>*pure* *vanilla* *extract*</u> or <u>*vanilla* *powder*</u>. All of course, free from *gluten byproducts*. These are

available at some regular and ethnic grocery food stores, most *health food grocery stores* and by *mail order*. (See *vanilla sugar*.)

Vanilla Flavoring: Vanilla flavoring is usually a type of *pure* and *imitation vanilla mixture*. Risky. Verify GF. (See *vanilla extract*.)

Vanilla Sugar: Vanilla sugar is a type of *sugar* (generally *refined sugar*) *flavored* with *pure* and/or *artificial vanilla flavorings*. Question the source. [You can home-make GF vanilla sugar easily.] (See *vanilla extract*.)

Vanillin: Vanillin is a *substance* that occurs *naturally* in *vanilla beans* or is a *synthetic chemical flavoring produced* from *eugenol* or *wood pulp*. Vanillin is often used in place of *vanilla extract* in countless products. Caution. GF. (See *vanilla extract* and *artificial*.)

Veal: A type of *meat*. *Pure fresh* and *plain* are GF. (See *meat*.)

Vegetable: Vegetables are certain *edible plants* and/or *plant parts*. <u>Not considering *grains* as <u>vegetables,</u> all *fresh* <u>raw</u> <u>vegetables</u> <u>are</u> *naturally* <u>GF</u>.</u> {Processed vegetables may contain added *thickeners*, *emulsifiers*, *preservatives*, *stabilizers*, *vegetable gums*, *oils*, *starch* and *flours*.} Avoid *fresh*, *cooked* and *frozen* vegetables in *forbidden sauces*, *gravies* and *creams*, with *pasta*, *breaded*, *batter dipped*, *coated* or *pickled* in *vinegars*, unless all ingredients are verified GF. Question commercially prepared *vegetable salads*. [Look up each type of vegetable product individually.] (See *sprouts*, *vegetables canned* and also see 'vegetables' in A & F charts.)

Vegetable Canned: Canned vegetables are vegetables commonly *cooked* and *preserved* in cans. Choose *plain* _canned_ _vegetables_. *Plain* canned vegetables are generally GF. {Canned vegetables may contain added *alkalis, antioxidants, buffers* and *flavor enhancers*.} Question the source of any added ingredient (e.g. *pasta, sauce* or *gravy*. Verify GF. (See *vegetables* and *canned*.)

Vegetable Flour: Vegetable flours are certain *flour milled* from *dried* _vegetables_, _roots_ or _tubers_. Caution: vegetable flours *mixed* with other *flours*. Question the term vegetable flour used to describe *grain flour*. Check for GF purity. (See *flour*.)

Vegetable Gum: Vegetable gums are various *gums* derived from *plant* sources. Types of vegetable gums include _corn_, _soy_, *oat*, or *wheat*. Caution: *forbidden oat* and *wheat* vegetable gums are widely used. Question the source.

Vegetable _Jello_: (See *agar*.) GF.

Vegetable _Juice_: Vegetable juices are prepared from a *vegetable base*. {Vegetable juices may contain *artificial substances*.} *Plain pure* and *fresh*-juiced vegetables are *naturally* GF. Question the source. Several vegetable juices are GF. Choose *100*% _pure_ _commercially_ _prepared_ vegetable juice or home-make. Verify GF. (See *juice* for additional details and specifics.)

Vegetable Lutein: Lutein produced from certain *vegetable plants*. Question the source. Verify GF.

Vegetable _Marrow_: A type of *fruit*. *Fresh* and *plain* are GF.

Vegetable Oil: Vegetable oils are different types of *edible oils* derived from *plants*. Question the source of vegetable oils and vegetable oil *blends*. Types of GF vegetable oils include certain brands of *pure* _corn_ *oil*. Forbidden *wheat germ* oil is referred to as vegetable oil. (See *oil, avocado oil* and *olive oil*.)

Vegetable Peeler: A vegetable peeler is a type of kitchen *utensil* with a blade specifically designed to cut away a minimum amount of *peel* from various *raw fruits / vegetables*.

Vegetable Protein: Vegetable protein is a type of *protein* obtained from *plants* (e.g. _corn_, _soy_, *oat* or *wheat*). Question the source.

Vegetable Protein Textured: (See *textured vegetable protein*.) Avoid.

Vegetable Shortening: (See *Shortening*.)

Vegetable Starch: Vegetable starch refers to *starch* derived from *plants* (e.g. _corn_, _rice_, _potatoes_, _soy_, *oat* or *wheat*). Question the source. (See *protein* and *hydrolysis*.)

Vegetal Albumin: (See *gluten*)

Vegetarian: Vegetarians are individuals who do not consume *animal foods* or *animal byproducts* of any sort. Eating as a vegetarian is done for any of a variety of reasons (e.g. economical, personal, religious, nutritional and/or ethical). The majority of vegetarian *foods* use *soy* and *wheat* products to imitate animal foods. You can have CD and still eat as a vegetarian. Always question the source of vegetarian foods.

Veined Cheese: Avoid all veined *cheeses* including *Blue Cheese, Danablu, Roquefort, Stilton* and *Gorgonzola*. [*Wheat-flour bread* is used in processing.] Avoid.

Vending Machines: Vending machines are convenient coin

operated machines from which you can buy packaged *processed foods*. You cannot count on a vending machine for a GF meal. Although convenient, most *foods* in vending machines are not GF. In some vending machines, you may find GF candy, soda and a limited amount of GF snack foods. Vending machine coffee is risky. (See *travel foods*.)

Venison: A type of *meat*. *Pure fresh* and *plain* are GF. (See *meat*.)

Vermicelli: A type of extremely thin *spaghetti* customarily made with *forbidden flour*. (See *pasta*.)

Vermouth: Question. (See *aromatic wine*.)

Villi: Villi are tiny fingerlike projections of the mucous membrane of the *intestine*. Villi line the *small intestines*. The villi help absorb the *nutrients* from *food*. The villi become damaged if a person with *celiac disease* eats *gluten* or *gluten byproducts* in even minute amounts. Damage to the villi leads to malabsorption of nutrients and this may lead to weight loss and other nutrient deficient related symptoms. *Acidophilus* is a good *bacteria* that will help restore *intestinal flora*. (See *acidophilus*, *flora* and *intestine*.)

Vinaigrette: Vinaigrettes are *oil* and *vinegar* mixtures. {Vinaigrettes may contain added *emulsifiers* and *seasoning*.} Question all *ingredients* in the *mixture*. (See *dressings*.)

Vinegar: Vinegar is a certain type of *fermented condiment* made from *natural* and/or *synthetic ingredients*. Types of vinegar include <u>apple cider</u>, <u>balsamic</u>, <u>cane</u>, champagne, <u>cider</u>, <u>white</u>, <u>grain</u>, <u>distilled</u>, spirit, fruited, herbed, spiced, flavored, malt, rice, sherry, shiso, umebosh, <u>wine</u> and *powdered vinegars*. Personal tolerance should dictate use.[Look up each type of vinegar individually.] Caution: *distilled* and other highly *processed* vinegars may be *synthetic ethanol*. Claims have been made that properly *distilled vinegars* do not contain *gluten peptides/prolamins*. {Vinegars may contain added *flavors*, *colors* and *sulfites*.} If just the word vinegar is listed as an *ingredient*, than it is most-likely an inferior *vinegar* (possibly *malt vinegar*). Apple cider and distilled vinegars are both GF and widely used as an *ingredient*, especially in *condiments*. Question the source of all vinegars. A variety of naturally GF vinegars are available. As a table vinegar <u>choose a pure naturally GF vinegar</u> such as apple cider vinegar, wine vinegar and/or balsamic vinegar. (See *condiments* and also see 'condiments' in A & F charts.)

Vital Wheat Gluten: A type of *hard wheat*. Avoid.

Vitamin: Vitamins are *essential organic compounds* for human existence. Vitamins are obtained *naturally* through *pure fresh foods*. Vitamins are also available in a *supplement* form. Verify GF. (See *supplement* and *nutrition*.)

Vitamin C Crystal: (See *ascorbic acid*.) GF.

Vitamin C Powder: (See *ascorbic acid*.) GF.

Vodka: A type of *distilled alcohol*. GF. (See *alcohol*.)

Wafer: Wafers are a type of crispy thin *cookie*-like *baked-good* usually made from *forbidden flour*. Avoid. *Commercially prepared* GF wafers are available through *specialty companies*. (See *cookie*.)

Waffles: Waffles are a type of griddle-*bread* customarily made with *forbidden wheat batter*. Avoid. Commercially prepared GF waffles and waffle mixes are available only through *specialty companies*.

Wakame: *A type of seaweed. Pure* and *plain* are GF. (See *seaweed*.)

Walnut: *A type of nut. Raw* and *plain* are GF. (See *nut*.)

Walnut Oil: A type of *oil* obtained from *walnuts*. Check for GF purity.

Wasabi: A Japanese *horseradish sauce/paste*. Avoid unless source is known. (See *paste*.)

Water: Water is a *naturally* GF *beverage*. Types of water include *distilled*, spring, reverse osmosis, charcoal filtered or home purified with an excellent filtration system. Question *flavored* water. (See *beverages*.)

Water Chestnut: A type of *vegetable. Fresh* and *plain* are GF.

Water Chestnut Starch: A type of *starch* obtained from *water chestnuts*. Verify GF. (See *starch*.)

Water Correcting Agent: Water correcting agents usually contain *compounds* and *acids*. Caution. Question the source.

Watercress: A type of *vegetable. Fresh* and *plain* are GF.

Water Ice: Water ice is type of *frozen dessert* made with *ground* ice and added *flavoring* (usually *artificial*). Most *water* ice is GF. Question the source of *flavorings*, especially *root beer* and *cream soda*. Verify GF.

Watermelon: A type of *fruit. Fresh* and *plain* are GF. (See *fruit*.)

Wax Bean: Wax beans are a type of *vegetable*. A type of yellow colored *string bean*. GF. (See *vegetable*.)

Waxed Paper: Waxed paper is a type of *kitchen* product used to store or package *foods*. Waxed paper is customarily made with a *wood pulp* base and *coated* with *paraffin wax*. [Waxed paper has no GF concerns.] Place slices of waxed paper in between slices of GF *breads* etc..., to keep them separated while *frozen*.

Waxy Corn: Waxy corn is a type of *corn* high in *starch*. GF. (See *sweet corn*.)

Waxy Corn Flour: Waxy corn flour is a type of *grain flour milled* from *waxy corn grains*. Check for GF purity. (See *waxy corn*.)

Waxy Cornstarch: Waxy cornstarch is a type of *cornstarch* made from *waxy corn grains*. Check for GF purity. (See *waxy corn*.)

Waxy Maize: (See *waxy corn*.) GF.

Waxy Rice: (See *sweet rice*.) GF.

Waxy Sorghum: A type of *sorghum*. GF. (See *sorghum*.)

Weakened Immune System: With a weakened immune system the body's interactive system that initiates the response to fight off sickness and *disease* is compromised because of sickness, disease, or *malnutrition* (e.g. *celiac disease*). A major concerns for *celiacs* is a possible weakened immune system. Individuals with *active celiac* disease will experience a rebuilding of the immune system by avoiding the offending *protein* from *gluten*. The *immune system* heals completely in most *celiacs*, although *celiacs* should always be concerned with their *immune system*. The *immune system* of certain *celiacs* must be monitored, especially for the elderly and infants. To help rebuild their immune system, some celiacs' *supplement* their *diet* with *nutrients* lost from prior *villi* damage in the *intestinal tract*. Celiacs must avoid *gluten* to maintain a healthy immune system. (See *supplement, immune system* and *celiac disease*.)

Weakfish: A type of *fish*. Pure *fresh* and *plain* are GF. (See *fish*.)

Wedding Cake: Wedding cakes are ordinarily not gluten free unless specially prepared with GF ingredients. You need to find a bakery that will create a GF wedding cake. (See *bakery*.)

Weight Gain: Weight gain is a concern for a number of celiacs, especially the newly diagnosed. [People increase their caloric intake to gain weight. People decrease their caloric intake, along with exercise to lose weight.] *Celiacs* routinely gain weight naturally, once the diarrhea stops and the *villi* start to grow back. Celiacs on average notice significant weight gain within one to three months after maintaining a strict GF diet. (See *villi, digestive system, calorie, malnutrition* and *diet*.)

Weiner: (See *frankfurter*.)

Wetting Agent: Wetting agents are *substances* that enable *liquids* to be absorbed. Wetting agents are used to make *foods spreadable*. Caution. Question the source.

WF: (See *wheat free*.)

Wheat: Wheat is a type of *forbidden cereal grain* from the *grass plant family*. Wheat has a *gluten prolamin* that is toxic to celiacs. It is the *gluten prolamins* in wheat (*gliadins* and *glutenins*) *toxic* to individuals with *celiac disease*. *Gliadin* is the *gluten*

prolamin in wheat. Other *forbidden* types of wheat include wheat flour, bleached wheat flour, bolted wheat, oriental wheat, common wheat, club wheat, white wheat, wheat bran, cream of wheat, ground wheat, cracked wheat, red wheat, crushed wheat, durum, kau fu, wheat germ, wheat gelatinized, hard wheat, soft wheat, whole wheat, wheat pasta, vital wheat, seitan, semolina, wheat starch and unbleached wheat. Avoid wheat grains and wheat grain relatives. Avoid *byproducts* of these *forbidden* grains. Avoid food made with these *forbidden* grains and *byproducts* of these *forbidden* grains. (See *grains, byproducts* and *gliadin*.)

Wheat Berry: Wheat berries are *wheat grains*. Avoid.

Wheatex: A type of *fat substitute*. Avoid. (See *fat substitutes*.)

Wheat Flour: A type of *grain flour milled* from *forbidden wheat grains*. Avoid. *Substitute* wheat flour with a combination of GF *flours* and *starches*. (See *specialty foods*.)

Wheat Free: Wheat free is a term meaning free of *wheat*. [Wheat free does not mean *gluten free*, because there can still be *gluten* from *forbidden barley* or *rye* and/or other *forbidden wheat grain* relatives.] A variety of gluten free foods are also labeled wheat free. Avoid all wheat free foods unless also verified gluten free. (See *gluten free*.)

Wheat Germ: The *germ* of *wheat*. Avoid. (See *sprouted wheat*.)

Wheat Germ Oil: A type of *oil* obtained from the *germ* of *wheat*. Avoid. (See *oil*.)

Wheat Gluten: *Gluten* from *wheat*. Wheat gluten is also a term used for *seitan*. Avoid both.

Wheat Grass: (See *sprouted wheat*.)

Whey: Whey is the *fresh liquid* that separates from *yogurt* or when making *cheese*. Whey is a *byproduct* of *milk*. Whey is available in either a *liquid* or *powdered* form. {Whey may contain added *fillers, gums, flavorings, alcohol,* or *enzymes*.} <u>Pure</u> GF <u>whey</u> powder <u>is</u> <u>available</u> at *health food grocery stores* and by *mail order*. Verify GF.

Whey Powder: Whey powder is the *liquid whey* to which almost all the moisture has been removed. <u>Pure GF whey powder is available</u> at *health food grocery stores* and by *mail order*. Verify GF. (See *whey*.)

Whipping Cream: Whipping cream is a *dairy product*. Whipping cream is a type of GF *heavy cream* used for *whipping*. Question the source of any added *gum*. Whipping cream is also an aerosol container of a *combination* of *natural* and *artificial* ingredients. Verify GF. (See *cream*.)

Whisk: A whisk is a type of *kitchen utensil* made with several looped wires. A whisk is used to whip *liquid ingredients* and aerate *dry ingredients*. Clean the whisk well between uses.

White Bean: White beans are *haricot beans*. White *beans* are white in color. GF.

White Corn: A type of *corn kernel* white in color. GF. (See *corn*.)

Whitefish: A type of *fish*. *Pure fresh* and *plain* are GF. (See *fish*.)

White Kidney Bean: A type of kidney *bean* white in color. GF.

Whiten: To whiten or *bleach* with chemicals or by age. (See *whitening agents*.)

Whitened Flour: A type of *wheat flour* whitened or *bleached*. Avoid.

Whitening Agent: Whitening agents are *substances* (usually *chemicals*) used to *bleach* or *whiten foods* (usually *flour*). Caution. Question the source. (See *bleach*.)

White Pepper: White pepper is a type of *seasoning* similar to *black pepper*. White *peppercorns* are *treated*. {Ground white pepper may contain added *filler*.} Risky. Question the source. [Black pepper can be used in place of white pepper in recipes, the only difference may be its visibility.] (See *pepper*.)

White Potato: White potatoes are a type of GF *tuber* considered an all-purpose potato. To cook: *bake, fry, boil,* or *steam*. (See *potato*.)

White Rice: White rice is a type of GF *rice grain* with the *bran* (outer layer) removed. White rice lacks the *nutritional* value of *brown rice*. *Commercially* packaged rice are commonly white *fortified, enriched, enhanced, polished* or *converted*. *Whole* white rice grains will *mill* into *flour*. Always question the source of *polished rice*. (See *rice* for details and specifics and *also* see *brown rice* and *white rice flour*.)

White Rice Flour: White rice flour is a type of *rice flour milled* from *whole white rice grains*. Avoid white rice flour *milled* from *forbidden polished*. 'Short' rice grains mill into a better *rice flour* than 'long' rice grains. [Brown *rice flour* is more nutritious than white rice flour.] Check for GF purity. (See *rice flour* and *brown rice flour*.)

White Sugar: White sugar is a type of highly *refined cane sugar*. White sugar lacks *nutrition*. Caution. GF.

White Vinegar: (See *distilled vinegar*.) Verify GF.

White Wine: (See *wine*.)
Whiting: A type of *fish*. *Pure fresh* and *plain* are GF. (See *fish*.)
Whole Foods: Whole foods is a term used to describe food that is not *denatured*. Whole foods may include *raw* and *fresh nuts*, *seeds*, *beans*, *roots*, *tubers*, grains, *fruits* and *vegetables*. [Look up each type individually.] You can obtain all the *nutrients* you need from a well-balanced whole foods *diet*. Simple basic and pure whole *foods* are less complicated. It is healthier, easier and possibly safer to *prepare* GF recipes with *whole food ingredients*. Some *whole* food recipes might require longer preparation time. Some *whole* foods and/or whole food *recipes* designed with a whole foods base are considered the safest for celiacs. [*Basic ingredients* with minimally *processed foods*, especially if *newly diagnosed* are generally safer.] Whole *foods* are available at regular *grocery food stores*. (See *whole grains, fresh, plain, basic, pure* and *organic*)
Whole Grains Whole grains are any *grain* not *denatured*. Whole grains still contain the *bran*. Avoid whole *grains* containing *gluten*. (See *forbidden grains*.)
Whole Meal: Whole meal is a term for any of a variety of *whole grains* and possibly *nuts* or *seeds* milled into a fine or coarse powder. Question the source. (See *whole grains*.)
Whole Meal Flour: (See *whole meal*.)
Whole Oats: The whole *oat grain* with its *hull intact*. Question. (See *oat* for details.)

Whole Rice: Whole rice is a term for *brown rice*. Whole rice grains still have their *bran* intact. [If the *bran* is removed then it becomes *white rice*.] GF. (See *brown rice*.)
Whole Rice Flour: Whole rice flour is a type of *rice flour milled* from *whole rice grains*. Check for GF purity. (See *whole rice*.)
Whole Wheat Flour: Whole wheat flour is a type of *wheat flour milled* from *whole wheat grains*. Avoid.
Wieners: (See *frankfurter*.)
Wild Cherry: A type of *fruit*. *Fresh* and *plain* are GF. (See *fruit*.)
Wild Rice: Wild rice is not a *grain*, but actually a *seed* of an aquatic *plant*. Wild rice is commonly *cooked* in a *mixture* with *whole grain brown rice*. Wild rice is great added in *omelets, pilafs, salads, stuffing* and other rice dishes. GF.
Wild Yam: (See *jinengo*.) GF.
Wine: Wine is an *alcoholic beverage fermented* from *grape juice*. Question the source of all ingredients in *fortified* wines (e.g. *sherry* and *port* wines), *aromatic* wines (e.g. *vermouth*), *malt* wines and *flavored* wines. Avoid wine with *sulfites* if possible. There are several US brand GF wines. Choose pure plain red or white GF wines. (See *alcohol* and also see 'alcohol' in A & F charts.)
Wine Vinegar: Wine vinegar is a type of *vinegar* made from red or white *wines* that were *fermented* from red or white *grape juice*. {Wine vinegars may contain added *colorings* and other *food agents*.} The best wine vinegars are *traditionally fermented* slowly and *naturally* in wood barrels (e.g., the "Orleans" method). A faster method

of *fermentation* usually involves heat. Various wine vinegars are GF. Verify GF. (See *vinegar*.)

Winged Bean: A type of *soybean*. GF. (See *soybean* and *bean*.)

Wintergreen: A type of *spice*. *Pure* are GF. (See *spice*.)

Wok: A wok is a type of *cooking pan* used to *stir-fry foods* on high heat. Woks in *restaurants* are only rinsed in between use, therefore *gluten residue* may *contaminate* your *food*. (See *Chinese food*.)

Wood Pulp: Wood pulp is a *substance* obtained from the wood of *trees*. Caution. GF. (See *tree*.)

Worcestershire Sauce: This is a type of *seasoning condiment* made with *soy sauce, molasses, vinegars* and *seasonings*. All ingredients must be verified GF. Verify GF. (See *condiment*.)

Wrapper: Wrappers are a type of *packaging material* (usually paper or plastic) used to wrap *foods* (*gum*, chewy *candy* or *cheese*). Caution: the wrapper may be *dusted* with *powders* (*wheat flour*, corn flour or *chemicals*) to prevent the foods from sticking to the wrapper. Question the source of any *powder* used to *dust* wrappers. (See *packaging material*.)

Xanthan Gum: Xanthan gum is a type of *gum commercially* grown in a laboratory from xanthomonas campestris *organisms*. Xanthan gum replaces *gluten* in some *recipes*. Xanthan gum helps *baked-goods* stick together. [Xanthan gum may be eliminated in some *baked-goods*, the only result may be a more crumbly *baked-good*.] Xanthan gum is available through *specialty companies* and can be purchase at *health food grocery stores* and by mail order. [Some individuals are *sensitive* to xanthan gum. *Newly diagnosed celiacs* may want to avoid xanthan gum for at least the first one-three months.] Caution. GF. (See *sensitivities* and *gums*.)

Xanthophyll: An *additive* derived from *egg* yolks or flower pedals. Verify GF.

Xylitol: A type of *chemical sweetener*. Caution. GF.

Yam: A type of *tuber* with orange flesh and skin. [Yams are not the same as *sweet potatoes*.] Remove the skin before cooking. GF.

Yamaimo: (See *jinengo*.) GF.

Yam Bean: (See *jinengo*.) GF.

Yankee Bean: (See Navy *bean*.) GF.

Yarrow: A type of *spice*. *Pure* are GF. (See *spice*.)

Yeast: Yeast is a type of *fungi* that cause the *fermentation* of *sugars* and other *carbohydrates*. Yeast is a *leavening agent* in *baked-goods* and *fermentation agent* in *wines* and *vinegars*. Not all yeast are *leavening agents*, some are used as a source of *nutrition* (e.g. *nutritional yeast* and *brewers yeast*). [Some individuals are *sensitive* to yeast. *Newly diagnosed celiacs* may want to avoid yeast for at least the first one-three months.] Other leavening agents may be used to *substitute* yeast in some *recipes*. Question the source of all yeasts. (See *leavening agent*, *yeast substitute* and *powdered vinegar* and also see 'yeast' in A & F charts.)

Yeast Bread: *Wheat bread* using *yeast* as a *leavening agent*. Avoid.

Yeast Extract: Yeast extract is a type of *yeast byproduct* used as a *flavor enhancer*. Avoid.

Yeast Food: *Natural* or *chemical substances* used in *dough* to activate the *leaving* process in *baked-goods*. Question the source.

Yeast Free: Without yeast. (See *yeast* and *yeast substitute*.)

Yeast Free Vinegar: (See *powdered vinegar*.)

Yeast Starter: A *mixture* of *sugar*, *yeast* and *wheat flour* used as a starter in *baked-goods*. Avoid it and all foods using yeast starters.

Yeast Substitute: Yeast substitutes are non-yeast leavening agents. Yeast substitutes are *leavening agents* used in place of *yeast*. Yeast substitutes include baking soda and *baking powder*. [Instead of *yeast* in *baked-goods*, use *batter mixes* with other *leavening agents*.] Question the source of all yeast substitutes. (See *batter mixes, baking powder* and *leavening agent*.)

Yellow Corn: Yellow corn is a term used for sweet corn and any *corn kernel* yellow in color. GF.

Yellow-Eyed Bean: A *heirloom* variety *bean*. GF. (See *bean*.)

Yellow-Eyed Finn Potato: A type of *tuber* with yellow flesh. To cook: boil. GF. (See *potato*.)

Yellow Wax Bean: Yellow waxed beans are a type of *green bean* yellow in color eaten as a *vegetable*. GF. (See *vegetable*.)

Yi Vi Rue: (See *Job's tear*.)

Yogurt: Yogurt is a type of *dairy food* produced from *fermented* and coagulated *milk*. {Yogurts may contain added *filler, gum, grain byproducts, sweeteners, flavorings, alcohols, stabilizers, thickeners* or *enzymes*.} *Plain* yogurt is made without the addition of *flavors*, as opposed to *flavored* yogurt with

added flavor. *Plain* yogurt with *freshly* added GF *ingredients* is ordinarily safer. Question all *fruited* and *flavored* yogurts. Avoid yogurt with *forbidden toppings*. Verify GF. (See *dairy*.)

Yuba: Yuba is the skin forming on top of *soymilk* during *cooking*. Verify GF. (See *soymilk*.)

Yucca: A type of *vegetable*. Fresh and *plain* are GF. (See *vegetable*.)

Yucca Starch: (See *tapioca flour*.)

Zein: Zein is a term for *corn* and also the *protein* in *corn*. GF.

Zest: Zest is a culinary term for the small thin pieces of *citrus peels*. GF. (See *citrus, citrus zester, rind* and *spices*.)

Ziti: Ziti is a type of tube shape *pasta* customarily made with *forbidden flour*. Avoid. (See *pasta*.)

Zucchini: A type of *vegetable*. Fresh and *plain* are GF.

Miscellaneous Definitions

_____: _____
_____
_____
_____
_____: _____
_____
_____
_____
_____
_____: _____
_____
_____
_____: _____
_____
_____
_____

Miscellaneous Definitions

_____: _____
_____
_____
_____

_____: _____
_____
_____
_____
_____
_____

_____: _____
_____
_____

_____: _____
_____
_____
_____
_____
_____

_____: _____
_____
_____

_____: _____
_____
_____
_____
_____

_____: _____
_____
_____

_____: _____
_____
_____
_____
_____

_____: _____
_____
_____

_____: _____
_____
_____
_____

Miscellaneous Definitions

_____: _____
_____
_____
_____

_____: _____
_____
_____
_____
_____
_____

_____: _____
_____
_____

_____: _____
_____
_____
_____
_____
_____

_____: _____
_____
_____

_____: _____
_____
_____
_____
_____

_____: _____
_____
_____

_____: _____
_____
_____
_____
_____

_____: _____
_____
_____

_____: _____
_____
_____
_____

ALLOWABLE & FORBIDDEN CHARTS

The allowable and forbidden charts are designed for quick and easy referencing. Look in the terms and definitions section for detailed information.

The headings in the charts are in order as follows

1. Dried Fruit
2. Eggs
3. Dairy and Dairy byproducts
4. Processed and Prepared Food
5. Beverages
6. Breads, Brownies, Cakes, Doughnuts, Muffins and Pies
7. Chili, Stews, Chowders and Soups
8. Vegetables, Roots, Tubers and Bulbs and byproducts of vegetables, roots, tubers and bulbs
9. Yeast and Molds
10. Fats and Oils
11. Seeds
12. Nuts
13. Seaweed
14. Fruit
15. Candy
16. Condiments and Herbs, Spices, Seasonings and Flavorings
17. Sweeteners
18. Desserts
19. Snacks
20. Beans
21. Grains and byproducts of grains
22. Alcohol
23. Meat, Fish, Fowl, Seafood and Shellfish
24. Vinegars
25. Cereals
26. Miscellaneous

ALLOWABLE

FORBIDDEN

1. Dried Fruit

ALLOWABLE	FORBIDDEN
Plain **sun dried fruits** are naturally gluten free. Types include certain brands of commercially prepared dried **apples, apricots, bananas, coconut, currants, dates, figs, peaches, pears, prunes, pineapples** and **raisins**.	Avoid dried fruit mixed with forbidden grain cereals (e.g. **trail mixes** and **granola bars**). Avoid dried fruit **dusted with forbidden** flours and **polished** or **coated with malt sweetener**. Purchase sulphur-free dried fruit if possible.

2. Eggs

ALLOWABLE	FORBIDDEN
Eggs are **naturally gluten free**. Gluten free prepared eggs include **plain soft** or hard-boiled and eggs **fried** in gluten free oil or butter.	Question **added fillings** and other ingredients in prepared eggs (e.g. omelets, or **quiche**). Avoid eggs **fried on a grill previously used to cook foods containing gluten**.

All food items need to be verified gluten free.

| ALLOWABLE | FORBIDDEN |

3. Dairy and Dairy Byproducts

| Gluten free dairy and dairy byproducts include certain brands of **aged cheese**, (e.g. Swiss, cheddar and parmesan cheese), **butter, buttermilk, buttermilk powder, cream, cream cheese, cottage cheese, ice cream, milk, milk powder, sour cream, whey** and **yogurt** (plain). Certain brands of **condensed, dry** and **evaporated milk** are gluten free. Milk is usually gluten free. | **Avoid** all **veined cheese** (e.g. blue cheese, Danablu, Roquefort, Stilton and Gorgonzola cheese). Forbidden ingredients are in some commercially prepared dairy products. Avoid dairy foods with added **forbidden grains** and forbidden grain **byproducts.** Question dairy foods for **added** fillers, alcohol, enzymes, flours, sweeteners, starch, emulsifiers, additives, gums, flavorings, preservatives, stabilizers and other **forbidden food agents.** Avoid **kefir**, commercially prepared **flavored milk,** some non-dairy **creamers** and **substitutes** and **yogurt** with added toppings. Question **ricotta cheese, cottage cheese, sour cream,** and all **processed cheese, cheese sauces,** and **cheese spread.** In dairy products forbidden **fillers** and **thickening agents** as ingredients are not always clearly listed (e.g., forbidden flour may be used to dust cheese so it does not stick to the package). Some celiacs are **lactose intolerant** (for most it is temporarily). Dairy contains lactose. |

4. Processed and Prepared Foods

| Gluten free processed foods includes **food made with allowable grains** and **byproducts** of allowable grains. This includes a **limited amount of certain brands of commercially prepared** and **processed** meals, meats, seafood, poultry, fish, dairy, fruits, candy, vegetables, tomato products, tortilla shells, tofu, polenta and an even less amount of certain brands of cereals, beverages, snacks and condiments. | **Avoid all processed foods containing** the **forbidden grains** and **byproducts** of those forbidden grains. This includes numerous brands of commercially prepared beverages, meals, poultry, meats, fish, seafood, dairy, fruit, candy, cereal, vegetables and condiments. Even if a product looks GF, it may contain gluten through cross **contamination,** in hidden sources (e.g. coating, flavoring and filler not listed as ingredients) and during manufacturing (e.g. forbidden flour on conveyer belts, airborne and in packaging material). Always question processed and prepared foods for forbidden additives. Question added fillers, flavorings, colorings, vinegars, thickeners, binders, emulsifiers, stabilizers, cereal protein, starch, sweeteners, preservatives, certain fats/oils, gums and other food agents. |

ALLOWABLE	FORBIDDEN

5. Beverages

Naturally gluten free beverages include and fresh juiced **fruits** and **vegetables** and pure **water**. Commercially prepared gluten free beverages include certain brands of **100% pure vegetable and fruit juice** and some coffee, soda, fruit drinks, dairy milk, non-dairy milk (e.g. almond, coconut, soy, rice and sunflower), pure herbal tea and regular tea.	**Avoid** commercially prepared **tea with barley, flavored milk, flavored coffee and tea, malted milk** and most **instant drinks, sarsaparillas, root beers** and **cream sodas**. Question commercially prepared **fruit drinks, punch, instant drinks** and **instant coffee**. Forbidden barley malt is often used to flavor and color beverages. **Always question added flavorings and colorings in beverages.**

6. Breads, Brownies, Cakes, Doughnuts, Muffins and Pies

Gluten free baked goods can be homemade or commercially prepared with acceptable ingredients; **grains** (e.g. amaranth, buckwheat, millet, quinoa, sorghum, milo, corn, rice, wild rice, job's tear ragi and teff), **flours** (e.g. amaranth flour, bean flours, buckwheat flour, corn flour, cornmeal, garbanzo bean flour, millet flour, quinoa flour, rice flour, nut flours, soybean flour, sweet rice flour, seed flours and dried vegetable flours), **starches** (e.g. arrowroot powder, corn starch, potato starch, rice starch, sago, tapioca flour, waxy corn starch and sorghum starch) and **leavening agents** (e.g. baking soda).	**Avoid** baked goods made with the **forbidden grains** and **byproducts** of those forbidden grains. **Certain brands of rice and potato breads contain wheat.** Always read labels. **If a baked good is truly gluten free it will be labeled 'gluten free'.**

7. Chili, Stews, Chowders and Soups

Gluten free chili, stew, chowder and soup can be homemade with acceptable ingredients. There are very few commercially prepared gluten free **chili** (e.g. meat and bean), **stews** (e.g. vegetable, beef, fish and tortilla), **chowders** (e.g. seafood and potato) and **soups** (e.g. bean, celery, pea, chicken and rice, lentil, onion, brown rice, vegetable and bouillons).	**Avoid** chili, soups, chowders and stews made with the **forbidden grains** and **byproducts** of those forbidden grains (e.g. unacceptable noodles, pasta, cooked grains, sweeteners and fillers). Question **added** starches, emulsifiers, flavorings, thickeners, preservatives, stabilizers, colorings and other **food additives**. Question all **canned soups, tomato soup, broths, stocks, bullions, soup bases** and **dry soup mixes** because of **hidden ingredients**.

ALLOWABLE   FORBIDDEN

8. Vegetables, Roots, Tubers and Bulbs and byproducts of vegetables, roots, tubers and bulbs

Allowable	Forbidden
Fresh raw and plain vegetables, roots and tubers are naturally gluten free. **Varieties include** alfalfa, aloe, artichokes, arugala, asparagus, avocado, bamboo shoot, bean sprouts, beet, beet green, broccoli, Brussels sprout, burdock, cabbage, cactus, carrot, carrot tops, cassava, cauliflower, celery, chard, charlock, collard green, colzo shoot, corn, cress, cucumber, dandelion green, eggplant, endive, escarole, fennel, grape leaf, gobo, green bean, jicama, kale, kohlrabi, kraut, leaf lettuce, leek, lettuce, lima bean, lotus root, malango, mushroom, mustard green, nasturtium, okra, olive, onion, parsnip, pea, peppers, poi, potato, pumpkin, radish, rhubarb, rutabaga, sago, scallion, shallot, spinach, string bean, sweet potato, Swiss chard, tapioca, taro, tomatillo, tomato, truffle, turnip, turnip green, water chestnut, watercress, yam, yucca and zucchini. You can eat vegetables raw (sliced, or juiced) or cooked (e.g. steamed, baked, broiled, sautéed or grilled). Gluten free **vegetable products** include certain brands of commercially prepared plain frozen and canned vegetables. **Gluten free vegetable, root and tuber flours and starches include** pure arrowroot flour/powder, potato starch-flour, tapioca flour and cornstarch. Gluten free **vegetable oils include pure corn oil, avocado oil and olive oil.** Choose salads plain and dry.	**Avoid** vegetables, roots and tubers, fresh, frozen or cooked **in forbidden sauces, gravies and creams, with pasta** and **breaded, batter dipped** or **coated,** unless all ingredients are verified GF. Question all additives especially added **thickeners, starch** and **flours.** Question prepared potato products. Avoid **commercially prepared vegetable salads** with **croutons, bacon bits, dressings &** other **toppings.**

9. Yeasts and Molds

Allowable	Forbidden
Gluten free leavening yeasts include certain brands of protected active dry yeast (**PADY**), bread machine yeast, cream yeast, instant yeast, fresh compressed yeast and rapid rise yeast.	**Question** all **brewer's** yeasts, **nutritional** yeast and instant active dry yeast (**IADY**). Yeast and molds are in fermented foods, some baked goods, gums, green olives, peanuts, wines, vinegars, teas, dry roasted nuts, mushrooms, alcoholic beverages, supplements, xanthan gum and mold based cheeses. **Question the source of all yeasts.**

Foods and ingredients in the allowable & forbidden charts are defined individually and extensively in the terms & definitions section.

ALLOWABLE	FORBIDDEN

10. Fats and Oils

Gluten free fats and oils include certain brands of 'pure' **grain oil** (e.g. corn), **vegetable oil** (e.g. avocado), **animal fat** (e.g. lard and butter), **fruit oil** (e.g. olive), **bean oil** (e.g. soy), **seed oils** (e.g. cotton, apricot kernel, pumpkin, canola, safflower, rape, sesame, sunflower and grape seed), **nut oils** (e.g. almond, coconut, hazelnut, peanut and walnut), **some margarines** and most **hydrogenated oils**.	Avoid **oils made from forbidden grains, wheat germ oil** and hydrolyzed vegetable protein (**HVP**) and **vegetable oils** with an unknown source. Question **cooking sprays**. Avoid **oils previously used to cook foods containing gluten, margarines with unknown fillers** and **wheatex**. Question fat **replacers, replace olestra, olean** and **oatrim**. Question **added** seasonings, spices, preservatives, colorings, flavorings, enhancers, emulsifiers and other food agents. The source of fats and oils are not always identified on labels.

11. Seeds

[Not considering grains as seeds.] Raw and plain seeds are naturally gluten free. **Varieties include** flax, rape, canola, apricot kernel, cotton, grape, sesame, pine nuts, pumpkin, safflower, squash and sunflower seeds. Commercially prepared gluten free **seed products** include certain brands of **seed butters** (e.g. sesame and tahini butters), **seed oils** (e.g. canola, pumpkin seed, grape seed, sesame seed, cottonseed, apricot kernel, safflower seed and sunflower seed oils) and **seed flours** (e.g. sesame seed flour, flax meal and sunflower seed flour).	**Avoid** seed butters with forbidden fillers. Question seeds that are **roasted, processed, dyed, seasoned, polished** and **flavored**.

12. Nuts

Raw and plain nuts are naturally gluten free. **Varieties include** almonds, acorns, beechnut, Brazil, butternut, macadamia, hazelnut, cashew, chestnut, hazel, coconut, filbert, pecan, hickory, peanut, pine nut, pistachio and walnut. Commercially prepared gluten free **nut products** include certain brands of **nut butters** (e.g. almond, cashew, hazelnut, macadamia and peanut butters), **nut oils** (e.g. almond, coconut, hazelnut, peanut and walnut oils) and **nut flours** (e.g. almond and chestnut flours).	**Avoid** nut butters with forbidden fillers. Question nuts that are **processed, dyed, roasted, seasoned, polished** and **flavored**.

Use the allowable and forbidden charts as a general guideline.

13. Seaweed

Fresh and plain seaweed is naturally gluten free. Varieties include pure **algae, arame, chlorella, chlorophyll** (from algae), **kelp, dulse, hiziki, kombu, nori, spirulina** and **wakame.** You can eat seaweed raw or cooked (e.g. sun dried, steamed, baked, broiled, sautéed or grilled).	**Avoid** fresh, frozen or cooked seaweed **in forbidden sauces, gravies** and **creams** and **breaded, batter dipped** or **coated** unless all ingredients are verified GF.

14. Fruit

Fresh raw and plain fruits are naturally gluten free. **Varieties include** apples, apricots, bananas, bayberries, berries, bilberries, black berries, blueberries, boysenberries, breadfruit, cantaloupes, carob pod, casabo, citron, cherimoya, cherries, citrange, coconuts, cranberries, dewberries, durian, elderberries, gooseberries, grapes, grapefruit, guava, honeydew, huckleberries, jackfruit, kiwi, kumquat, lemons, limes, litchi nuts, drupes, loganberries, loquats, mangos, melons, musk, mulberries, nectarines, oranges, papayas, passion fruit, pawpaw, peaches, pears, persimmons, plums, pineapples, plantains, pumpkins, pomegranates, quince, raspberries, sago palm, sapodilla, starfruit, strawberries, tamarinds, tangerines, tomatoes, vegetable marrow, watermelon and wild cherries. You can eat **fruits** raw (e.g. juiced), or cooked (e.g. stewed, sun dried, steamed, baked, broiled, sautéed or grilled). Commercially prepared gluten free **fruit products** include certain brands of **plain frozen or canned fruits.**	**Avoid** fresh, frozen or cooked fruit **in forbidden sauces** and **creams** and **breaded, batter dipped** or **coated** unless all ingredients are verified GF. Question additives especially the addition of **thickeners, starch** and **flours**. Avoid **commercially prepared fruit salads** with forbidden **sauce, dressing, granola &** other **toppings**. Avoid **some pie fillings**. Avoid dried fruit **dusted with forbidden flour**. Avoid **sulfured** dried fruit if possible.

15. Candy

Gluten free candy can be homemade **with gluten free sweeteners** and other ingredients. GF commercially prepared candy products include certain brands of **hard candy, pure chocolate** and **many others.**	Avoid candy prepared with **forbidden grains** and **forbidden grain byproducts**. Question added emulsifiers, flavors, colors, coatings, preservatives, stabilizers, sweeteners, fillers, gums and other food additives. Avoid candy dusted with forbidden flours. Question **licorice, caramel candy, marshmallows, jellybeans,** and candy made with **toffee, flavored syrup, butterscotch, malt, filling or crunchy cereal.**

ALLOWABLE

FORBIDDEN

16. Condiments, Herbs, Spices, Seasonings and Flavorings

'Fresh' and 'dried pure' **herbs** and **spices** are naturally gluten free. **Varieties include** absinthe, allspice, angelica, anise, basil, bay leaf, beech, bergamot, birch, burdock, camphor, caraway seed, cardamom, catnip, cayenne, celery seed, chicory, chamomile, chive, cilantro, cinnamon, clove, colts foot, comfrey, coriander seed, cumin seed, dong quai, dandelion, dill, Echinacea, elderflower, fennel seed, fenugreek, feverfew, garlic, ginger, goldenrod, goldenseal, hawthorne, hemp, hops, horehound, horseradish, horsetail, hyacinth, hyssop, juniper berry, laurel, lavender, lemon balm, licorice, lobelia, mace, mallow, marjoram, marigold, marshmallow, mint, mullein, mustard seed, nutmeg, oat straw, oregano, oyster plant, paprika, parsley, peppercorn, peppermint, phsyllium, poppy seed, prickly ash, pyrethrum, rose hip, rosemary, rue, sage, sarsaparilla, sassafras, savory, shavegrass, skullcap, slippery elm, spearmint, spikenard, tobacco, tarragon, thistle, thyme, tumbleweed, turmeric, ura ursi, wintergreen and yarrow. **Natural gluten free condiments include** certain brands of agar, baking soda, liquid aminos, carrageen, cream of tartar, unflavored, gelatin, guar gum, kudzu, pectin, salt, some tomato products and xanthan gum. Other **gluten free condiments include a limited amount of specific brands** of baking powder, BBQ sauce, mayonnaise, ketchup, miso, lecithin, mirin, mustard, olives, pimentos, pickles, polenta, salsa, sauerkraut, shortening, tamari sauce, tofu, some vinegar, chili mixes and seasoned salt.

Avoid condiments, herbs, spices, seasonings and flavorings made with **forbidden grains** and **byproducts** of those forbidden grains. Question added fillers, vinegars, stabilizers, dyes, colorings, sweeteners, flavorings, food agents and additives normally found in dried herbs, dried spices, ketchup, dressings, sauces, marinades, dips, dry seasoning mixes, mustard, tamari sauce, soy sauce, mayonnaise, bouillon, BBQ sauce, gravies, gravy extracts, ground pepper, miso and spice blends (e.g. curry powder, chili seasoning and taco seasoning). Question all **seasonings, condiments, herbs, spices and flavorings** for added **forbidden fillers.** Filler in foods are not always listed on the label as ingredients. **Always question hidden ingredients especially in spices, sauces, gravies, dips** and **spreads.** Question the source of MSG (glutamic acid) and avoid if possible. **Question added flavors** in most condiments and flavorings. Condiments are easily **contaminated with utensils (e.g., leaving crumbs behind).**

17. Sweeteners

Gluten free sweeteners include certain brands of **artificial sweeteners** and pure **chocolate, carob, corn syrup, date sugar, fructose, fruit spread, honey, maple syrup, molasses** (e.g. black strap and sorghum), **rice bran syrup** (e.g. without barley malt) and **sugar** (e.g. raw, granulated, milk, unrefined, table, confectioners and white sugar).	**Avoid** sweeteners made with **forbidden grains** and **byproducts** of those forbidden grains. **Avoid** sweeteners made with **barley malt.** Question **brown sugar** and **invert syrup** and **invert sugar with additives. Avoid rice bran syrup** with barley malt. Question that all sweeteners are 'pure'. The source of sweeteners as an ingredient on labels is not always identified.

18. Desserts

Gluten free desserts can be **homemade or commercially prepared with acceptable ingredients.** Gluten free dessert include **some specific brands of gelatins,** sorbets, ice creams, frozen yogurts, some frozen dairy and non-dairy products and a few puddings.	**Avoid** commercially prepared desserts made with **forbidden grains** and **byproducts** of those forbidden grains. Question **commercially prepared desserts** for added preservatives, gums, emulsifiers, fillers, flavorings, colorings, sweeteners, stabilizers and other food additives. Avoid **desserts with crusts, crumb toppings and breading.**

19. Snacks

Naturally gluten free snacks include fresh **fruits,** fresh **vegetables,** plain **nuts,** plain **seeds,** plain **popcorn** and pure **sun dried fruit.** Commercially prepared gluten free snacks include certain brands of **rice cakes, popcorn cakes, rice crackers, tortilla, potato** and **taro chips** and **sticks.**	**Avoid** snacks **made with forbidden grains** and **byproducts** of those grains (e.g. **cookies, pretzels** and most **puffs** and **crackers**). **All snacks are questionable.** Avoid snacks dried on conveyer belts **dusted with forbidden flours.**

20. Beans

Plain beans are naturally gluten free. **Varieties include** anisazi, adzuki, black-eyed pea, great northern, garbanzo, black, kidney, lentil, lima, mung, navy, soy and pinto. Gluten free **bean products** include pure **bean flours** (e.g. garbanzo, soy, mung and adzuki), **bean oils** (e.g. soy) and **bean pasta** (e.g. lentil, and mung).	**Avoid** bean flour and bean pasta **made with both acceptable and forbidden flours.** Avoid **beans coated, polished or dyed with forbidden substances.** Question all **seasoned beans.**

ALLOWABLE   FORBIDDEN

21. Grains and byproducts of grains

ALLOWABLE	FORBIDDEN
Gluten free grains include **amaranth, millet, quinoa, buckwheat, wild rice, job's tear, ragi, teff, sorghum** (milo), **corn** (white, blue or yellow- regular, popcorn and flour corn kernels) and **rice** (long and short grain- brown, white and sweet rice grains), **Gluten free flours** include **amaranth** flour, **buckwheat** flour, **corn** flour, **cornmeal, millet** flour, **quinoa** flour, **rice** bran/polish, **rice** flour (brown, or white), **sorghum** flour (milo) and **sweet rice** flour. Certain brands of commercially prepared **gluten free processed foods** include pure rice, bean or corn pasta, vermicelli, bean thread noodles and a limited amount of crackers, cereals and snacks. **Any baked good truly gluten free will be labeled.** A limited amount of grain food products made with gluten free grains are labeled gluten free.	Grains to avoid include **wheat, barley, rye** and possibly **oats.** Other grain foods to avoid include **bulgur, diploid, durum, einkorn, emmer, far, farro, hexaploid, kamut, mir, seitan, semolina, tetraploid, tsampa, spelt, triticale** and **triticum. Avoid all byproducts of forbidden grains.** Avoid **processed foods made with any forbidden grain.** Avoid **processed foods made with any** byproducts of the forbidden grains (e.g. **breading, croutons, stuffing, macaroni and cheese, noodles, cereals, pasta, snacks** and **some rice mixes**). Avoid **contaminated gluten free foods** (e.g. commercial cornmeal mixed with wheat flour and rice coated with gluten for sheen). Question all gluten free processed food prepared in an environment with both gluten and non-gluten foods. Question all treated rice (e.g., **polished** or **converted**).

Find additional information about grains under 'Details and Specifications' and look up grains in the 'Terms and Definitions' section.

22. Alcohol

ALLOWABLE	FORBIDDEN
Gluten free alcohol includes certain brands of **potato vodka, rum, gin, brandy, tequila,** corn **whiskey** and some **wines.** Certified and medical distilled alcohols are GF. **Properly distilled alcoholic beverages are gluten free** (e.g., any distilled alcohol 80 proof or more). Pure distilled alcohols include **whiskey, rum, gin, vodka, scotch, brandy, bourbon, vermouth** and **pure liqueurs.**	Avoid **ale, beer, lager, flavored wines** and **malt wines.** Distilled alcohols with **additives** are not gluten free. Avoid wines with **sulfites if possible.**

23. Meat, Fish, Fowl, Seafood and Shellfish

Pure fresh and plain meat, fish, poultry, seafood and shellfish are naturally gluten free. Types of meat include beef, buffalo, caribou, deer, venison, elk, goat, lamb, mutton, sheep, liver, kidney, moose, pork, rabbit and veal. **Types of seafood and fish include** abalone, albacore, amberjack, anchovies, bass, blackfish, bluefish, bluegill, bonita, bream, cackle, carp, catfish, chimaeras, chub, clams, cod, crab, crappie, crayfish, cuttlefish, crustaceans, dab, drum, eel, flat fish, flounder, grayling, grouper, haddock, halibut, herring, hake, kippers, limpet, lobster, marlin, mackerel, menhaden, minnow, mullet, mollusk, mussel, octopus, oysters, perch, pike, pilot, pollock, pompano, porgy, prawn, sailfish, salmon, sardines, scallops, shad, shark, shrimp, shrimp worm, skipjack, sole, skates, slug, smelt, snapper, snail, sockeye, steelhead, squid, stingray, sturgeon, sunfish, swordfish, tuna, trout, turbot, weakfish, whitefish and whiting. **Types of fowl include** chicken, dove, duck, goose, guinea, partridge, pheasant, pigeon, poultry, quail, squab and turkey. You can eat meats, seafood, fish, fowl and shellfish **baked, steamed, broiled, sautéed** or **grilled** plain or seasoned with gluten free seasonings. **A limited amount of certain brands of commercially prepared** fish in oil, brine or water and pure bacon, frankfurters and lunchmeats are okay.

Avoid meats, fish, fowl, seafood and shellfish dusted with **forbidden flours**, batter dipped or breaded and with unknown **seasonings** and/or condiments. Avoid **self-basting** fowl (e.g. turkey and poultry). Avoid **scrapple**. Avoid **imitation** bacon and seafood. Avoid ham **injected** with barley malt, **tuna canned in vegetable broth** and some meat and poultry **patties**. Avoid **some prepared sardines, hot dogs, salami, sausage corned beef and pastrami**. Question all meats, fish, fowl, seafood and shellfish that are pickled, canned, preserved, fermented, smoked, pre-seasoned, dried, marinated, sweetened, flavored or treated with additives unless all ingredients are verified gluten free.

24. Vinegars

Gluten free vinegars include certain brands of pure **apple cider, balsamic, cane, cider, wine** and some **powdered vinegars. Distilled vinegars are gluten free** (e.g., **spirit, grain** and **white**).

Avoid **flavored vinegars** and **malt vinegars**. Question fruited vinegar, herbed vinegar, spiced vinegar, **shiso, umebosh** and some **champagne, wine** and **rice** vinegars. [Properly distilled vinegars do not contain gluten peptides/prolamins. Malt vinegar is not distilled and therefore still needs to be avoided.] Distilled vinegars with **additives** are not gluten free. The source of vinegar as an ingredient is not always identified on the label.

ALLOWABLE	FORBIDDEN

25. Cereal

Commercially prepared gluten free cereals include certain brands of **puffs** (e.g. corn, millet and rice puffs), **whole grain cereals** (e.g. amaranth, millet, buckwheat, corn, quinoa, sorghum, rice job's tear, ragi and teff) and **corn grits, cream of rice** and **hominy.**	**Avoid cereals made with forbidden grains** (e.g. wheat, barley, rye and possibly oats). Other grain cereals to avoid include, bulgur, diploid, durum, einkorn, emmer, far, farro, hexaploid, kamut, mir, seitan, semolina, spelt, tetraploid, tsampa, triticale and triticum. Avoid **most cereal beverages.** Avoid rice cereals from forbidden polished rice. Avoid forbidden rice cereal coated with barley malt.

26. Miscellaneous

	Avoid communion wafers. Avoid licking the paste on **stamp** and **envelopes.** Question some **packaging** materials.

Fill this section in with your personal notes.

Acceptable:	Avoid:

See Book Ordering Form on page 211
See Celiac Associations/Groups on page 210

NOTES

NAMES, ADDRESSES, & PHONE NUMBERS

☞ _____

_____

_____

#_____ - _____ - _____

☞ _____

_____

_____

#_____ - _____ - _____

☞ _____

_____

_____

#_____ - _____ - _____

☞ _____

_____

_____

#_____ - _____ - _____

☞ _____

_____

_____

#_____ - _____ - _____

☞ _____

_____

_____

#_____ - _____ - _____

☞ _____

_____

_____

#_____ - _____ - _____

☞ _____

_____

_____

#_____ - _____ - _____

☞ _____

_____

_____

#_____ - _____ - _____

CELIAC ASSOCIATIONS/GROUPS

For updated information about celiac disease (CD) and the gluten free (GF) diet write, call, or visit the web sites of the following organizations.

CSA/USA
P.O. Box 31700,
Omaha NE. 68131-0700
Phone # 402-558-0600
Fax # 402-558-1347
Web Site www.csaceliacs.org

CELIAC DISEASE FOUNDATION
13251 Ventura Boulevard,
Suite 1, Studio City CA. 91604-1838
Phone # 818-990-2354
Fax # 818-990-2379
Web Site www.celiac.org

GLUTEN INTOLERANCE GROUP
15110 10th Ave SW, Suite A,
Seattle WA 98166-1820
Phone # 206-246-6652
Fax # 206-246-6531
Web Site www.gluten.net

CANADIAN CELIAC ASSOCIATION
5170 Dixie Road Suite 204
Mississauga, ON L4W 1E3
Phone # 1-800-363-7296 or 905-507-6208
Fax # 905-507-4673
Web Site www.celiac.ca

Consult your doctor about any decisions regarding your health.

I would very much like to hear from you.
If you have a comment, suggestion, question or anything else, you can contact me through the publishing company.

Guide Books Publishing Company
2113 Washington Lane, Bensalem PA. 19020   U.S.A.
www.GlutenFreeCentral.com

BOOK ORDERING FORM

1) Fill in your phone number, name and mailing address.

Phone Number (_____) _____-_____ E-Mail_____

Name and/or Business_____

Mailing Address _____

City_____

State_____ Zip Code_____

2) Fill in the number of books requested followed by their costs plus S & H and postage.

☐ **GLUTEN FREE FOOD PRODUCT LIST**
The Manufactures List of Commercially Prepared Gluten Free Foods
Amount of Books_____
$19.95 USA $23.95 CANADA   *1) Book Costs_____*
$3.00 for S & H and postage   *2) S & H and Postage_____*

☐ **GLUTEN FREE RESOURCE GUIDE**
A Consumers Guide for Living Gluten Free
Amount of Books_____
$8.95 USA $10.95 CANADA   *Book Costs_____*
$2.00 for S & H and postage   *S & H and Postage_____*

☐ **GLUTEN FREE REFERENCE GUIDE**
The Complete Book of Terms and Definitions
Amount of Books_____
$19.95 USA $23.95 CANADA   *Book Cost_____*
$2.50 for S & H and postage   *S & H and Postage_____*

3) Total the costs

Total Book Costs_____

Total S & H and Postage _____

Sub-Total (The total of both amounts) _____

4) Make check or money order payable to:

Jan Marie Silcox

5) Mail order form and check or money order to:

Guide Books Publishing Company
2113 Washington Lane,
Bensalem PA. 19020   U.S.A.

Discounts are available for large book orders. Write for details.